Republics of Difference

Religious and Racial Self-Governance in the Spanish Atlantic World

Religious and Racial
Self-Governance in the
Spanish Atlantic World

KAREN B. GRAUBART

OXFORD
UNIVERSITY PRESS

OXFORD

UNIVERSITY PRESS

Oxford University Press is a department of the University of Oxford. It furthers
the University's objective of excellence in research, scholarship, and education
by publishing worldwide. Oxford is a registered trade mark of Oxford University
Press in the UK and certain other countries.

Published in the United States of America by Oxford University Press
198 Madison Avenue, New York, NY 10016, United States of America.

© Oxford University Press 2022

CIP data is on file at the Library of Congress

ISBN 978-0-19-023384-6 (pbk.)
ISBN 978-0-19-023383-9 (hbk.)

DOI: 10.1093/oso/9780190233839.001.0001

1 3 5 7 9 8 6 4 2

Paperback printed by Marquis, Canada
Hardback printed by Bridgeport National Bindery, Inc., United States of America

Republics of Difference

To Mateo

Contents

Contents

Acknowledgments

THIS BOOK HAS taken many years, friends, critics, and interlocutors to complete. It has also required significant material support, both for research and for writing time. First, I thank the National Endowment for the Humanities for two cycles of funding, as well as their contribution to a yearlong fellowship I held at the John Carter Brown Library. I am also grateful to the American Council of Learned Societies for a fellowship for writing, and to the Institute for Advanced Study (Princeton), where I completed revisions while in residence. The JCB and the IAS also contributed to my intellectual development by placing me in communities of generous scholars with ample resources; this kind of privilege can be life-changing, and I am forever grateful that these institutions flourish.

At the University of Notre Dame, I received financial support from the Kellogg Institute, the Institute for Scholarship in the Liberal Arts, and Notre Dame Research, which allowed me to travel relatively freely to archives and conferences and underwrote aspects of the book's publication. The University's ongoing commitment to excellence in the humanities should be a model for all.

The archives I consulted included the Archivo Arzobispal de Lima (with thanks to Laura Gutiérrez Arbulú); the Archivo General de la Nación in Lima (particularly Yolanda Auqui Chávez and Celia Soto Molina); the Sala de Manuscritos of the Biblioteca Nacional del Perú (with thanks to Sra. Cleofé Cárdenas); the Biblioteca Nacional de España and the Archivo Histórico de Madrid; the Archivo de Protocolos and the Archivo Municipal de Sevilla; the Archivo General de Indias, both in person in Sevilla and online; the Institución Colombina at the Archivo Arzobispal de Sevilla (with gratitude to María Isabel González Ferrín); the John Carter Brown Library; the Hispanic Society of America (especially Dr. John O'Neill, Curator of Manuscripts and Rare Books and Dr. Patrick Lenaghan, Head Curator of Prints and Photographs, who solved a photographic mystery); and the New York Public Library, especially its Map Division and Art and Architecture. The Fundació Institut Amatller d'Art

Hispànic in Barcelona gave me kind permission to reproduce a photograph from their gorgeous collection.

This project required a great deal of new learning, not least of which involved studying Qur'anic Arabic and reading the dense historiographies of medieval Iberia and of enslavement across the Spanish empire. I have counted upon generous and critical colleagues and friends, among them Jovita Baber, Herman Bennett, Jeffrey Bowman, Ross Brann, Sherwin Bryant, Kathryn Burns, Kaja Cook, the late Douglas Cope, Max Deardorff, Carlos Gálvez Peña, Carlos Jáuregui, Katy Kole de Peralta, Brais Lamela Gómez, Sara Vicuña Guengerich, Kris Lane, Jane Mangan, Victor Maqque, the late María Elena Martínez, the late Joe Miller, Iris Montero Sobrevilla, Anna More, Jeremy Mumford, John Najemy, Dan Nemser, Marcy Norton, Rachel Sarah O'Toole, Eddie Paulino, David Powers, Francisco Quiroz Chueca, Susan Ramírez, Amy Remensnyder, Michael Schreffler, Stuart Schwartz, Karen Spalding, Francesca Trivellato, María Cecilia Ulrickson, Miguel Valerio, Teresa Vergara Ormeño, Elvira Vilches, Belén Vicéns-Saiz, Lisa Voigt, Margaret Washington, and too many more to list. Patricia Morgado contributed her research on early Lima as well as her brilliant maps. In Lima I thank Natalia Sobrevilla and her family, who were wonderful hosts. In Sevilla, Lourdes Távara Martín and her transnational family (especially Adriana and Natalia) have long been my extended kin, making my stays a delight. And the informal dean of the AGI, Luis Miguel Glave, has been a friend and colleague in Lima and Sevilla alike.

Renzo Honores not only read my work and suggested books and articles to me, but he took me on a memorable walking tour of Lima's former Cercado early one Sunday. We never found its wall, but walking the site and talking with a brilliant friend and scholar taught me much more. José Carlos de la Puente Luna has likewise been a constant interlocutor, careful reader, and friend. I am grateful we constantly find our projects running into one another in fruitful ways. Michelle McKinley has been not only an important critic but was a dear friend at a crucial moment, a kindness I will never forget. And Mariana Candido has been an inspiration as a colleague and co-conspirator. It was a privilege to briefly teach with her and run our Gender, Slavery, and Atlantic History seminar, both experiences that contributed to my own intellectual development.

Those who read and commented on chapters (or the full manuscript!) include the valiant and generous Ana Lucia Araújo, Ana María Echevarría Arsuaga, Ebrahim Moosa, and Bethany Aram. The late Tom Abercrombie provided extraordinary guidance under horrific circumstances; I am grateful to him and to Beth Penry for their unwavering support, critiques, and generosity. I thank the anonymous readers for Oxford University Press for engaging with a project that seemed, at times, untamable. I hope they see how I engaged with their critiques in these chapters.

I have a special debt to two departed colleagues, the beacons who brought me to Notre Dame in the first place: Sabine MacCormack and Remie Constable. Both of their imprints are on pieces of this work, but mostly I think of them as stars who helped me chart my way forward as well as friends with whom I shared many delightful meals and glasses of wine. Academia is dimmer without them.

Two collectives have shaped this project and, even more, how I wish to live in the strange world of academia. The Tepoztlán Institute for the Transnational History of the Americas, especially its visionary founder Pamela Voekel, has been my home since I first attended in 2005 with a baby in my arms. It is difficult to express what that community has meant to those of us fortunate enough to spend time there; it has been a space for experimentation, collaboration, critique, and support. Its model of expecting hard work but providing comfort and love— and childcare!—informs every event I program. I have met too many wonderful scholars in Tepoztlán to list, but I wish to recall María Elena Martínez in particular, with whom I clashed and argued and eventually became friends before her untimely death. I am also grateful to the local families who cooked and watched our children, making all of our intellectual labor possible. The second collective emerged out of Tepoztlán, and became La Patrona Collective for Colonial Latin American Scholarship. Initially an attempt to keep María Elena Martínez's light alive through collaborative work and support for our graduate students, La Patrona produced a series of events that also deepened our friendship, including a miraculous ten days in Rome, for which I also thank the Kellogg Institute, Princeton University, and Dartmouth College. During the first year of pandemic it was a lifeline, with regular Zoom cocktail hours that held us together across long distances and a great deal of uncertainly and anxiety. I am grateful to Pamela Voekel and Jennifer Hughes for conspiring with me to create it, and to Jessica Delgado, Ivonne del Valle, Anna More, Bianca Premo, and David Sartorius for making it a true source of mutual support during good and trying times. Anna More, especially, has cheered me many times when things were hard, and I want to acknowledge how friendship is foundational to good scholarship.

I was privileged to receive research assistance from undergraduate students at the University of Notre Dame: Deanna Kolberg, Rebecca Jegier, Angelica Inclan, and most notably Natalia Ruiz (who even learned paleography on the fly). Asmaa Bouhrass and Silvia Escanilla Huertas both assisted with documents in Sevilla. Marcia Tucker at the Institute for Advanced Study helped make an old photograph publishable.

Local friends were also key to surviving this long period of research and writing. In particular, I thank Christina Wolbrecht, Sara Maurer (holding her close), and Alexandra Guisinger for always being present via text and sometimes in person. My brother Barry, his wife Patty, and their daughter Katie have always been kind and supportive, and welcome me home to New York City every year. Laurie Prendergast has been a friend, cheerleader, and critical interlocutor since we were babies. Three families took in my son so I could travel over the years: Ted and Michelle Beatty, Elena Mangione-Lora and Juan Lora, and Maria and Mark McKenna. I thank them and their children for being our extended family here.

Matthew Sisk, then of the Navari Family Center for Digital Scholarship at the University of Notre Dame, produced the ArcGIS maps in the initial chapters. He patiently met with me to think about what geolocational software could do for this project, and tweaked each map multiple times until we agreed that they were meaningful and beautiful. He is also a thoughtful teacher and a talented researcher, and my work was greatly improved by our collaboration.

My writing group, which originated through the Omohundro Institute, "Archival Fragments, Experimental Modes," and is run by Sarah Knott and Sara E. Johnson, has been a source of inspiration, discipline, and joy during the pandemic. I thank them all for holding me up and keeping me on task.

I have presented portions of this research in progress in many welcoming venues, including the Tepoztlán Institute for the Transnational History of the Americas; Karin Kupperman's Atlantic World seminar and Tom Abercrombie's Latin American Studies lecture series, both at New York University; the Early Modern Workshop at the Huntington Library, hosted by María Elena Martínez and Kaja Cook; the luncheon series at the John Carter Brown Library; Sherwin Bryant's "The Early Modern Atlantic World: Slavery, Race, Governance" at Northwestern University; the Círculo Andino at the University of Michigan; a number of Comparative Early Modern Legal History events at the Newberry Library organized by Lauren Benton, Richard Ross, and Brian Owensby; the Protection and Empire Conference convened at Harvard University by Bain Attwood, Lauren Benton, and Adam Clulow; the University of South Florida; Johns Hopkins University's History Seminar; the Center for Medieval and Renaissance Studies at the Ohio State University; the Max Planck Institute; MECILA (Köln); the Brown University Program in Latin American Studies; Francesca Trivellato's Early Modern Empire+ seminar at the Institute for Advanced Study; the Program in Latin American Studies at Princeton University; and Jesús Velasco's Iberian Connections Seminar at Yale University. These and other venues were important not only for receiving feedback on the developing project but for deep conversations with scholars with intersecting interests.

I am grateful to my editor at Oxford, Susan Ferber, for her thoughtful and unwavering support of this project. She has stepped up innumerable times when things were going awry and has always expressed confidence while also being clear about the work needed on the road ahead. She also edits brilliantly, and her sharp voice eventually overrode my verbiage.

Finally, all my love and gratitude to Mateo Graubart, who has literally grown up with this book. He traveled all over the Americas and Europe with me, putting up with new babysitters, camps, and day cares. He learned Spanish and ate new cuisines and entered more museums and churches than he cared to (as he let me know). He received love from a network that now stretches across the world. He was also my friend and companion in unfamiliar places, and a great excuse to return home when things were going too long. All of my work is dedicated to him, and this book is no different.

Republics of Difference

Introduction: Republics and the Politics of Self-Governance

ON A SUNDAY in October 1475, two Jewish men, Raby Mosé Matutel and his son-in-law Muysé, and a Christian friend, Alfonso de Córdoba, walked into the office of one of Seville's many Christian notaries.[1] The two Jewish men "renounced the law of Moses," indicating that they were temporarily placing themselves under the jurisdiction of Christian judges for the purpose of this visit. Along with other unnamed Jews, they had abandoned their synagogue and were praying together in another house. The document they asked the notary to draft obligated them to return to the synagogue and not to pray or hold *cabildo* (council) meetings elsewhere with any other Jews, under a substantial cash penalty. Whoever violated the agreement would pay the sum to the third party, Córdoba, a member of the household of a powerful Castilian nobleman.[2] Matutel and his son-in-law gave authority to "whatever judges of this city" to exact the penalty, renouncing as well their right to appeal and their right to customary law.

This odd document—wherein men who embraced Jewish law as upheld by their local Jewish judges willingly subordinated themselves to a Christian notary and unnamed Christian judges for the sake of accountability to their religious community—reveals one way that law informed group formation in the early modern Spanish kingdoms. Muslims and Jews in the Christian kingdom of Castile could and did live under their own authorities and judges until the late fifteenth century expulsions. They also had access to local and royal Christian authorities, which, as here, enabled them to venue-shop for particular outcomes. Two laws coexisted, albeit in a distinct hierarchy where one was significantly more powerful. In this case, Jewish subjects gained an outsider's enforcement of their oath not to splinter their own religious community. Perhaps the rabbi also made a pledge within his own faith and law not to exit with a minyan (the quorum of ten Jewish adult men needed to perform public worship and certain other

Republics of Difference. Karen B. Graubart, Oxford University Press. © Oxford University Press 2022.
DOI: 10.1093/oso/9780190233839.003.0001

obligations) or to form a new congregation, under a spiritual rather than financial penalty. Christian courts might be more effective in collecting his penalty, and paying a Christian for failure to carry out a Jewish obligation would confer additional shame. Thus the men invited a Christian to enforce a Jewish obligation, renouncing Jewish judges' authority in the matter, in the public space of the Christian notary's office.

The coexistence of multiple competing jurisdictions and legal authorities, requiring mutual negotiation and advocacy to produce stable and legitimate rule—what scholars have called legal pluralism—shaped everyday life in the Iberian world.[3] The existence of multiple legal jurisdictions did not imply equality or equivalence, though the disparate political forms were largely united through their loyalty to the crown. While medieval Iberia has been seen by some as a place of romanticized *convivencia* (coexistence), prejudice and even violence underwrote official toleration.[4] Christian monarchs, like their Muslim and Jewish counterparts, were certain of their religious and legal superiority; moreover, they often had the power to enforce their will. They also benefitted from access to and control over sometimes-wealthy minority communities, as well as the claim that those communities flourished under royal protection. Minority legal spaces offered participants a way to assert their own practices and exercise their own notions of justice, however fragilely. At the same time, non-hegemonic jurisdictions marked consequential difference. The claim that certain practices were "customary" for a group could externalize supposedly inherent differences. If Jews and Muslims used law differently than did Christians, that might be used to explain how they differed in other ways, including the makeup of their bodies, minds, and emotions.[5]

People in the late medieval European world were often subject to multiple legal jurisdictions. The thirteenth century had ushered in massive changes, producing a canon law of the Roman Catholic Church along with secular legal systems embedded in urban centers, manors, and kingdoms. Customary law, which legal historian Adriana Chira calls a versatile community justice, was a recognized means for resolving local conflicts both formally and informally.[6] A unified modern legal system was still far away in fifteenth-century Iberia, much as some monarchs hoped to construct one.[7] Instead, Christian rulers on the Iberian peninsula recognized multiple legal jurisdictions that were simultaneously subject to the justice of the monarch and of the Catholic Church. This meant, among other things, that the king or queen was the judge of last resort and could reserve jurisdiction to him- or herself for certain types of offenses.

Iberian monarchs governed by delegating certain kinds of jurisdictions through corporate political units they often referred to as *repúblicas*. The late medieval and early modern republic was a vehicle for producing the common good of a group of people who were largely similar and had shared interests.[8] These republics promoted good governance through accountable rule and attention to law, and they were headed by officials who served limited, and usually elected, terms. A classic example is the guild, formed by a group of qualified and certified artisans who constituted themselves as arbiters of regulations designed to promote their professional well-being.[9] They elected a leadership body that established procedures for learning the craft and moderated behavior within it through penalties and punishments. They might receive royal or municipal permission to set up shops on particular streets, which could become a locus for group communication and interactions. They collected dues or fees to pay for celebrations, mutual support, and other expenses.

The republic was an important instrument for Iberian monarchs during periods of rapid change, allowing them to expand and maintain their territorial reach. Kings and queens empowered frontier settlers, city councils, desirable foreign merchants, resident Muslims and Jews on the peninsula, and Indigenous peoples in the Americas as republics. The institution served royal needs to hold and govern all kinds of populations, while also providing a means for groups to define themselves. For those excluded from power, whether minorities or majorities, the republic was a space for constrained self-invention. Members made financial sacrifices in order to promote certain kinds of collective action, which could include attempts to push back against royal and local interventions.

This study examines how largely disenfranchised peoples crafted and utilized the political form of the republic on both sides of the Atlantic, in Seville and Lima, as spaces of self-governance and as consequential markers of difference within an imperial system. The republic was central to the ways that disempowered peoples articulated their own needs. It could also dictate the ways they should function in order to be intelligible to outsiders. In that sense, the ways that republics acted contributed to how their members were perceived by the dominant society. *Republics of Difference* does not search for continuities between these two linked places, nor is it a comparative analysis intended to demonstrate simple equivalences or contrasts. Instead, it examines how diverse peoples, in distinct political moments, reacted to and reanimated a mechanism intended to give them a proscribed form. It brings together groups usually studied in isolation—not only juxtaposing Spain and its colonies, but examining the interactions of Muslims, Jews, and West Africans within Seville and Indigenous and Black residents within Lima—by focusing upon the institutions that shaped their experiences in consequential ways.[10]

Republics had many different names. In Seville, Muslims and Jews lived as minority communities with access to their own religious judges, learned elite, and political leaders. By the twelfth century, Castilian authorities generically referred to these political entities as *aljamas*, borrowed from the Arabic *al-jamāʻa*, "collectivity" or "community," though communities likely referred to themselves in other ways.[11] Fifteenth-century Castilian monarchs appointed a man of West African descent to act as judge for men and women of African origin or ancestry in Seville; he was known as the *alcalde* or *mayoral de los negros*. That community also participated in other republican forms like the city's *cofradías* (confraternities, or lay Catholic brotherhoods that came together to celebrate masses, collect alms from the public, do charitable works, and process on feast days). In the Americas, native polities had innumerable forms and names at conquest, but Spanish officials reorganized them into *pueblos de indios* (Indian towns) headed by hereditary native leaders they generically called *caciques* along with new colonial officers. All of these institutions served both the common interests of the communities and the needs of royal authorities; they also interacted with other republics such as city councils (*concejos* or *cabildos*). As part of a larger system of law and culture, republics became vehicles for the articulation of internal and external notions of belonging and status in the Christian Iberian world.

The peoples discussed in this book were perceived as different and lesser in fluid and sometimes ambivalent ways. All of them were expected to be able to convert to Christianity and, while the completeness of their conversion might be questioned in practice, the Church and monarchs had no doubt that they should, and could, become Christians. At the same time, all were thought to have significant and possibly inherent differences embedded in their bodies, sometimes visibly and other times not. Republics were one of the structures that Christian authorities used to manage those populations, to protect those (like recent converts) who might be infected or otherwise damaged by them in metaphorical or material ways or to protect them as members of fragile communities. Scholars have disagreed over whether these differences should be categorized as racial, but there is no doubt that the tension between sameness and difference was integral to policy and to community organization. While race is not the central topic of this work, the republics studied here emerged both to control difference and to shape its many forms in racialized ways.

The Beginnings of the Iberian Republics

In 711, the Iberian peninsula was drawn deeply into the Islamic world, as a small contingent of Berbers and other North Africans under Arab leadership crossed the Strait of Gibraltar from the Maghreb, entered Andalucía, and defeated a Visigothic army. From the south, these forces would take control of most of the peninsula up to the Pyrenees, forming al-Andalus, which was eventually unified under the Caliphate of Córdoba and incorporated into commercial networks that extended from the Mediterranean to the Indian Ocean. Islamic rule was characteristically urban. While a city of some kind had sat on the Guadalquivir River since ancient times, Muslim Išbīliya (later known as Sevilla) was transformed into an extraordinary metropolitan center. In addition to its well-known architecture, characterized by an abundance of neighborhood mosques marking residential areas, the city was undergirded by a complex irrigation system, supported by an effective administrative and taxation structure, and enhanced by famous centers for ceramics and metallurgy. Its site on a navigable river allowed for the exchange of people, agricultural products, and merchandise between the peninsula and North Africa.[12] Christians and Jews also continued to live in al-Andalus as *dhimmī*, resident non-Muslims with a protected status, limited internal autonomy, and a special tax burden.

After a brief period of unity under the Caliphate, the peninsula deteriorated into sectarian factionalism, and Christian armies began to move out from the northern mountain fringes of Asturias where they had retained hold. In the eleventh century, Christians took Toledo, and the Taifa ruler of Išbīliya called for support from the Almoravid dynasty across the straits in Marrakesh. The Almoravids responded by taking control of al-Andalus briefly until a new wave of fragmentation led to the incursion of another Berber Muslim group, the Almohads, in the 1140s.[13] In the thirteenth century, the warring Christian kings of Aragón, Castile, and Navarre joined to defeat the Almohads. The last Islamic kingdom on the peninsula, Granada, fell to Castile in 1492. The Christian monarchs largely absorbed the Islamic infrastructure; cities like Córdoba and Išbīliya were among the most magnificent in Europe at the time. In addition to co-opting urban planning and borrowing political language (the Castilian *alcalde* taken from the Arabic *al qadi*, for example), Christian kings kept Muslim farmers on the land much as they were, supported Muslim and Jewish artisans in towns, and recruited elite Muslim and Jewish immigrants to anchor their frontier cities.

The eleventh through thirteenth centuries were periods of conflict but also of territorial expansion for Christians, who eventually reorganized under the monarchs of Aragón, Navarre, León-Castile, and Portugal.[14] Despite the consolidation into a smaller number of kingdoms, the monarchs did not rule alone. Historian John Elliott has called these "composite monarchies," kingdoms fashioned by acquiring territories and integrating them with other dominions, whether under a single law or while recognizing constituents as distinct entities.[15] Characteristic of such composite states was the monarchs' need to negotiate with the high nobility of the kingdoms as well as with urban elites in order to govern. The key to the stability of the early modern Spanish monarchy was its success at integrating leading political actors, from a variety of interests and locations, into a form that largely left the substance of power in local hands.[16]

Nobles, also called *ricos hombres*, were members of the great houses that controlled extraordinary territories and wealth and had some level of jurisdiction over large rural populations. They were buttressed by *hidalgos*, members of the lower nobility, who enjoyed lesser privileges and properties, and pledged military aid to the Crown. The Crown delegated powers to other bodies as counterweights to the aristocracy; urban centers had councils (*concejos*), which sent representatives or procurators to parliamentary assemblies (*cortes*), and monarchs issued charters (*fueros*) to settlers on frontiers, offering privileges and self-rule as a condition of holding the territory. These regional and local elites formed important power bases for the monarch and held leverage over their own urban citizens.

Resident Muslims and Jews were also recognized as members of semi-autonomous bodies. They paid taxes that guaranteed them the ability to self-govern and to practice their religions with limited interference, in a fusion of dhimmī status with that of the republic. The multiplication of republics—especially the urban concejos and the Muslim and Jewish aljamas—functioned as a brake on the power of elites, creating dependencies on the monarch and competition over resources and jurisdiction. They were also a rich tax base.

Muslim and Jewish aljamas were not simply collections of residents who worshipped in a particular faith. These were political institutions that represented the interests of the group to other authorities via elected or appointed officials. That common interest would be identified through their own mechanisms, including regulating whose voice might be heard in political decision-making. But even poor and disenfranchised Muslims and Jews might have a relationship to the aljama, as the institutions often assisted in the manumission of enslaved coreligionists. Wealthier Muslims contributed to purchasing freedom for enslaved Muslims, and communities aided in communications across the Mediterranean to their families.

The Crown gave the form of a republic to another disempowered population in Seville: non-Muslim Africans, often from West Africa (sometimes called "Guinea" in documents) and increasingly referred to as Black. Andalucía is separated from the Maghreb by the narrow Strait of Gibraltar, and had received its visitors and ambassadors throughout the centuries. By the late fourteenth century, the incipient Portuguese-African slave trade stretching from Senegambia to Angola, including the Canaries and other coastal islands, was bringing enslaved non-Muslim Africans to Lisbon and Seville, where contracts for their sale began to appear in the registers of local notaries. In the fifteenth century, Black men and women were a common sight in Seville, as were those of mixed heritage, often called *mulato* or *loro*.[17] The community was defined by association with both slavery and foreignness, as the emerging Atlantic trade created a constant stream of new and involuntary immigrants. Authorities created new institutions to assist and manage them: an archbishop opened a hospital and confraternity, and monarchs named their alcalde. Through these and other mechanisms, they built community. Black men and women participated in cultural and religious events throughout the city, including welcoming Queen Isabel when she entered the city in 1497.[18]

The use of the republic as a vehicle for governance shaped but did not determine the form political entities took. Republics were not autonomous but they were intended to carve out legitimate juridical spaces, safe from competing groups. The fact that those spaces only protected practices that the Crown deemed minor or inoffensive did not make them less powerful to community members, who clearly relished their ability to choose their leaders and define their actions. Community members pushed back against royal and local constraints in important ways, defending their officers and judges against outside appointees and litigating on behalf of resources. They also cooperated with other minority or coreligionist groups, and often borrowed practices from outsiders. Collective action—whether distributing tax burdens, participating in festivals, providing mutual aid, or funding lawsuits—was one of the main ways that the communities constituted themselves beyond the expression of religion or heritage.

Republics across the Atlantic

By the late fifteenth century, three major changes had affected this political landscape. In January 1492, the monarchs Isabel and Fernando entered the Islamic kingdom of Granada and claimed it. While Granadan Muslims retained the right to practice Islam legally for another eight years, the conquest coincided with the decades-long rollout of the requirement that all free inhabitants of the Castilian kingdom be Christians.[19] In periodic waves buoyed by the establishment of an Inquisition designed to identify and correct false or lapsed converts, Jews (1483, 1492) and then Muslims (1501) were forced to receive baptism or emigrate. While corporate governance would continue for many, including Africans who converted without shedding their distinctiveness, Jewish and Islamic law were no longer recognized.

Second, the peninsula was increasingly reshaped politically. Navarre, like Granada, came under Castilian annexation. The marriage of Isabel of Castile and Fernando of Aragón in 1469 set the stage for joint rule, though the kingdoms retained political independence even when each took their respective throne in 1474 and 1479. After Isabel's death in 1504, the kingdoms split briefly; they reunited under Charles V, though Aragón maintained much of its independence. Portugal would later (1580–1640) unite dynastically with Spain. These Castilian expansions concealed significant tensions. Even within composite Castile, regional anti-monarchical conflicts could turn violent, as during the revolt of the "*Comuneros*," citizens of its autonomous cities in 1520–1521.[20] Despite periodic attempts to centralize authority, institutions, and law, the peninsula remained fragmented in important ways, including in terms of wealth and power.[21]

Finally, Iberian explorers and traders were setting out to expand their own, and thus their rulers', political and economic reach. Portuguese and Castilian expeditions arrived at ports along the coast and coastal islands of north and western Africa, and eventually ventured west into the Atlantic. The Portuguese made few inroads on the African continent, where they sometimes negotiated the right to trade with coastal elites, including for captives.[22] In contrast, African islands and the Caribbean offered greater imperial possibilities.

Spanish and Portuguese invaders laid claim to the Americas in a variety of symbolic, economic, political, and brutally militaristic acts, but also by redefining the sovereignty of its natives. The Spanish crown claimed its "New World" territories through the mechanism of parallel republics. It recognized soldier-settlers as *vecinos* (political citizens) on the cabildos of its frontier cities, and it turned pacified native peoples into royal vassals organized into small polities or *parcialidades*, dismantling the larger networks or empires that had previously bound them. Each of these republics was intended to check the expansiveness of the other, via limited self-governance, and to produce an income stream for the Crown.

As with the Muslim and Jewish aljamas of the peninsula, the negotiated contortion of diverse native polities into republics transformed them. By the late sixteenth century, viceroys had relocated and reorganized much of the diminishing Indigenous population. Andeans responded, migrating to escape notice and taxation. The republics that transformed into pueblos de indios directed their political engagement toward litigating and petitioning, to defend the resources they still controlled.[23] They also reinvented their practices, created competing genealogies of nobility and legitimacy, and found ways to establish justice in local affairs.

Conquest and the transatlantic slave trade inserted West and West Central African peoples into this new connection between the Americas and Europe. The collapse of the Indigenous populations of the Caribbean, due to epidemic disease, warfare, flight, and overwork, led Spanish officials to turn to the African slave trade as a solution to their labor and ethical problems. Sixteenth-century debates over the morality of enslaving or coercing natives—tellingly coded as "fragile"—enabled officials to characterize the African trade as more just.[24] By the middle of the sixteenth century, cities housed as many Blacks as Spaniards. The Catholic Church organized them into confraternities, which arguably became Black subjects' most important vehicle for constrained cultural expression and political organizing.[25] But in most cases, they were denied secular spaces for self-governance; only under extraordinary circumstances were they recognized as republics. This refusal was linked to a fear of resistance and conspiracy, but it created difficulties when authorities wished to coerce free people of African descent to pay taxes or perform collective labor.

Transformational Self-Governance

Despite the varieties of ways that members participated in religious rites, ethnic cultures, political representation, and local economies, the republic—as the vehicle of official recognition—inherently transformed communities. These transformations can be characterized in four ways.

First, the particular form that a republic took was historically contingent and reflected how outside forces attempted to contain, segregate, or mark the community, as well as the desires of participating community members to constitute themselves as an entity. The republic was not permanent or unchanging, nor was it simply the aggregate of people named by the adjective appended to them. It was a strategic and informed act of collectivization. Just as all of the permanent residents of a city were not participating members in its cabildo or concejo, a Muslim or Jew who could not afford to contribute to the head tax might not be a political member of an aljama, even if he or she was at times subject to the jurisdiction of one. Indigenous men and women sometimes fled rural obligations, or moved to urban centers and lost kin-group resources. People of African descent in the New World only belonged to republics under very specific conditions, which might include the loss of autonomy and the embrace of repulsive actions such as slave-catching. A republic was an ongoing act of exclusion as well as inclusion.

Second, the political forms of the Spanish empire emerged out of this interaction and were, therefore, concurrently established with the subaltern republics rather than imposed upon them. While the republics were intended to contain or protect particular subject peoples, those subjects also pushed back and shaped imperial policy. The Crown encouraged competition over workers and resources, demanding constant conflict and negotiation that constrained town and city councils. These contentious interactions spread local knowledge across institutions, since each had to investigate the other in order to better argue their position. This was an imbalanced dynamic; leaders of minority or subaltern groups had to be fluent in multiple legal languages to bring their concerns to judges in different arenas, but even dominant groups had to make their claims intelligible and responsive.

This mutuality also reshaped the officials who executed the law. The leader-judges of Jewish, Muslim, Indigenous, or African-descent communities subordinated to the Spanish-Christian monarch had to walk the knife's edge of legitimacy within the community, among other people of the faith or larger polity, and with the external powers that dominated them. Rulers sometimes, and usually unsuccessfully, sought to impose their own officials on subordinate groups. The more subtle move was to pare away at jurisdiction, for example by removing criminal cases and those involving parties from different jurisdictions. There were also prohibitions on all sorts of cultural expression, curtailing the ways that communities could celebrate or mark status. Disparagement could also come from within the groups. Famously, the Maghrebi Islamic scholar (*mufti*) al-Wanšarīsī issued fatwas to Andalusian Muslim qādīs, instructing them to leave places conquered by Christians.[26] To remain as a judge or leader under imperial rule required not only flexibility and finesse, but also a willingness to be called a traitor or worse.

The leaders who emerged had control over material resources. Republics were usually stewards of their own finances. They collected taxes to meet external obligations, and they accumulated and administered institutionally held wealth and property. Elected or appointed officers had to manage these, and the body had to make decisions about their use or liquidation. Communities had to instruct new generations in forms of literacy and accounting, to ensure that important documents were archived and protected. If membership in a collective came at a cost, it could also provide access to useful knowledge and resources.

Third, republics had porous borders; it could be difficult to discern who was a member of a community and who was not, and definitions could shift over time and space. The early modern Spanish world was the site of loosening social categories, which compounded the difficulty of determining who was a New Christian or an Old one, or an Indian or mestizo.[27] The association of status, privileges, and fiscal obligations with republics made the stakes high even for plebeians. Members of the lower and subservient classes occasionally became wealthy and acquired the trappings of that status: property, clothing, jewels, enslaved servants. It was difficult to assign status based upon visual indicators.[28]

At times, imperial authorities tried to establish geographical boundaries for some republics, assigning Jews or Muslims to particular parishes or relocating native towns throughout the New World. Some republics benefited from a specific location, like the artisan guilds or foreign merchants who sold wares on certain blocks. But for subordinate groups, the requirement to live in a particular place could be onerous or even dangerous. Seville's Muslims and Jews, like urban Indians in Lima, sent lawyers to defend their choice to remain outside the assigned boundaries, and Lima's men and women of African descent made themselves difficult to locate or move. The desire for containment could also reflect a desire to police physical relationships; the mixing of peoples who were considered members of distinct groups with distinct legal status created problems of categories. Castilian monarchs issued laws prohibiting sexual relationships between Christians and non-Christians, often under penalty of death. Because of the lack of physical distinctiveness between members of different religious groups, authorities called for the wearing of insignias or specialized clothing. But they proved mostly unable or unwilling to enforce either segregation or the wearing of such symbols.

In the New World, such sexual relationships were not usually considered dangerous and were encouraged if they could aid conversion and cement political and economic hegemony.[29] However, Spanish women were initially scarce enough to be able to marry men of higher status, and Spanish men balked at marriage to plebeian native women, preferring informal sexual relationships with them (and with other non-Spanish women) while reserving Catholic rites and legal formality for Spanish women.[30] Many, if not most, of these "informal" sexual relations would today be considered rape or assault, but Spanish law did not protect the bodies or virtue of Indigenous and Black women. Sex did create a category problem: to what republic did the children of mixed parentage belong? Under what law did they live, were they free or enslaved, to whom did they owe taxes, and who was charged with collecting them?

Finally the republics of Muslim, Jewish, Indigenous, and African-descent peoples were understood to require containment or transformation. Containment was rarely successful, but attempts to change them had deeper effects. Jews' and Muslims' special tax payments made them the "treasure" of the monarchs, and their wealthier members were invited to participate in the royal court, giving Christian rulers an incentive to maintain Jewish and Muslim populations. Even so, archbishops, preachers, and congregations periodically called for their conversion. The aljamas were forced to keep their celebrations and rituals silent and invisible in order to avoid harassment. The language of crusading echoed in Castilian streets, and while riots were not common, they could spread rapidly and dangerously.

The apparent success of the conversion project, mostly due to threats and violence, contributed to the demise of Muslim and Jewish aljamas. By the late fifteenth century, growing numbers of men and women who had converted to Christianity or were descended from converts became the focus of anger and paranoia. The institutionalization of a Spanish inquisition in Seville in 1480—to prosecute judaizers, or infectious, backsliding converts from Judaism—was followed in 1483 by the expulsion of any Jews in Andalucía who refused to convert. In 1492, the remaining Jews in Castile were forced to convert or leave, and in 1501 Castilian Muslims had to follow suit. These terrible events reflected internal political struggles as well as questions of religion and culture. The invention of a third category between Jew or Muslim on the one hand, and Christian on the other—the inadequate convert who cannot help reverting to old customs when surrounded by unconverted kin—inexorably tipped the balance of power. In a world of Old and New Christians, heritage was made to explain difference: the statutes of *limpieza de sangre* (blood purity) reflected a new desire to see religious difference as inhering in the body over generations, despite conversion.[31] Eventually *moriscos* (converts from Islam) would be expelled from Spain for fear they were conspiring to rebel, and *conversos* (converts from Judaism) and their descendants would live under suspicion and accusation as well as barriers to their advancement.

In the New World, Indigenous and Black subjects were expected to convert to Catholicism, and conversion did not change their status as tribute payers. The new converts would, however, be considered fragile neophytes, both because of their recent introduction to the faith and their supposed intellectual and emotional limitations.[32] They were perceived to require education in civility and urbanity (*policía*), which involved changing their physical environments as well as religion, work discipline, and culture.[33]

Indigenous subjects would receive that education through their republics, in new physical spaces, and under the guidance of Catholic priests and native leaders, the latter trained in Christian catechism, the Spanish language, and good labor habits. When hereditary leaders proved incapable of this guidance, they could be removed, but new sorts of officials were also put in place to cultivate promising Christians and good colonial subjects.

Slavery removed most Black people from self-governance. When enslaved, they were intended to have access to Catholic priests as well as the just rule of their masters, both mostly honored in the breach. Confraternities were one of their scarce spaces of any autonomy. But even freedom granted few opportunities for self-governance, other than the rare Black republics the Crown imposed on men and women who refused work discipline in one form or another. These could replicate the conditions of enslavement, or they could be free towns with arduous labor and tax obligations. The republics, then, were not simply a means for self-governance but also served as vehicles for transforming the temperament and behavior of conquered peoples.

Not all of this transformation came from without. Members of the collectives themselves pressed for change, as defensive strategies and as innovations. Muslim and Jewish communities reformulated religious practices to accommodate their particular deprivations and circumstances, sometimes in communication with distant religious leaders. Andean collectives litigated, redefining notions of property in order to protect resources in a form that would meet colonial expectations of good governance. They declared herds, lands, deposits of foodstuffs, and even the act of litigation itself to be surplus assets that protected communities in contingent circumstances.[34] The act of forming a collective organization—a republic—could produce a social good distinct from the one imagined by authorities.

Self-governance under conditions of unequal power could be dangerous. In 1562, don Gonzalo Taulichusco, the son of the *kuraka* (ruler, renamed cacique in Spanish documents) of the Lima Valley at the time of the Spanish conquest, wrote his last will and testament before a Spanish notary.[35] Don Gonzalo was navigating a changing political and economic landscape that created tensions between his personal advancement and the collective good of his subjects. Most crucially, he was entangled in a variety of property relations that threatened the community's survival. His experiments with land sales, rentals, and partnerships with Spanish settlers had left them financially, and thus politically, vulnerable. Most egregiously, he had sold lands over which he had no personal or political rights under the current regime. In his will, he attempted to undo these acts, and he sought to disable his successors from repeating his offense by collectivizing much of the property now attached to his office and turning it into a community fund jointly overseen by the new cacique and a Franciscan friar. Don Gonzalo simultaneously critiqued the ease with which Spanish law could mischaracterize and redefine Andean practices and utilized that law to dismantle native forms of ownership.

Like Raby Mosé Matutel, don Gonzalo Taulichusco found himself confronting a crisis by drawing on the notions of justice being articulated within his community as well as the forms of justice that surrounded and threatened it. Seville's Jewish residents, like the Lima Valley's Indigenous populations, understood their own historic practices as well as the challenges of their present. They utilized a jurisdiction granted them by dominant powers, in a legal language that was external to them, to assert their control. For them, the republic was neither a way to preserve tradition nor to supplant old forms entirely with the new, but was a pliable and negotiable institution that created new, often exclusive, and contentious ways of maintaining communities.

As these examples reveal, the republic can serve as a device for tracking the ways that communities formed and reformed themselves within the emerging Spanish empire. It provided a form through which groups struggled against interventions, constituted and disciplined their membership, and invented their practices over time. It was also the public face of disempowered communities, and could bolster negative stereotypes. Raby Matutel's use of a financial incentive might fuse with stereotypes about Jews and money; don Gonzalo's illegal land sales could underscore popular beliefs that Andean leaders were corrupt or inept. The variety of republics, including the ones that occasionally existed for people of African descent, illustrate how flexible an instrument it could be—weak or strong, transformative or conservative, collective or elitist.

These republics, tethered within imperial structures that siphoned their resources and constrained their actions, were not places of total freedom, nor were they sites of pure subjection. Law became an instrument through which difference could be articulated both from within—as a carving-out of practices that should not be erased and that encode forms of justice and identity—and also from without—as an externalization of inherent or metaphysical difference that could be read on the body, as a harbinger or marker of race. The difference of Jews, Muslims, and Indians could be summarized by their law, which catalyzed and naturalized what was Christian and Spanish. Blackness, generalized as the absence of that law, would be encoded as the impossibility of legal integration.

———

Republics of Difference is organized into three parts, each moving between late medieval Seville and early modern Lima in parallel chapters. The first part, "Space," introduces the two locations in terms of the ways that their authorities tried, often unsuccessfully, to place subordinated peoples into segregated spaces. *Juderías* (Jewish quarters), *morerías* (Muslim quarters), and pueblos de indios were conceived as sites to contain members of those republics for the purposes of protecting them or protecting others from them. But a series of arcGIS maps, created by extracting spatial and demographic information from notarial records and censuses and projecting them onto contemporary urban maps, demonstrate that these policies had mixed results. While kings, archbishops, and municipalities fought over placing Jews, Muslims, and Indigenous subjects into particular parishes, in reality, occupation, social class, and place within their own community's hierarchy proved far more instrumental to the ways they used the city. Residential and workplace geography reflected the opportunities available to people of different skills and advantages, their aspirations, and their internalization of subaltern status. Notably, placing these cases into conversation demonstrates how different they were from one another, in terms of access to resources and power. Mapping Seville (Chapter 1) and Lima (Chapter 2) reveals the distinct internal structures of the Muslim, Jewish, and native republics as well as the ways they related to outsiders.

While they were popularly associated with physical space, republics truly functioned through law. The second part, "Jurisdiction," analyzes how they were integrated into larger social structures through law and politics. Chapter 3 introduces the legal frameworks of late medieval Seville. By the fifteenth century, religious minorities in Castile still retained the right to worship in their faith, but other aspects of coexistence required energetic vigilance from political actors. This meant entering into contests with royal, municipal, and ecclesiastic authorities. Aljamas fought with all of these over jurisdiction, generally losing their ability to prosecute crimes among their members or their civil conflicts with Christians. But they were able to retain jurisdiction over their own civil law, which was the material basis for much of everyday life. They were sometimes aided by royally appointed *alcaldes mayores*, wealthy and well-connected Muslim and Jewish men who acted as appellate judges and mediators between Crown and aljama. A similar framework was offered to Seville's non-Muslim African community under their *alcalde de los negros*, a royally appointed man of African heritage who managed relations within the diverse Black community and between it and the rest of the city. Although subordinate to the Crown, these republics could be dynamic and inventive.

Chapter 4 details what the aljamas actually did and how they were organized. Because their internal records are lost, it rebuilds the life of the aljama by, first, understanding the limits that other jurisdictions imposed on its actions, and then searching for traces of practices within the documentation that survives. This includes how ritual life was carried out, what kinds of property the aljama held institutionally, and how religious and legal leaders interacted with outsiders and insiders. The chapter also reconstructs something of the interior world of Muslims and Jews in Seville, including some religious practices (particularly worship, education, and marriage), property distribution and inheritance, care for the dead, and tax collection. Seville's residents operated competently in a variety of jurisdictions. If the aljama was not a space of complete autonomy, its members crafted practices collectively by drawing upon shared knowledges.

Chapters 5 and 6 turn to the institutionalization of community leadership in greater Lima, the capital of the viceroyalty of Peru. The Spanish conquest of the Americas dismantled large imperial structures in order to replace them with the Spanish monarch, while identifying or crafting smaller polities that would function as native republics and conduits for Spanish rule. As in Castile, these would act as checks upon municipal cabildos formed of wealthy new citizens who sought control over Indigenous labor, territory, and natural resources that ranged from water to silver. Andean communities and their leaders could only hold off these invasions by learning to craft intelligible narratives about resources and power; unlike Seville's Muslim and Jewish judges, Peru's caciques did not always share notions of land tenure, political succession, and resource management with their conquerors. Caciques and communities survived by reinventing themselves, co-producing a body of law that governed property, succession, and resource management that gestured at a compatible Andean past.

The final part, "Order and Disorder," presents two case studies that illustrate how the characterization of the republic was consequential. Chapter Seven begins in Seville, where enslaved and free residents of African descent were granted institutional existence through the creation of the alcalde de los negros in the fifteenth century. His job was to adjudicate civil conflicts, and to oversee marriages and other festive or ritual acts. The city also boasted a number of confraternities founded for African-descent Christians, which enjoyed some popularity but also received public animosity. The idea of organizing Black subjects into a republic faltered in the early Caribbean and mostly disappeared, although the confraternity model flourished. The Black republic, or pueblo de negros, re-emerged in mainland schemes for disciplining *cimarrones* (fugitive slaves), supplying slave labor to mines, and forcing free urban Blacks to labor and pay tribute. It became a fallback measure for Spanish monarchs and viceroys who grew frustrated with their inability to control the masses of men and women who eluded slavery by manumission or self-theft. If people of African descent were considered foreigners and refused citizenship, they were also denied a history of customary law and nobility in their homelands. Instead of protecting them, as they did Indians, Spanish authorities theorized that citizens had to be protected from them, cast as they were as people whose only relationship to property was theft. The erasure of Black institutions in much of the Spanish Americas can be traced to the refusal to grant them a legal collective personality.

The second case, in Chapter Eight, is Santiago del Cercado, a walled pueblo de indios built at Lima's eastern edge, under the auspices of the Jesuits in the 1570s. Cohorts of forced native laborers lived there in temporary housing, joined by more permanent migrants. The town was subject to many different legal jurisdictions, including the natal caciques of temporary workers, an Indian alcalde and cabildo, a Spanish *corregidor* (magistrate), the royal *audiencia* (appeals court), the viceroy, and the Jesuits. These interests can be seen to clash in conflicts over property regimes, including collective lands purchased by the native communities who sent their labor drafts and private holdings created and traded by some of the permanent residents. These cases demonstrate how different levels of jurisdiction articulated colonial indigeneity in distinct ways, from encouraging urban Indians to embrace private and heritable paths to wealth, to insisting upon tying their common good to collective holdings. The depiction of Indians as too fragile to live according to the rules of policía that they were being taught had traction across the empire, even inflecting the language used by Indigenous litigants. Self-governance came to require embracing aspects of colonial discourse.

The republic proves a key mechanism for understanding how Spanish rule functioned on the local and imperial levels. It created space for communities to express their changing shared interests and produce their own forms of justice. It allowed for the continuity of beliefs and practices within a form that was plastic enough to respond to new incentives and threats, including when outsiders attempted to make its institutions more pliable so as to extract resources more efficiently. It provided a semblance of security, although it was not adequate to guarantee safety.

The republic was far from the only way that members of dominated groups organized themselves. There were significant costs to living in the republics, leading many Jewish, Muslim, Black, and Indigenous peoples to live outside their structures. These costs were often material—the republic distributed and enforced tributary and labor obligations—but they could be mortal, as when violent rioters invaded Seville's *judería*. In the Americas, native people vigorously migrated with the intention or the effect of abandoning their republics. Presenting oneself through the republic of a marginalized group was an action rather than an identity.

The republic was a norm in the late medieval and early modern Spanish world. Members of different corporate institutions knew that they would interact within and through these relationships, between judges and between distinct forms of law. They inhabited the same space, making interactions quotidian and often frictionless. The Crown's many subjects believed they knew something about one another, because they understood each other's republics, even superficially. This made the republic a stand-in for the community whose interests it represented, for better and worse. The monarch's Jewish, Muslim, Indigenous, and Black subjects would be known through (often unkind) representations of their collective practices. They would even have to articulate their demands through those refractions of their practices, in order to be seen and heard.

PART I

Space

Cities often mark historical sites associated with marginalized inhabitants, as if they had not been residents like any other. The neighborhoods might be called quarters or ghettos, words that signify poverty, victimization, or simply unequal differentiation. They might have been cut off from other spaces by walls or by reputation. Seville and Lima both bear these traces today, locating the cities' historical Jewish or Indigenous neighborhoods in ways that suggest that the rest of the city belonged to a "normal" and unhindered inhabitant. Authorities' attempts to contain the minority republics reflected the opposite truth: cities required ease of movement, and individuals connected with one another across many categories of belonging. To the extent that these quarters existed historically, they were part of contentious political processes that etched the hierarchies of the minority republics into larger urban social stratification.

Instead, members of the republics occupied the cities in distinct and meaningful ways. Jews in Seville centered themselves on a neighborhood that gave them prestige, while Muslims formed occupational enclaves with their Christian co-workers. In Lima, Indigenous people turned marginal mixed neighborhoods into their own centers, but royal policy also pushed many into Spanish households and workshops. In all cases, the ways that members of the minority republics occupied space engaged with the other ways they experienced the city, as members of their own communities but also as economic actors in larger spaces they did not control.

I

Religious Republics in Seville, 1248–1502

ON TUESDAY, FEBRUARY 15, 1502, nine Muslim men gathered in their mosque in San Pedro parish in Seville "at the hour of mass" to hear a royal order (*cédula*) delivered by a representative of the Catholic monarchs Isabel and Fernando: "We have decided to order all the *moros* [Muslims] from our realms to leave." The Muslims' *alcalde* (qādī, judge) Çayde Blanco, was absent, perhaps already having emigrated or converted. Royal officials seized the mosque's property and sequestered its belongings. Each of the nine men "took the order from Their Highnesses, and kissed it, and placed it on their head, and they said that they obeyed it and were obeying it as a letter from their King and Queen and natural lords, may God our Lord let them live and reign for a long time in His Holy service."[1]

As the nine Muslim men enacted this ritual of submission to their king and queen, they disbanded their republic and acknowledged the end of their membership in the legal category of *mudéjar*, or Muslim living under Christian rule. They followed Andalucía's Jews, who had been required to convert or emigrate in 1483. As of 1502, it was no longer legal to live as a free non-Christian within Castile or to use Jewish or Islamic law individually or within a body.[2] The Inquisition would continue to grapple with the ambivalent distinction between religious law and custom or culture as it claimed to identify backsliders among the baptized. But the royal order rendered the juridical institution of the aljama—the congregation or community of Muslims living under their own law, a Muslim republic—illegal in Castile.

The location of this ritual was significant: the Muslims gathered in their only mosque, in the parish of San Pedro. Twenty years earlier they had been forced to relocate to the parish from their homes and businesses around the city. Seville's Muslims and Jews had periodically struggled over physical space with their Christian rulers, both on a symbolic and a material level. Separation could be

Republics of Difference. Karen B. Graubart, Oxford University Press. © Oxford University Press 2022.
DOI: 10.1093/oso/9780190233839.003.0002

protective or it could make a vulnerable community an easy target. The *judería*, or Jewish quarter, was at different times a space of protection, a death trap, and a prestigious neighborhood for Jewish families. Muslims, in contrast, did not have a *morería* or Muslim quarter and came to occupy the city through occupational networks embedded in streets and neighborhoods. Their forcible relocation to San Pedro in 1483 was a sign that their future was limited.

Most Castilian subjects enjoyed freedom of movement, and migration between and within cities was common.[3] The wartime settlement of frontiers necessitated enticing large populations to relocate, and individuals also moved in response to economic crisis and disease. Law enshrined the right of subjects to be mobile, though in the sixteenth century anti-vagrancy laws would attempt to restrict some subjects, often the poor and those perceived as not meeting the obligations of local citizenship.[4]

The right to occupy a particular space was not guaranteed. Most land was reserved to the Church, the Crown, or the municipality, for their temporary or permanent distribution. When towns were founded, land distribution (a formal process called *repartimiento*) established hierarchies as well as patterns of use, including the placement of markets, mills, ovens, and other public goods. But it was uncommon to hold people in particular places from which they could not move. Lepers, wrongly thought to convey highly contagious disease, were detained, as were the voluntary members of religious orders or others subject to temporary or permanent enclosure.[5] Prisoners were sometimes incarcerated, though they were more likely to be exiled or placed on galleys. But these were exceptions.

The aljamas that governed religious minorities in Castile were political, economic, and cultural institutions, but legislation often conceived of them as groups of people who could be contained. Attempts to place the aljama on a map or—a related move—to mark its members with insignia were generally unsuccessful but the attempts could be costly, even deadly, for the community. Instead minority religious communities occupied urban space in ways that drew from their collective self-invention but also as individual residents with political and economic interests. Jewish and Muslim aljamas differed in their resources, their access to power, and their reliance upon the Christian city. Using documents that trace aspects of their economic and social lives, this chapter maps out the distinct ways each occupied the fifteenth-century city.

Conquest and Transformation

The foundations of the Muslim and Jewish aljamas in Seville were laid in 1248. Fernando III took the city after its military leader Axataf refused to surrender during the long conflict. As he prepared to claim the city, Fernando refused all of Axataf's terms, including a request to rehouse Muslims in a walled sector "so that everyone would be safe."[6] Instead he cleared the city for a theatrical reconsecration and attempted to attract loyal immigrants as settlers.[7] Alfonso X, his son and successor, worked to bring in Jewish notables from Toledo, and he attracted some Muslim leaders, including the son of the king of Baeza, who became the judge or qadi of the new Muslim aljama. Much of the displaced Muslim population returned, and were joined by Muslim immigrants.[8] It took multiple rounds of property distributions to stabilize Christian occupation.

Seville soon had one of the largest Jewish populations in Castile. Some lived in an enclosed urban neighborhood, described as the judería, set between the Alcázar and the city walls, where three mosques were given to them for their synagogues.[9] These notables gave shape to the institutional form of the aljama, the body that would govern the urban Jewish community. The most illustrious early immigrant was don Çuleman ibn Sadoq, an ambassador and revenue collector in the royal court. Alfonso endowed don Çuleman with significant properties in and around the city, including houses, vineyards, and olive groves. He awarded Rab Yuçaf Cabaçay a store in central Seville near the Cathedral. There was also a Jewish town founded outside the center, Paterna. There Alfonso granted twenty-seven Jewish men, many identified as *Rab* (here likely meaning religious scholar), *almojarife* (tax collector), or *alfaquí* (legal scholar), generous plots laden with olive and fig trees.[10] These acts constituted the sites as new political and religious centers, whose elites were endowed with properties that would generate wealth they could use to support the monarch, and provide employment for the region's laborers. The men and their families enacted a new structure of Jewish governance, while they also represented strong ties to the Castilian monarch.

Some notable Muslims also immigrated, joining the large community of laborers and artisans that remained. Alfonso X appointed Abdelhaq al-Bayyāsī as the new Muslim aljama's first qadi or judge. He granted him a significant rural estate at Alcalá de Guadaira as well as a house in the parish of San Pedro near the *alhóndiga*, or public granary, which also served as a hostel for visiting Muslim merchants.[11] A handful of Muslim immigrants received minor grants of rural land among Christian settlers.[12] Neither monarch established a morería. Muslims, like Jews, purchased or rented real estate from the new Christian owners, paying the Church the *diezmos* or ecclesiastical taxes.[13] From the very beginning the aljamas had differential access to resources and to power.

The aljamas were tasked with meeting Jewish and Muslim obligations to higher authorities, particularly their fiscal contributions. Alfonso X's founding ordinances for the city already identified Jewish and Muslim communities as targets for raising funds for public works, such as the repairs to the city's bridges after the long siege.[14] They also paid significant annual head taxes that were assigned at the level of the kingdom and then distributed according to the size and wealth of particular aljamas by Muslim and Jewish officials within the royal court. Tax records surviving from 1292 to 1294 show the city's Jewish aljama paying the large sum of 115,333 *maravedís* (mrv) annually. The larger but poorer Muslim aljama paid about 5,500 mrv in each years.[15] Each aljama organized the collection of taxes for the monarch, ecclesiastic institution, or endowed individual to whom income was owed. The leadership also represented the community's interests to outsiders. To carry out their tasks they drew upon their own intellectual traditions with attention to local distinctions. The aljama was a specific and contingent response by particular Muslim and Jewish communities to the new administrative demands of Christian authorities.[16]

A City of Republics

Christian settlement drew upon the physical organization of the Almohad city, whose dense population (estimated at 65,000–83,000 people) had been divided into many neighborhoods, each with its own mosques or oratories, markets, bakeries, ovens, residential spaces, and bathhouses.[17] The settlers divided the city into twenty-four *collaciones*, or parishes, each with a church and two (non-voting) political representatives (*jurados*) in the municipal concejo. Each collación also served as a fiscal unit for taxation purposes.[18] The remainder of the concejo were royally appointed and locally elected officers who were required to meet in the presence of the jurados, non-voting officials who reported their work back to the citizenry.[19] The concejo represented the interests of the city to the monarch at the assemblies called Cortes, in a relationship of mutual obligation that bound the kingdom together.[20]

Castilian monarchs delegated some governance and tax collection to other urban republics that supported their economic and political aspirations, many of which also occupied physical space within the urban center. Genoese merchants, who had had ties to Seville since the Almohad period, were installed with privileges negotiated between their state and Fernando III in 1251, including tax reductions and jurisdiction over commercial litigation among their compatriots. In the middle of the fourteenth century, these privileges were expanded to include the right to purchase homes on the Calle de Génova; their own legal jurisdiction under their consuls using Genoese law; and special jurisdiction in debt-related lawsuits with non-Genoese, releasing them from local courts and giving them direct access to higher authorities.[21] Their *barrio*—though many owned homes in other parts of the city—became a commercial center with shops, ovens, baths, and a church. Similarly, the neighborhood of "Los del mar" was identified with

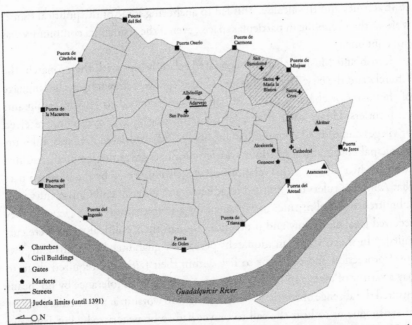

FIG. 1.1 Late Medieval Seville, with relevant sites identified. Drawn by Matthew Sisk, Navari Family Center for Digital Scholarship, University of Notre Dame.

those involved in the maritime industries, shipbuilders and sailors who received rewards for past service and privileges to encourage their enterprise in Seville. Their alcalde managed maritime disputes and the community was exempted from serving in the land-based military. The neighborhood had its own butcher shop, and its residents could sell merchandise from their homes.[22]

Non-Muslim Africans could call upon the office of the *mayoral* or *alcalde de los negros*, though this judge was not elected by his peers but appointed by the monarch. They had no residential neighborhood—enslaved Black subjects lived either with their masters or independently in poor neighborhoods near their jobs, and free Black men and women, insofar as they can be identified, were scattered across the poorer parts of the city.[23] But their republic was associated with marginal neighborhoods. Their confraternity was hosted in the chapel of Nuestra Señora de los Ángeles at the far end of the parish of San Roque, outside the city walls and across from the Puerta Osario and the Jewish cemetery.[24] Their alcalde was instructed to hold their public gatherings facing the church of Santa María la Blanca in the former judería. Officials wished to keep non-Muslim Africans at a distance, because their festive activities were perceived as disruptive, while also incorporating them into the city through the controlled mechanisms of the

confraternity and the alcalde. This led to anchoring some of the political framework of their republic in particular spaces, even if the residential community was
not contained.

Jewish and Muslim aljamas negotiated relationships with the monarch, the
Church, and the city. Their rights and obligations were drawn from the language
of the *fueros* or charters that Castilian monarchs issued to Jewish immigrants
on frontiers. Under their terms, Jewish settlers occupied royal lands, received
privileges and limited community autonomy, and negotiated tax rates. Like any
municipal corporation, Muslims and Jews formed governing councils and distributed their offices.[25] This relationship was also informed by the dhimma pact
that Almohad rulers had granted to adherents to Judaism and Christianity who
submitted to Muslim rule: in exchange for a payment of tribute (*jizyah*), they
received legal autonomy and protection, though their political rights were curtailed.[26] In short, Castilian monarchs personally guaranteed Muslims and Jews
royal protection and the right to live within their faith, but required them to
pay a variety of taxes and fiscal impositions. Institutional tolerance by no means
ensured the absence of conflict—even the right to worship at a particular mosque
or synagogue or to hear the call to prayer had to be negotiated—but Jews and
Muslims had access to the counsel of their own judges, could distribute their tax
burden as they chose, and were guaranteed places of worship, butchers, bathhouses, ovens, and cemeteries.[27]

The aljama offered Muslims and Jews a space for making political claims
within a society that treated them ambivalently. Although some were referred to
as *vecinos* of their municipalities—literally meaning neighbors, the term increasingly defined residents with obligations and privileges—theirs was a limited
citizenship at best.[28] Jews and Muslims did not serve in municipal concejos, but
they were periodically called upon to pay taxes or perform services for what these
articulated as the common good.[29]

Taxation also defined their relationship to the monarchy. At least from the
twelfth century, Muslim and Jewish tenants were a "special property" or "royal
treasure" of the monarch who derived fiscal benefits in the form of taxes and
forced loans. Expansionist monarchs like those in Castile and Aragón also
strengthened their royal authority through these relationships, which could be
displayed as redemptive gestures.[30] Jews and Muslims could not be held by other
individuals without the Crown's permission, and monarchs shored up support
by distributing shares of their labor and financial contributions to royal retainers and religious institutions.[31] Revenues from Jewish aljamas in particular were
presumed to be destined for the war chest in exchange for their right to settle on
royal lands. In 1190, Alfonso VIII called Castilian Jews *servi [camarae] regis*, or
dependents of the king (or of his treasury) in the fuero he issued to Cuenca, a

characterization that followed them throughout the kingdom. In Castile, Jews were assigned a symbolic annual sum of thirty *dineros* to the church, a payment meant to remind them of the coins for which Judas betrayed Christ to the Jewish Sanhedrin.[32] Jews were vassals in a "relationship of dependency and obligation that bound [them] to render a special service to their lord, the king of Castile."[33]

In contrast, Castile's Muslims were a large, mostly rural labor force with a small elite.[34] They paid royal head taxes, tithes to the Catholic Church, and taxes to the concejo.[35] Like Jews, Muslims paid special taxes on monopolies that served them separately, including public ovens, bathhouses, and hostels. They were sometimes subject to labor drafts, particularly for the upkeep and stocking of castles and fortifications.[36] Their artisans and masons were required to contribute labor, by building cathedrals, churches, and city walls.[37] The Crown also required Muslims to fund Castile's war against Granada in the late fifteenth century. Seville's most prominent Muslims received *francos*, or tax abatements, but they would have been responsible for such obligatory loans.[38] Both Muslim and Jewish communities played central roles in the kingdom's finances, and both were directly connected to royal authority through the aljama. As with many European composite monarchies, Castile's sovereigns drew power from the corporate entities with whom they negotiated rule. Jewish and Muslim aljamas did so with access to different resources, but both communities existed in tension with both local and royal needs.

Differentiation

As frontier societies absorbing large laboring and tax-paying populations, the Christian kingdoms could hardly reject assimilation and acculturation. But intimacy also invited concern, particularly because Jews, Muslims, and Christians could not be superficially distinguished. Christian leaders and rulers often embraced discourses of separation, spouting dangerous canards about Jewish and Muslim contamination, but in practice relationships were generally more pacific. Efforts to mark or move Jewish and Muslim populations were rarely implemented because they threatened local economies, undermined revenue collection, and dislocated foundational relationships. This changed in the late fourteenth century, as Castilian politics became bloodier and discriminatory rhetoric became associated with anti-elite positions. But even then there was no consistency in application.

The centuries between conquest and expulsion were marked by repeated, usually failed attempts to impose symbolic and material controls over religious minorities. These largely took two forms: requiring superficial distinctions like clothing, insignia, and hairstyles, and calling for physical separation. Unlike early

Muslim and Jewish calls for neighborhoods where they could feel safe, these controls were intended to delineate hierarchical differentiation between populations that were more similar than not. Popes, archbishops, and monarchs were their usual authors, though the discourse of segregation also manifested at the local level, and no institutions were consistent in their messaging. The socioeconomic implications of these controls could be devastating even for those not targeted—kingdoms faced the loss of tax revenue from migration, neighbors feared inflationary effects on real estate, consumers and artisans worried about barriers to everyday trade as well as the destabilizing effects of violence—and many parties fought them or dragged their feet on implementation. Indeed, the periodic reissuing of similar orders is a clear signal that they were not being implemented. Nonetheless, the discourse cast a long shadow, and false memory of the physical separation of members of religious minority communities tends to dominate the historical narrative.

The precarity of Muslims and Jews in Christian Europe was formalized with Pope Innocent's Fourth Lateran Council of 1215, though prohibitions on their actions had circulated throughout medieval Christendom.[39] Lateran denounced Jews holding public office and called for both Jews and Muslims to be physically distinguished by a marker or insignia on their clothing, intended to humiliate them but also to prevent sexual contact with Christians. Castilian monarchs were reticent to alienate their Jewish vassals. Fernando III complained in 1217 that unhappy Jews would leave for Muslim lands, diminishing his treasury. The Pope exempted Castile from the dress codes.[40]

Castilian monarchs were even slower to impose restrictions on Muslims, a less wealthy (and therefore less concerning) population.[41] In the early fifteenth century, Castilian monarchs demanded that Muslim men wear a yellow *capuz* or cowl, and that both men and women sport a visible turquoise crescent on the shoulder. These were, again, probably unenforced most of the time.[42] Hairstyle was another popular target. In Aragón a cut known as the *garceta* was first prohibited to Muslims, and then required for them, as Christian fashions changed. Castilian Muslims were subject to more lax regulations about hairstyle than those in Aragón, leading some Aragonese Muslims to request exemptions on the grounds that they often traveled to Castile.[43]

More pointedly, Castilian monarchs issued sumptuary legislation. Most aimed at prohibiting plebeian Christians from wearing luxury goods, but occasionally monarchs differentiated between wealthy and powerful Muslims and Jews, on the one hand, and Christian nobles, on the other. Legislation issued in 1268 and 1351 prohibited Jews and Muslims from wearing fabrics and jewels that suggested nobility, and royal ordinances issued in 1412 stated that they could not wear cloth costing more than 60 mrv the *vara* (a little more than a yard), or use the honorific title "don."[44] In 1476, Isabel and Fernando denounced the ambiguity that accompanied wealth: "It is not possible to tell if the Jews are Jews or if they are clerics or learned men of great estate and authority, or if the Muslims are Muslims, or if they are gently bred courtiers."[45] Laws that prohibited Muslims and Jews from owning Christian slaves, employing Christian salaried workers, and having Christian domestic servants, while somewhat ineffectual, were part of a refusal to normalize noble status among Muslims and Jews, and to deny them power over Christians.

Muslims, Christians, and Jews purchased cloth, tailoring services, and clothing from one another without much differentiation, at least as documented in the fifteenth century. When Yantob Pollegar, a Jewish tailor, placed his teenage son Jacob in apprenticeship to a Christian *toquero* (a maker of women's sheer headdresses), the employer was required to give the young man, at the end of his placement, a *corocha* (long coat or cape), a *capirote* (a cap with long folds of cloth that hang to the shoulders or beyond), and a *sayo de florete* (a fine cotton jerkin or garment that goes over the doublet).[46] Jacob was to acquire the skills to produce clothing worn by the well-off, and he would be rewarded with fine clothing that would not mark his Jewishness.

Further evidence of actual wardrobes comes from the items sequestered by officials when Muslim artisans defaulted on debts. Alí Oberí, a *borceguinero* (maker of a soft leather boot or buskin), was relieved of a new carpet of Spanish wool, a grayish-brown cowl, a velvet cap, a new *contray* (a Flemish fabric) mantle, a green dress with a lot of sewn trim, and an ounce of seed pearls.[47] When the mason Haçan de la Puente failed to repay a debt to an Italian merchant, officials seized a white *fustián* (twill) waistcoat with silk sleeves and appendages, a new embellished purple *capuz*, and another worn *capuz*.[48] These clothes marked the wearer's gender and economic status, but not his or her religion. Jews and Muslims had special garments for prayer and ritual, and occasionally they might have been forced to wear an insignia, but in their everyday life they dressed like their Christian neighbors.

Space and Separation

The discourse on physical separation emerged with the Christian conquest, as the Crown established a judería composed of parts of what would later be the parishes of San Bartolomé, Santa María la Blanca, and Santa Cruz, behind a high wall with three gates. The exterior gate, known as Puerta de la Judería, gave way onto a field, the main Jewish cemetery, and the slaughterhouses that give the site its modern name, Puerta de la Carne. Two internal doors opened onto the parishes of San Nicolás and Santa María. The three mosques donated by Alfonso X to serve as synagogues lay within, as did the community's ovens and baths.[49] Not all of the Jewish immigrants lived within it, but it was intended to serve as a safe and convenient incentive to settlement.

In contrast, Fernando denied the Muslims the wall they requested. Like Jews, they wanted access to community resources; they also articulated a need for protection from Christian economic and physical violence. Moreover, they worried about the theological implications of living under Christian rule. As al-Andalus fell, many Islamic jurists argued for emigration and some muftis even ruled that those who remained were no longer Muslims. Al-Haffar, for example, contended that Muslims who lived among Christians exposed themselves to corruption.[50] As

FIG. 1.2 Surviving remnant of wall of the judería. Photo by Karen Graubart.

the city changed hands, the effects of Christian hegemony over space and place became evident: the sound of church bells drowned out or replaced the Muslim call to prayer, former mosques were reconsecrated as churches and synagogues, and public signs of Catholic religiosity and pomp displaced banned public rituals of other faiths.[51]

While Jews and Muslims lived within an environment that circulated anti-Jewish and anti-Muslim discourses, relations in Seville were largely peaceful through the middle of the fourteenth century until local tensions set off episodes of violence. After cycles of economic crisis and epidemic disease, exacerbated by high taxes and indebtedness, attacks on Jews were incorporated into all manner of conflicts. Most notably, Enrique of Trastámara, fighting his half-brother Pedro for the Castilian throne in the 1360s, claimed that Pedro was influenced by the kingdom's wealthy Muslims and Jews. His success, enthroned as Enrique II, escalated hostility between his followers and Pedro's loyalists, and anti-Jewish discourse became an instrument of that conflict.[52] The men who allied themselves with the House of Trastámara began to reshape local politics in cities like Seville, and anti-Jewish polemics provided them with a focus.

In that context, the anti-Jewish sermons of Ferrán Martínez, the archdeacon of nearby Écija and a member of the propertied class indebted to Enrique, were an accelerant.[53] Martínez began to preach in Seville's public plazas in 1378, courting citizens who felt excluded from power and who had suffered through decades of war and crisis. He called for Jews to be excluded from the city's community and offered to defend any Christian who attacked one. The Jewish aljama, led by the cloth merchant don Hia ibn Ataben, complained to Juan I, who issued letters of protection to the aljama. In 1388, don Hia approached the royal court tasked with hearing complaints against municipal officials in Seville, to remind them of the aljama's protected status. Don Hia had the public scribe read out the king's words against the cleric:

> [Y]ou walk daily among them preaching many evil things. . . . We are much amazed at your claim that you are so intimate with us that you know our and the Queen's intentions, and that you do such things. Therefore we prohibit you to walk around preaching these sermons and saying these things against [the Jews], and if you want to be a good Christian, that you stay in your house rather than go running around like that with our Jews, lest the aljama of this city is destroyed through your action and they lose what is theirs.[54]

The aljama's legal victory was undermined by Martínez's public response denouncing their alleged crimes. He continued to incite crowds, despite the efforts of local and royal officials.[55]

With the deaths of Juan I and the archbishop of Seville in 1390, Martínez stepped up his campaign, which fueled more generalized urban unrest against those perceived as unduly powerful, including the very visible Jewish royal tax collectors.[56] Royal and local officials continued to defend the Jews, ordering some Christians whipped for verbal abuse and arresting agitators at a riot on Ash Wednesday in 1391. In June, another mob rioted in Seville, and the rebellion spread across Iberia that summer. Seville's judería was sacked.[57] Its three collaciones rapidly became majority-Christian, and two of its three synagogues became the Catholic churches of Santa Cruz and Santa María la Blanca.[58] Many of the judería's former residents fled or converted, and the Jewish population declined precipitously as indicated by diminished tax payments. Enrique III responded to the concejo's failure to protect his Jews by fining it 135,000 doblas to make up for his lost revenue.[59]

The pogroms of 1391 marked a shift in politics across Castile. Jews became symbolic extensions of those entrenched in power, and disempowered audiences could be roused by attacks on them, even when fomented by the also-powerful. Castilian monarchs brought back policies around insignias and sumptuary laws, which had new valence because of the mass conversions of the period.[60] Catalina of Lancaster, who briefly acted as regent for her minor son, Juan II, issued drastic policies in the early years of the fifteenth century, shaped by her relationship with the Dominican preacher Vicente Ferrer. Ferrer warned of the wavering practices of new converts, and called for Jews and Muslims to be contained, in part to protect conversos from bad influences.[61] Conversos moved away from Jewish neighbors and kin to demonstrate their distance from their past. But they remained a focal point for Ferrer, who stated to an audience in Zaragoza in 1415, "many Christian men believe their wife's children to be their own, when they are actually by Muslim and Jewish [fathers]."[62]

In addition to calling for Muslims and Jews to live in segregated neighborhoods with severe penalties for mobility, Catalina's ordinances attacked the legitimacy of the aljama as a juridical institution and prohibited Muslim and Jewish use of the honorific don.[63] In Seville, municipal authorities at least considered separating the populations. Converso chronicler Alvar García de Santa María wrote that Seville's Jews and Muslims had been ordered to move to the parishes of San Julián and Santa Lucía, at the far northeast limits, near the Puerta de Córdoba. Some converted to Christianity rather than move; others complained to Fernando, who suspended the ordinances in the regions he ruled. The law's main legacy was that it was opposed and reversed.[64]

Even more moderate royal policies came wrapped in calls for physical separation and symbolic designations. Juan II issued new legislation intended to protect Jews and Muslims from interventions by the church and the nobility, and expressed familiar concerns that Jewish emigration would lead to "great dimi-nution and damage to my rents and taxes."[65] But he expressed frustration that municipalities refused to implement his calls for separation. In 1437, he wrote a letter to the Archbishop of Seville, don Diego de Anaya, noting his intention to compel the city to create segregated neighborhoods.[66]

The monarch was correct in his assessment that the municipality was block-ing the move. Concejos represented interests that could not be reduced to reli-gion. Jews and Muslims were men and women with occupations, wealth and assets, and political allies and enemies: local conflicts could draw attacks upon them, as in 1391, but they could also protect or bypass them. A group of Jewish residents petitioned Juan II, claiming that they were unable, not unwilling, to meet his conditions. They were too poor to buy or build new homes in the for-mer judería, and its Christian and Jewish landlords were asking opportunistically high rents. The neighborhood was simply too small to accommodate the new population without removing existing Christian residents. The petitioners closed by requesting that the king appoint "two or three good persons, faithful and of good conscience, in whom [he] trusted" to oversee the operation. The committee would help select a location that served the good of the Jews and their Christian neighbors, and would set reasonable prices and rents on those homes. Juan II named Archbishop Anaya to lead the commission.[67]

But the structure of municipal politics undermined this effort. The jurados, representing each of the city's collaciones, had strong opinions about the location of a potential judería and morería. Christian residents of Santa Cruz filed a peti-tion claiming that the Jews were planning to wrest homes away from the parish's Christian owners at unfair prices. Instead, the residents recommended that the Jews be resettled in another neighborhood, at the eastern edge of the old judería, where not only would the Jews be protected, but Christians would also be safe from the "infamy" of their interactions.[68] They suggested the Barrio Nuevo, the "Barrera que llaman de doña Elvira," or the Postigo del Jabón, all of which they claimed were already populated by Jews and would provide the distance neces-sary to protect Christians.[69] It is difficult to calculate the fifteenth-century tip-ping point for turning a Christian neighborhood too Jewish, but clearly well-off Christians were more tolerant of a few rich Jewish neighbors than they were of a mass of poorer ones.

The debate in the concejo had no material effect: Seville's Jews were never relocated. It was only in 1483, with the conversion order for Andalucía's Jews, that Muslims were finally forced into a designated morería. That morería lasted barely two decades, ended by the expulsions of 1501.

Separation was a blunt political instrument that used the specter of Jewish (and to a lesser degree, Muslim) contamination to gain support for other political

motives. Even Christians who endorsed the sentiment disagreed about implementation. The policy was a distraction for city councils, one with dark implications. To dislocate Jews or Muslims was also to dislocate Christians and create
economic and social disruptions. And Jewish and Muslim communities were
not homogeneous; their internal divisions reflected the distinct roles they played
within the city, which often found them in partnership with Christians. Those
differentiations also explain the distinct paths taken by the city's Muslim and
Jewish aljamas.

The Spatial Organization of Seville

Religious minorities did live in residential clusters, but these followed logics
other than separation. They reflected people's occupations, their aspirations, their
socioeconomic status, and the housing barriers they faced. This can be shown
with a series of GIS (Geographical Information System) maps that connect data
that notaries took down about residents to physical locations in the city. To create
them, I turned the register of Jewish and Muslim notarial clients into a database
that included residential or work parishes, occupations, kin, and the other frag-
mentary bits of information that notaries recorded when they drew up contracts
and other documents.[70] Those names were coded with geographical information
and distributed onto historical maps of the parishes using ArcGIS software. These
mappings must be analyzed in the context of the history of Seville's urbanization.

The maps reproduce the shortcomings of their documentary base, notarial
records, which are predominantly economic contracts between individuals.[71]
They mostly involve Muslim and Jewish subjects who desired or were required
to work with a Christian notary; no Jewish or Muslim notaries in the city left
records that have been located. They overrepresent the moderately well-off,
professionals, and artisans, precisely the people who dominated aljama governance. Other kinds of clients appear occasionally, including farmers who came
to buy or sell goods in the city or women who purchased textiles for their own
use. Occasionally there are oblique references to Jewish and Muslim neighbors
of properties under contract to Christians. But most Muslims and Jews went
undocumented in this genre, most concerningly the poor.

It is difficult to estimate what part of the total population these records represent. There is no accurate count of either confessional population, whose numbers
would have been in constant flux due to waves of conversion and emigration.[72]
The best estimate is that the city held some 450–500 Jewish heads of household
prior to the 1391 pogrom.[73] The failed attempt in 1437 to move Jews into a segregated neighborhood called for some sixty-five houses, a loss of about 85 percent.

Muslims prove even more difficult to count. Scholars suggest that there were fifty or so Muslim vecinos (as heads of households) in the early fifteenth century, falling to thirty-two or thirty-five families by midcentury. Tax records demonstrate a steep decline: the Muslim aljama paid 8,000 mrv a year in 1463, but generally only 4,000–4,500 annually between 1480 and 1501. The tax records—a distribution of the total sum of 150,000 mrv spread unequally across all of Castile's Muslim aljamas—indicate relative demographic shifts rather than head counts. They might reflect falling absolute numbers, or a decline in the number of wealthier families that could contribute.[74]

Nonetheless, the database and maps reveal patterns in the dispersal of Jewish and Muslim residents, including how these changed over time. There are distinctions between the groups and key inflection points, reflecting changes in the city's economy and the increasing threat (and reality) of expulsion. The exercise presents a previously unknown view of how certain Muslim and Jewish families occupied the city, and their kin, coreligionist, and occupational networks. They show the emergence of political structures out of the larger mass of the faithful.

Jewish Seville

Jewish families lived or worked in at least eight of the city's twenty-four collaciones, mostly scattered around the eastern sector of the city associated with the former judería. Fully 72 percent of the Jewish notarial clients resided in Santa Cruz, Santa María la Blanca, and San Bartolomé. Others gave the notary addresses in neighboring collaciones, such as the commercial center Salvador, the wealthy collación of San Isidoro, and the poorer San Nicolás. Two families lived or worked across the river in Triana. The concentration suggests the deep connection between the economic and political heart of the aljama and the synagogues, cemeteries, and other resources in that space. But even this small sector of the city was economically, socially, and religiously diverse.

The parishes of Santa Cruz, Santa María la Blanca, and San Bartolomé were far from ghettos. The median cost of a home in one of them ranged between 14,900 and 16,000 mrv, which was slightly below the median city price of 22,608; thirteen parishes had cheaper housing stock.[75] Some of their neighborhoods, like the Corral de Jerez in Santa María la Blanca, were quite wealthy. Other streets were humbler: parts of Santa Maria la Blanca were considered a magnet for ruffians, and Cervantes would place "an infinity of Black men and women" in its small plaza at the Puerta de la Carne, near the church that housed the Black confraternity of Nuestra Señora de Los Ángeles.[76] But most residents of the former judería were well-off Christian families.[77]

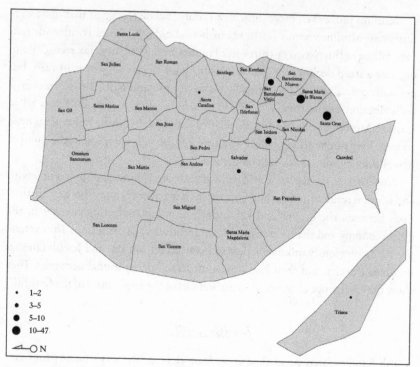

FIG. 1.3 Distribution of Jewish residences, drawn from notarial records between 1441–1484.

Source: Wagner, *Regesto*. Map by Matthew Sisk, Navari Family Center for Digital Scholarship, University of Notre Dame.

This corner of the city was the epicenter of Jewish political life, and home to the families that constituted its aljama. They included families notable for their wealth or their connections to the powerful. The commercial merchants David de Illiescas and David Pardo had homes in the Corral de Jerez. Yudá Aben-Sancho, of Santa Cruz, was one of the collectors of the 5 percent tax on dried and green fruits in 1474; he paid more than 6,000 mrv per year to the city's *mayordomo* for the privilege. He also acted as guarantor for a Christian who collected the tax on grapes.[78] Members of the Briviesca family also lived in Santa Cruz, including Ysaque Castillo, a bookseller who held the contract to collect the thirty dineros the aljama owed to the church each year.[79] His brothers David and Samuel lived nearby, and in 1493 a house in that parish was sold that had belonged to Yantob de Briviesca and his wife Luna before expulsion.[80] Abrahán de Briviesca was a tailor, but he was connected to powerful local figures including one of the city's Christian jurados, who loaned him money, and Rab Yucef of La Algaba, who acted as guarantor. Briviesca had multiple real estate properties beyond his home in Santa Cruz, including a house in La Algaba and a workshop or store in San Salvador.[81]

There was little sign by of the Castilian Jewish nobility in Seville, but they would have seen themselves as vassals of the monarch and members of his court rather than subject to the obligations of the aljama. They mostly appear as transitory collectors of royal rents, such as Vidal and Yucef Bienveniste, members of a wealthy and powerful family that included don Abraham Bienveniste, who served as *alcalde mayor* (representative at the royal court) of the kingdom's Jews under Juan II as well as his financial advisor.[82] A handful of Jewish owners of rural estates also appear in the records, such as Rab Yucef of La Algaba, who was called an *escudero* (squire) or high-status landowner.[83] But the Jewish community's political center was urban and plebeian.

The heart of the aljama, its governing cabildo, was composed of artisans and professionals. A record from a cabildo meeting in 1454 listed Mayr Abensemerro as the aljama's judge and nineteen other members, who included a medical professional (maestre Ysaque *cirugiano*), four tailors (Mosé el Leuy, Ysaque Anigo, Janto [Yantob] Pollegar, and Ysaque Aborrabe), a leatherworker (Ysaque Benhabib), and a silversmith (Frayme Barchilón). Some of these men came from notable families, despite being artisans by trade. Silversmiths were part of a heavily regulated guild, and the cost of entry—raw materials—was prohibitive. Many prominent Jewish families had members in the prestigious trade.[84] But even a tailor like Yantob Pollegar was far from disadvantaged.[85] After his teenage son completed an apprenticeship, the father and son formed a partnership, with salaried Christian employees. They lived in San Isidoro, among wealthy Christians, rather than in Santa Cruz.[86] Many of the men who held cabildo offices had at least distant ties to Jewish notables or intellectuals.

The cabildo's plebeian status is, however, signaled by the absence of the honorific don before any of their names in the 1454 document. The title was originally endowed by the monarch on grandees as a sign of high nobility, but over time it was appropriated by minor nobility (*hidalgos*) and then by the upwardly mobile more generally. Jews and conversos were popularly accused of using it too flagrantly; the title came to be associated with Jewishness, and some Christian nobles eschewed it altogether. Despite royal ordinances limiting its use to Christians, monarchs referred to Jewish aristocrats in their court as don, and many less notable Jews used it within their own communities.[87]

In Seville, the Christian notary utilized the don with eight Jewish clients including the silversmith don Yucef. Frayme Barchilón, also a silversmith, was denied the honorific in the 1454 document but received it twenty years later before a different notary when arranging the financial affairs of his late son, there called don Çuleman Barchillón. The status of the Barchilón family might have changed, or a different notary in another moment might have been more flexible.[88] Women in general used doña more freely, and twenty-nine Jewish women were recorded this way by Christian notaries. Plebeian Jews were only marked in documents as *judío* or *judía*.

Notaries designated some Jewish men with Rab or Raby, which could indicate either an ordained religious leader or a Talmudic scholar. Men using this honorific were the anchor of Santa Cruz and Santa María la Blanca, and none lived in San Bartolomé, a less prestigious address but home to the city's surviving small synagogue. Six Rabs visited Christian notaries in the second half of the fifteenth century, two of whom were likely from nearby towns. These men did not state secular occupations, an argument for considering them ordained leaders rather than scholars. Mayr Abensemerro, who served as the aljama's judge, received a "donation" from the city's cattle ranchers in 1460 as a fee for pasturage; the money was characterized in the documentation as payment for the kosher butchers.[89] Such fees might have provided salaries for Jewish officials and ordained leaders.

Jewish families were integrated within economic enclaves in these parishes, often among Christians of their social class. Ysaque Abenbaça, a Jewish man who lived in the Barrera del Çofer ("Neighborhood of the Jewish Notary") in Santa Cruz, resided next door to the Catholic Church canon Fernando Cataño.[90] Two well-off Jewish men contracted bookseller Ysaque de Castilla to sell a home they owned in Santa María la Blanca, which sat next to houses owned by a converso clothing seller and a Christian of unknown occupation. A 1466 rental agreement for a home in San Bartolomé shows that "Mosé, Jew" and Anton López, a Christian silkweaver, were its neighbors.[91] Jews and Christians might even occupy the same house; the Christian borceguinero Juan de Jerez rented the attic of his home in Santa María la Blanca to a Jewish tenant in 1472.[92]

Jewish families also lived outside the old judería. The less fortunate, often working in textiles, lived either at its outskirts—in the parish of San Bartolomé, where housing was cheaper—or in neighborhoods like San Nicolás among others of their trade.[93] The tailors Mosé Toledano and Yehuda Santaren lived in San Nicolás, as did a shoemaker called Yantob. Symuel de Talavera, also a shoemaker, shared a workshop in San Salvador with Yantob. The very poor are invisible in these notarial records, though the argument Jewish residents made in 1437 against forced relocation to the judería suggests that many of those who struggled financially resided outside its boundaries. The poor clustered with those of their occupation or marginal economic status, or perhaps they rented rooms or outbuildings on properties owned by better-off coreligionists.

At the other end of the social scale, members of the distinguished Pollegar family were the only Jews to reside in the wealthy parish of San Isidoro. While

Jews of more comfortable status might have preferred to live among rich Christians, they apparently encountered barriers. This can be seen through the residential patterns of wealthier conversos, many of whom had converted to protect their livelihoods and secure their children's futures. While most conversos remained in the eastern part of the city, they occupied nearly every parish in some number; some of the spread surely reflects an anxious desire to disassociate from Jewishness. The wealthiest, however, moved into elite addresses previously unavailable to them.[94] Prominent merchants did so: Diego de Susán lived in San Isidoro, Juan de Córdoba lived in San Ildefonso, and Alfonso González Abenino had a home in San Esteban, all alongside wealthy Christian neighbors. Some conversos rented out their former homes in the judería while living elsewhere with their families. Converso merchant Diego González let an expensive house in Santa Cruz to Symuel Abenxuxen, who had not converted. Next door lived a silversmith and a member of the Jewish cabildo.[95] This all suggests that wealthy Jews faced discrimination in housing and responded by turning the former judería into a prestigious neighborhood, known both for its economic power and for its association with a Jewish identity.

After the 1391 pogrom shattered their neighborhood, Jewish residents of Seville fought off attempts to force them to congregate. But the heart of the aljama remained in the former judería. These collaciones became spaces where, in the face of discrimination, materially and politically enfranchised Jewish families could enact their own prestige. While some Jews would have preferred to reside alongside the Christian nobility, for many the judería was an aspirational location.

Muslim Seville

In contrast, Muslims had no true geographical center prior to their 1483 removal. Abdelhaq al Bayyāsī, their first qadi, received a home in the collación of San Pedro in 1253, but by 1281 he lived among the Muslim goldsmiths in Santa María la Blanca.[96] In the absence of a great mosque, the city probably hosted many small neighborhood places of worship, though no certain sites have been identified.[97] In the middle of the fifteenth century, Muslims were scattered across at least fourteen collaciones, especially among the less-well-off sectors to the north. The largest number of families were in San Marcos, near the Puerta del Osario and the Muslim cemetery, likely also the site of a mosque. Nearby San Pedro, which would eventually house the morería and the community's last mosque, was home to a small cluster of Muslim families.

This dispersion reflects the community's humbler social status. If they had links to aristocratic families such as the Belvís of Guadalajara or the Xarafí of

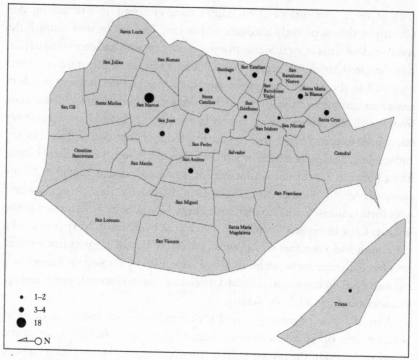

FIG. 1.4 Distribution of Muslim residences, drawn from notarial records between 1441–1483.

Source: Wagner, *Regesto*. Map by Matthew Sisk, Navari Family Center for Digital Scholarship, University of Notre Dame.

Toledo, it was not obvious.[98] No Muslim men received the honorific don from a Christian notary, although nearly a dozen women, including the wives of the qadi and cabildo members, were called doña in what was likely a gesture toward their family's local prominence.[99] The aljama's political class included some religious authorities, or *faqihs*, men of religious and juristic education, but they, like most of Seville's Muslims, were also artisans.

Work largely determined where Muslims lived in Seville. Their most common occupations were borceguineros, masons, ceramicists, and producers and sellers of various kinds of textiles. The city's numerous Muslim masons lived in the center-north of the city. Textile workers, both Muslims and Jews, predominated in the area near the judería and the alcaicería or silk market. Borceguineros, who made a soft leather buskin or boot popular with aristocratic horsemen, lived and worked in the more upscale neighborhoods of San Esteban and San Ildefonso.[100] There were other smaller clusters: in Triana, Muslim ceramicists—who produced and designed the famous azulejos seen in elite residences and churches throughout the city—had homes and shops alongside Christian practitioners, many of whom learned their craft from and alongside them.

Families passed crafts between generations—the Blanco family were blacksmiths; the Agujas were ceramicists; the Carmonís made buskins—so kin networks would explain some of these patterns. Many popular arts had Islamic roots, giving Muslim plasterers, buskinmakers, ceramicists, and masons a cachet that differentiated them from Christian artisans and tied them to one another. Mudéjar artistry was in high fashion, and Muslim craftsmen were particularly sought after.[101]

The identification of skills with place was reinforced by apprenticeships that placed those learning the craft inside the households of masters. Most apprenticeships were likely managed within each faith, perhaps within families, but cross-religious placements were occasionally notarized. The contract assigning Jacob Pollegar to a Christian headdress-maker in 1465 specified that the Jewish boy would be allowed to "keep his religious festivals and Passover and Sabbaths" during his four-year apprenticeship.[102] Apprenticeships could extend to enslaved workers, who might learn new skills and generate income for their masters. Francisco de Rueda placed Mahomad de Alfamad, an enslaved Muslim from Granada, with a Christian weaver of esparto fibers in exchange for room and board and a monthly fee of 200 mrv.[103] City officials also embraced apprenticeships as a way to occupy marginal laborers, placing men like thirty-year-old Mahomad, a "*moro blanco*" (white Muslim slave, possibly North African), with a Christian wineskin-maker and his wife for three months in 1493.[104] These required conditions as well, including an appraisal of the slave in advance of placement and the artisan's responsibility for "risks" other than natural death or illness. All of these created occupational networks for Muslims that had roots in Christian homes and workshops.[105]

Artisans produced their own distinctions. Many crafts were organized by guilds or Catholic confraternities; in the early sixteenth century the city would issue formal regulations that reveal some of these structures.[106] For example, the city's borceguineros were required to elect two officers annually, an alcalde and an inspector. After an apprenticeship, candidates were examined by those officers along with six elder artisans, and sworn by the concejo. To earn the title of maestro an artisan had to prepare three pair of buskins of different thicknesses and styles before those judges.[107] The city's ceramicists' early regulations have not been found, but by the sixteenth century their leaders were suing artisans and using as evidence their official stamp, which depicted the Giralda, the Muslim-built belltower of the cathedral.[108]

Muslims and Jews almost certainly encountered barriers to full incorporation in these incipient guilds, which mixed their control over artisans with participation in Catholic confraternities, under the banner of a patron saint. At the very top of their trades, a handful of mudéjar artisans held salaried municipal offices called *maestro mayor*, or master supervisor. They would presumably have been certified or approved by the guilds associated with their trades, and hired by the concejo to oversee large projects. These men often practiced technical trades associated with the city's Islamic past. The master mason Abrahán Gynete was in charge of overseeing the maintenance and repair of the aqueduct that supplied Seville with water, earning him over a thousand mrv in 1488.[109] Mahoma Agudo was the master supervisory mason for the royal *Alcázares* (palaces), where he and a team of three Muslim masons repaired wind damage to its roofs in 1484.[110] These structures all dated to the Almohad period, and Muslim masons were considered experts in their construction.

But accomplished mudéjar artisans who did not hold salaried offices used the honorific *maestre* rather than the maestro used by Christians. In an earlier period, the two terms were largely interchangeable, both indicating someone examined in their field who had paid relevant fees and was entitled to run a workshop and teach apprentices. As Christians excluded Muslims and Jews from their organizations, which used maestro to indicate licensed masters, Seville's Muslims and Jews likely developed their own apprenticeship programs and examinations, perhaps also adopting the mutual assistance strategies that artisan confraternities used to support their widows and orphans. Their use of the more archaic maestre would have signaled their own licensing process.[111] Jewish medical practitioners who had passed the guild's licensing exam also used the title, like maestre Ysaque *cirugiano* and maestre Juan Leví. Doña Leal, married to a silversmith, was called a *maestra de sanar ojos*, or an examined curer of eye diseases: gendered language here obscures distinctions between Jewish and Christian practitioners.[112]

Whatever its origins, maestre carried significant political implications within the city's Muslim community. Every man listed as a member of the aljama in 1501 used the title, including maestre Abrahén Recocho, no artisan but owner of a vineyard and a tavern.[113] All of the women were called doña and were listed as widows, some of them likely running their late spouse's workshop.[114] The padrón was the record of taxpayers: the thirty-two Muslims it registered were the aljama's leadership and tax base. In this case, maestre might have indicated men who were eligible to hold cabildo office, a convergence between the political and professional distinctions.

Economic status affected where Muslims lived within these enclaves, though it is harder to capture because notarial records show less status variation for Muslims than they do for Jews. Only a few Muslims lived in prestigious locations, such as the master mason Çayde Castellano who owned a house in the parish of Santiago, next door to the city's alcalde mayor. His municipal office gave

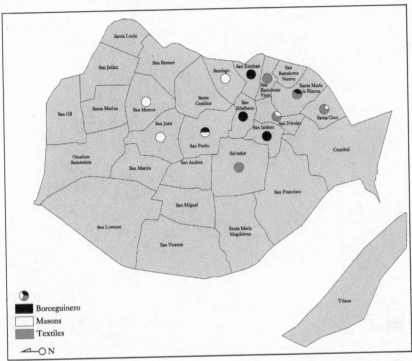

FIG. 1.5 Distribution of three common occupations for Muslims and Jews, drawn from notarial records between 1441–1483.

Source: Wagner, *Regesto*. Map by Matthew Sisk, Navari Family Center for Digital Scholarship, University of Notre Dame.

him a salary and offered privileges that stretched beyond his own community.[115] But mapping honorifics like maestre and offices like maestro mayor allows for some visualization of economic status. Those with titles tended to be concentrated toward the urban core, while those without lived farther away, especially in poorer neighborhoods. While they were more dispersed than Jewish families, Muslims with economic security and aljama authority also inhabited the southeastern parishes close to the judería. Prejudice and economic means limited the way they occupied the city, but the aljama gave their residential patterns structure.

Muslims seem to have garnered less social standing from holding an office within the aljama than did Jews. They likely received no financial compensation; maestre Cayde Blanco continued to work as a blacksmith while serving as qadi, and maestre Ali was both *alfaquí* (faqih, Islamic legal advisor) and a borceguinero. They relied upon their professional networks to be recognized as specialized artisans and parlayed that into status within their political-religious community. The face of the aljama was its maestros mayores and maestres, as demonstrated in its

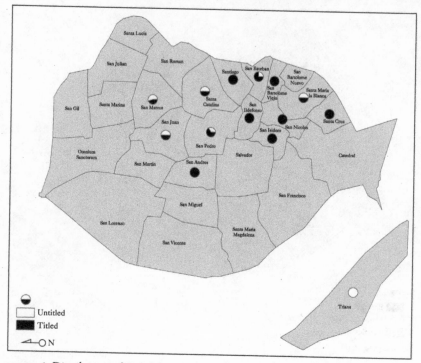

FIG. 1.6 Distribution of Titled (maestre, maestro mayor) and Untitled Muslims, drawn from notarial records between 1441–1483.

Source: Wagner, *Regesto*. Map by Matthew Sisk, Navari Family Center for Digital Scholarship, University of Notre Dame.

dealings with Christian officials. Their dispersal around the city was not random; instead it reflected enclaves of Muslim and Christian craftsmen.

Expulsion Strategies

After the Jewish expulsion of 1483, the city became more stratified. The city's Jews did, indeed, leave or convert. Only a handful of notarial documents named Jewish clients in 1484 and none thereafter. The Crown collected the small sum of 500 mrv in special taxes that year from the few still arranging their affairs.[116] The archival record also tracks the tasks associated with emigration. In the first months of 1484, members of the Abensemerro family visited Christian notaries, collecting debts and rents on behalf of themselves, other Jews, and Christians to whom they were obligated, and arranging for Christians to take over their rent-farming.[117] Symuel Frontyno, a Jewish weaver who was perhaps planning to convert, appeared before the notary in February 1484 to rent his house in

Santa María la Blanca (next to the "house of the King and Queen our lords, that used to belong to Leví," presumably expropriated) to a Christian named Diego González el Conde, for a year.[118] Beyond these last few Jewish names, the record is silent.

In August 1483, Fernando wrote to Seville's concejo demanding that they establish, at last, a separate zone for the city's dwindling Muslim residents.[119] His representative, the *regidor* of Toledo, Ramiro Núñez Gusmán, chose the Adarvejo (alley) of San Pedro, the parish that had been home to Seville's first qadi and the old grain market that hosted Muslim merchants.[120] Seville's concejo objected, asking him to designate instead the collación of San Marcos where some Muslims were living, leaving the more central location for their own urban expansion. While the concejo claimed that this would cause the Muslims less "aggravation," the Muslim response is undocumented.[121] Fernando required the concejo to form a committee with his representatives to make the final decision: they would establish an official morería in San Pedro. If there was no mosque there already, one was established for the community's use.[122] Most—but not all—Muslims eventually relocated.

The forced removal caused obvious problems. The notarial records do not show a massive sell-off of Muslim property or new purchases or rentals in the Adarvejo, but expropriations, transfers, sales, and rentals must have taken place. The organization of artisan workspace and shops presented its own concerns: if Muslims artisans had to move to San Pedro, would their clients follow?

Some appear to have resolved this by retaining old properties while acquiring new addresses in San Pedro. The city's artisans had been buying multiple properties for some decades, either to accommodate residences separate from workplaces, or as an investment strategy. Maestre Çuleman Oberí, a borceguinero, lived in San Isidoro and had a store in San Ildefonso in 1480.[123] His brother maestre Ali, alfaquí and a borceguinero, had property in three different neighborhoods in the 1470s, including in San Esteban. Artisans seem to have been especially drawn to rental properties, perhaps as a hedge against inconsistent income. In 1454, doña Fotox, widow of maestre Hamete Carmoni, rented out one of the two houses she owned in San Andrés to a Christian couple.[124]

After 1483, this strategy took on a new meaning, as retaining real estate outside San Pedro either violated or stretched the intentions of the separation order.[125] Given the possible loss of their livelihood to Christian competitors, it is no surprise that many retained workshops (where they might also have lodged informally) in other neighborhoods. Mahomad Oberí gave his official address to the notary as San Pedro in 1493, while he rented a site in Salvador near other ceramicists; he also rented a store in Santa María from a Christian artisan in 1498.[126] Some artisans owned numerous properties with no clear indication of whether they were used as workshops, income properties, or second homes. In 1499, the borceguinero maestre Mahoma Carmonil gave his residence as San Andrés while he rented a house he owned in San Marcos to the chaplain of the church of San Juan. That house sat next to another one he owned and one belonging to maestre Abdallah Agrudo.[127] Maestre Çayde Blanco, the blacksmith and qadi, owned a home in San Juan through 1480, but he also purchased properties in the morería of San Pedro, in San Román, and in San Marcos. The last was next to a place belonging to Ali Aguja, a mudéjar potter. The borceguineros especially embraced this strategy. Maestre Abdalla Nayal changed his official residence from Santa María (in 1493) to San Pedro (in the 1501 padrón) but continued to have professional connections with Christian borceguineros in Santa María at the later date.[128] While some Muslims might have been permitted to retain multiple properties, they might have simply hoped to evade authorities by having many addresses.[129]

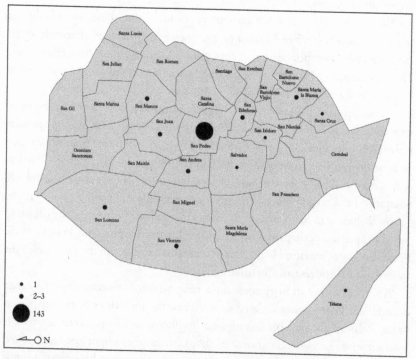

FIG. 1.7 Distribution of Muslim Residences and Workplaces, drawn from notarial records between 1484–1501.

Source: Wagner, Regesto. Map by Matthew Sisk, Navari Family Center for Digital Scholarship, University of Notre Dame.

Entanglements

The organization of the city into occupational sectors promoted separation but also forced daily interaction. Artisans and vendors were particularly likely to have connections across faiths. These relationships are particularly important for revealing the ways that entire communities might become vulnerable. The Jewish aljama, because of its relative wealth and its distant connection to the royal court, could be self-sufficient even in crisis. However, this very strength made it a target of Christian political leaders who wished to attack monarchical power. In contrast, the Muslim aljama had little wealth and was deeply integrated into certain Christian artisan communities. When crises came and the Jewish community could not offer protection, Muslim artisans found themselves exposed.

The integration of non-Christian artisans into the economy is most easily seen through the borceguineros. As the footwear style became more popular, Christians came to dominate the field numerically. Thirteen Muslim borceguineros appear in notarial records in the second half of the fifteenth century, probably a fraction of the total number working in the city at any given point.[130] By 1477 the city's borceguineros were organized under an elected alcalde and inspector, their practices were regulated by the municipality, and many of them worked on a street that bore their name next to the Cathedral.[131] It is unclear whether they admitted Muslims as full members, but there is documentation of Muslim borceguineros acting in concert with their Christian counterparts.[132]

For example, with the leather buskins' vogue, the growth of the trade precipitated action against the artisans and they responded collectively. By 1472 there were so many working and selling on Borceguinería Street that their stalls illegally spilled onto the sidewalks and steps around the Cathedral. The archbishop threatened them with excommunication, which would annul all their contracts, if they did not retreat.[133] Numerous artisans, Christian and Muslim, signed a letter to the concejo requesting intervention in the conflict. During another disagreement with the city three years later, thirty-eight borceguineros (including two Muslims), represented by the guild's alcalde, signed an agreement to use only high-quality goatskin (*cordobán*) rather than cheaper sheepskin.[134] While it is difficult to gauge whether Muslim artisans were treated as equals to Christians within or outside the guild, they occasionally saw their individual fates tied to collective action.

Muslim and Christian artisans also worked closely together in adjacent shops, combining their buying and selling power. Muslim borceguineros and potters joined with Christians to purchase bulk leather and clay from Christian sellers. These arrangements might have enabled Muslims to have access to better credit terms than they might receive independently.[135] Muslims also sold wholesale

FIG. 1.8 Relief of borceguí or leather buskin, emblem of the Barcelona shoemaker's guild, on facade of Barcelona Cathedral. Photograph with permission from Fundació Institut Amatller d'Art Hispànic, Barcelona.

to Christians: in 1474 two Muslims sold a large shipment of their buskins to a Christian shoemaker, receiving 14,000 mrv for their product.[136] The occupational enclaves facilitated collaboration with Christian artisans, who were neighbors and colleagues with shared interests, despite religious differences. These networks and the larger guild structure of the city provided Muslims especially with access to some protections from the majority, as long as trust continued.

The documented use of credit signals most graphically the distinct ways that Muslims and Jews were integrated into the urban economy. Notarial records favor moderately sized transactions that involved payment on installments or at a future date, and a notarized contract enabled injured parties to go to court for enforcement. Seville had twenty-three official notaries, appointed by the Crown, and they mainly stationed themselves near centers of business and commerce: the Alcaicería market, the Cathedral's steps, the Calle de Génova, the Plaza of San Francisco. While the great merchants doing extensive or international business wrote up their own bills of credit, which are not stored in Seville's public archives, smaller enterprises and individuals visited a notary.[137] The records show the patterns of lending, and, especially, the absences of certain types of loans that were key to economic life.

The absence of significant documented lending activity to religious minorities indicates that most received loans within their confessional groups. During the period 1441–1502, only twenty-three outright loans of cash were drafted by notaries between members of different faiths. Most of those, ten, were Christians lending money to Muslims. These ranged from straightforward cash transactions—Maestre Çayde Castellano received 4,000 mrv from Francisco de Algesira for a one-month term, using his expensive home in the collación of Santiago as collateral—to more complicated scenarios. For example, in 1483 Fátima accomplished her manumission from slavery by borrowing 8,000 mrv from Juana Rodríguez. In exchange she contracted to be Rodríguez's servant for at least the next two years. Moreover, the loan was guaranteed by her coreligionist, mason Maestre Mahomad, who had to borrow an additional 700 mrv from Fátima's owner to make up a shortfall in the payment.[138] The Muslim blacksmith maestre Çayde [Blanco] had a large outstanding debt with converso blacksmith Juan Martínez when he was reconciled (that is, confessed and punished) by the Inquisition in 1488. Maestre Çayde defaulted, leaving a Christian couple who had acted as guarantors to pay for him when Seville's treasurer confiscated the funds as part of Martínez's reconciliation. It is not clear whether the original loan was made before or after Martínez's conversion, which would have taken place in 1483 or prior.[139] These were all relatively rare occurrences, suggesting that Muslims arranged for cash loans either with coreligionists, or from Jewish lenders who processed their own contracts.

And while Jewish men were broadly caricatured as voracious lenders who preyed upon Christians, they do not show up in great numbers in these records. Only six Jewish men made loans to Christians, and usually in partnership with Christians. Çuleman Abensemerro, from a prominent Jewish family that included rent farmers, teamed up in 1460 with the Christian royal notary Pedro Fernandez to lend a large sum to a Christian couple, as well as to a Muslim man from nearby La Algaba.[140] In a more unusual case, two Jewish men, Mayr and Yuda Abentabe, made substantial loans to three Jewish women on behalf of or in partnership with the Marqués of Santillana. The women's artisan husbands were being held in prison, so the lenders excused them from turning over goods as collateral.[141] Larger sums might have changed hands in different venues, but Christian borrowers had many options in a city full of merchants and money-changers.

Six Christians made cash loans to Jewish borrowers between 1441 and the 1483 expulsion, and most of these were small and somewhat inconsequential. Two illustrate why these might appear in a notary's register: these were made to

Jacob Barchilón, who was leasing vineyards in 1472 and arranged small loans from the property owners at the same time, perhaps an advance to help him establish a wine or olive business.[142] Jewish families who needed cash loans could probably approach Jewish lenders or better-off members of the community rather than turn to Christian lenders, who might also refuse their business or offer poor terms. The case of Jacob Cohen suggests that loans within the faith might have been more desirable. He had a 400 mrv commercial debt with a Christian textile merchant in April 1472; Yantob Saltiel, a Jewish lance-maker, acted as his guarantor. At the end of that year, Saltiel paid the merchant 420 mrv to clear Cohen's debt. If Saltiel and Cohen drew up a new contract between them, they did not do so at the office of the notary who handled the original document.

Very occasionally, loans within the minority religious community were made before a Christian notary. Often these happened because a Jewish or Muslim individual was in danger of default and a coreligionist stepped in to pay the debt and set up a new loan. Aljamas likely played a role in arranging loans between members as well as in protecting those who fell behind on payments. Maestre Alí, a mason, kept four mudéjar artisans from defaulting to a Christian lender in 1450 by lending them the sum himself.[143] In 1454, when Jewish silversmith Abrahén Camarero and his wife Çadbona defaulted on a debt to a Christian, Camarero was sent to prison. Ysaque, a Jewish furrier, lent the family 4,000 mrv to free him.[144] But the overall absence of evidence suggests that when Muslims or Jews needed cash, they did not get loans from Christians.

In contrast, Muslim and Jewish borrowers were more likely to arrange credit as part of everyday commercial transactions with Christian vendors. Even those numbers never became truly significant, particularly when measured against the larger commerce of the city.[145] These smaller loans were formalized before a notary, especially those with offices in the city's commercial centers, particularly the Alcaicería, Sierpes Street, the Calle de Génova, and the Gradas or steps of the Cathedral, which served as an informal slave market and was near artisan stalls.[146] Those notaries would have been familiar with the legal intricacies of inter-faith contracting, and their documents sometimes describe whether a Jew "swore within his law," or whether he "renounced the privileges that Jews have," namely, the right to a Jewish witness and to sue before Jewish authorities.

These credit transactions most often made possible the purchase of raw materials, bulk agricultural goods, and other commodities related to work. They described relatively small amounts and they often featured people of different faiths in partnership.[147] Smaller purchases of bulk cloth in the Alcaicería were most common. Merien, a Muslim woman, bought 415 mrv worth of cloth from two Christian brothers; Malfate and her daughter Xencia, also Muslims, spent

1,850 mrv on textiles, to be repaid at 800 mrv a month.[148] Perhaps these would be used to make clothes for the family, or a small-scale business.

The documentation for credit-based sales shows us the entanglement of faiths in the urban economy, but also how fortunes changed over an intensely difficult period, in terms both of political upheavals and of cycles of famine and plague. Whether because of local conditions or an unrelated effect of what has survived in the archive, the 1470s were a high point for credit-based interactions as well as real estate transactions involving religious minorities.[149] Between 1470 and 1480, contracts involving nearly thirty Muslims and Jews can be identified. Many were farmers, who relied upon credit to market their crops before harvest and allowed purchasers to speculate on prices. Yoná Aben-Núñez, a Jewish farmer from Utrera, came into Seville to sell barley that he was about to harvest in late summer 1472. The Jewish tailor Haxa Rubio came to Seville in 1468 to sell his own barley harvest to the merchant Pedro Rodríguez de Arahal, receiving cash in May and agreeing to bring the crop in August.[150] Jewish brothers Abrahán and Mosé Palas and Mosé's son contracted with Juan Mexia to buy a large quantity of grapes and figs from his land for 8,000 mrv in August 1473.[151] The Palas men were probably planning to make wine, as they also attempted to hire a building with brewing equipment at the same time.

Most common were contracts to buy needed raw materials on installments, allowing an artisan to produce his goods. Five potters, two Muslim and three Christian, joined together in 1475 to buy a large shipment of clay from two Christians. They paid an advance of a thousand mrv for the delivery.[152] Yuda Huerta, a Jewish shoemaker from Gerena, required hides; he took a shipment from Juan Ruiz in Sevilla and promised to pay 662 mrv in six weeks.[153] Finished products could also be sold in large units over time: maestre Alí Alfaqui and maestre Abdalla Nayal sold 14,000 mrv worth of buskins to the shoemaker Juan Rodríguez de la Merced, to be paid over six months.[154] Credit smoothed operations during typical and atypical economic cycles.

But the credit market was also a barometer for the crisis in the latter part of the century. By the 1480s, the market had shifted dramatically. The Jewish expulsion and the inquisitorial attacks on conversos dampened Muslim access to commercial credit, and those contracts came nearly to a halt for a decade. But a new wave appeared in the 1490s, a harbinger of what was to come.

As Muslim residents dealt with the Jewish expulsion, the ongoing pressure to convert, and the political effects of war and unrest in Granada and the Alpujarra mountains, their futures were no longer certain. Emigration was costly—the price of a license was more than double what had been demanded of Jews—but those who stayed lived in increasing precarity.[155] In the fifty years before 1490, only eleven Muslims made contracts with Christians that involved credit. In the decade from 1491 to 1501, and despite the dwindling number of Muslim residents, there were seventeen, of which seven appear to be outright sums of cash from a money-lender.

The expulsions created a new need for credit, but it also made default far more likely. The records prior to 1488 only show one Muslim defaulting on loans; Aly Sobrino's possessions were embargoed for nonpayment of a 600 mrv debt to another Christian potter.[156] But between 1488 and 1498, charges were pressed against eleven Muslim men, mostly ceramicists, borceguineros, and masons, for defaulting on debts that ran to many thousands of maravedís.[157] This crisis must have touched nearly all the Muslim families in the city. The debts were mostly for the purchase of raw materials, and the goods embargoed were raw and finished products, but also anything with resale value. Maestre Mahoma Carmoní and his wife turned over six pairs of borceguíes and a linen quilt against a debt of more than 10,000 mrv to a Christian merchant.[158] The incipient crises caused defaults and legal problems that led many Muslims to draw up powers of attorney to empower others to represent their interests in a variety of venues. A few called upon relatives, but most asked one of the city's Christian procurators to step in for them in legal fora.[159]

Credit is a revealing guide to the economic positions of Muslims and Jews in the city. The archival documentation demonstrates that, while religious minorities were deeply integrated into the city's economy, they faced serious barriers to credit. Jews were able to draw upon the hierarchies of the aljama to keep one another afloat, and they may also have sustained Muslims before 1483. But Muslims turned to Christians for smaller commercial transactions with staggered payoffs, because they could not source shoe leather or clay within their communities. Their ongoing partnerships with Christians made this kind of trust possible, but also left them exposed after the Jewish expulsion. The entanglements that supported them could also be devastating.

———

Rather than a Christian city with Jewish and Muslim neighborhoods or ghettos, Seville was a complex system of social and economic relationships that drew the faiths together, for better and for worse. Muslims and Jews were entrenched in the city as laborers, property owners, and taxpayers. They were also members of aljamas with their own hierarchies and interests. Increasing Christian anxiety about distinguishing between Christians and non-Christians and about separating Christians from Jewish or Muslim contamination was expressed by periodic calls for physical insignias and separate neighborhoods. While ideologues presented these as simple solutions to a serious problem, the reverse was true: the proposed solutions were difficult to implement and, in most cases, few found the problem of distinguishing the faiths concerning. In a city where most residents would come into regular contact with Jewish and Muslim neighbors and colleagues, adherence to a faith was likely obvious and often irrelevant. And Jewish and Muslim residents represented a needed tax base as well as access to all sorts of services and trades that were integral to urban life.

This changed with the pogroms of 1391. The fifteenth century would be far more contentious and dangerous for Jews and Muslims. And yet they continued to occupy the city much as before. Their distinct origin stories—expropriated Muslim plebeians who had to reinhabit their conquered city on the one hand, recruited Jewish elites and intellectuals who received incentives including a walled neighborhood for their community needs on the other—in retrospect partly explain that geographic dispersal, with Jews forming close communities near their synagogue and Muslims living within occupational enclaves.

Mapping these spaces shows how the Jewish community—because of a certain level of wealth and authority, and under increasingly dangerous political conditions—succeeded, to an extent, in creating a self-sufficient neighborhood. Even after its collapse, the judería retained cachet for the city's Jews. Their connections with Jewish notables at the court allowed them to turn the former judería into a center for the aljama's and their individual social and economic identities. Their relative wealth and networks enabled them to support one another financially and to represent their interests compellingly to the municipality. There were clearly barriers to their integration in the fifteenth century; even the wealthiest were excluded from the best neighborhoods, and when they converted to Christianity they moved more freely toward Christian elites. The absence of notarial records describing their loans and credit operations speaks to either their inability to break into certain Christian sectors, or their desire to keep their acts within the community.

Seville's Jews, then, were both integrated and not integrated into urban society. They were part of an elite with Christian allies and supporters, even when they were championing anti-Jewish rhetoric. But they were also vulnerable when royal support abandoned them at the end of a century of bloody politics. The fact that their expulsion rendered the city's Muslims powerless is a sign of the power that they once wielded.

In contrast, the Muslim aljama was tied to the Christian economy in the same way that they were spread across the city, through networks of craftsmen and laborers. The professional class of artisans formed the aljama's hierarchy, and the laborers—mostly absent from notarial documents—would have worked for Christian or Muslim employers. This entanglement with a Christian society that could turn off access to credit and employment proved deadly. They were not self-sufficient, though they also enjoyed some cachet. Their ways of making a living were deeply integrated into the Christian artisan economy, which rarely had the desire or ability to protect them when threatened. The wave of debt and foreclosures that heralded their own expulsion demonstrates how that interdependence could easily turn to economic collapse.

The shape of the aljama as republic, as giver of law and producer of hierarchy and order, tells us a great deal about Seville's Jewish and Muslim populations. There were many people who worshipped as Jews and Muslims who cannot be traced through the aljama's workings; they are not irrelevant to its history, but they do not explain how Jewish and Muslim administration functioned. Instead, these mappings have shown how minority religious institutions occupied and used the city, and how vulnerabilities emerged from their structures.

2

Lima's Indian Republics, 1532–1650

IN 1599, FOURTEEN Andean men and nine Andean women gathered in a
notary's office in Lima to draft a power of attorney enabling a representative to
argue their case before the king in Spain. Most were artisans and shrimp fishers.
They stated that they had previously lived in a section of the parish of San Lázaro
known as San Pedro, on the banks of the Rimac River, over the bridge from the
city proper. They had lived there quietly, they said, paying their taxes, attending
church, and seeing to their occupations as well as performing labor for the city.
But "by force and against their will," in 1590, the viceroy had had them removed
to the walled Indian town of Santiago del Cercado and placed under the supervision of the Jesuit order.[1]

The "Indians of San Lázaro," as they were known, rapidly organized to protest their removal.[2] Some fled the Cercado but could not return to their homes,
which the viceroy confiscated and sold to Spanish residents to placate them for
their loss of the Indians' labor. With the support of the city's archbishop, Toribio
de Mogrovejo, who lost jurisdiction over them with their transfer, they fought
for their right to leave the Cercado and return to San Lázaro. The viceroy and the
Jesuits continued to transport Indigenous artisans to the Cercado, arguing that
they were living without supervision and failing to receive a Catholic education;
they were not under the guidance of any republic.

The Andean complainants argued that this was incorrect. Their town, San
Pedro de los Camaroneros, had a church and an active Catholic confraternity,
and Lima's *real audiencia* or highest court had formally recognized its native
cabildo in 1573. Within that republic they paid their tribute obligations by provisioning the city with fish and shrimp, maintaining the riverbeds where they
fished, and clearing its rubbish.[3] They were self-governed, presenting their officers
(an alcalde or judge, and three *alguaciles* or constables) annually to the Spaniards
who sat on Lima's cabildo.[4] Indeed, two of the complainants served as judge and

Republics of Difference. Karen B. Graubart, Oxford University Press. © Oxford University Press 2022.
DOI: 10.1093/oso/9780190233839.003.0003

constable, and their number also included men using the honorific don, indicating they were part of the native nobility. They continued to function collectively even while exiled to the Cercado, joining with artisans to found a new confraternity. Despite the physical disappearance of their town, they continued to live in a visibly Christian republic.[5]

The king and his Council of the Indies agreed and issued a royal order in favor of their freedom in 1595, but authorities in the viceroyalty of Peru failed to implement it. Viceroy Velasco stated in a letter to Philip II, dated May 1598, that their "complete liberty" would enable their inherent "bad inclinations" and that he would await proper instructions for their permanent placement; to implement the decision, he argued, would undermine the common good.[6] Velasco's language suggested they were vagrants, in need of work-discipline, rather than members of a republic.[7]

Not until 1606 were the terms of the king's order implemented, belatedly confirming the right of the Indians of San Lázaro and their artisan allies to live outside the Cercado as free vassals. Their ultimate success was a result of their alliance with powerful Spanish interests in Lima, but also of their own harnessing of the republic and its political language, through their cabildos and confraternities. In the end, viceregal authorities and the Jesuit order had to recognize the limited jurisdiction of that Indian republic.

If the end of Seville's aljamas was signaled by the Muslims' relocation, Spaniards began their colonial project in the Americas by moving populations. In Peru, this had to do with two central aspects of that project: conversion and labor provision. The mountainous landscape and dispersed kin groups of the Andes were obvious barriers to both, and Spanish officials and clerics understood that concentrated populations would be more easily reached. As part of this project they also intervened in governance but, as on the peninsula, maintained an expectation that communities would govern themselves under their own law, to ensure the efficient delivery of labor and tribute to Spanish grandees. This was even true in cities like Lima, newly formed of immigrants who did not necessarily share political traditions or a hereditary nobility. Indigenous and Black inhabitants experimented with forming ad hoc urban republics, but none found universal traction. The old language of separation and removal was omnipresent in the colonial Andes but it had distinct meaning when the expressed object was to convert millions of inhabitants and drive them toward new forms of labor.

Indigenous and Black inhabitants of the Americas participated in many republics. Two were unambiguously successful: native populations were gathered into colonial towns called *pueblos de indios*, and Christians of both heritages joined confraternities. Other republics went either unseen by authorities (and uncaptured by the archives) or were marked as unauthorized and criminal, such as maroon communities and the Andean kin groups that supported spiritual practices that the Church denigrated as idolatry. Urban Lima and its greater rural environs offer case studies for many of these, exposing how they interacted with officials intent on extracting wealth and producing what they termed *policía*, a civic virtue that involved Christian behavior and productive activity.[8] Indigenous and Black residents understood the benefits and dangers of living in recognized republics, and responded in complex ways.

Founding Lima

At the turn of the seventeenth century, Lima was large and diverse: a census in 1613 identified 11,867 Spanish, 11,130 *negros* and *mulatos*, and 2,170 Indian or mestizo permanent residents.[9] The large transient populations within and at the edges of the city went uncounted, including native laborers and vendors who commuted within the greater Lima Valley, hundreds of residents of the mostly Indigenous Cercado, and newly arrived enslaved people of African origins, who were quarantined and awaiting their sale.

Unlike Seville, Lima had not been densely populated or particularly urban prior to its conquest. The site was a ritual center within the realm of two brothers, the *kurakas* (rulers) Taulichusco and Caxapaxa, who had been recently imposed on the population by the Inka to maintain imperial peace. It sat within a swathe of valleys sliced by three rivers descending from the Andes, and organized under two dominions or *señoríos*, now known as Collique and Yschma. These contained many smaller kin-based units, which Spaniards called *parcialidades*, each split into two *ayllus* headed by kurakas, whom the Spaniards also called *caciques*.[10] Like other coastal polities, they organized themselves into fishing and agricultural communities as well as specialized trades like weaving.[11] Lima was subordinate to the Yschma señorío, which included the important religious center of Pachacamac.[12]

In 1532, the Spanish conquistador Francisco Pizarro had abruptly captured and then assassinated Atahualpa, one of two half-brothers at war over control of the Inka empire after the death of their father, Huayna Capac. Pizarro, his small band of Spaniards, and an army of native allies made their way through the highlands toward the Inka capital, Cusco. En route they claimed control of a site called Jauja and left behind a group of settlers organized into a cabildo to assert a fragile dominance. The mountainous terrain was bad for their horses and good for their adversaries. Cusco was even more hostile to Spaniards, as Inka lineages were not readily convinced they were out of power. It would take more than a decade before Spaniards could effectively govern, and even then an Inka outpost remained in the jungle to trouble them.[13]

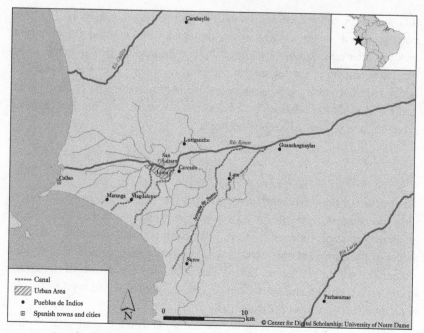

FIG. 2.1 Lima and Surrounding Valleys. Map by Matthew Sisk, Navari Family Center for Digital Scholarship, University of Notre Dame.

Instead, they turned to the Rimac River Valley as a command center. Caxapaxa lived in Cusco among the Inka, and so Taulichusco met with Francisco Pizarro and his forces in 1534 and struck up an amicable relationship.[14] It was a gentler environment, a flat, desert landscape fed by rivers that descended from the Andes mountains, and it had access to the Pacific Ocean through the port of Callao. Spaniards recognized the potential for a permanent Spanish settlement.[15]

With royal authorization, Pizarro founded la Ciudad de Los Reyes (the City of Kings, or Lima) on January 6, Three Kings Day, in 1535. He designated its central plaza and a place for a church, which he ceremonially founded in a ritual using some stones and wood, declaring that they had taken possession not only of the site but also of the ocean and the "discovered and yet undiscovered lands." He also drew up Lima's *traza* or core plan, assigning *solares* (standard plots of land) to each of the settlement's new *vecinos*, or politically empowered permanent residents.[16] Pizarro called upon the vecinos to protect the site "among these barbaric peoples who have until now been incognizant" of the Catholic faith and to keep it safe "from the dangers of its enemies and those who would do it damage and ill."[17] Taulichusco's thoughts went unrecorded, though the notary's final words attest that the document was drawn up within his territory.

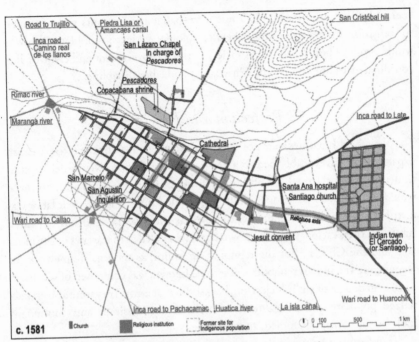

FIG. 2.2 Lima in 1581. Map by Patricia Morgado (with permission).

Spaniards moved Taulichusco's subjects to a nearby site called Chuntay, and drew up a plan that would be built directly over the existing town, extending a grid from an open-air plaza they found near the Rimac River. The five pyramidal *huacas* or sacred sites around the plaza were repurposed or swallowed by new buildings, including the cathedral and Pizarro's residence.[18] Christians intended their new spaces to undermine the power of Lima's spiritual geography and coax Andeans toward conversion. Settlers (and their Indigenous and Black laborers) borrowed adobes from the most important huaca to build the cathedral, and used the rest for a hospital dedicated to Santa Ana that was intended to serve native patients. They eventually placed the Inquisition's building on the route from the plaza to Santa Ana and the great huaca, as a reminder to idolators of the dangers they faced. The spaces of Lima looked different through the eyes of Spaniard and Indian, although each would have been aware of the existence of the other's perspective.

Spaniards brought with them a belief that physical space contributed to the production of sound values and behaviors; cities in particular were places that cultivated civilization.[19] In order to extirpate Andean spiritual practices they would dismantle the structures that had housed them; conversion required reshaping public and private spaces. Rural Andeans would be gathered into gridded towns centered on a Catholic church. These new spatial arrangements were intended to transform the behavior and beliefs of colonial subjects: well-planned towns would produce policía, an urban society with just government and civilized life, coordinated around the axes of Christianity and labor discipline.

Protection and Policía

The New World colonies were not to be multi-confessional. By the 1530s, Spanish expansion was irrevocably tied to a program of conversion, even if debate continued to flare over methods and the policing of faith.[20] Governance, however, would still be exercised through multiple jurisdictions. Although their labor was distributed in a form of entailment known as *encomienda*, Andeans remained subject to their caciques and their own civil law, as well as to the laws of the monarch and the Church. But the república de indios, as the legal framework for recognizing the Indian republics came to be known, was composed of Christian novices in danger of willful rejection, backsliding, or error. They were also characterized, popularly and in legal texts, as intellectually, physically, and emotionally frail—easily corrupted, fooled, and cowed.

Transforming fragile souls required dedicated oversight. The royal Laws of Burgos (1512) had ordered not simply that Caribbean natives attend church regularly, but that they adopt good customs such as exchanging goods for money in markets, providing labor on demand, and adopting stone buildings, beds, European-style clothing, and cutlery. This necessitated bringing them to live near Spanish cities and towns.[21] As Charles V ordered, "the Indian natives should arrive at a knowledge of our holy Catholic faith and live in the settlement and manner that Spanish Christians do, to be saved and kept healthy, and for this purpose, as experience has shown, the main way is to promote interactions between the Indians and Christians . . . having trade and enterprise by means of exchange and commerce."[22] But the forced resettlement of Caribbean natives to sites near Spanish towns—often accomplished by destroying their former residences—led to abuse, contributing to the genocide set in motion by the conquest and epidemic disease.

This contradiction was addressed by calling the reorganization of native society an act of protection.[23] By the middle of the sixteenth century, the Crown and the Catholic Church placed Indians collectively in the legal category of *miserables*, literally those deserving of compassion, joining widows, underaged orphans, and "rustics" or ignorant people.[24] The category recognized the weak structural position of Indigenous subjects, who were considered endangered because of their ignorance of law and their intrinsic timidity. Thus plebeian "Indians," as a legal category, were entitled not only to the jurisdiction of their own lords but also to the assistance of Spanish institutions and legal counsel to protect them from exploitation.[25] Judges would have to temper verdicts against them, they could dissolve contracts they had signed in ignorance, and they received free—if thinly spread—legal assistance.

As part of this protection, the Crown called for the preservation of native political organizations, but through a process of reordering and relocation known as *reducción* (in Peru) or *congregación* (in Mesoamerica). These terms referred to the creation of centralized, intentional towns whose previously dispersed residents could efficiently provide labor to encomenderos, receive catechism from missionaries, and self-govern as a republic.[26]

From Utopias to Indian Republics

The first major experiment with reducción came at the hands of Vasco de Quiroga, judge of the Audiencia of Mexico and later bishop of Michoacán. He founded two *hospital-pueblos* in the Valley of Mexico and Michoacán in the 1530s to protect Indigenous peoples against enslavement and epidemic disease, but also to root out what he considered their barbarous customs. Quiroga purchased lands from local owners and populated them with men, women, and children he recruited or removed from missions.

The towns' governing ordinances emphasized Christian doctrine and communal labor "according to what each, given his or her *calidad* (status) and needs, means, and condition, finds necessary for self and family."[27] Borrowing from Thomas More's *Utopia* and Bartolomé de las Casas' *Remedios*, Quiroga established how families were to live, how they were to dress (all in cheap, "clean and honest" white cotton and wool), and the workings of their political system.[28] Each family unit would elect a *padre* or father, who in turn would select a *principal* for a three-year term as well as a series of annual officers. Stripped of the institutions that had governed them in "barbarity," the hospital-pueblos were intended to transform natives into political citizens.[29]

Quiroga's hospital-pueblos were intended to create and protect a society of communal Christian laborers who did not express differentiated ethnicity and status. His vision contrasted with contemporary colonizing experiences in Mexico and the Andes, where both kinds of distinctions were valued. Spanish incursions into Tenochtitlán (Mexico) and Tawantinsuyu (Peru) introduced them to civilizations that rivaled those of Europe. The Mexica and Inkas produced grand manmade structures using stone and metals that led conquistadors to dub them Indian *mezquitas* or mosques, perhaps having Seville's Great Mosque-turned-Cathedral in mind. They laid out large plazas and pyramidal structures to define public and private ritual spaces. Tenochtitlán boasted extraordinary cities and markets. In the Andes, Inka rulers had their subjects build wide roads to move armies and tribute across their vast empire, and placed receptacles storing goods outside each town. Mexica and Inka imperial religious practices, while still marked as alien and sometimes barbaric, had enough in common with Christianity that they were recognizable as elements of a hierarchical, priestly religion.

Indigenous elites not only dressed sumptuously and demanded deferential behavior from their subjects, they also received material and ideological benefits that the Christians admired. In the 1530s and 1540s, Charles V confirmed the status of ruling dynasties across much of central Mexico and in the Andes, issuing patents of hereditary nobility to many heirs of dynastic houses, especially those who could make a strong claim to having aided the Spanish conquest such as the Tlaxcalans of central Mexico or the Chachapoyas and Cañari of the Andes.[30] He also recognized the lower nobility—caciques and nobles called, generically, *principales*—as equivalent to Spanish hidalgos. Once formally titled through a petitioning process, they received limited privileges including exemption from paying tribute, income from their subjects, and the rights to ride a horse, receive a coat of arms, and bear a sword. Charles II issued a royal order in 1697 to regularize these norms because "in pagan times they were nobles whose inferiors recognized vassalage and paid tribute, and whose particular nobility still remains in effect, retaining as much as possible their ancient fueros and privileges."[31] Native polities across the Americas, led by these natural lords, were brought into the Spanish kingdom as republics. They likely experienced this as a kind of continuity, especially those emerging from prior imperial networks.

Resettlement presented challenges, especially in the Andes. The region's large urban centers were generally administrative sites with temporary residences. Most people lived in dispersed hamlets associated with kin-based ayllus distributed over expansive mountainous territories that they exploited for access to the resources of different microclimates.[32] In many cases, this obviated the need for markets, as ayllus distributed local products internally and used long-distance trade only for specialized goods.[33] While in Mesoamerica reducción entailed concentrating somewhat scattered towns, in the Andes it could cut communities off from essential but distant pockets of resources, sacred landscapes, and habits of neighborly cooperation. It is estimated that 1.5 million people were dislocated in the 1570s when Viceroy Toledo universalized the process, although the scope of those moves, their permanence, and the particular forms the new towns took are still debated.[34]

Toledo pressed for physical reorganization for at least three reasons. The first was economic: reducción rearranged agricultural practices, enabling the Crown to expropriate what were deemed "excess" lands and sell them to eager Spanish entrepreneurs. It also involved censusing the population to set tribute rates and the schedule for forced labor or *mita* drafts. Second, reducción enabled a political shakeup: new towns elected new kinds of officials who could be a brake on powerful hereditary nobles like caciques. Toledo's final intention was spiritual: by creating new towns around Catholic churches, Indigenous communities could be reoriented toward conversion and socialized as Christians.[35] The vision of policía promoted by Toledo's reforms was encapsulated in the reduced urbanized town, organized hierarchically along an orthogonal grid, making labor and church attendance compulsory.[36]

Reducción was not intended to paralyze communities, but to establish clear lines of obligation and authority. As the king assured the Indians of San Lázaro, his subjects were free to move. The economy required mobility. Mita labor drafts pulled large numbers of adult men, sometimes accompanied by their families, into cities and mining regions every year. Temporary migrants often became permanent residents. Others fled to other communities where they were not listed on tributary rolls. These movements were a problem if the migrants evaded paying tribute or serving in the mita. The king's vassals enjoyed freedom of movement as long as they met their obligations.

Royal authorities attempted to restrict outsiders' access to Indian towns. Encomenderos were repeatedly banned from living among the Indians assigned to work for them because of their tendency to abuse them. Unmarried Spanish men were considered particularly dangerous to native women and girls, for fathering *mestizo* (mixed Indigenous-Spanish ancestry) children, who were not required to pay tribute.[37] In 1535 and regularly thereafter, men and women of African descent were excluded for their "poor customs." The ban was extended in 1563 to include "Spaniards, Blacks, mulatos, or mestizos."[38] Non-Indians were also characterized as threats to native conversion:

> the [Blacks, mulatos and mestizos] teach them their bad habits and laziness and also some errors and vices that could ravage and impede the fruit that is desired for the salvation of the soul of the Indians, and so that they live in policía . . . given that the said mulatos, Blacks and mestizos are universally so poorly inclined.[39]

More bluntly, a priest reported, "For the same reason that there cannot exist a good form of republic and friendship between wolves and sheep, there cannot exist a good form of republic, confederation, and connection between Indians and Spaniards."[40]

By the late sixteenth century, much of the rural Andes was reorganized into pueblos de indios. The rhetoric around reducción muddled the language used against Castilian aljamas: the converts to be protected lay within the pueb-lo's perimeter rather than without, and the supposed predators included the Christian invaders. Nonetheless, Indian towns were relentlessly permeated by outsiders, including Spanish landowners and Black slaves purchased by Andeans and Spaniards alike. But the reducción model did have profound effects on self-governance and law.

Expanding Lima

The settlements within the valleys formed by the Rimac, Chillón, and Lurín rivers—the Lima Valley—were reorganized early on because of their proxim-ity to Lima, which became the seat of the viceregal court and the metropolitan archbishopric around 1542.[41] The nineteen pre-Hispanic kurakazgos were reor-ganized into numerous encomiendas and distributed to Pizarro's family, soldiers, and allies.[42] Most were too small to be a major prize and were generally paired with larger highland ones.[43]

In 1573 these kurakazgos were turned into the six pueblos of Magdalena, Surco, Late, Lurigancho, Carabayllo, and Pachacamac.[44] Their tributaries sent wheat, corn, vegetables, fruits, fish, fowl, and cattle to the city, and supplied labor for urban construction.[45] They maintained and expanded the existing system of irrigation canals and staffed *tambos* (inns) for the numerous travelers who passed through the region.

Epidemic disease, years of civil war between Spanish factions in the area, and the magnetic pull of Lima rapidly depopulated the coastal pueblos, which lost perhaps 5 percent of their population annually between 1525 and 1600. As Lima grew, the agricultural lands around the city rose in value and left communities' control. Even those who remained in the valley's pueblos de indios often traveled to Lima to work or to sell their produce and goods. By the seventeenth century, the valley's lands would be mostly owned by Spaniards who worked them with hired Andean and enslaved Black laborers.[46]

Yet Lima remained an Indigenous city. Its original inhabitants were replaced by voluntary and coerced permanent migrants. But the mita, the labor draft that usually sent Andeans to mines like Potosí, also had a hand in these changes. The Spanish settlers of Lima complained that, unless they were encomenderos, they had desperate need but little access to cheap workers. Sixteenth-century viceroys demanded periodic contingents from Indian towns to deal with labor crises, and Toledo formalized this as an annual draft, for which he hispanized the Quechua term for a labor turn, *mit'a* becoming *mita*.[47] As in Potosí, many men (and their families) relocated permanently.

The city was also Black. By the time of Lima's foundation, African slavery was fully normalized in the Spanish Americas as a supplement to or replacement for the shrinking Indigenous labor force.[48] Some Spaniards brought enslaved men and women from the peninsula, and merchants supplied the city with ever-growing numbers from the Atlantic trade. About 1,500 enslaved people of African descent were counted in the city in 1554, growing to 6,700 in 1593. In 1613 some 11,000 free and enslaved Black men and women were counted as permanent residents, about one for every Spaniard.[49] The African origins of this community can be traced as far as ports in what are now Senegambia and Guinea-Bissau, until the turn of the seventeenth century, when Angola and the kingdom of Kongo became the most common ports of departure. They also arrived from other parts of the Americas, including Panamá and New Granada.[50]

Many enslaved people earned their liberty through self-purchase, gifts and contingent arrangements with owners, and flight.[51] Constant labor shortages in Lima created opportunities for enslaved men and women to earn income, the foundation of eventual self-purchase. People of moderate means, usually Spaniards but occasionally Indigenous and free Black men and women, purchased slaves whom they could rent out for the *jornal*, a daily wage that might be shared between enslaver and enslaved. Artisans bought assistants, who learned a skill or a trade that they could continue to exercise once free. These conditions meant that many enslaved men and women found resources that placed them in a liminal space between free and unfree.

Rapid population growth overwhelmed the intentional social hierarchy of the original urban grid. Pizarro had placed the most powerful closest to the plaza: the cabildo, the church, residences for himself and the founding vecinos. Indians were understood to belong in the valleys, at the city's edges, and on a handful of urban plots distributed to valley caciques to house temporary workers. The cabildo continued to distribute more distant solares to new vecinos, pushing back the urban margins. But natural boundaries like the Rimac River limited that growth, and property owners divided their lots and allowed the streets to be bisected by alleys and *callejones* that created space for the less fortunate and rents for the propertied. The poor congregated in the cheap *corrales* and *rancherías*, informal housing structures built around an alley or open-air passageway between houses, with multiple units for tenants and a shared patio that functioned as a collective kitchen.[52] The city's outer margins were also irregularly gentrified, displacing the poorer families who lived there in informal housing. Elites viewed all of these residential arrangements as unsanitary and disordered, and associated them with immorality and vagrancy. Lima's growth brought the entwined problems of poverty and housing to the cabildo's agenda.

Legislating Social Order

By mid-century, royal and municipal officials were producing legislation that aimed to resolve Lima's emerging urban problems, which they theorized as a failure of social order and labor discipline.[53] As part of a contemporary wave of attempts to control itinerant vagabonds and paupers across the Spanish empire, Lima's legislators used structures of governance to impose order on Spaniards, including the unemployed men who streamed into the city, but they singled out Indigenous and Black residents in distinct ways.[54] If the Indian was described as a fragile novice in need of protection and civilizing education, the Black subject was criminal and predatory in his or her mobility or mis-occupation of space. In both cases, proposed solutions would involve controlling urban space, either by curtailing free access to certain locations, or by physically placing the poor in the custody of Spanish masters for discipline and socialization.

Among the most common concerns expressed through law was the lack of supervision. The Real Audiencia argued repeatedly that urban Indians were outside their caciques' jurisdiction, which left them without Christian guidance and open to exploitation. The Audiencia attempted to create jurisdiction by making them the subjects of the valley's caciques or ordering temporary laborers in the city to live alongside their own cacique, but their exasperation with the swelling numbers of immigrants continued. In August 1550, the Audiencia gave native men and women living outside the control of a cacique thirty days to return to their communities of origin or to place themselves with a master to learn a trade.[55] Viceroy Cañete issued orders in 1560 demanding that all the free Black men and women in Lima contract themselves to Spanish masters within eight days "unless they are black women married to Spanish men, under penalty of permanent exile from these kingdoms of Peru, and they cannot have their own houses to sleep or reside in, but will sleep and reside by day and by night in the house of the said masters with whom they contract."[56] The uncontrolled flow of Black and Andean men and women throughout the city had to be resolved by placing them into Spanish households.

There was no mass exile or relocation of Black and native people from Lima in the 1550s and 1560s. But the policy returned more quietly in the 1580s, as local authorities began to respond to complaints about vagabondage by placing non-Spanish men, women, and particularly children into Spanish households as apprentices and servants. Many of those contracts were voluntary, but others were probably the result of sweeps of the poor and unhoused. While nowhere near the massive program that authorities intended, the placement policy was effective at creating a large sector of skilled service workers and artisans. In 1603, when the corregidor and his Jesuit allies called for all of the city's Indians to be resettled in the Cercado, Lima's cabildo fought back because "the Indians are so useful and beneficial in their arts . . . that [the city] could not support itself without them."[57]

Other policies, especially those targeting free people of African descent, tried to control how they occupied space.[58] In 1549 the cabildo prohibited Black men and women from congregating in groups, claiming that they were coming together for dances, robbery, and drunken fiestas "under the guise of a cofradía." Black confraternities were subject to special restrictions: they could only meet on Sundays and holy days, in the hours between communion and mass, and in the church itself.[59] And Spanish slaveowners were warned not to leave enslaved laborers unsupervised in the countryside, though they balked at being told how to use their own property. Authorities in Lima associated good governance with control over the use of space by unruly residents.

Visualizing Policy

Unsupervised Andean immigration to the city also had fiscal ramifications. Indigenous mobility implied the evasion of obligations like tribute and mita, which were enforced by the leadership of rural communities. In 1613, Viceroy Juan de Mendoza y Luna called for a census of Lima's Indians, one that would identify the cacique and community to which they owed tribute payments. Carried out by Miguel de Contreras, a royal notary who went house-to-house to question residents, the long narrative document displays how they occupied Lima as well as the history of their migration and labor.[60] Contreras entered each house on a street, writing down the name, age, birthplace, and occupation of each resident he judged to be an Indian. He asked how long they had lived in Lima, the name of their cacique, and whether they paid tribute. He also noted information about their children and any absent spouses. In the margins he kept a reckoning of the salient facts about men he decided owed tribute: their ages, where they came from, their occupations.[61] He summarized the information in a few sentences, including, occasionally, his disagreements with his subjects' statements.

The census missed many residents, especially the informally employed, who fled or hid to avoid being counted; all the city's Indian officials were brought in to attest to absent workers. It did not count the Cercado's residents, who lived under many layers of jurisdiction and made their fiscal contributions through their caciques or the Jesuits. Among its nearly 1,900 entries occur small numbers of "Indians" from Goa and Manila, enslaved Indigenous children from Chile, self-disclosed mestizos, and the free Black and mulato landlords who rented rooms to tributaries. The census overrepresents those in trades and in domestic service: some 80 percent of male respondents called themselves artisans.[62]

FIG. 2.3 A page of the 1613 census of Lima, with Contreras' marginal annotations. Contreras, *Padrón de los indios que se hallaron en la ciudad de los Reyes del Perú*. From the holdings of the Biblioteca Nacional de España, Mss/3032. Biblioteca Digital Hispánica, Accessed January 9, 2022. http://bdh-rd.bne.es/viewer.vm?id=0000028573&page=1.

When data are extracted from the census and mapped onto the city streets using arcGIS software, the results show urban apprenticeship and service policies distributing Andeans across nearly every city block.[63] The maps document how those occupations came to characterize the ways that native peoples inhabited Lima, and how the city's new republics came into being through those spaces. Certain neighborhoods, indicated with darker tones, had a denser Andean presence, especially San Lázaro across the Rimac River and the blocks leading eastward toward the Cercado. These were residential spaces that welcomed Indigenous and Black professionals but also provided cheap and informal housing for new migrants and the poor. But markedly, native residents were ubiquitous in commercial centers like the area below the Plaza Mayor and in elite neighborhoods. Few parts of the city did not depend on Andean workers or tenants.[64]

By far the greatest source of residential integration was the Spanish reliance upon Indigenous servants. Spaniards expected access to native and Black labor, both to carry out tasks and to display their place in the colonial hierarchy. Elites dressed their help in livery and finery to indicate their own status, flouting the sumptuary laws that prohibited Indian and Black women from wearing luxurious

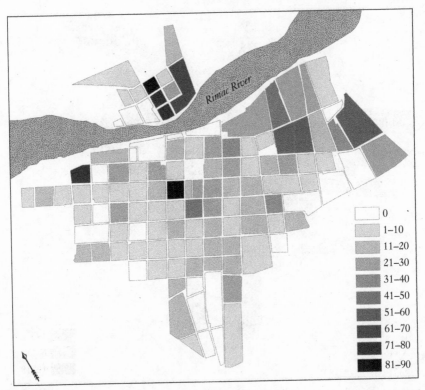

FIG. 2.4 The 1613 Census of the Indians of Lima, mapped.

Source: Contreras, *Padrón de los indios de Lima*; Bromley and Barbagelata, *Evolución urbana de Lima*, 8. Map by Matthew Sisk, Navari Family Center for Digital Scholarship, University of Notre Dame.

items. The pageantry of controlling non-Spanish labor in public spaces was part of the culture's symbolic economy and a prerequisite for asserting privilege.[65]

The largest concentrations of Indigenous servants were in wealthier neighborhoods, where elite families owned large residences that required staff. They were also ubiquitous in religious households: the city's churches and especially its residential convents and monasteries were their largest single employers. Massive institutions such as Santo Domingo, San Francisco, and Santa Clara (from west to east, just below the Rimac River) were virtual islands of native and Black labor.[66] Further, sorting by gender demonstrates that, despite their smaller overall numbers, women and girls were the agents of the city's integration through their work as household servants. While most women did not indicate a profession to the notary, 146 of those who did were in service (of a total of 546), as opposed to 226 men (of 1,127). The notary did not bother collecting most women's occupations, as they only owed tribute through their participation in family units.

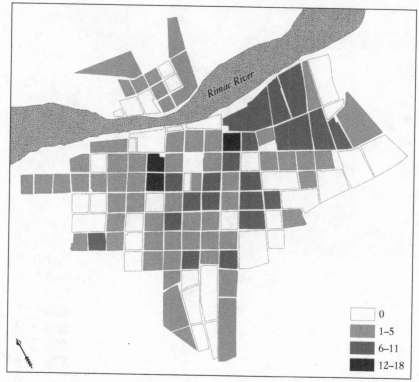

Rimac River

□	0
▨	1–5
▦	6–11
■	12–18

FIG. 2.5 Distribution of Indigenous Servants and Slaves in Lima, 1613.

Source: Contreras, *Padrón de los indios de Lima*; Bromley and Barbagelata, *Evolución urbana de Lima*, 8. Map by Matthew Sisk, Navari Family Center for Digital Scholarship, University of Notre Dame.

The policy of placing unsupervised individuals with masters reinforced the hierarchical structure of the city while dispersing non-Spaniards across it. In part, it was an answer to the common practice elite Spaniards made of removing natives from their communities and bringing them to city homes. As the Crown tried to restrain such exploitative "personal service," anti-vagrancy policy met the need. Placement was largely carried out by the *corregidor de los naturales*, the royal magistrate with jurisdiction over the region's indigenous inhabitants. His notary's records from the turn of the seventeenth century demonstrate this focus, particularly on placing children. He situated ten-year-old Alonso Liviac with priest Lucas de Ressa and sent twelve-year-old Agustín Quina to serve Andrés Ramírez for two years.[67] Some of these children were placed with their families' explicit consent, as when Pablo Carpapumbi from

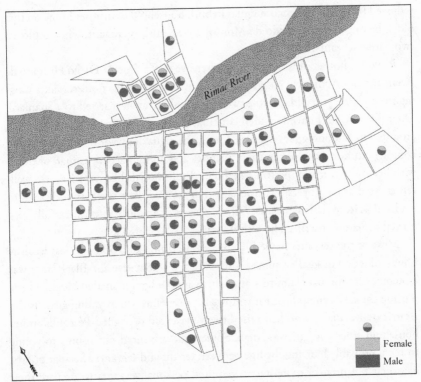

FIG. 2.6 Distribution of Indigenous Residents in Lima by Gender, 1613.
Source: Contreras, *Padrón de los indios de Lima*; Bromley and Barbagelata, *Evolución urbana de Lima*, 8. Map by Matthew Sisk, Navari Family Center for Digital Scholarship, University of Notre Dame.

Huaylas was placed with his uncle Hernando Quispe to learn tailoring and help in the workshop.[68]

One block in the census is particularly illustrative of the way elite spaces were integrated. The church of La Merced, built in 1541, sat two blocks below the plaza mayor. Eleven unmarried Andean men served or cooked for the priests in that massive structure. The rest of the street was occupied by city notables, including the home of Doctor Montalvo, chief justice of the Real Audiencia. In between, two sons of conquistadors established their households. One was don Martín Pizarro, the city's regidor and an encomendero, and the other don Martín Ampuero (Yupanqui), the son of the Spaniard don Francisco de Ampuero and doña Inés Huaylas (daughter of the Inka Huayna Capac), himself a former *regidor* of the city. Contreras found young Indigenous servants removed from familial encomiendas in both households. Another home on that block belonged to Bernardo de Montoya, a Spanish merchant, who employed two native servants.[69]

Powerful households were run by extensive staffs. Doctor Diego Hurtado de Avendaño, an Audiencia judge, employed five young Indigenous servants ranging from a nine-year-old girl to a twenty-year-old woman married to a Spaniard. Their duties would have included cooking, cleaning, tending children, running errands, and shopping. Severino de Torres, the alguazil mayor of the city, signed contracts to hire two men in their twenties and an unmarried woman of thirty with her eight-year-old mestiza daughter.[70] Professionals like notaries were well-represented as employers. Occasionally they trained their servants and slaves to read and write as their assistants.[71] These centers of Spanish power were fully supported by native and Black household staff.

Most of the servants named in the census, however, worked in less wealthy households and in smaller numbers, because access to native and Black labor was a prerequisite for any claim to status: these are the lighter-shaded blocks a little outside the city center. Spanish widows kept servants, often young girls, as did Beatriz de Betanzos, who had raised twelve-year-old orphaned Petronila in her household since the girl was small. Some widows rented out rooms to young women, probably blurring the line between tenant and servant.[72] Secular priests, like their brethren in monasteries, required personal servants to prepare their meals and clean their homes.[73] Some merchants owned young enslaved girls from Chile, where Indian slavery was legal until 1679. It is notable that some employers expressed little knowledge or curiosity about their servants. Francisco de Villanueva, a muleteer, employed a nine-year-old girl and a thirteen-year-old boy, both of whom he had brought to the city from the highlands fifteen days before Contreras' census. Villanueva's wife provided this information in his absence, stating that she knew nothing more about them, perhaps a function of the language barrier.[74]

Even the less notable neighborhoods were full of servants and assistants. On a road that left the city to the north, María de Contreras, a Spanish grocery store owner, employed Inés Carua, twenty-four, and an unnamed eight-year-old boy.[75] A sixteen-year-old orphan, Alonso Llaguas Cabilca, noted that he had worked for a Spanish fisherman near Callao "since he was small."[76] Two children of the provincial Andean nobility were placed into service in San Lázaro. Spanish embroiderer Juan Ortiz kept a seven-year-old Indian girl in his home as a servant.[77] She told Contreras that her father was don Carlos of Huánuco. Juan Carrasco, who slaughtered young bulls, employed a sixteen-year-old boy whose father was the cacique of Checras, located to the city's northeast. Slaughtering bulls and domestic service were not prestigious careers, but they were portable skills that would provide steady income, including for the downwardly mobile children of the declining non-Inka nobility.[78]

A handful of non-Spaniards, especially members of the city's new Indian leadership, also employed native servants. The Indian alcalde of the Cercado, Andrés Ramírez, employed a twelve-year-old boy in his household.[79] Don Francisco de Sanzoles, captain of the Indian infantry company and a tailor, owned three houses in San Lázaro and employed nine-year-old Juana Chagua. The infrequency of these placements suggests that Indigenous servants created less prestige for native masters, who were more likely to purchase Black slaves. People of African descent occasionally had Indigenous servants and employees. They included Francisco de los Reyes, a mulato carpenter with a workshop on Malambo Street (where many free Black Limeños lived); Bernarda de Córdoba, a mulata who lived in a corral; and Diego Hernández, who employed a twelve-year-old girl from Chile. Maria de Angulo, *morena* (Black, implying free), and her Spanish husband Francisco Díaz de Illán not only managed a crew of native fishermen, but also had Alonso Loche, a disabled fourteen-year-old boy, in their service.[80]

The embedded and intimate nature of domestic service was both a danger and an opportunity. Subservient employees were at risk of sexual and other abuse, and the large number of children in service (in the census, 193 were under the age of sixteen) invites speculation. Adults were also at risk, and only 27 percent of female and 9 percent of male adult servants reported being married. The marked tendency for unmarried female servants to mention their mestizo children in wills and other documents is evidence that masters considered sexual access part of the implicit labor contract. The other side of intimate service relationships, though, is that they might have provided access to political, economic, and legal knowledge. Indigenous women occasionally benefited materially through gifts and inheritances for themselves and their children. Household staffs would have shared gossip and information with one another. The uncanny success of some domestic servants and slaves, often women, at litigating and maneuvering through colonial institutions has been attributed to practical and legal knowledge they learned around the household.[81]

Apprenticeships

If domestic service placed Indigenous men, women, and children literally across the map, policies regarding apprenticeship were more targeted but no less consequential. In addition to determining the ways that native and Black workers occupied the city, the drive for apprenticeships drew men, especially, into a narrow stream of jobs, creating a city full of petty artisans.

Apprenticeships were both sought by laborers desiring training and imposed on underemployed young men by authorities and parents. Men like Baltazar Cacuna of Guayaquil, Cristóval Guana Xulca of Cusco, and the free mulato Diego Pérez apprenticed to learn shoemaking from local craftsmen.[82] Textile arts and tailoring were also popular. In 1596, a Spanish-speaking *muchacho* (a pre-adolescent) from Cajamarca was placed with a silkmaker, and ten-year-old Juan Carhua of Jauja was placed with a Spanish tailor for a year.[83] Some found placements to develop more unusual talents: swordmaker Pedro de Godoy hired Pedro Yasaima, a "Spanish-speaking Indian" from Trujillo, for a year in 1597.[84] These men and boys were likely recent arrivals—their places of origin span the Andes—and placement for a fixed term offered room and board and the promise of new skills.

Apprenticeships were common for poorer young men, but they had particular implications for Indigenous and Black men. They provided a technical education and placed laborers under the authority of a male adult. This transfer of patriarchal authority, which was often conducted by an Indian or Spanish official rather than a parent, undermined the minors' legal rights to dissolve the contract and left them in the hands of artisans who had broad latitude to correct their behavior.[85] Many contracts specified that apprentices could not leave their situation and occasionally required that parents imprison and return them if they fled home.[86] Apprenticeship thus imitated the rigors of enslavement in temporary ways, but many parents saw such contracts as a way to provide opportunities and material support for their children. They likely understood the contract, despite the vagueness of its guarantees, as a protection of certain rights. In 1596, Juan Moyo, from Surco, appeared before the corregidor de los naturales in order to formalize service contracts for his eight- and twelve-year-old sons with two Spanish employers. The servitude had already begun, but Moyo returned to request a written contract, perhaps because he worried that they would not receive their contractual requisites over the five years of labor. [87]

Apprenticeship concentrated young people in the area around the plaza mayor in the workshops of Spanish tailors and shoemakers. Some Indigenous and Black artisans took on apprentices, as did Luis Vernal, a tailor, when he hired a nineteen-year-old native man to work in his store near the Jesuit church.[88] Some apprentices found placements across the river in San Lázaro or in the streets leading to the Cercado, spaces already dominated by Indigenous and Black residents. But the vast majority of apprentices were placed with Spanish shoemakers and tailors in the city's center.

By the early seventeenth century, tailor and shoemaker were among the most common occupations for Indigenous men in the city.[89] Apprenticeship continued to be key to the transfer of knowledge and the occupational structure of the

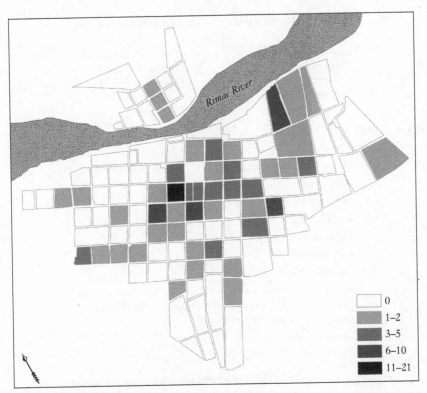

FIG. 2.7 Distribution of Indigenous Apprentices in Lima, 1613.

Source: Contreras, *Padrón de los indios de Lima*; Bromley and Barbagelata, *Evolución urbana de Lima*, 8. Map by Matthew Sisk, Navari Family Center for Digital Scholarship, University of Notre Dame.

city. Indeed, by 1631, the Franciscan Salinas y Córdova claimed that most owners of tailoring and shoemaking shops in the city were non-Spaniards, though the Spanish-run establishments likely had far more employees.[90]

The Hierarchy of Workshops

Apprenticeships channeled young men into a labor structure that shaped Lima's occupational hierarchy. But in contrast to the way that Muslims trained within families to pass trades across generations, in Lima Indigenous youth learned their trade from Spanish masters. About half of all artisans in the city were Spaniards, about 30 percent were native, and the rest were of African origins, but Spaniards were far more likely to be masters and employers.[91] The structure of artisan workplaces and the geography of the city ensured that while individuals were interdependent across races, the hierarchy was maintained.

Table 2.1 Most Common Occupations in 1613 Census
of Lima

Occupation	Number of "Indians"*
Servant	408
Tailor	262
Tailor's apprentice	73
Shoemaker	117
Shoemaker's apprentice	21
Silkweaver	45
Silkweaver's apprentice	11
Farm laborer	68
Fisherman	52
Chicha vendor	15
General vendor	21

*This count includes a few dozen "Indians" of the Philippines, Goa, and other parts of Iberian Asia.

Source: Contreras, *Padrón*.

The plaza mayor was the city's great market with stalls set along its porticos and informal vendors selling on blankets and boxes and under improvised shelter throughout its open space. Vendors sold the produce and other foodstuffs brought from the nearby valleys and far afield including Trujillo, Chile, Guayaquil, Panamá, and Nicaragua. Imported goods arrived from Europe at the port of Callao, and many of those items made their way into the surrounding shops. This abundance wound itself around the plaza's more official functions. With wooden buildings assigned to the cabildo and jail, the viceregal palace where the Audiencia met, the cathedral, notarial offices, and a gallows, it was the site of public pageantry as well as minor social and economic dramas. It was the city's most vibrant space.[92]

The eight streets leading into the plaza were full of storefronts and workshops. Mercaderes (Merchants) Street had the most expensive shops, and the census shows it also had the city's densest concentration of Andean tailors.[93] Tailoring in Lima required purchasing woven textiles—expensive imported goods or cheap coarse cloth from nearby *obrajes* or textile workshops—and cutting and sewing them into garments according to European designs. These were bought by Spanish, Indigenous, and Black consumers, though Andeans also wore and sold clothes in their own styles, either handwoven or made of imported fabrics.[94] Andean tailors in Lima had to learn a new trade from European artisans to meet the demands of the local market.

Contreras visited seventeen tailors' shops on Mercaderes street, all but one run by a Spanish master. Each employed between one and eight native craftsmen or apprentices; he counted forty-seven tributaries on this block alone. The largest workshop belonged to Andrés Núñez, described as the tailor to the viceroy. Among his staff were eight Andean men: three tailors and five apprentices. Miguel Camacho, a Spanish tailor, had five such employees, including don Francisco de Jesús, who insisted that the notary take down his honorific. These were all significant businesses, most described as having a store attached or at the back of the workshop. The sole Indigenous business owner was Lorenzo Comel, originally of Cajamarca, who worked as a hosier in a store next to a pharmacy.[95]

Shoemakers clustered in the three square blocks below the plaza. As with the tailors, their workplaces were mostly owned or managed by Spaniards, and their craft was European in origin. On Roperos Street, for example, the shoemakers Diego Xaramillo and Juan Galván had small workshops collectively employing

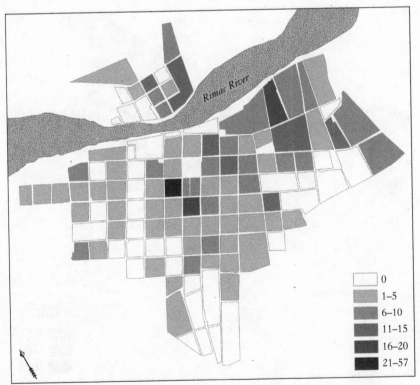

☐	0
	1–5
	6–10
	11–15
	16–20
	21–57

FIG. 2.8 Distribution of Indigenous Tailors in Lima, 1613.

Source: Contreras, *Padrón de los indios de Lima*; Bromley and Barbagelata, *Evolución urbana de Lima*, 8. Map by Matthew Sisk, Navari Family Center for Digital Scholarship, University of Notre Dame.

three adult male craftsmen and one eighteen-year-old apprentice, all of whom were registered by the notary as tributaries. Shoemakers on these streets tended to have smaller enterprises than tailors, with one or two Indigenous employees, possibly enabling more social mobility. Also on Roperos Street, Francisco Llauca, an Andean shoemaker, had a store in "the house where the Licenciado Duarte stays," alongside two more Indigenous shoemakers and a young teenager named Pedro "who apprentices to this master." While the grammar of the entry is ambiguous, the master tradesman seems to be Llauca, who rented the shop.[96]

Historian Frederick Bowser noted of the artisan trades, "[i]n no other area of endeavor did Spaniard, African [sic] and Indian work together so closely, on so wide a scale and under such relatively equal terms."[97] That equality was not readily seen on streets like Mercaderes, where no Indigenous or Black artisan appeared to own a shop in 1613, although a block away, Phelipe Domínguez, a mulato tailor, owned a house and store and employed four native men.[98] But moving even a

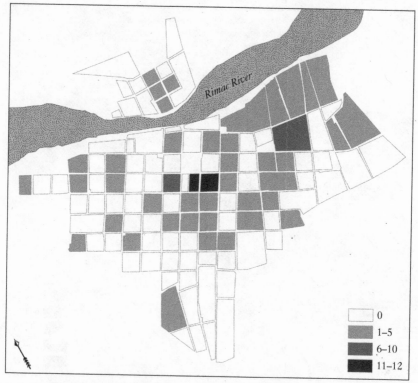

FIG. 2.9 Distribution of Indigenous Shoemakers in Lima, 1613.

Source: Contreras, Padrón de los indios de Lima; Bromley and Barbagelata, Evolución urbana de Lima, 8. Map by Matthew Sisk, Navari Family Center for Digital Scholarship, University of Notre Dame.

few blocks away from the plaza, social relations softened. On the street leading east from the church of San Francisco, an older Andean man named Francisco Xuárez had a store where he employed a younger assistant. One of a very few Indigenous men described in the census as a *maestro*, or master artisan, Xuárez's self-presentation raised the prejudices of the notary, who called him "a master shoemaker, with his shorn hair and dressed in the clothes of a Spaniard."[99] A second Indigenous maestro was Juan de Gavira, twenty-two years old and from highland Huamanga, who had his own shop and was also described as dressing like a Spaniard.[100] Contreras often used this racially coded language to suggest that subjects were attempting to pass as Spaniards to evade tribute payments, while clearly registering them as tributaries in his margins. In such a context, these men must have struggled to achieve their status as examined masters—a qualification that only eighteen indigenous and nine Black men received, according to Francisco Quiroz's analysis of sixteenth century records.[101]

Andean tailors and shoemakers with their own shops were mainly concentrated in San Lázaro and on the streets leading to the Cercado. These neighborhoods were home to an emerging sector of artisans that featured a powerful Indigenous political class.[102] At the city's north edge, and home to a leper hospital, quarantine barracks for newly arrived slaves, and slaughterhouses, San Lázaro was the site of numerous small businesses, organized more randomly than in the city's center. On a street that led to the slaughterhouses, don Francisco de Sanzoles reported that one of his adult sons was a tailor like him, the other employed as a dance master. Other craftsmen on the nearby streets shared rental spaces, like Juan de Torres and Domingo Ramos, tailors who rented a storefront at the end of Malambo Street from Anton Martín, perhaps a Spaniard. On the same block the Andean tailors Juan Bautista and Pascual Paucar Poma both rented space from a woman they called "Beatriz Madalena known as *La Rica* (the rich woman)."[103] The nickname was earned. In 1631, Beatriz Madalena would purchase another house on Malambo street for 1,050 pesos in cash, an astonishing amount for an Indigenous woman in Lima at the time. A few months later, she sold a female slave on credit to a Spanish infantry captain for 700 pesos.[104]

The labor model in these neighborhoods differed from that of the center in that they were based on horizontal partnerships or cooperative rentals of workspaces without a master or apprentices. Here, a workshop was most likely a series of rooms rented from a landlord where independent artisans worked and lived. Sometimes they were connected by their place of origin. On Malambo Street, Juan Guaman lived in a house his wife owned and they rented a room to a younger man from his hometown of Cajamarca. Next door, a saddler, also from Cajamarca, opened his home to his recently arrived brother, a young tailor.[105] While these relationships were surely important for recent immigrants, they also extended over time. Across Malambo, a blacksmith named Geronimo de Ayala owned a rooming house where he rented to three fishermen, all from the beach town of Huanchaco (Trujillo), which they had left two or three decades earlier.[106]

The Creolization of Lima

While the census-taker tried to impose his logic on urban Indians, the brief ethnographies he wrote down reveal their resistance to his assumptions. Viceroy Mendoza may have called for the census in response to a letter from Juan Vélez, a mestizo from the Jauja Valley, the Quechua interpreter-general, and a *protector* or public advocate for Indians.[107] Vélez had argued that migrants who relocated to urban centers were destroying their natal communities, which struggled to meet their fiscal obligations. He proposed removing them from Lima and returning them to their small republics. But the viceroy and notary Contreras were more focused on securing payment. Contreras asked each resident to sketch their geographical origins and their place in the taxpaying hierarchy. He tallied ages to calculate when young people would become obliged to pay tribute and elders would become exempt. The census was preamble to tax-extraction.

Contreras' subjects resisted this narrative. Men and women claimed not to know who their cacique was, because they had come to the city as children or were long out of touch with their community of birth. Very few claimed to be up to date with their payments. Some simply stated the fact without excuse: they did not pay. Juan Sánchez, a tailor living near the Cathedral with a shop in San Agustin, named his cacique and encomendero back in Saña. He noted, "he has been in this city for three years and he is single and twenty years old, and until now has never paid tribute."[108] Others offered reasons. The disabled were exempted; at the home of a blacksmith the notary found "a blind Indian who operated the bellows" and noted in the margin "do not count this one."[109] More controversially, many argued that they were not "Indians" at all, but mestizos. Contreras tended to disbelieve them, characterizing them as "Indians in the garb of a Spaniard" and marking them as Indians in his marginal tallies.[110]

Limeños justified their exemptions with arguments about the communities to which they were attached. Many used the term *criollo*, usually understood to describe both enslaved people of African descent who had assimilated Spanish language and culture, and people of Spanish descent who were born in the New World and were considered (and increasingly considering themselves) to have different interests and physical constitutions than their peninsular relatives. Lima's residents may have coined the term *indio criollo* to describe an Indigenous person born in the city, without claims on a rural kin group or an obligation to them or a cacique.[111] Vélez warned of the politics of this discourse in his letter to the viceroy: "most [Indians in Lima] have abandoned their pueblos and reducciones, fleeing the payment of tribute and personal service, considering that because they live among Spaniards and are so naturalized among them, calling themselves criollos, and for this reason they are all or mostly exempt from paying tribute."[112]

Not all were tax evaders. Some argued that they were still part of distant pueblos de indios whose obligations were met outside the usual tax system. A Filipina woman married to a Tlaxcalan man noted that her husband did not pay tribute, as the Tlaxcalans "had neither cacique nor encomendero," referring to their unusual legal status as an autonomous polity within the viceroyalty of New Spain.[113] A fisherman from Trujillo stated that "the Indians of his hometown do not pay tribute because it is paid by *censos* that their ancestors imposed upon Spanish property"—that is, they taxed Spaniards who rented collectively owned properties and used the proceeds for tribute payments.[114] Luis Hernández, a shoemaker originally from Ica, claimed that the Indians of his town had an arrangement with the city's cathedral, wherein they "decorated bridges and acted as *chasquis* (postal agents) and did whatever they were asked" instead of paying tribute.[115] While these immigrants no longer contributed labor to their republics, they remained on the tribute rolls along with the kin that did not leave.

Others insisted that they were residents of Lima, and not of those distant pueblos. In the words of don Carlos de Mendoza, who claimed to be the cacique of Yungay but lived in Lima, his wife doña Ana García was a criolla of Lima "and as such she knows no cacique nor encomendero."[116] Wills from the period also utilize the language of creolization in order to establish a legal link with Lima and an exemption from obligations elsewhere, especially for people who had no ability to mobilize the weak privileges they might be owed by their parents' birthplaces.[117] Eighty years after the founding of new urban settlements in the Andes, it was difficult to gauge when migrants ended their relationship with the communities of their birth, with dispersed families, or even with their ancestors. As Miguel Sánchez, the alcalde of the city's Indian tailors, stated, while he was born in the town of Chimbo, "he has no idea about the succession [of his encomendero or cacique], he has been in this city for more than thirty years."[118]

While Contreras considered identifying Lima's tributaries a simple task, he uncovered a web of developing beliefs about status, law, and identity. The vast majority of respondents were able to offer a reasonable answer to the question of where they were from and to whom they owed tribute, but many also argued that their migration had undone the fiscal obligations to their republics. The city had republican structures but not the ones that Contreras was seeking, rendering the lines of authority invisible to him. Lima's Indian republics were strong in some ways but, with no means or will to enforce them, markedly weak in terms of tax collection.

New and Old Hierarchies

One useful marker of status in Indian Lima was old: the honorifics don and doña. The Crown policed claims to nobility, issuing titles to a relatively narrow group of claimants. But members of the lesser provincial nobility and many Andean commoners simply appropriated the don, much as the Jews had been said to do in medieval Castile. Andean author don Felipe Guaman Poma de Ayala, himself grievously deprived of his family's inherited privileges, noted that "there are many dons and doñas in this life not worth a fig."[119]

The census is a good barometer of how those claims functioned: they produced a narrative about status with no material privileges attached. A city of immigrants would have been an ideal place to reinvent oneself, but only thirty-six men and women could convince Contreras to report the honorific title with their name. Undoubtedly this reflected Contreras' paranoia that it was yet another tax-evasion scheme: caciques, at least, were exempt. But many Indigenous and a few Black men and women used the honorific in daily life, as a claim that they merited status, at least within their own community.

Nine of the nobles recognized in the census were women. As elsewhere in the empire, women might have been given more latitude with the term than men, particularly since, as non-tributaries, it did not accord them many material advantages. Two women claimed descent from Inkas: Petronilla from Huamanga, who called herself *Ñusta*, and Juana Cusi, who called herself a *Palla* from Cusco. Both terms were used for female members of the royal Inka lineage. Neither woman had great wealth, each lived in a room she rented from a Spanish shopkeeper, and neither used doña.[120]

Four of the dons lived on a block that carried the nickname "Calle de Pobres," so called, according to Juan Bromley, for its "modest housing."[121] This otherwise unnamed street ran from the church of the Incarnation onto private fields and gardens on the southern route leaving the city. Most of its houses were owned by Spaniards, who let rooms to fishermen from the north coast, or hired single and widowed native women as live-in servants. But among these were also doña María de Vega of Huarochirí, married to a Spanish tailor. The couple had a workshop and an Indigenous apprentice. A few houses down was the residence of don Francisco Mecomo, the son of the cacique of north coastal Catacaos, and his wife doña Catalina Chumbi. The couple was raising a young girl, the daughter of a potter from Surco who also took the honorific doña. Don Francisco had been in the city for four years, managing litigation for himself or his community.[122] A few yards away was the house of captain Alonso Gómez, who rented a room to don Juan González Cornejo, an Indigenous fisherman from Trujillo who had lived in Lima for twenty years. He stated that he was the cacique of the Indians of Trujillo, but "in his absence an Indian named don Diego del Salto governed."[123]

These men and women, many of them members of the provincial nobility, lived away from the commercial centers and the homes of high-status Spaniards. They were not wealthy and they lived at the city's southern edge among the rooming houses and corrales of the poor, but not near plebeian San Lázaro or the Cercado. While some caciques continued to exert leadership roles while in Lima—mostly among their subjects within the Cercado—the provincial elites were relatively disempowered without the men and women they might have commanded in their hometowns, though they were proud of their genealogies. When Contreras interviewed them, they insisted on their honorifics and repeated their backstories, but he indicated them as tributaries in his records.

Eighteen dons and doñas did not claim to be caciques or Inkas, suggesting that they had earned status through other means. Those included service in the military: by 1620, Lima had ten Indian infantry battalions, each with a captain and sergeant, and 500 members in total, creating a significant social ladder.[124] These battalions functioned as small republics, producing hierarchies, networks, and a support system that interacted with the city's other representative bodies. Don Francisco de Sanzoles, a tailor, served as an infantry commander as well as an Indian alcalde. Don Pedro Gonzalez was the captain of the Cañari Indians in the city, the ethnic group that had rebelled against the Inka and formed a military flank for Pizarro.[125] Don Juan Curivilca was the brother of the cacique of Condormarca, a tailor in Lima, and an infantry sergeant.[126] Militia service, which involved public performances at important ceremonial moments in the city's life, would be among the most important ways Indigenous men cultivated status in Lima.

In contrast to the down-on-their-luck Andean nobles and provincial caciques, by far the most mobile sector was its successful artisans and farmers. They reinvented the republic in the city, weaving together a panoply of elected positions or *cargos* that they circulated through over their careers. Their status drew upon multiple institutions, including cabildo offices, the infantry, and the Catholic Church.[127] They had connections to the Andean nobility, through marriage, godparentage, and memberships in confraternities. But many began as unpropertied immigrants, building careers that allowed them to accrue property and employ others, and also accumulate other forms of power, such as enslaved men and women.

Status and Slavery

Slave ownership was a powerful symbol in Lima, and it was eagerly adopted by many upwardly mobile Andeans. Don Juan Curivilca drew upon his status as infantry sergeant in 1612 when he approached the corregidor de los naturales seeking permission to sell Beatriz, a fifty-year-old enslaved African woman of the

Casanga nation, to the Spaniard Juan Reyno for 825 pesos.[128] The law largely prohibited Indians from engaging in the African slave trade, requiring a license from the corregidor for all related commerce. While he might have balked at giving permission to an Indian tailor, the corregidor had no qualms about approving the request of a military officer.

Nor was it only men associated with the infantry who bought and sold slaves. Gregorio Hernández, a farmer and landlord who served as the Indian alcalde in 1613, owned three enslaved Black men and was a minor slave trader. His political and economic contacts enabled this occupation: he sold slaves to don Gaspar Maldonado, a lawyer with the Real Audiencia, and to Josephe Godoy Delgadillo, a Spanish farmer.[129] Only twelve Indigenous households listed in the census owned Black slaves, for a total of twenty enslaved persons (seventeen were women or girls, three men or boys). At least a few more lived in the uncensused Cercado. Slave ownership correlated strongly with the same occupations as political leadership: six families were in tailoring, four were in agriculture, one was a cobbler, and one a painter. An outlier was don Martín Capuy, the Quechua interpreter general for the Real Audiencia, arguably the highest status position available to an Indigenous man in Lima at the time.[130]

Such purchases would have been far beyond most households' abilities, and Andean families found loans with difficulty. Slave merchants were reluctant to issue credit to those who lacked significant collateral, and informal credit markets rarely provided such large sums. Instead, purchasers took advantage of numerous smaller opportunities. Luis Pérez, who appears in the census in 1613 as a farmer living on the street leading to the Cercado, wrote a will ten years later that demonstrated his improved station.[131] His new wife brought a large dowry of 400 *patacones* in cash, which they turned into a house, three horses, and five enslaved men. They did so by using the dowry as collateral to acquire loans from other Indigenous Limeños, including 200 pesos from Beatriz Magdalena "La Rica" and smaller sums from a number of men in the Cercado. In addition to purchasing slaves to serve as farm laborers, Pérez also placed one enslaved child in an apprenticeship, receiving a small fee and future returns on his skills. Others found loans in more unexpected places. Pedro Panara in 1626 reported that he had purchased three enslaved persons (two adults, one child) for his farm by borrowing money from the Cercado's rector Padre Vázquez. In his will, he returned 70 pesos and a harvest of wheat to the priest.[132] These credit networks offer glimpses of the ways that urban Indians were reconstituting communities, creating trust through occupational frameworks, through proximity, and through the Catholic Church.

Gender also affected the decision to purchase slaves. Single Indigenous women did so, perhaps because they had particular needs for flexible and mobile forms of capital. Slaves could be sold, rented, or even pawned, as doña Catalina

Llacla did with an enslaved adult and child when she grew sick while traveling through Lima. A Spaniard had given her 450 pesos for the pair, which she hoped her executors would recoup.[133] They also assisted with laborious tasks. Catalina Payco, a *chicha* (corn beer) vendor, owned an adolescent boy she called Juan *negro criollo* in 1575; he would have helped brew the drink and haul it to market.[134]

Some of the city's free people of African descent came to similar conclusions: owning slaves could offer status and smooth income streams during economic crises. Black men and women faced innumerable economic barriers, beginning with achieving freedom. Self-purchase took enormous time and discipline, making the accrual of intergenerational wealth almost impossible. This experience also impressed upon freedpersons the need to invest for their futures. Like Andean men and women, they chose real estate and slavery as their instruments toward prosperity. These were also in part gendered decisions. Free Black men largely invested in agricultural land that they could till, although some couples bought real estate to generate rental incomes.[135] Wealthier free Black women, like their Indigenous counterparts, more often purchased slaves. Of seventeen Black women who left wills in late sixteenth- and early seventeenth-century Lima, fifteen owned at least one enslaved person and seven of those owned three or more; one woman owned six.[136]

These investments generated income through the jornal, the vehicle that had brought incremental freedom to so many enslaved men and women. That wage probably explains the prevalence of slave ownership among some unmarried women, who relied upon such payments to tide them over during bad times. Juliana Nuñez, whom the notary termed "mulata in color, a free unmarried woman," purchased twenty-eight-year-old Francisco Biafara from a Spanish hatmaker in 1596 for 350 pesos in cash, perhaps as an investment against economic uncertainty.[137] That crisis came in 1578 for Mencia López, a Black woman who spent time in jail and, upon release, tried to collect the wages of the four slaves she had placed with paying clients during that time. She had also pawned one for 150 pesos and sold another for 500.[138] While most of these slave owners were a few generations removed from enslavement, their collective knowledge of the workings of self-manumission informed their decisions to buy and rent out their own slaves.

With few credit markets available to people of African descent, whatever wealth they had must have always seemed tenuous. María de Bilbao, a Bran (Upper Guinea) woman, had freed herself by 1625 and had purchased Pedro Casanga's freedom for 700 pesos before she married him. She did not erase that debt with the marriage because it represented her children's inheritances. In her will, she called upon her son and daughter to forgive part of Pedro's debt and to work out a payment plan with him for the rest, but she also threatened her husband with lawsuits and prison if he failed to make timely payments. Her husband's freedom would not come at the expense of her children's future.[139]

Like Andeans, Black Limeños also created their own credit markets. The free probably made many loans to the still-enslaved, few of which were recorded. María de Huancavelica, a freedwoman who identified herself as a Folupa (Floup) born in Guinea, had lent 750 pesos to Antonio Carabalí and Jacinta Folupa to purchase their freedom. On her deathbed, she forgave Antonio's debt but ordered her executors to collect from Jacinta.[140] Ana Biafara had, along with her husband, lent 160 pesos to Sebastián de Loyola for his manumission, and asked her executors to collect her share of the debt in 1586.[141]

A structural solution might have come from one of the few self-governing institutions available to Black subjects. Confraternities collected fees from members and alms from the public, and used both to assist cofrades. Despite the poverty of Black members, the confraternities could manage relatively large accounts. When Sebastián Zape's term as *mayordomo* (elected administrator) of the Rosario confraternity ended in 1608, he did not turn over the account books or treasury box to his successors as required by their constitution. The new mayordomos had him imprisoned. They noted in their lawsuit that "when he was elected and named mayordomo he was a slave, subjected to servitude, and his wife was as well, and now both are free and have freed themselves with the charitable gifts for burials and other income for the confraternity."[142] Sebastián Zape eventually produced account books and receipts for the year that showed that, if he had embezzled, it was not as significant a sum as they claimed—he had taken in 504 pesos and expended 425—but it was consequential. Those funds were regularly used for such charitable causes as supporting cofrades and their families in illness or funeral costs. Contributions toward freedom papers have been documented in some cases.[143]

Credit presented risks, especially for those whose only collateral was their ability to work. Similar to arrangements already noted in Seville, María Conga agreed to serve Gerónima de Montiel for five years as repayment for a loan of 150 pesos she had used to purchase her freedom in 1596.[144] The brutal reality behind such a contract is revealed in the case of Ysabel Folupa, who sought freedom from her master in the middle of the seventeenth century. She received a loan of 400 pesos from Maria Angola, a free Black woman, who used doña María de León y Salvatierra as her intermediary. Ysabel was to give doña María seven pesos a month until the loan and interest were repaid; María Angola would use those funds, in turn, to purchase her own husband's freedom. By 1666, Ysabel Folupa was in arrears, leaving María Angola on her deathbed without enough of an estate even to pay for her funeral. Her executors recognized this transaction not as a loan but as a property transfer. From their perspective, María Angola had purchased Ysabel Folupa, who would be sold to doña María de León to settle the estate. Apart from these funds, María Angola was not wealthy, with only some clothing, a little jewelry, and twenty-two chickens and a rooster to her name.[145]

In short, while some well-off free people of African heritage could be found in Lima, their stories can be deceptive. Most clearly occupied an insecure place. If free, their friends and families might still be enslaved, and they were surrounded by evidence of the precarity of their lives. The lack of institutional and political structures was both a cause and a result of this fragility. While confraternities provided some material as well as spiritual support, free Black men and women were often financially adrift. Inconstant freedom and unstable incomes created suspicion and competition between residents, and likely made it difficult for Black people to see themselves as part of a collective body.

In contrast, Indigenous residents—while also mostly very poor—found more paths to status and mobility in Lima. They did so by inventing new and somewhat amorphous republics that reconfigured colonial institutions for their benefit. While the old Andean nobility struggled to maintain status in the urban setting, new possibilities were raised by military service, confraternity memberships, and offices within the church and Indian cabildo. The apprenticeships and service contracts foisted upon immigrants could be paths to networks that offered them jobs, credit, and investments. The vast majority could not benefit from these paths, becoming one among hundreds of city tailors or servants. But the most successful learned to use capital to acquire more capital.

———

The Spanish settlement of Lima required removing and reordering the region's native peoples. Taulichusco's subjects were replaced by immigrants from the coastal valley and then, due to waves of forced and voluntary immigration, from across the Andes and beyond. As Lima became the seat of the viceroyalty of Peru, its coastal site and temperate climate attracting Spanish settlers and merchants, it also acquired a multiethnic Indigenous population. Men and women of African descent were brought in great numbers to the city and became its single largest sector. Unlike Seville's Muslim and Jewish inhabitants, Lima's Black and Indigenous residents were not united through a belief system. They arrived from heterogeneous regions with distinct languages, religions, and cultures. Even when they could maintain relationships with distant kin or others of their origins, they lived within a system designed to transform them. Eventually Catholicism and Lima itself could serve as unifying factors. But the absence of cohorts, reinforced by only limited republican self-governance, left a political vacuum.

Spanish authorities sought to discipline that diverse city. While in rural areas officials were concerned with keeping Spaniards and others out of pueblos in the interest of protecting Indians as they acquired policía, in Lima policy dictated the opposite. By the middle of the sixteenth century, officials had settled on a program of attaching permanent Black and Indigenous residents to Spanish masters. Mapping the census shows how profoundly this affected the ways that the city was inhabited. Apprenticeships grouped Indigenous and Black men in skilled crafts, feeding them into workshops in the city center or in their own businesses on the margins. For some, that proximity gave them the connections they required to advance in their careers, to negotiate loans, and to assume leadership positions. Indigenous women overwhelmingly spent time in service, thereby integrating elite households, or they congregated in urban markets to sell food, beverages, and other goods. These locations gave some access to elite resources and horizontal networks of support. Black men and women were also often attached to Spanish households or workshops, as enslaved laborers or as free servants and apprentices. While they were certainly the least powerful people in the city, some drew upon these relationships to borrow funds or acquire knowledge. Lima rapidly became a complex city of extremes, whose governing elite was Spanish but where non-Spaniards could find brotherhood and, occasionally, security.

Mappings of the city are a way to contemplate how its native residents utilized all the space available to them to learn crafts, gather wealth, find solidarity, and produce new forms of status and hierarchy. When Spanish authorities tried to coerce the separation of republics, they were usually rebuffed—both by those being removed and by the local people who relied upon their labor. But the intersection of notions of community with designated but not compulsory neighborhoods also created the possibility of internally focused social hierarchies and power structures. The use of honorific titles, the invention of indios criollos, and the coalitions between artisans across racial and ethnic categories were meaningful and could be used instrumentally. They offered viable frameworks for crafting collective ways of being that met the dominant powers' expectations but also had space for internal solutions to local problems that could be invisible outside the community.

PART II

Jurisdiction

Legal culture and practice were effective at binding communities together. To be a member of the Jewish or Muslim aljama or the pueblo de indios was to be bound by obligations and privileges that were institutionalized through horizontal local ties and an internal hierarchy that communicated with external forces. Jurisdiction, like spatial organization, was the target of external interference that chipped away at its autonomy. But the lines of jurisdiction, particularly at the very local level, created the structure through which communities could reproduce themselves as cultural organisms, that preserved and invented meanings.

These chapters explore the ways that law became central to the formation of difference in these republics. Minority self-governance was useful to monarchs, but only within certain limits, leaving communities to scrap with them over the extent of their jurisdiction. Those tensions also shaped the experience of belonging to the republic, particularly in the ways members of the republics articulated status and hierarchies, and produced rules for collective living in an unfavorable environment. Muslim and Jewish aljamas in Seville and Indigenous pueblos in Lima scripted their institutional existence in distinct and consequential ways.

3

Institutionalizing Legal Difference in Castile

IN THE EARLY years of the fifteenth century, don Muhammad ibn Yusuf al-Quaysi, the royally appointed *alcalde mayor* (provincial magistrate) of all the Muslim aljamas of Castile, wrote an impassioned letter to the concejo of the city of Sepúlveda.[1] The municipality had criticized don Muhammad for naming a *qadi* or local judge for the city's small community of Muslims. Don Muhammad's reply indicates that the concejo had argued not only against the particular candidate but against the need for any Muslim judge in Sepúlveda.

Don Muhammad conceded the concejo's position regarding the particular candidate, who, he noted, had been pushed upon him by "great lords of this kingdom," but argued that the community required a qadi. What happens, he asked, when a Muslim man or woman dies, leaving small children, and there is no one to protect their inheritance? What prevents a widow or widower from remarrying and assigning their late spouse's estate to their new family? Who will ensure that Islamic inheritance law is enforced? Don Muhammad attempted to protect the mudéjar republics as juridical spaces where Muslim judges could pronounce Islamic justice within the constraints of Castilian power.

This letter provides unique insight into the ways that contestations over the limits of juridical autonomy shaped the experience of being a member of a religious minority community. Don Muhammad's intervention articulates the ongoing tension between an increasingly hegemonic Christian society and its religious minorities, whose right to worship in their faith might be conceded theoretically but required persistent institutional guarantees. In particular, their ability to protect civil law—here, the material practice of taking care of the community's physical and spiritual needs—was regularly challenged by local Christian actors eager to assert jurisdiction. This was not only an issue of power but a reflection of the constant and mundane interrelations that took place between Christians,

Republics of Difference. Karen B. Graubart, Oxford University Press. © Oxford University Press 2022.
DOI: 10.1093/oso/9780190233839.003.0004

Muslims, and Jews in daily life, where Islamic or Jewish justice could easily be permeated or overwhelmed by Christian justice.

The local arena was also a stage for larger political tensions. Muslim and Jewish communities were often pawns in contests between monarchs, nobles, church officials, and urban elites. The aljama served a dual institutional purpose: it guaranteed Islamic or Jewish justice for its members, but was also a structure that conveyed the collective's wealth and labor to the Crown. As a result, it had to resist external attempts to constrain or take over the mechanisms of justice delivery and fiscal extraction, which often targeted the men who held its local and royal offices. This chapter defines those struggles over the juridical structures of Jewish and Muslim republics through the centuries between the conquest of Seville and expulsion.

Institutionalizing the Aljama

After Christian forces settled in the former Muslim kingdoms, they began transforming the temporary relationship of conqueror to conquered into a practical one of negotiated rule. Monarchs, archbishops, nobles, and settlers helped to identify authorities who could speak for and to the conquered and created networks to communicate their demands and expectations. Muslim and Jewish subjects of Christian monarchs responded by creating viable institutions for producing a coherent social, political, and religious identity. The result was a new group of political-religious offices that built upon long-standing practices in Judaism and Islam, but reforged them to accommodate the shifting needs of communities under Christian rule, the increasingly limited set of men who could fill those roles, and the threat of interventions from outside.

Conquest was contractual, in keeping with the Iberian peninsula's long history of political pluralism. Castilian political theory called upon communities to designate their leaders and transfer political power to the monarch willingly. Alfonso X explained in the *Siete partidas* that "wise men have declared that the greatest and most perfect authority that an emperor can exercise *de facto* in his dominions is when he loves his people and is beloved by them."[2] Lords swearing vassalage negotiated customary law, their obligations to the monarch, and the extent of jurisdiction they could exercise over their subjects. The founders of cities and towns received fueros, or municipal charters from their monarch, but they also expected to negotiate terms and to enact their subjecthood in ways that reflected their understandings of custom as well as their knowledge of what their neighbors had received. Muslim and Jewish aljamas enjoyed a certain degree of autonomy during this formative period because their success was crucial to Christian projects of long-term settlement and urbanization.

Pluralism did not give equal weight to all jurisdictions. The monarch reserved the right to intervene at his or her pleasure, and many Christian institutions exercised power over non-Christians. As a negotiated entity, jurisdiction could always be redefined or taken away. Yet pluralism produced and sustained a political class among the conquered or integrated, providing rewards to those who could make legitimated claims to speak on behalf of their community. While monarchs often asserted their right to choose their conduits to the aljamas from among their Jewish and Muslims circles at court, local politics raised up new leaders who worked through conflicts with municipal officials.

For conquered Muslims and incorporated Jews, this hierarchical pluralism led to a fraught legal complexity. Muslim and Jewish leaders negotiated relationships with their own religious communities, with the monarch (or lord) who claimed them; with the representatives of municipal bodies such as the *concejo* in the towns and cities where they dwelled; and with various institutions within the Catholic Church. These relationships were often characterized by conflict, but they also allowed for powerful alliances.

The same large patterns that conditioned the issuing and derogation of separation policies also affected independent jurisdictions for non-Christians. Until about 1350, monarchs more or less officially tolerated limited autonomy, predicated on the idea that separation could protect Christians from Jewish or Muslim contamination, but a vital society was going to require Jewish and Muslim participation. By the middle of the fourteenth century, local and kingdom-wide political rivalries instrumentalized popular anti-Judaism, culminating in the 1391 assault on Seville's judería that grew into a series of pogroms. Across Castile, many elite Muslims and Jews converted to Christianity to hang on to their status, leaving the communities with less wealth and power as well as fewer leaders to secure governance. Converts understandably feared association with their former communities and kin and, if they maintained relations, they did so privately and quietly. Local officials and preachers took advantage of their weakness to chip away at aljamas' ability to act independently and govern their own affairs. The fifteenth century brought a paradigm shift as monarchs periodically attacked the idea that the aljamas could oversee their own legal affairs, and ended dismantling them. While it was legal, the republic served as a vehicle for self-governance, but it was in constant danger of losing so much jurisdiction as to be incapable of delivering justice.

Creating Political Space for Difference

In 1251, Alfonso X confirmed upon the settlers of Seville the fuero previously given to Toledo, supplemented by specific privileges issued to particular classes of individuals, as well as local customary law.[3] The fuero set out the distribution of taxes to the king and the Church, established norms for the city's repopulation, and recognized the tax-exempt status of certain groups of settlers. In language that the monarch would use again in other legislation, it also asserted the right of Christians not to be judged by Jews or Muslims in their courts, but had little else to say about religious minorities.[4] The fuero was characteristic of charters issued to many Andalusian cities at the time. Local particularities were addressed with subsequent privileges, such as one allowing residents to pasture their herds and cut wood on commons outside the city, another creating a fund to repair the city's water system, and others regulating wheat mills.

In 1272, Seville's concejo issued ordinances for governing the city, also confirmed by the king.[5] These established the roles of municipal officers, some named by the king, others elected locally, and some, the jurados, representing each of the city's twenty-four collaciones. Eventually the king would insert his own presiding officer, a corregidor, into the institution. The concejo also filled a variety of minor offices including notaries, mail service, town criers, and market and building inspectors.[6] The ordinances themselves deferred to existing "use and custom" regarding everything from running the markets to maintaining towers and walls, leaving space for the concejo's interpretation.[7]

In its early years the concejo recognized religious minorities as participants in shared urban life and focused on managing conflict. The members set rules for controlling animals who might damage crops and prohibited residents from cutting down olive and fig trees for firewood. They ensured that the city's ovens were staffed and banned city officials from being found in the company of prostitutes or panderers. They ruled that Jewish salt-sellers must ensure that their product was clean and properly measured, and that Muslims could not carry a knife in the city "because they are so likely to get into debt and from this comes much lunacy."[8] Market regulations set out in 1279 established fees that Muslim and Jewish butchers paid to inspectors, indicating that ritually prepared meats were readily available and were separately taxed.[9] The concejo's debates and legislation show that its jurisdiction only overlapped with Jewish and Muslim citizens when they were regulating common markets or collecting particular fees.

In turn, Muslim and Jewish communities created religious, political, and legal institutions to enact their limited autonomy. While some of the city's Jews and Muslims arrived from other regions already bearing authority, the new conglomerations of immigrants and natives would have to invent institutions that served the needs of diverse residents.

The Islamic debate over emigration only added to this social complexity. Jurists in Mālikī fiqh (law), the dominant legal tradition for Andalusian Muslims, issued fatwās stating the obligation of conquered Muslims to emigrate to lands under Islamic rule (*dār al-Islām*).[10] Those who remained among Christians, or under Christian rule, were derided by some Muslims in Granada and North Africa as traitors or "the people of submission."[11] The vast majority of the population of al-Andalus remained in place, most notably the poor. Migration was costly, both materially and emotionally, and only realistic for elites.[12]

Few who remained had formal training in law. Over time, the loss of scholars transformed the political community. By the fifteenth century, the term *alfaquí* no longer designated a student of fiqh, but rather the holder of an office charged with carrying out legal tasks in the service of the aljama, such as the partition of inheritances.[13] Muslims in Seville maintained relationships with jurists in the greater Islamic world to manage complex legal affairs.

The early Jewish community, led by Toledan immigrants, had especially strong ties to the Castilian crown. Some held prominent offices: as ambassadors, astronomers, and scribes, as well as collectors of rents (*almojarifes*) and political governors or intermediaries (*alfaquíes*) to the Jewish aljama.[14] They received rural properties in the initial land distributions that befitted men of their stature, to encourage their permanent settlement. By the end of the thirteenth century, Seville's Jewish aljama was wealthy and heavily taxed, Castile's second largest after Toledo.[15]

The Jewish aljama's leadership in the early years seems to have been drawn entirely from those with relationships to the royal court, including don Jucef, its first alfaquí, and its first chief rabbi, don Todros ben Joseph Halevi Almalafia.[16] Don Zag, who served as Alfonso X's rent collector for Seville, was endowed with a significant rural estate, and his four sons received properties equivalent to those given to Christian aristocrats.[17] In the early fourteenth century, Alfonso XI asked Pope Clemente VI for permission for the city's Jews to pray in a new synagogue donated by his rent collector, don Yucef de Écija, because the Jews "had contributed so much to the city's prosperity and often allied with Christians to fight [foreign] Muslims, not fearing to risk their lives."[18] While most of the Jewish community was far from wealthy and illustrious, its leading members tied the city to the royal court and contributed to its economic growth.

Early documentation has little to say about Christian intervention into aljama politics, suggesting that the communities mostly managed their own fiscal and civil concerns. Occasionally, this limited autonomy became explicit. When Alfonso X required that the Muslims of Morón, a Muslim town forty miles outside Seville, relocate to a new site, he signed an accord with their qadi Çabah ben Hamet Aben Çabah, broadly affirming the qadi's position as "the judge over all the Muslims of Morón who would come to live in Siliébar, as appropriate to their religious and civil law." The agreement—which freed up the Muslims' lands on the frontier for Christian purchase—also allowed the Muslims of Siliébar to build "bathhouses and stores and ovens and mills and granaries" according to Islamic practice.[19] The king spelled out property rights, which could infringe upon Christian desires, while he left issues internal to the Muslim community unstated.

The aljama thus was an institution that produced the conditions for Jewish or Muslim life under Christian rule through religious, fiscal, and legal acts. A qadi or rab served as judge and adjudicator, along with a variety of other officers who protected and defined the community's religious, cultural, and economic practices, from religious leaders to tax collectors and enforcers of market regulations. The aljama defined confessional status within the minority community as well as to the outside world. Aljama membership cannot be simply deduced from an act of worship, a payment of taxes, or a Christian accusation of non-Christian practices. It was a mutable thing—a kin-group, a set of networks of power, wealth, and knowledge, a body of celebrants, and a group with the ability to accept often heavy obligations.

Jurisdictions

As law defined institutionalized religious difference (and religion was often referred to as *ley* or law), the ability to interpret, confer, and judge was central to what it meant to belong to an aljama in a particular time and place. The existence of multiple republics within a Christian society already strained by political competition made jurisdiction a contentious issue. It was articulated in two situations: regarding community autonomy over internal (civil or criminal) conflicts; and regarding the question of what venue, judge, and law oversaw contests between Christian and non-Christian parties. The ability of Muslim and Jewish aljamas to adjudicate among their own, or between their own and other subjects, diminished over the centuries. But many Andalusian aljamas were able to retain some control nearly until the end.

Intra-Community Autonomy

Jurisdiction for conflicts within communities largely remained there, and were judged according to that law. This is a truism, as most of those conflicts would have been invisible to the outside, involving the fulfillment of contracts, property transfers, partition for inheritance, the distribution of tax burdens, and care for community members. But it was also, at times, explicit royal policy. The common thirteenth-century fueros often referred obliquely to this autonomy. Alfonso X's Fuero Real allowed Jews to "read and have all the books of their law, those given to them by Moses and by other prophets," and the common requirement that Christians not be judged by non-Christians implied the existence of non-Christian courts.[20] Aljamas might require external support in order to enforce or execute sanctions, but most often internal jurisdiction was indiscernible to outsiders.

Legal pluralism functioned as a means to contain contamination as well as a way to keep the peace. Alfonso X's Partida VII demanded that Jews "pass their lives among Christians quietly and without disorder, practicing their own religious rites, and not speaking ill of the faith of Our Lord Jesus Christ," yet it also required that they be allowed to rest on their sabbath, and not be summoned to court on a Saturday.[21] Enabling Jews and Muslims to resolve their own conflicts was less a privilege granted than a means to manage their difference.

Monarchs sometimes responded to local challenges to this limited autonomy, especially when they threatened fiscal exactions. In 1351, when Castilian Jews complained that local concejos were attempting to assert jurisdiction over them, Pedro I ordered that they retain control "because the Jews are foreigners and require support, and because if they bring their cases before all alcaldes they might receive great damage and great loss of their wealth, as the Christians could impoverish them with warrants and lawsuits."[22] Until the fifteenth century, Castilian monarchs mostly presumed that Muslims and Jews could adjudicate their own civil conflicts.

Monarchs did ultimately assert jurisdiction over criminal complaints and particularly capital crimes. Although Alfonso X's *Siete partidas* claimed that jurisdiction from Muslims and Jews, Castilian practice was initially uneven. Certainly, Rab Solomon ben Abraham ibn Adret (1233–1310), a member of an aristocratic family in Barcelona, thought Jewish judges had more leverage in Castile. In a legal opinion he wrote regarding a case where a Jewish citizen challenged his communal authorities by shouting, in the presence of Christians, that Jews were exacting usurious interest rates, Rab Solomon stated that the man would deserve the death penalty as an informer "had we the same powers here as in Castile."[23] Not until the middle of the fourteenth century, when Trastamaran legal reforms centralized judicial authority in the alcalde mayor, was criminal jurisdiction explicitly removed from the Castilian aljamas. The cortes held in Soria in 1380 heard a dramatic (if largely unsubstantiated) claim that Jewish conspirators had recently executed the king's chief accountant, Yucef Picho, in secret and on false grounds. The assembly found that it was a "great sin" to allow "rabbis and other judges" to exercise privileges that had been denied to them since the advent of Christ. Thereafter, Jews had no standing in cases whose punishment included death, dismemberment, or exile.[24] But within the aljama, many criminal penalties could be exacted without external notice. A document from fifteenth-century Aragón lists *huddud* (Islamic penalties) for crimes including insulting the qadi, arguing with him about sentences, and throwing dirt in his face.[25] These did not rise to the level of capital punishment, nor did they involve Christian parties.

The fifteenth century marked a paradigm shift, beginning with Catalina's unenforced ordinances of 1412 that explicitly challenged legal autonomy, directing that:

> The aljamas of Jews and Muslims not have their own judges who might hear their civil or criminal complaints, but that these be heard by the alcaldes of the cities, towns or places where they reside; and that these (Christian) alcaldes, in the civil lawsuits, enforce the customs and laws of the Jews and Muslims; the privileges they enjoyed in this matter are revoked.[26]

As with the other ordinances of 1412, these had little effect and were followed by a brief period of royal tolerance of community autonomy. Under royal patronage, Castile's Jews even assembled in Valladolid in 1432 to produce statutes (*taqqanot*) for the internal organization of aljamas. While these statutes were "more utopian than real," in historian Tamar Herzog's words, they reflected an optimism that communities would continue to be given the space to self-govern despite shrinking numbers.[27] Even the civil war that destabilized Enrique IV's reign, wherein his opponents characterized him as a "*filojudío*," Jew-lover, did not undo local aljama autonomy, though it hastened the coming of the Inquisition in Castile.

It was the cortes of Madrigal (1476) that announced the final contractions of aljama autonomy. During the council, Isabel and Fernando performed the well-used theater of calling for separation while asserting protection (of Seville's Jews, in this case).[28] Their main design in the assembly, however, was to establish centralized control over the kingdom in the wake of the nobility's uprising. They did so in part by removing criminal jurisdiction from all local officials and by interposing the Santa Hermandad and royal corregidores into municipalities to exercise control over the factions that were undermining their administration.[29] While Muslims and Jews were increasingly policed in this period, the removal of criminal jurisdiction from the aljamas should be seen within the larger context of the royal guarantee of urban peace.

Even when access to Jewish or Islamic law was guaranteed, it was not always delivered through a Jewish or Muslim judge. Christian judges might oversee Jewish and Muslim cases and pronounce sentences according to their understanding of that law. Christian monarchs may have seen this as an inevitable move as they adopted policies of settling Christians within Muslim towns and resettling mudéjar populations, thus concretizing local hierarchies between occupiers and occupied.[30] Many Muslim populations became too small to constitute a functioning aljama, and others either lacked the power to force independence or, in at least a few cases, preferred not to have a qadi at all.

The Castilian city of Burgos, for one, seems never to have had a Muslim qadi, leaving Islamic law in the hands of Christian judges almost from the time of its conquest. As Fernando IV confirmed in 1304,

> the lawsuits which occur between the Muslims are to be judged by the alcaldes of the city, as had been the custom during the reign of other kings . . . and [as] they did not have a separate alcalde or *merino*, they asked me a favor. . . . I have deemed it right, and order that the lawsuits which occur between the Muslims living in the city of Burgos and its surrounding district are to be judged by the alcaldes of the city, as they used to . . . and that they will not have other alcaldes.[31]

But Muslims often reacted angrily to the selection of Christian judges. In Aragón, some Muslim scholars were so disturbed at the intervention of Christian officials into the choice of qadi in the fourteenth century that they refused the office. In 1391, their monarch Juan I issued an order enshrining their right to refuse, though other monarchs insisted that royal appointments be accepted. But the effect of the scholars' decision to refuse politicized posts is to make them disappear from view of the Christian archives, leaving the appearance that they had no authority. A valiant reconstruction of Arabic-language records in Aragón demonstrates that scholars were indeed active in local legal life, but that their activity went unrecorded by Christian scribes.[32]

In the cases where Christian judges did preside over Muslim cases, they might have had access to translated Islamic law books, commonly known as *Leyes de moros* or *Brevario sunni*, to assist them in their deliberations.[33] They also consulted with or co-judged with Muslim alfaquís and Jewish rabbis, though probably in an advisory capacity.[34] There was some overlap between Muslim, Jewish, and Christian jurisprudence in Iberia, particularly in terms of contract and commercial law, given the deep economic integration of the communities. But when Muslim or Jewish parties came before Christian judges, there is little doubt that they experienced this as a disenfranchisement.

Cross-Religious Jurisdiction

Christian authorities were not ambivalent about who should manage legal actions that involved Christians.[35] Cross-religious interactions were commonplace, and there were formal and informal means for them to be carried out legitimately and for broken commitments to be resolved. But within a majority-Christian city, Jews and Muslims recognized their dependence upon Christian justice. While each faith had its own scribes, Muslims and Jews regularly approached Christian notaries if they thought they would need Christian enforcement of their contracts.

Courts with Christian judges had to accommodate Muslim and Jewish litigants and witnesses. Some fueros required that trials include witnesses from the defendant's faith, a custom that also benefitted Christians indebted to Jewish moneylenders.[36] Alfonso X invented guidelines to ensure that Muslims, Jews, and Christians could swear effective oaths when testifying in mixed proceedings. According to his directions, each would go to their house of worship accompanied by the person requiring the oath and an audience of coreligionists; the Jew would swear upon his or her Bible, the Muslim by raising a hand to the *al-qibblah*, and the person requiring the oath would ask them to swear according to their own precepts—by God who made Adam, and the ten commandments of the law that God gave to Moses, or by the truth that God placed in the mouth of Muhammad. After the reading of the (fictional) script, the Jew or Muslim would reply, "I swear," and, being warned of the curses and plagues that would befall the one who swears falsely, he or she would state "Amen." In parallel fashion, the Christian was required to swear in the name of the Father, Son, and Holy Spirit while holding a cross or touching the altar.[37]

But the customary practice of guaranteeing coreligionist witnesses eroded over time. In the cortes of 1371, Seville's procurators requested that, in spite of the Jews' "charters and privileges," Enrique end the practice of requiring coreligionist testimony because "this covers up many thefts and robberies among the said Jews and Muslims." The king upheld the custom except in capital criminal cases.[38] In 1436, Abdalla, the procurator for the Muslim aljamas in the kingdom, petitioned Juan II to keep the practice in general. The monarch issued a letter across the kingdom stating that Christian judges could not condemn Muslims in any trials, civil or criminal, solely on the basis of Christian witnesses. Even for practices well enshrined in customary law and restated in privileges, enforcement was always a concern for religious minorities and required intervention at the highest levels.[39]

Not all cross-religious conflicts went to court; most were likely worked out informally or with non-compulsory guidance. Yuda Gagui, a Jewish man, rented a house in Santa María la Blanca from Catalina Guillén, a Christian widow. A broken pipe in the street flooded the house and he repaired it. That Gagui and Guillén went to a notary to draw up a receipt for his costs suggests that they had reached an extrajudicial settlement. Such interactions were surely commonplace, and obviated the concerns over jurisdiction.[40]

But when the courts were needed, who was to judge, and where, in litigation between mixed parties? While most Castilian courts gave the right of forum to the defendant, aljamas never had control over complaints involving Christians.[41] Without aljama judicial records it is difficult to state that they never heard mixed cases, but the Christian records occasionally provide indications that Jews and Muslims brought their suits there. Abrahan Abensemerro, who was Jewish, collected 3,333 mrv from Catalina Fernandez in 1484, the outcome of a suit Abensemerro brought against her before bachiller Diego Gomez de Baeza, the magistrate of the high court in Seville.[42] In addition to the fact that the high court would have been more effective at enforcement, this was a conflict between two distinct jurisdictions settled by an appellate court.[43]

The jurisdictional issue was politicized in part because of lawsuits over Christian debtors to Jewish lenders. In the middle of the thirteenth century, Alfonso X prohibited Christian moneylending, turning it into a royal monopoly associated with a small cohort of Jews.[44] Alfonso taxed those Jewish loans, essentially taxing Christian borrowers. As the Crown pursued its revenue, Jewish lenders became more aggressive with their collections, supported by royal policies and privileges. Christians continued to lend at interest, often writing loans into contracts for the purchase of goods, but moneylending (like tax farming) came to be associated with Jews as well as with the Crown.[45] Concejos considered royal support for debt collection as an unwanted intervention into local concerns.

Because of the sensitivity of these relationships, as well as the Crown's unwillingness to establish the superiority of either local jurisdiction, royal officials were often placed in the middle of these proceedings. Alfonso X sent agents called *entregadores* to oversee the collection of delinquent property from Christian borrowers.[46] Some Castilian fueros called for alcaldes from each religious community to collectively oversee such cases. The deep connection between jurisdiction over mixed cases, royal interference, and debt made venue a prickly issue for town councils as well as religious communities.[47]

The Crown was also attentive to jurisdiction around the lending and commercial activities of Genoese merchants working in Seville, though those activities were usually described with less venom. Monarchs issued privileges to that corporate group to articulate the complexities of relationships between nonresident foreigners, Genoese permanent residents, and non-Genoese residents. The Genoese in Seville were entitled to elect two consuls to judge any civil conflict that emerged between Genoese citizens, using the laws of Genoa. Seville's city council, however, functioned as an appellate court and heard civil cases between its citizens and the Genoese. In 1350, the community successfully petitioned the monarch to remove them from municipal jurisdiction, and thereafter Genoese merchants who needed to collect debts and loans from non-Genoese vecinos of Seville could take their case to a royal alcalde or judge.[48]

Because aljamas were distinct jurisdictions or republics within the kingdom, they mostly resolved irreconcilable conflicts with Christians in their localities through royal appellate courts, which might be sensitive to their customary law but not bound by it. The Crown also operated in the opposite direction, by utilizing Jewish and Muslim members of their inner circles to affect policy within aljamas.

The Alcalde Mayor

Castilian kings had long appointed a *rab mayor*, or chief justice, across all Jewish communities, and as Muslim aljamas came under their authority, monarchs created offices variously called *qadi mayor* or *alcalde mayor de las aljamas*.[49] Wealthy and well-connected Muslims and Jews purchased the offices, with support and patronage from Christian allies. The incident in early fifteenth-century Sepúlveda suggests that alcaldes mayores might view themselves as safeguards for religious independence and thus occupy the role of intercessor between the aljama, the concejo, and the monarch. Because of their politicized position, they might also have negotiated with religious authorities outside the kingdom. While the alcalde mayor was associated with the Crown's desire to manage religious difference and assert control over his Muslim and Jewish subjects, he also served as a reminder of the collective power of aljamas and their customary right to receive justice from their coreligionists.[50]

Before the Christian conquest, Iberian Muslims had lived under a similar tension between local authorities and the caliph, and there was a certain element of continuity as the office first developed under Christian rule. In Muslim al-Andalus, high offices such as *qādī al-qudāt* or *qādī al-jamāʿa* were likewise deeply politicized: they were appointed by the head of state rather than chosen by a local population, they tended to come from a small number of elite families, and they had the ability to name their direct subordinates excepting the local qadis.[51] This politicization meant that changing relationships between monarchs (or caliphs) and their vassals and subjects profoundly affected the role of the qadi. If previously the qadi negotiated between local (and ethnic) demands and those of the Muslim ruler and the Islamic world, under Christian rule he managed negotiations between mudéjares, the Christian monarch, city councils, and—to varying degrees—parts of the Islamic world.

As historians of colonial Latin America have shown, the tension experienced by middlemen between a variety of colonial authorities and the Indigenous or minority subjects upon which they depended was not easily resolved to anyone's satisfaction.[52] As Christian monarchs moved toward limiting actual governance by Muslims and Jews, the alcalde mayor had to negotiate in an environment hostile to his own position. The few scholarly analyses of medieval Jewish and Muslim alcaldes mayores have emphasized this as a religious difference, explaining the existence of the alcalde mayor as well as the subsequent constraints upon his rule as a function of antipathy to Islam and Judaism.[53] Without discounting this, it is useful to place the alcalde mayor within a broader political context to see how minority religious communities experienced changes in greater Castilian society.

Alfonso X was largely the architect of the institution in Castile, appointing alcaldes mayores to intervene in unresolved adjudication within aljamas by referring cases to a tribunal headed by a royal official who acted as appeals judge and who also supervised Jewish or Muslim judicial matters at the level of the kingdom. Alfonso also set the price for the office, requiring the alcalde mayor of either faith to pay the Chancery 100 mrv, but the local Jewish alcalde paid 200 and the Muslim alcalde 20.[54] The fee structure was revised a number of times, reflecting the falling fortunes of the communities, and by 1476 an alcalde mayor paid 600 mrv for a lifetime appointment, plus 200 more for the letter with its official seal. A shorter appointment would cost half as much, and an appointment as judge of a city or town would cost between 50 and 100 mrv.[55] That Muslim and Jewish holders of the highest office were charged the same rate suggests that, while Castilian Jewish communities were still far wealthier than Muslim ones, the few men eligible for court appointments were of their economic class.

The alcalde mayor played another important role that placed him directly in the line of fire between the aljama and the Crown. He was the tax collector for the kingdom, the sole non-Christian on a council of *repartidores* who distributed the tribute burden upon local aljamas. That council decided how to impose the regular tributary head tax, special assessments, and the extraordinary contribution known as *servicio* and *medio servicio* across the many small aljamas subject to the crown of Castile.[56] There were also exceptional irregular contributions, especially to support warfare against Muslim states. Given the extreme disparities in wealth within and between communities, conflicts abounded, and aljamas often fought their assessments with the help of procurators who represented their interests before the repartidores and the alcalde mayor.[57]

The alcalde mayor could have been a simple political appointee owing little to religious authority or local standing. At times, this may well have been true, as with the wealthy and politically connected Belvís family who had a powerful grip on the qadi general's office in Valencia.[58] Yet some alcaldes mayores stood out for their religious and intellectual commitments. One was Rab don Todros, named by Alfonso X for the Jews of Castile. An exceptionally learned member of an

aristocratic family in Toledo, Rab Todros was a mystic and ascetic. His appointment spoke to contemporary Jewish intellectual traditions rather than patronage.[59] But alcaldes mayores also formed part of a strategy for inserting royal
authority into municipal venues.

By the fifteenth century, alcaldes mayores understood their role to include the
need to maintain the aljama as a meaningful institution. When the rab mayor
Abraham Bienveniste called a Jewish tribunal to write *taqqanot*, or community
statutes, in 1432, he did so also to cement his position as head of Castile's dispersed Jewish communities and right-hand man to Álvaro de Luna, Juan II's close
advisor.[60] The Jewish authors of the statutes called for communities to choose
their own local judges and other officials through general assemblies, asking the
rab mayor to step in to resolve conflicts. They did not, however, address the question of who appointed the rab mayor—the monarch's prerogative to do so was
understood, although the tribunal asserted that the candidate had to be steeped
in Talmudic law. They did note that Bienveniste, while appointed by Juan II,
was also named by a Jewish assembly in Valladolid.[61] The language suggests that
Jewish officials were struggling with the increased pressure from above and their
dependence on Christian authority for social position within and without their
religious community.

The Problem of Royal Patronage

The alcalde mayor derived his power from his association with the Crown
as well as his standing among elites of the three religions, and he had great
distance from the base, who daily had to work out the practicalities of being
Muslim or Jewish among Christians. He served at royal pleasure and was often
subject to court intrigue. The story of don Abrahem Xarafi, named alcalde
mayor by Isabel and Fernando in 1475, is illustrative of the inherent problems.
Xarafi was a member of a very well connected mudéjar family in Toledo and
served as the personal physician to Isabel's uncle, the Archbishop of Toledo.[62]
He lost his job a year later, perhaps due to a falling-out between Isabel and
her uncle. Many alcaldes held positions in the royal court prior to appointment, including that of the "tax-farmer general," in charge of the Jews who
collected taxes from Christians within the kingdom, the Crown's auditor of
accounts, and the personal physicians to the royal family.[63] The close relationship reflects the requisite level of trust but also the dependence on a small elite
of wealthy members of the religions who were sources of income and loans as
well as advice.

The fifteenth-century Jewish experience demonstrates the continuing politicization of the office. The appointment of Bienveniste, a man with independent

political intentions, as rab mayor owed a great deal to High Constable Álvaro de Luna's effort to reinvigorate the Crown's treasury with new funds from the aljamas. But when Bienveniste died in 1450, Luna appointed Pedro de Luján, a Christian (and possibly a converso) in his place. The appointment of a Christian likely had to do with anti-tax and anti-converso uprisings the previous year in Toledo, as well as Luna's own political agenda against the local nobility. Jewish elites were displeased.[64] Almost immediately, Juan II issued a letter promising his continued protection of the Jews and rescinded the appointment. In this reversal, Juan II offered the Jewish community the *merced*, or privilege, of electing their own slate of judges, from which he would select half as officeholders. This sleight of hand preserved Juan's power as ultimate decision maker and his reputation as a monarch of great prudence and generosity.

Sometimes the close royal patronage turned the alcalde's position into almost a heritable office. Don Farax de Belvís, who replaced don Abrahem Xarafi, had the patronage of don Diego Hurtado de Mendoza, a relative of the royal family. Queen Isabel's 1476 letter appointing don Farax reveals how insular the circle of candidates could be. Her father Juan II had appointed don Farax's father, don Yahya, to the same office and Isabel stated her wish that don Farax's son, also called Yahya, inherit it after his father's death.[65]

Such reforms did little to calm municipal concejos, who saw alcaldes mayores much as they saw corregidores, as external agents who protected royal interests. The municipality of Toledo, deep in conflict with the Crown, refused to recognize Isabel and Fernando's appointment of don Farax de Belvís, instead recognizing a mudéjar carpenter named maestre Lope—an individual not connected to the royal court, but probably the son of an official in charge of construction projects in Segovia. Maestre Lope had received his office from Isabel's half-brother Enrique IV, and now Toledo's concejo claimed that its aljama was not subject to Castile, but was its own jurisdiction. By 1480, Isabel had conceded and issued a letter of confirmation to maestre Lope as "alcalde mayor de las aljamas de los moros destos nuestros regnos" (alcalde mayor of the Muslim aljamas of these our kingdoms).[66]

The ongoing conflicts with Toledo must be seen in the context of the Castilian crown's policy to limit the power of its Christian competitors, as well as curtail the autonomy of Jews and Muslims.[67] Tension with the Crown intersected with anti-Jewish and anti-Islamic rhetorics, leading to political machinations that invoked prejudicial fears. For this reason, aljamas often found themselves aligned with Christian municipal officials and their neighbors, even while local anti-Jewish and anti-Muslim sentiment ran high. While religious difference was at the center of the creation of the aljamas, it was corporate status that maintained them as a political entity.

Corporate Changes

To contextualize this analysis of the politics of structural difference, it is helpful to examine two more institutions that also experienced constraints on autonomy in Seville during the fifteenth century. These institutions—the corporate forms of the communities of people of (non-Muslim) African descent and of sufferers of leprosy—were constituted as republics and entitled to the political representation of their common interests before citizens and the king. But they also found themselves embroiled in questions of legitimacy and the recipients of heavy-handed intervention by the Crown. Marginalized subjects seized on the space opened by the republic as a political form, but it was always subject to the political winds of the kingdom.

By the late fourteenth century, Seville's archbishop and its municipal officials increasingly viewed the city's residents of West African origin or descent as a body in need of closer management. In addition to increasing numbers of enslaved people, the city now had a substantial free Black population, which included emigrants from the African continent as well as manumitted men and women and their free descendants. They posed a problem similar to that of the conversos following the city's pogroms, in that they not only had to live as Christians but had to be perceived as adequately Christian by critical outsiders. Seville's archbishop don Gonzalo de Mena y Roelas created a hospital and confraternity to serve their spiritual and physical needs.[68] These institutions were also responses to popular representations of the Black population as excessively exuberant and predisposed to criminality.[69] In the fifteenth century, Castilian leaders began to see Black slaves and free persons as a community requiring discipline.

At the turn of the fourteenth century, Enrique III named what appears to be the first *mayoral* or *alcalde de los negros sevillanos* (leader or judge of the Blacks of Seville). The chronicler Ortíz de Zúñiga wrote in 1677 that the first mayoral was an enslaved man in the royal household who represented the interests of enslaved people to their masters and "reconciled their quarrels with the authorities."[70] In keeping with the assumption that his role was to maintain public peace among the community of enslaved and free Black men and women, he was made to act not only as ombudsman or arbiter of grievances, but also as a cultural leader and a model for Catholic conversion.

By the reign of Isabel and Fernando, the alcalde de los negros was an amalgamation of the local qadi and the kingdom's alcalde mayor, a political appointee chosen from the subject population to govern them according to "use and custom."[71] Like the Muslim or Jewish judge, he managed marriages, lawsuits, and contracts between community members. He seems also to have had a role arbitrating between enslaved people and their owners, or between Black members and Castilian authorities, presumably in non-binding arrangements and perhaps more in the service of translation, enforcement, and compliance. If attached to a hospital or confraternity, he might also have distributed charity to the deserving poor. He received an unstated salary and privileges.

The alcalde de los negros required legitimacy within his diverse republic. The letter from Isabel and Fernando appointing Juan de Valladolid to the position in 1475 recognized him as a man of "noble lineage." Whether this supposed lineage granted him legitimacy among Africans or before the monarchs is unstated, although a clause appointing him to the office "in spite of any elections that may have taken place" suggests that legitimacy came only from the monarch and could flout the community's will.[72] The order commands the city's municipal officials to recognize Juan de Valladolid in this capacity and no one else; the contemporary experience with Toledo's Muslims was surely present in their thoughts. Not only was Juan de Valladolid imposed upon his republic, but he was given authority before municipal authorities who might have preferred other candidates. Those alternative candidates might have carried more weight among enslaved people or their masters.

A similar tension arose with the appointment of leaders of the community of lepers who resided at the hospital of San Lázaro outside Seville's limits. San Lázaro was founded under royal patronage, and among its privileges was to name "one hundred men in one hundred cities across the archbishopric of Sevilla and bishopric of Cádiz," who would collect alms, free of taxes.[73] Its patients were led by a salaried mayoral or administrator who, according to participants, was elected from their ranks. After the death of the mayoral in 1476, the hospital's patients held elections and chose Juan de Sosa from among them as leader. At the same time Rodrigo Maldonado, a presumably healthy member of the city's elite, approached Queen Isabel and requested the office, making what the monarchs later assessed to be "false claims." Isabel appointed Maldonado, who proceeded to Seville to claim his new position, where he was firmly rejected not just by the hospital's residents but by all the officials of the city.

In May 1476, the monarchs issued an order rectifying the situation, revoking Maldonado's title and naming Juan de Sosa, "*enfermo*" (ill, i.e., a patient), the new mayoral according to the customary law of the hospital. By August, Maldonado had sued in royal courts for his position, claiming to have documents that demonstrated the legitimacy of his royal appointment over the election of the lepers, presumably evidence that previous mayorales had been appointed by monarchs. Juan de Sosa, though he was publicly called upon to appear in court and defend himself, failed to show, was declared "in rebellion," and was replaced with Maldonado. The new mayoral continued to have difficulties with the municipality, which ignored his requests to increase revenues for the hospital by appointing wealthier alms collectors, an action requiring yet another royal intervention in 1483.[74] The administrative position, which involved management of large sums of money and other resources, was likely a royal appointment that was legitimated customarily by the hospital's residents, much like the kingdom's Jewish and Muslim alcaldes mayores. The fact that some of San Lázaro's infirm were well-off made it difficult to foist an unfavorable candidate on them.

Contests over jurisdiction were inherent in societies composed of multiple self-governing republics. They took place at many levels, from relatively horizontal conflicts that emerged from attempts to guarantee justice within or across specific communities, to power-laden moves by or against royal officials, which sometimes pulled aljamas and other institutions into larger battles. By the late fifteenth century, relatively disempowered corporate entities, like the aljamas of Muslims and Jews, the Black population in Seville, and the lepers at San Lázaro hospital, all experienced conflict as the monarchs insisted upon their right to name their leaders while the communities rejected those interventions. Minority communities sometimes found allies in municipal government, where the specificities of local politics could generate support against royal demands. The degree to which communities triumphed through this strategy is uncertain, but they certainly exploited confusion and their geographic distance from the powerful for the space afforded them.

Jurisdiction and autonomy were essential to the survival of minority republics. They guaranteed the community's ability to produce justice, as they chose to define it, for their members. A community that could not participate in choosing its leaders, especially one whose leaders were imposed from the dominant group, was in danger of disappearing into insignificance. For this reason, aljamas fought to protect even the slim jurisdictional independence they enjoyed. Civil jurisdictional spaces for formalizing marriage, divorce, inheritance, taxation, and property relations were central to group identity and daily interactions, although they cemented relationships within the community rather than preserved its existence in the Christian world.

This chapter has contextualized the constraints on Muslim and Jewish political elites by viewing them within a larger politics. It served the needs of the Crown to maintain Muslim and Jewish aljamas with their own customary law, because they were a source of revenue and sometimes acted as counterweights to municipal governments and the nobles that dominated them. Yet the Crown also wanted to shape those aljamas, which it did by creating royal representatives with appellate powers over them and by redefining religious law such that it could at times be dispensed by Christian judges. Aljamas sometimes fought these constraints, though at times they appear to have worked to their advantage, and often they were powerless to stop them. But the tensions between royal, noble, and municipal actors, and the Muslim and Jewish commitment to hold space for religious practices produced meaningful legal difference until late in the fifteenth century.

4

Aljama, or the Republic of Difference

A CASTILIAN MANUSCRIPT titled "Leyes de Moros" circulated in multiple editions in the fourteenth century. Written in Latin script, and adapted from a tenth-century legal treatise by the Iraqi Mālikī scholar Ibn al-Jallāb al-Basrī, the text explains a strain of Islamic jurisprudence to a general audience. It was most likely written to assist Christian judges who presided over Muslim courts in places like Burgos, Madrid, and Segovia.[1] While some of its positions were incongruous for Muslims in fourteenth-century Castile, it articulates concerns that Muslims brought to their judges and, through that, gives insight into the aljama as a meaningful social institution. The aljama was the institution that offered justice within the community, whether that meant moral guidance, enforcement of contracts, or care for the most precarious.

The text focuses on family and inheritance law, establishing the obligation a husband has for his wife's material support (even when living apart), how a husband should divide his time among multiple wives, and the conditions under which grandmothers might inherit estates. It establishes rules for judges and witnesses (for instance, excluding menstruating women from giving testimony). The text also offers guidance for dealing with matters of the market. Title 60, for example, is called "Of those who buy bread, stating 'this is so much' but it is not that much," arguing that sellers must adjust prices when they sell underweight commodities. Similarly, fruit vendors must not sell unripe fruit or sell fruit trees without explicit statement of whether the trees are already bearing fruit. Other titles constrain a seller's ability to sell on installments or to charge interest on installment payments.[2]

While the local practice of Islamic law varied, the *Leyes de Moros* offers a lens onto the experience of living as a mudéjar in cities such as Seville. Muslims, Christians, and Jews all shared similar worries in normal times: of resolving their familial and neighborly conflicts, collecting payment for work completed or

Republics of Difference. Karen B. Graubart, Oxford University Press. © Oxford University Press 2022.
DOI: 10.1093/oso/9780190233839.003.0005

goods purchased, ensuring care for minors and the elderly, and managing complex households. In addition to regulating religious practices, the aljama provided institutional support for specific ways of living. Muslim and Jewish worshippers negotiated their social, political, and economic relationships through and within the institution.

The relationship between individual and aljama was inconsistent over time and space; Muslims and Jews were not required to utilize their aljama's governance structure, nor were they necessarily prohibited from participating in the city's institutions. Their relationship to municipal services was locally determined: they paid some taxes toward its upkeep, though they were unlikely to participate in the concejo or military service, and they could bring complaints to their own or the city's judges. When they committed criminal acts, they were most likely to end up in the city's jails.[3]

Some Muslims and Jews deployed limited citizenship across multiple jurisdictions. When in 1455 the mudéjares Zulema and her son moved permanently to Seville, they petitioned the concejo to register them in the collación of Santa Marina.[4] This inscribed them in the parish rolls for the purpose of assessing taxes and other obligations. They might also have created a relationship to the Muslim aljama by attending prayers, contributing to the annual head tax, receiving religious education at the *madrasa*, or seeking guidance or support from its officials. These local relationships defined individual citizenship and options for justice more compellingly than the Crown's definition of their status. They offered the protection of law and kinship, though these promises were also contingent and fragile.

This chapter discusses the membership, the structure, and the materiality of Seville's Muslim and Jewish aljamas in the fifteenth century through an analysis of Christian notarial records. In addition to information about Muslim and Jewish clients, the records also offer instructive negative space; missing actions probably took place before a Muslim or Jewish notary or judge, whether written or not.[5] The aljama's autonomy was limited if examined from the perspective of what Muslims and Jews were denied, but members found it expansive. Its domain stretched from organizing and codifying ritual practices to the management of funds, to governance and the transmission and enforcement of law, to control over property, and to external relationships with distant coreligionists or with local Christendom. These were meaningful places where justice could be asserted, if not always guaranteed.

The Ritual Community

While the institutionalized aljama was distinct from the congregation, faith and ritual were its foundation. The Arabic root, *al-jamāʿa*, refers to a "meeting or assembly of the whole body of believers united by their common faith," such as a congregation.[6] These congregations gathered in particular buildings, which hosted many of the actions that distinguished them from their Christian neighbors. In addition to prayer, their mosques and synagogues also facilitated the finalization of marriage and dowry contracts and solemn and festive ceremonies. Legal tribunals and cabildos met in aljama buildings, and their officers distributed charity and alms, and enforced codes of behavior there. The faiths defined themselves within mosques, synagogues, and churches.

Some of the locations of these buildings are known: the original three synagogues were located within the judería, though by the fifteenth century two had been reconsecrated as Catholic churches.[7] Little is known of where Muslims prayed, except that eventually there was a mosque in the Adarvejo, in San Pedro parish. There were surely other sites as well. Rabí Mosé Maturel's promise to return to the synagogue from a "house" in 1475 illustrates the ways that buildings could be informally repurposed for changing religious needs.[8] The Crown asserted control over the foundation of new synagogues and mosques. In Toledo in 1460, when a group of Jews returned to a house they had used for prayer forty years earlier, King Enrique IV forbade them because "the house is ... distant from the judería" and their presence would be an offense to its Christian neighbors.[9] He instituted a 10,000 mrv penalty each time they used the house for prayer. For such reasons, prayer that took place outside officially sanctioned buildings is (and perhaps was) largely invisible.

Something of the ways that Seville's Muslims carried out ritual life can be gleaned through an analysis of the edict of their expulsion, read out by Lorenzo Çomeno, deputy assistant to the count of Cifuentes and alferez mayor (standard-bearer general) of the monarchs, at that mosque on February 15, 1502. The brief statement ordered that "the mosques be emptied and closed," and the deputy embargoed the movable property in the San Pedro mosque and listed it for his scribe:

> In the said mosque was found the following: two brass lamps, a wooden almsbox, two new doors, sixteen rush mats, new and old, a small water basin, a pulley and rope, thirteen slates for teaching children, a wooden pallet for burials, a pike, two old basins, a small earthen jar.[10]

The absence of a Qur'an or any books suggests that the community had already removed objects of value to them. Nonetheless, the embargoed items were indicative of ritual life. The prayer mats were few in number, suggesting that some men brought their own. Their condition, "new and old," indicates that the community continued to supply ritual goods even as they recognized the coming of the end of their legal existence. The basins were also a key part of daily religious practice, as a purifying ablution was required before each of the five daily prayers and other ritual events. Jews would have had access to a *mikvah*, or ritual bath, in or near their own buildings.[11]

The children's slates are a reminder that traditions and beliefs were transmitted through formal schooling and literacy. Seville had a madrasa throughout the period in question, described by seventeenth-century chronicler Ortiz de Zúñiga as "one of their celebrated schools, in the mosque or near it," and identified by the Arabic inscription on a stone.[12] If the community did not have a resident teacher, an itinerant scholar might arrive from time to time, given Seville's proximity to Granada and North Africa. Mosques and synagogues held books as well: the scrolls of the Torah, the Qur'an, the Testaments of the Bible, and probably scholarly and legal texts. These would promote literacy as well as the retention of at least bits of Arabic and Hebrew even though Castilian was the hegemonic tongue.[13]

The alms box attests to the role of charity in uniting the community. Islam articulates at least two forms of benevolent charity: *zakat*, or obligatory annual giving, and *sadaqāt*, righteousness or sincere faith, a voluntary form of support for other Muslims. Both could be material, as in money, property, or goods; sadaqāt could also take the form of deeds. These contributions were part of the formation of a distinct cultural identity, much as confraternity membership defined the practice of many Catholics. That identity also crossed geographic boundaries, and almsgiving could include ransoming distant (or locally captive) Muslims out of slavery as well as supporting a neighbor in need. Participating in charitable works created cohesiveness and an identification with a global Islamic community.[14]

A number of the objects speak to the centrality of death and burial ritual in the community, which, like the rest of Seville, struggled with plagues and famine. Muslims require burial of the dead before sunset or within the next day, after a ritual washing performed by experts or family members of the deceased. Community members would carry the body, wrapped in shrouds, on the wooden pallet to a cemetery, and lower it into a grave, perhaps using the pulley and rope. All of these actions would have been accompanied by prayer, and done in the presence of some portion of the Muslim community. Women might have been excluded from some rituals, though the Castilian *Brevario sunni* of this period indicates flexibility.[15] Archaeological evidence from Muslim cemeteries in other parts of Castile demonstrates that communities used traditional practices as well as innovations necessary under their subjugated condition.[16]

Jewish rites also required ritual washing before the body was wrapped in a shroud or placed in a coffin for burial. A tombstone would be laid about thirty days after the burial. Like Islam and Christianity, Judaism calls for family and community to pray and grieve together for a period.

Seville had dedicated spaces for Muslim and Jewish interments. Not only were non-Christians prohibited from burial in Christian cemeteries, but Muslim and Jewish families rightly feared interference and the disturbance of graves. Their sites lay outside the city walls, as cemeteries were considered unhealthy for urban residents. The main Jewish cemetery was near the gate of the judería, with a second in the barrio of San Bernardo. Queen Isabel seized the San Bernardo site in 1482 because she had heard that *conversos* were being interred there with Jewish rites.[17] The Muslim cemetery sat next door to lands belonging to the church of Santo Domingo de Silos and vineyards belonging to Nuño Fernandez de Cueva, near the eastern Puerta Osario, situated not far from the Adarvejo of San Pedro.[18] These locations allowed funeral processions to take a direct route from the mosque or synagogue, thereby limiting mourners' contact with potentially hostile Christian neighbors.

Control over the cemetery allowed for greater control over ritual, including the proper positioning of bodies (for Muslims, on their right side, oriented toward Mecca; for Jews, with head to the west and feet to the east so that they would face Jerusalem when they rose), and the placement of appropriate markers. Māliki jurisprudence largely prohibited elaborate monuments and frowned upon inscribed gravestones, though some Andalusian stones still bear Qur'anic passages and other Arabic texts, Christian designs, and the names of the deceased, particularly in elite families.[19] The two Jewish cemeteries, which have been excavated, have both graves and brick tombs bearing coffins made of iron, nails, and wood.[20]

Finally, the aljama was the place where religious and cultural practices were policed and affirmed. Seville was home to at least four men who used the honorific Rabí in the second half of the fifteenth century: Yucef Abensemerro (documented 1454), Yocef Brudo (1460), Mosé Matutel (1475), and David (1473–1474).[21] The Muslim community was likely led in prayer by an alfaquí, such as Abrahén Gynete (1486–1501), Alí (1472–1475), or Abdalla de Málaga (1501). The aljama extracted certain kinds of penalties for heterodox or prohibited activities. In some parts of Castile, this even included the death penalty.[22] More commonly, religious leaders regulated moral issues including respectful behavior, attendance at services, drinking and petty criminality, and concerns about familial and sexual relations. Some ostensibly religious issues had to be taken outside the community but the alcalde or juez might ensure compliance with the practice of the faiths, such as the keeping of the Sabbath, the character of fasts, prescribed vestimentary conventions, and adherence to dietary laws.

Public Ritual and Public Threats

In February 1489, notary Luis García de Celada wrote in the margin of a document, "Today fifty persons, men and women, were reconciled [confessed], from the sequestered ones; among them went Pedro González, public scribe of Sevilla, and his brother."[23] These men and women, previously held in secret in a castle in Triana, included conversos, and they were processed through the city streets on the way to their punishment.[24] Over the following months, the Inquisition auctioned off the belongings of those convicted and those simply accused and detained.[25]

The audience for the *auto-de-fé* would have included many conversos, as the Inquisition intended to terrify them with spectacle. The city's mudéjares would also have been struck with new fear from the realization that their own horizons were narrowing, leaving them few good choices. At the turn of the new century, Muslims would face property sequestration and auction, as their economic difficulties manifested in defaulted loans and their opportunities began to vanish.

The terrible processions of 1489 are a reminder that, while Jewish and Muslim rituals were circumscribed, hidden, and sometimes literally walled off, Catholic ritual often took place in the streets. Processions in particular functioned as street theater; Seville's Holy Week rituals drew the entire city into a week of spectacle, music, smoke, and crushing crowds. The attack on Seville's judería in 1391 was spurred by Ferrán Martínez's sermons during Holy Week, a time when medieval Christians often theatrically re-enacted vengeance against Jews.[26] Interacting with even the smaller daily public rituals conditioned what it meant to be a Jew or a Muslim in Seville.

While Castilian life was punctuated by such traumatic moments, religious minorities more often experienced everyday acts of hostility. Jews and Muslims did not need to be told to avoid Holy Week processions. It is not surprising that they muted their rituals to the point that they are almost invisible within the Christian archives; to do otherwise would have courted disaster. But part of how they enacted their ritual life was formed by their reaction to this hostile environment.

The Taxed Community

Part of the humiliation placed on Muslims and Jews involved the payment of extraordinary taxes to the royal treasury and the Catholic Church. The Crown's repartidores assessed each aljama with an apportioned quantity and the aljama redistributed that obligation among its membership, according to an internal logic. While taxation marked subordination, it also guaranteed the aljama privileges it needed to operate.

Castilian Jews in the fifteenth century argued for reduced payments as, due to conversions by the wealthy, their numbers were dwindling and most who remained were quite poor. In 1439, they were taxed at 5,000 mrv for the *cabeza de pecho*, an old head tax, but upon appeal, the amount was reduced to 2,000 mrv because they were "few and poor." The *cabeza de pecho* was replaced midcentury by the *servicio y medio servicio*, and between 1464 and 1479, greater Seville's Jews paid 2,500–3,800 mrv annually.[27] While the community still boasted powerful families, it was largely a group of artisans and vendors.

In 1454, Mayr Abensemerro, the judge of the Jewish aljama, brought together nineteen men in a special meeting of the cabildo at a synagogue in the presence of Christian notary Andrés González. González drew up a power of attorney enabling Rab Yucef Abensemerro to subcontract the collection of rents for two years to whomever and at whatever price he chose.[28] These two rents were likely a tax on the sale of kosher meat at a market stall, and the annual tribute owed by Jews to the Crown.

The decision to have a Christian notary write up the power of attorney suggests that the subcontracting rent collector could theoretically have been a Christian or a Muslim, or at least someone whom they would have preferred to sue in municipal or royal courts. The rabbi's choice that year is unrecorded but, in 1465, Mayr Abenbilla, a silversmith and cabildo member, subcontracted the tax on wine and meat to Ysaque Abensemerro, and in 1472, Ysaque Castillo, a bookseller, was the collector of the thirty coins owed to the Catholic Church.[29] On the receiving side, the archbishop's agent to collect the tax was Juan González, the archbishop's porter, who also subcontracted the collection.[30]

The Muslim aljama was also taxed. In 1489, a notary copied out the demand for payment from the *receptor* of the Catholic monarchs and presented it to the Muslim aljama, for 7,500 mrv. It appears to have been a generic request to aljamas in Castilla, as the sum included Seville's expelled Jewish community.[31] In 1501, in the midst of a clear economic and social crisis in the mudéjar community, the Crown had its agent Juan de Cáceres present alcalde maestre Çayde Blanco and maestre Abrahén Blanco with a royal order demanding payment of the previous year's servicio y medio servicio and cabeza de pecho, in the amount of 4,000 mrv. The document is undated and was likely an attempt to collect an amount in arrears.[32]

Aljamas negotiated their status, which could differ greatly. Seville briefly hosted two Muslim aljamas, with distinct legal privileges. In July 1485, Castilian forces captured the Muslim city of Ronda (near Málaga), and under the terms of surrender the monarch affirmed the city's residents' right to live freely where they chose.[33] A group requested permission to move to Seville. The monarchs granted this, issuing special privileges to a group of about thirty Muslim men and women (and their servants and children) to live in Seville, with the monarchs' protection of themselves and their possessions, and an exemption from all of the taxes paid by Muslims in the kingdom. They and their alguazil and alfaquís remained independent of the already-existing aljama; their names do not even appear in the notarial registers for the short period they remained in the city. Eighteen months after receiving permission to settle in Seville, they requested passage to North Africa, where they could once again "live in Muslim lands." While their experiences living under Islamic rule likely affected their decision not to integrate with Seville's mudéjares, their special tax status would also have been an incentive for maintaining institutional independence.

Taxation policies helped define the aljama. The taxes themselves maintained institutions key to aljama existence. The tax on meat, for example, was linked to the presence of Muslim and Jewish butchers and a table or stall at the market. In 1476, Symuel Abenbaça, described as the mayordomo of the Jewish aljama, paid 300 mrv to Isabel de Fuentes as "tribute" for their kosher butcher shop. Fuentes presumably received that annual income as a privilege from the Crown.

The archives give no indication of how the tax burden was distributed among the aljama's membership. Since Muslims organized themselves according to a hierarchy wherein master artisans and their families represented the institution and held its offices, these families likely paid the bulk of its taxes. In the Jewish community, economic inequality was even sharper, and its most elite members would have enjoyed exemption from taxes. In that case, perhaps the council of elders, men of moderate means, represented the taxpaying base, supplemented with voluntary contributions from the wealthier noble class. The men and women who prayed in the city's synagogues and mosques but who, because of their relative poverty, do not appear in notarial records might have paid little or nothing. Some likely received aid from the aljama's charitable funds. Whether they would have been considered members of the aljama or could have made any demands upon it without making a payment or another obligation remains unclear.

The Governing Body

An institution of governance and law, the aljama was often interchangeable with its cabildo, its officers, and those eligible to hold its offices. This is patently the case in documents from Seville notarized by Christians. In 1454, when the Jewish cabildo agreed to produce a power of attorney for tax collection, the twenty participants were identified as "Jews of the said aljama, being assembled in our cabildo, in our synagogue."[34] The collapse of "Jews of the aljama" into its cabildo is notable, as are the descriptions of the congregating men: none was called "don," and only a few had occupational titles, the highest status was a silversmith. The named officers included Mayr Abensemerro, its judge, and Symuel Abenbaça, a mayordomo, probably a treasurer and financial officer. Also present was Ysaque Abensemerro, a rent farmer and part of a prominent family.

The census of the Muslim aljama a few months before expulsion can be read in a similar fashion. Thirty-two men and women came to a site in the morería to declare themselves to the scribe Luis García de Celada, who had previously recorded many of their private contracts. Each Muslim man was identified as maestre, and every woman as doña; the men were potters, construction workers, architects, blacksmiths, boot and shoemakers, tailors, an inn-keeper, and the master of the city's waterworks; the women were widows of artisans.[35] The membership of the Muslim aljama was equivalent to the heads of households of councilmembers. The alcalde was the blacksmith maestre Çayde Blanco, who first appeared with that title in documents in 1498. In addition to Blanco, the document indicates three Muslim men with whom the monarchs' representative interacted directly: Abdalla the alfaquí, and two maestres without aljama titles, mason Hamete Ginete and ceramicist Abdalla de la Rosa. The four men perhaps served as a formal or informal cabildo.[36]

Contemporary Islam and Judaism offered guidelines or long-standing custom for arranging for the proper governance of a community. In Iberian Jewish communities, known in Hebrew as *qahál*, the community was a group of individuals who elected a rabbi by majority vote to be their legal and religious advisor, and an administrative or juridical leader. The tribunal would be formed of three judges with knowledge of Jewish law, though they were not necessarily men of formal legal education; in the absence of theologians, any wise man might do. When communities lacked adequate men of scholarly training, they could be imported from outside. The tribunals generally also included a *sofer* (scribe).[37]

In Islam, any community that reconstituted itself as a minority was required to form a representative body with an *amīn*, a political or religious leader. Castile's initial Muslim aljamas must have been resilient, having lost so many religious leaders to emigration. Over time they reconstituted themselves, likely through contact with scholars and jurists in the nearby Islamic kingdom of Granada.[38] Seville's aljama would have included teachers, scribes, religious leaders, and officers. Women might have been among its educated members, as was the case in other places. Muslim women were regularly involved in their families' commercial enterprises, which necessitated familiarity with bookkeeping and Islamic contract law.[39]

Fifteenth-century Christian notaries used the Spanish term *juez* or *alcalde* for the Jewish judge and *alcalde* for the Muslim. The choice of juez suggests that the Jewish community still had access to men of scholastic training, while the Muslims did not. Both communities' judges were confirmed by the kingdom's alcaldes mayores de las aljamas. In 1439, Yahia, then alcalde mayor, named maestre Alí Oberí, an artisan, to be Seville's Muslim alcalde, probably after a local election.[40] Alí Oberí came from a prominent family of artisans including bootmakers, turners, and construction workers; his support was local rather than royal. In regions where Muslims were not directly under Crown control, other authorities appointed or confirmed. In Cantillana (Castile), the Muslims were issued a founding charter by the archbishop of Seville in 1345, which allowed them to name their own qadi, subject to the archbishop's approval.[41]

We have no particular insight into the content of Muslim or Jewish law as practiced in fifteenth-century Seville, though legal texts in circulation articulate contemporary religious jurisprudence.[42] Jewish and Islamic law were both living traditions, with distinct interpretations across time and space, and religious scholars in Castile debated with one another, sought external approval, and produced local understandings of their practices. There were often multiple men (or perhaps women) who were described as scholars in each community, and important legal centers were located nearby (Granada for Islam and Toledo for Judaism).

Shari'a, or Islamic law, is derived from multiple sources. God's ordering of human activities was partially revealed to Muhammad between 610 and 632. These revelations, which Muslims consider to be the word of God, were collected into the Qur'an. The revelations are fairly brief with respect to actual law and are partially filled out by the hadith, "narrative reports that embody the model behavior (*sunna*) of the Prophet and his companions," which were collected into authoritative texts in the ninth century, serving as accounts of how Muslims understood law in historical time.[43] Beyond these texts, shari'a was generated by jurists who utilized the Qur'an and the hadith to find solutions to contemporary juridical problems, following complex rules of analytic and syllogistic reasoning. In the ninth century, four scholars with large followings gave their names to the major schools of law in Sunni Islam: Mālikī (the school with influence over Andalucía), Hanafi, Shafi'i, and Hanbali. Individual jurists within these schools published commentaries, handbooks, lawbooks, and treatises. By the tenth century, a fully formed shari'a was "embodied in a vast corpus of commentaries and lawbooks."[44] The qadi, as judge, was part of an Islamic intellectual, political, and religious sphere, one of a number of scholars who might have maintained an active intellectual relationship with Islamic centers and jurists.

Jewish law derives from the Torah, the first five books of the Old Testament, but more importantly from learned interpretations and legal commentaries, many of which were produced in Muslim Iberia and Northern Africa. After the Christian conquest, Castilian Jewish intellectuals were increasingly drawn into

European cultural orbits, both Ashkenazi Jewish and Christian. Toledo, with a Talmudic school, was a center for Jewish philosophical and theological debate in the fourteenth century, while kabbalistic mysticism simultaneously revived lay religiosity across parts of the kingdom. The various centers of Jewish thought in Spain were not under external coordination, and the 1432 assembly to write *Taqqanot* in Valladolid was unsuccessful even in creating internal order. This dispersion made Jewish law heterogeneous across the Iberian kingdoms and particularly dependent upon the productivity of local religious scholars and philosophers. Scholars in Valencia and Toledo produced revivals, while Seville declined as an intellectual center in the fifteenth century.[45]

A small but telling scrap of evidence of legal practice in Seville exists in the form of a brief notarized receipt dated October 8, 1499. The receipt attests to payment by alcalde maestre Çayde Blanco to Alfonso Fernández, a Christian, for carrying unspecified paperwork from a lawsuit to the Granadan alfaquí Hamete Xarafi.[46] Xarafi had been called upon to judge a suit between maestre Hamete Carmoní and two Muslim widows, doña Merien and doña Fotox, for undisclosed reasons. Whether the absence of trained jurists meant that Xarafí had to be consulted in all mudéjar lawsuits, or whether he was advising on a particularly thorny question, is unknown.[47] But the receipt verifies the long-assumed communication between local qadis and legal specialists, as well as the aljama's place as the site for resolving civil conflict.

Muslim and Jewish alcaldes sought to coordinate with or appeal to the Christian concejo when dealing with issues that crossed jurisdictions. In 1447, the Jewish alcalde Abraham Barchilón appeared before the concejo of Seville to ask that they constrain the activities of Rodrigo Rodríguez, "who is greatly injuring and aggravating certain Jews."[48] Whether this was an individual conflict or a sign of larger unrest, it was in the municipality's interest to keep the peace.

The concejo could also assist aljamas with their internal enforcement issues. In 1450, the "Muslim taxpayers of the aljama of Sevilla" requested the concejo's intercession to enforce a judgment against maestre Hamete Carmonio, a Muslim and the owner of a mill, for 684 mrv.[49] The aljama had sued Carmonio before the city's Christian alcalde Juan Cerón and won, but the miller refused to pay. The circumstances suggest that Carmonio owed the aljama funds toward their tax bill or for a license or rental fee, but that they lacked the ability to force him to make the payment.

Jewish and Muslim judges were not the only leaders of their communities. There were legal experts, tax collectors, inspectors, lawyers, notaries, and treasurers who oversaw the internal organization of the community and its interaction with external actors. Few of these are identified in Seville's notarial documents. Three Muslims bear the title alfaquí or jurist. While in the Muslim world faqīh indicated a person learned in *fiqh*, Arabic scholarship generally, or Islamic law more narrowly, in Christian Spain the title named a profession. An alfaquí was a person who carried out religious and legal tasks in the service of the aljama.[50] He could also have led the community in prayer. Yça Gebir (or Gidelli), an eminent alfaquí in Segovia, also held the positions of imām and qadi of that aljama.[51] If Seville's alfaquíes led prayer at a mosque, that would explain the absence of another religious leader in the records.

The three men identified as alfaquí in Seville held the position over different decades: maestre Alí Alfaquí (1470s) was a borceguinero and a landlord, and maestre Abrahén Gynete (1490s) was an architect and the supervisor of the city's waterworks. Abdalla de Málaga was called alfaquí when he assisted in the census of the city's mudéjares in 1501, perhaps brought in from outside to assist in this task as elders emigrated. They may have served serially, using the title only while holding office, as Gynete was also present at the registration and listed prominently but without the title.

Maestre Abrahén Gynete also appears in a unique document that reveals the ongoing role of Muslim judges in the city.[52] When an enslaved Muslim girl named Catalina was accused of theft in 1492, Gynete presided over what seems to be an informal interconfessional tribunal. Catalina was accused of stealing a silver spoon from her Christian master and turning it over to Fátima, a Muslim slave from Granada, who sold it. In proceedings described by a Christian notary, Gynete took testimony from Fátima's mistress, doña Catalina de Mendoza, as well as from Muça, the Jewish silversmith who received the reportedly stolen goods. According to legal norms, a minor criminal trial that crossed all three religions should have been under a Christian jurisdiction. In this case, a Muslim judge presided and Muslim and Christian witnesses participated. It is possible that the Christian accuser thought a Muslim judge would be a more effective enforcer of penalties in this case. The woman's status as a slave might also have influenced the choice of venue. It stands as evidence of the continuing role of the Muslim judge in the city, and as a reminder that local practices did not always follow the strict prescriptions of law.

Gynete's role in this hearing suggests that he might not only have been the aljama's legal expert and advisor, but also its notary, a key occupation missing from both Jewish and Muslim records. A document from Granada in 1492 tells us that Hamete Xarafi was both alfaquí and scribe of Islamic law in that kingdom.[53] Miller documents this mixed role for alfaquíes in contemporary Aragón, who she argues often took the dual position because it carried a salary and prestige at a time when the legal scholar's own authority was challenged by Christian rule.[54] The Crown used the lucrative office of notary to reward personal favorites. In Aragón, members of the Muslim Bellvís family received the office in a number of different aljamas. They then subcontracted the position to others, who collected fees per document or instrument.[55]

The 1501 padrón, overseen by alcalde Çayde Blanco and alfaquí Abdalla de
Málaga, also suggests the intertwining of the roles of jurist, judge, and notary as
the men were required to swear "according to their law" that the list of Muslim
residents drafted by the Christian notary was complete and correct.[56] As was
likely the case when Gynete presented the Granadan immigrant Fátima's testimony, the alfaquí might have acted as interpreter. Seville's Muslim community
was by this point too small to have enough educated men to carry out multiple
legal roles requiring literacy and language skills. Educated men like Abrahén
Gynete, Abdalla de Málaga, or Alí Alfaquí might have shared a variety of roles,
regardless of any particular title they bore.

Seville's notarial records do not document a Jewish scribe either. Rabbis would
have been literate, as were the royal courtiers such as tax collectors and *alfaquimes* (who were either medical professionals or interpreters to the court, occupations that were linked because of the Jewish medical scholar's need to translate
works to and from Arabic, Castilian, and Latin). Jewish alfaquimes sometimes
acted as scribes as well as interpreters, including in Arabic, as was the case for don
Abraham ibn Wacar, a physician who served as interpreter, scribe, and cultural
mediator in the court of Alfonso X.[57] Seville's archives do not attach any particular men to these roles as jurists or notaries, though it is clear that the cabildo continued to function until expulsion and presumably kept its own records. Given
that many of the city's Jews were men of professional standing, they might have
shared the task of keeping records.

Finding Missing Archives

Despite the lack of documentation of record-keeping within the aljamas, legal
acts certainly took place there. The clearest evidence is the absence of key Muslim
and Jewish documents in Christian notarial archives. Muslims and Jews must
have made wills, contracted with one another, distributed taxes, assigned tutelage,
and performed a range of similar actions. They did not do so before a Christian
notary, so they must have done this in the aljama.[58] These can be reconstructed
partially through an analysis of Christian evidence that reflects those acts as well
as informed speculation about what cannot be seen.

Wills and Inheritance

The most glaring absence in the Christian notarial record is the most obvious: the
last will and testament. These documents were ubiquitous in both communities. A prophetic hadith urges Muslims, "Do not spend two consecutive nights
without your last will and testament being written and placed underneath your

pillow."[59] No Muslims or Jews asked a Christian notary in Seville to put their affairs in order, presumably because they were handled internally.

In Castile, each religion managed the disposition of property within the community of the faithful. An undated post-expulsion document notes that "successions and inheritances and partitions of goods done up until the date of this order that were carried out according to Muslim law, let those be valid and firm, but from this date on, the laws of our Kingdoms and the fuero of this City must be kept with respect to the said successions and inheritances."[60] In each of the three traditions, notaries drew up documents of final disposition according to their law, clarified the distribution of property where not governed by their law, and described the funerary and post-funerary practices desired by the dying man or woman. Wills had to be enforceable as well as religiously sound, and individuals largely depended upon professionals to draw them up.

Christian wills in late medieval Castile were simultaneously secular and religious documents. Generally opening with a protestation of faith, the rest of the document included boilerplate language regarding funeral services and masses, burial, and a description of property and its distribution according to civil inheritance law.[61] The legal practice has origins in Roman law—giving independent, competent, adult males the privilege of distributing their property before seven competent male witnesses—but also in the medieval practice of making donations to ecclesiastical institutions, written up by priests and maintained in church records. By the early thirteenth century, with increasing lay literacy and changing concepts of piety and property, wills were "resecularized," written in Castilian by public notaries, and they distributed property to a variety of people and institutions as well as to the Church.[62] They remained expressions of religiosity, and the process of will-writing involved a contemplation of the rituals around death and the cultural and spiritual processes necessary for the desired outcome of Christian salvation.[63] The Christian will also required small contributions to pious works. The formal linkage of social status and religious performance made it difficult for non-Christians to see this contract as a secular document.

Nor could they expect a Christian notary to understand Islamic inheritance law, which was complex and mathematical, requiring "a knowledge of square roots and algebra in order to be fully understood."[64] Distribution of an estate required identifying heirs who fell into one of two categories, compulsory and agnate. Compulsory heirs were certain close relatives including husbands, wives, parents, siblings, and daughters who would each receive a fractional share of a minimum of two-thirds of the estate after debts were paid off. The agnate category included the closest male relative, beginning with the son, according to a hierarchy debated by Muslim scholars, who received the rest of that two-thirds.

The final third could be distributed as bequests to anyone not already receiving a fractional compulsory or agnate share.[65]

In practice, Muslim inheritance was more flexible. Legal specialists weighed anthropological and sociological considerations when drawing up testaments. They debated the precise hierarchy between male agnates and established the primacy of compulsory heirs over bequests. This gave local authorities like alfaquís some power when it came to distributing complicated inheritances. But the Islamic inheritance system also provided the possibility of establishing, prior to the deathbed, a family endowment, wherein immovable property could be designated as an endowment for a child and his future lineal descendants, thus removing that property from testamentary inheritance. An endowment could effectively disinherit a spouse, siblings, and other heirs. Such a tactic let testators "[define] the meaning of family for their lineal descendants and insured the physical integrity of their resources in perpetuity."[66]

One form of this endowment was known as *waqf*, and it appears in Seville's archives. Alcalde maestre Cayde Blanco and his wife Merien made a "donation between living parties" in 1492, granting a house in the *morería* of San Pedro to their son Yuça Blanco, a blacksmith like his father. Why the alcalde made this document before the Christian notary is a puzzle. It may indicate that, by 1492, there was no Muslim able to draw it up, or he might have had concerns that the gift would not be recognized in the current hostile climate or that it would be contested by other heirs, including those who had converted to Christianity.[67] Mason Haçan de la Puente drew up a similar document in favor of his daughter Malfate and her husband Maestre Alí de la Puente around 1496.[68] These donations are perhaps the strongest evidence that Muslim inheritance practices continued to have relevance, even towards the end.

Medieval Jewish wills are less commonly found in Iberia than Christian or Muslim ones. Although Jews also had a long and vigorous practice of written dispositions, they were often done informally, within the family.[69] Jewish written practice diverged from Christian in a number of ways. The Jewish documents present the wishes of the deceased through the words of the witnesses, who attest to the person's physical and mental condition and recall his or her desires. In terms of property distribution, after the return of dowry and contracted spousal gifts, "the first-born son normally got a double share, a husband received the estate of his wife, a daughter as only child became the sole heir, a wife did not inherit her husband's estate."[70]

In practice the forms often converged, with Muslims, Christians, and Jews borrowing from one another's traditions. The overlaps were facilitated by the use of one another's judges and notaries. Iberian Jewish wills written in Romance languages by Christian notaries often differed very little from Christian wills of the same time and place, often diverging only in their religious invocations, places of interment, and charitable gifts.[71] A set of Jewish wills from Catalonia show the effects of a very integrated commercial and even spiritual world. The wills refer to Jewish feast days and mourning practices, but they also mirror Christian tendencies to leave legacies for the poor and to call for the remission of sin.[72] Muslims, Jews, and Christians shared understandings of property and finance as well as desires to protect family members, legatees, and institutions, resulting in venue-shopping and entangled practices.[73]

But in the second half of the fifteenth century in Seville, there is no evidence that any Muslim or Jewish client approached a Christian notary to write a will. Muslim and Jewish men and women either managed their affairs through custom or had their own notaries draw up documents to be enforced by their religious judges. Without extant documentation, the content and structure remain unknown. But the choice to work through coreligionists suggests that Seville's Muslims and Jews sought to maintain differential traditions rather than seek commonalities with Christian law.

Enforcement was a different problem, and sometimes required intervention from Christians. Seville's Christian notaries helped local Muslims gain possession of inheritances in other cities by documenting a death or providing a power of attorney.[74] When one exited one's own community, even to perform actions in a distant community of coreligionists, a Christian notary could prove valuable.

An unusual notarial document that sheds light on internal inheritance practices among Muslims was registered in 1499, after Çuleman Oberí's death left his wife Xencia Castellana a widow.[75] Oberí, a Muslim, had a brother who had converted to Christianity and had taken the name Diego de León. León approached Castellana, demanding to inherit his brother's estate on the grounds that his conversion to Christianity did not disinherit him. León was drawing upon Christian legal doctrine—the *Siete partidas* had ordered that Jews who converted to Christianity "shall possess all their property, sharing the same with their brothers and inheriting it from their fathers and mothers and other relatives, just as if they were Jews."[76] The widow responded that she was not her husband's heir, rather their daughter was, and that her husband had left no estate in any case, as their debts exceeded their possessions.[77] This exchange reflects the debates within the Muslim community on the order of inheritance, as a brother (a male agnate) could have had priority over a daughter unless the daughter was specifically endowed with the (theoretical) inheritance. It is also possible that the Oberí family had embraced the Spanish-Christian model of requiring that living children of any gender inherit from their parents. In any case, the widow's apparent poverty made it impossible for the Christian brother to collect.

Loans and Debts

Seville's Christian archives lack contracts and loans made within minority communities, though a handful of documents, discussed in Chapter 1, refer to such interactions. They include cases where a Muslim intervened when coreligionists were in danger of defaulting on loans to Christians, and a Jewish tanner lent cash to an Jewish silversmith who had defaulted on a loan and was imprisoned. In these cases, the Muslim or Jewish party used a Christian notary to create an enforceable contract in a situation where there was concern about credit, but also to produce legal evidence of repayment to a Christian for the courts.[78]

The absence of documentation from within the aljama leaves open the question of how those contracts might have differed from the ones they did write. For example, the ritual calendar shaped Christian contracts, using feast days as a common marker. Christians writing contracts involving Muslims and Jews took care to accommodate the different calendar, as when employment contracts insisted on employees' right to their sabbath and holy days. Loan conditions might be different in non-Christian documents: Christians required payment over a limited time frame, while Jews could demand payment indefinitely, making the final cost much higher.[79] No documentation reveals anything about interest, pricing, or time frames in non-Christian practices, but there is reason to expect that Jews and Muslims might have done some things differently within their cohort, due both to legal distinctions and to close ties.

Dowries and Children

Marriage and divorce (or repudiation), as religious rituals, were carried out within confessional communities.[80] Muslims, Jews, and Christians all utilized some form of dower and arras, or payments from the families of the bride and groom, respectively. Mayr Brudo, son of a rabbi, married Cimilia, daughter of a deceased Jewish physician. In 1460 he appeared before the notary Gonzalo de Plasencia to acknowledge receipt of his bride's dowry of 40,000 mrv from his new mother-in-law.[81] The Christian notary was called in because Cimilia's mother had had to sell two houses to another Jewish couple to raise the funds. Muslims, too, utilized dowry and arras, as Xencia Castellanos' argument with her brother-in-law demonstrates.

Finally, recall the insistence of the alcalde mayor de las aljamas in Sepúlveda that the city needed a qadi to protect Muslim children. In Islamic law, children belonged to the husband's family, and a father's death would likely have placed his minor children in the hands of the father's male relatives.[82] Tutelage arrangements can occasionally be intuited, as when the death of don Çulemon

Barchilón in 1474 left his wife Clara a widow with three young children. At the time of his death, don Çulemon was selling land with don Mayr Abenbilla to a Christian couple. With Barchilón's death, his underage children were co-owners of the property. The widow, Clara, and her father-in-law don Frayme Barchilón (member of the Jewish cabildo) appeared jointly as their guardians, along with Abenbilla and the Christians to notarize the final papers. While the tutelage contract itself is invisible, its effects are clear.[83]

The archive also presents evidence of other ways of caring for children, as detailed in arrangements for apprenticeships for boys and domestic service for girls. Nearly all cases of Muslim or Jewish participation in apprenticeships come from contracts across faiths. Some contracts explicitly attempted to create space for children to meet the needs of their faith, but placing a Muslim or Jewish child into a Christian workshop or household undoubtedly exposed them to pressures to convert.[84] The pressures might go both ways. In 1485, the Inquisition in Toledo accused a converso named Juan Alvarez de Sevilla of judaizing. In his first confession he testified that, while living in Seville twenty-five years earlier, he had been apprenticed to or worked for a Jewish silversmith and at least three Jewish toqueros (headdress makers), whom he had watched "carry out certain ceremonies of the Mosaic law" with their families. He explained that don Mayr Abenbilla, the silversmith and a member of the Jewish cabildo, had explained to him that "this was the truth and that he must save himself according to this law." The young man accordingly brought the rituals to his parents' home and continued to attend synagogues, interact with practicing Jews, and carry out various rituals until the Inquisition called him in for judaizing.[85] Álvarez's testimony is suggestive of the ways that Christians surely imposed their beliefs on Muslim or Jewish charges and created intimate social pressure to convert.

Most apprenticeship relations probably took place within religious communities. Trades largely stayed within extended families, and these would have been arranged informally or with the cooperation of religious judges. The sole exception in the archives was when an outsider, Mahoma "El Gordo," of Almagro, apprenticed to maestre Hamete Ginete for two years to learn masonry in Seville. As in similar cases involving outsiders, it was desirable to register the contract with a Christian notary.[86]

While young men apprenticed to learn skills and trades, young girls were placed in households to earn dowries. Three contracts placing young Jewish girls with Christian masters survive, from 1472 and 1476. They are largely similar, each placing an adolescent or preadolescent for a lengthy period of unspecified service in exchange for a significant sum. No details in the contracts speak to protections for young girls within these very intimate relationships. One other contract stands out. In April 1496, Caçan Moguel and Merién Candil, a Muslim couple, placed their nine-year-old daughter Xencia with another Muslim couple, maestre Bucar and doña Haxa. She would live with them for ten years, and they would educate her, supply her needs, and remunerate her at their discretion at the end of the period.[87] At such a distance and with so bare-bones a document it is difficult to read between these lines. This might be yet another placement to gain a dowry, but it might also indicate the fragility of the Muslim community in the years before expulsion. It is possible that the parents intended to leave Seville and were entrusting their daughter to another family or simply that they feared for her future. In any case, they felt compelled to bring their situation to a Christian notary.

The Possessing Community

The aljama was also an agent for management of the community's commonwealth. The king issued communal property to the Jewish aljama at the thirteenth-century repartimiento, and throughout their existences both Muslim and Jewish communities managed common goods including synagogues and mosques, cemeteries, warehouses, mills, ovens, baths, and other real estate.

The aljamas shared a common understanding of property regimes with Christians. In Castile, property could be held collectively, by the Crown or another institution such as the Church, or privately by individuals.[88] Notarial records overemphasize the importance of urban private property, the least common form of holding, but it was also one recognized by Christians, Muslims, and Jews. They largely agreed with respect to how it might be alienated and how it was valued. If they disagreed with respect to specifics, these existed within a larger agreement about the status of property in the kingdom.

Property could be expropriated at the monarch's pleasure. The case of don Çulemon ibn Sadoq (or Pintadura) would have been instructive for many religious minorities. Don Çulemon was Alfonso X's financial officer, and he received extensive rural holdings in the thirteenth-century resettlement of Seville. Over time he collected many urban properties as well, including a garden at the judería's gate next to the Jewish cemetery; warehouses in the Alcaicería and the Puerta del Arenal; and mills, olive oil storage facilities, baths, and bakeries. But at his death in 1274, despite his family's close relationship with the monarch, Alfonso X seized most of those properties and turned them over to Seville's cathedral. While don Çulemon likely considered himself the owner of these properties, they were—like all lands taken in conquest—at the king's disposition.[89]

Seville's Muslim aljama managed property, including at least one mosque and the cemetery outside the city walls. When royal officials embargoed those in 1502, they took care to clarify possession. The notary asked the Muslim officers to "state

that they are all collectively-held goods, the said mosque with all the said property." The officers had to swear both "according to their [Islamic] law and according to [royal] law" that these were the aljama's sole collective goods. At expulsion,
the Crown also took possession of a house and a *corral* belonging to the Muslim
aljama. These were located in the Adarvejo, next door to the mosque. These may
have been the same properties that the alcalde Çayde Blanco and alfaquí Abrahén
Gynete went to court over in 1498, a house and a mill described as being in the
parish of San Nicolás.[90]

The Jewish aljama also owned a house and corral that they leased to members
of their community for income, and that property reveals something about intra-
confessional contracts. In 1466, Yucef Abensemero, as judío mayor and in the
name of the aljama, issued a long-term lease to silversmith Mayr Abenbilla on a
house he owned in Santa Cruz. Under the terms, Abenbilla paid an annual fee of
315 mrv. He was prohibited from selling or trading the property to a member of
the nobility or aristocracy, to a religious institution, or to a foreigner, and could
only alienate it to someone from whom the aljama could collect the fee.[91] While
Muslim, Christian, and Jewish parties all understood such contracts and agreed
about the meanings of property, Jews and Muslims knew that they were at a dis-
advantage in terms of enforcement if a Christian failed to make payments.

Venue-Shopping

Aljamas were sites of law, intersecting with other jurisdictions in complex, hierarchical ways. The common notarial formula whereby Jews "renounced the law
of Moses" in order to contract with a Christian indicates how easily Muslims or
Jews exited the jurisdiction of their judges and shopped for venues or shifted to
other kinds of juridical spaces. The archives present evidence of two particular
ways that Muslims and Christians left their religious jurisdiction: by engaging
a Christian notary or by taking a case directly to the municipal concejo. They
might also have settled informally (extrajudicially) or brought a case to a royal
court, neither of which left traces in the notarial records. At times moving out
of religious jurisdiction gave a better outcome, and at times it was required. But
often shifting jurisdiction was simply a matter of seeking better enforcement.

Neighborly and contractual conflicts regularly crossed religious jurisdictions.
When Muslims and Jews needed to complain about Christian neighbors, they
took it to civil court or to the concejo. Mayr Abensemerro, himself the judge of
the Jewish aljama, did that in 1455 when his neighbor in the barrio Santa Cruz,
a Christian named Juan Díaz de Cea, damaged Abensemerro's roof while adding
new beams to his own home.[92] A year later Abensemerro appeared in court to sue
a shepherd in nearby Triana for undisclosed damages.[93] While the outcomes of

these suits are unknown, Abrahán Abensemerro, another family member associated with the Jewish cabildo, successfully sued Catalina Ferrández before the
city's alcalde de la justicia, Diego Gómez de Baeza, in 1484, and collected his payment.[94] Municipal and royal courts were really the only hope that Muslims and
Jews, including the judges of their own religious communities, had for enforcement against Christians.

Muslims and Jews also turned to Christian authorities when they needed legal
muscle, inside or outside their community. They wrote up powers of attorney
before a Christian notary in order to ensure that they would be widely accepted.[95]
When Yehuda and Mayor Santarén, a Jewish tailor and his wife, sold their house
to a Christian tailor and his wife, Mayor had to give power of attorney to her
husband to manage her share of the sale. She did so before the same notary who
wrote the contract.[96] Occasionally, a Jew or Muslim gave power of attorney to
a Christian to represent them in legal affairs, as when Clara Aben Sancho, the
widow of don Çuleman Barchilón, gave hers to the city's scribe, Pedro Guillén, in
1480.[97] These instruments were useful for collecting debts in other regions as well
as in other jurisdictions, as surely Don Ysaque Abensemerro knew when issuing
one to his nephew, don Çuleman Abensemerro of Toledo, to collect a debt from
a Christian couple in Talavera.[98]

As their communities entered crisis, Muslims and Jews often found themselves in the hands of city and royal authorities, in jurisdictions that offered little
protection. The threat became clear as numbers of Muslim artisans defaulted on
loans and taxes at the end of the century and Christian officials went to their
places of business to execute sequestration orders. In 1493, Abdalla de la Rosa, a
potter working in Triana, was presented with an order prohibiting him from fir-
ing his kiln until he paid the *diezmo* and *almojarifazgo* that he owed the Catholic
church.[99] Later that month, the mason maestre Haçan de la Puente had property
embargoed for defaulting on payment to a merchant.[100] Between 1493 and 1498,
the authorities sequestered property nine times from Muslim debtors, usually
placing it with either a coreligionist or a practitioner of their occupation, against
payment. No longer able to call upon wealthier community members to guarantee their debt, they were left at the mercy of Christian jurisdictions. In addition to
the economic pain these narratives reveal, the interventions of Christian authorities represented a very public humiliation, rendering flight and conversion reasonable tactics for survival.

The Connected Community

The Jewish and Muslim aljamas were also in touch with coreligionists outside
the city. In the case of Jews, the relationships were most powerful for elites, who

might have had residences in Seville but acted on behalf of the Crown in other cities, often as rent collectors. They did so as part of powerful Jewish families, who benefited from connections to conversos as well as to the Crown.[101] The Abensemerro family, a presence in Seville as well as Cádiz, is one such case.[102] Mosé Abensemerro was the rent-farmer for Xerez de la Frontera in 1472, and Rabbi Frayme Abensemerro collected the sales tax on feral cattle in Alcalá de Guadaira. Ysaque Abensemerro, an elder of the family, had collected a variety of rents in the middle of the fifteenth century.[103] In 1484, with the Jewish expulsion finally underway after a delay, Mosé Abensemerro, who was responsible for collecting the sales tax on hides and furs in Utrera, hurried to close the books on old accounts from his home in Seville. Seven men described their debts to him, mostly in payments of units of barley, for taxes on the sales of oxen. A blacksmith drew up a contract to pay Abrahén Abensemerro for the tax on the sale of his home.[104]

Jews from other regions also entered Seville on business. Vidal and Yuçaf Bienveniste—members of a prominent Jewish family from northern Spain—came as inspectors in 1467.[105] Many of those engaged in rent-farming were members of the great merchant families and would have had a presence in Seville's economic life. They would have frequented the Alcaicería's shops, streets like Sierpes, and the markets that surrounded the Cathedral's steps.

Seville's mudéjares had ties with more plebeian or commercial partners, including rural Muslim aljamas such as nearby La Algaba and merchants from farther afield. Traders from North Africa enjoyed favored status at times. In 1460 Enrique IV reminded Seville's concejo to respect the special tax privileges he had issued them.[106] When the city experienced a grain shortage in 1471, residents demanded that the concejo bring grain from North Africa and be prepared to pay with coins that Berber traders would accept.[107]

Commercial agents also came to the city from Granada when political affairs between the kingdoms allowed. Throughout the fifteenth century, relations with the kingdom of Granada cycled between warm and hostile. In 1450, Juan II of Castile announced a five-year ceasefire with don Ysmael, king of Granada, allowing goods and prisoners of war to move between the two kingdoms.[108] Seville's concejo issued a general order in late 1452 that the "Muslims who come from Granada with their merchandise" be given safe passage because of the truce.[109] The truce was periodically violated—in 1453 some Muslims were accused of stealing cattle from Marchena—but Castilian monarchs often found the relationship productive and the city of Seville considered it particularly beneficial.[110] Muslim long-distance merchants were part of the life of the city, subject to regulation from the time of Alfonso X to the Catholic monarchs' attempts to segregate their rooming houses in 1491. They were visible in public and private spaces, from the alhóndiga where they bought and sold grain, to the *mesones* or hostels where Christians charged them rent.

Finally, the Muslim aljamas in Seville's rural environs sent men and women into the city for work. The members of La Algaba's aljama, mostly agricultural workers, often came to Seville to do business. In 1495, Gonzalo de Stúñiga rented some farmlands near Gerena to six Muslim men from La Algaba. The contract ran for six years, with rents payable in wheat and barley on the Feast of the Assumption each August.[111] Others sold their crops in advance for cash, as three farmers from La Algaba arranged in June to turn over a large load of straw to a *vecino* in August.[112] And in the late summer and early fall, as olive harvests came in, rural Muslims signed contracts with land owners to extract and bottle olive oil. In the harvest season of 1486, Gonzalo Gómez de Cervantes of Seville hired two Muslim men from that village to grind the olives into a paste and press it through mats; the canon of San Salvador church also hired a Muslim for this task. In each case, the workers were paid an artisan's salary of about 400 mrv a month, and one man received a cash advance.[113]

The final important way that the aljamas interacted with outside coreligionists involved the institution of slavery. Medieval Mediterranean slavery had been largely premised upon ransoming captives. Most Christian cities had an *alfaqueque*, a Muslim official charged with negotiating ransom from the families of captives, and vice versa. There is no indication that Seville had a permanent officeholder, although in 1470 Enrique IV informed the city that he had named a Christian as his *alcalde de alfaqueques*, to work in conjunction with an *alfaqueque mayor entre cristianos y moros*.[114] These men might have been involved in trading higher-value prisoners across the borders with Muslim territories. The aljama and Muslim individuals occasionally facilitated the release and redemption of less-well-off Muslim captives in the city.

Recent scholarship has challenged the long-standing belief that manumission by owners was common in medieval Iberian slavery, thereby critiquing a tradition that considered Iberian slavery more virtuous than its Atlantic counterpart.[115] There is little in Seville's notarial archives to indicate that slaves of any background were more than occasionally granted freedom papers in the fifteenth century.[116] There is, however, evidence that they fled their masters, as Mahoma, Yça, Fátima, and the baby Mahomico did in 1496. Their owner, doña Juana Enriquez, the duchess of Escalona, sent her husband's servant with a power of attorney to bring them back.[117]

Muslim slaves differed from most West African slaves in an important regard: Muslims had the advantage of being able to raise funds to purchase their freedom from coreligionist communities, who saw their contributions as a charitable act.[118] Thus in 1497, Mahoma Cinçar, a free Muslim weaver of rush mats, contractually agreed to substitute for Isabel Rodríguez's slave, Mahoma Çayate, in that craft, while Çayate went "to search for donations in all the places, cities, and towns he wishes in this kingdom of Castile." The donations would purchase his freedom, which Rodríguez had evaluated at 18,000 mrv. Çayate also arranged a 2,000 mrv loan from one of his mistress's servants to pay for his journey. A month later, Çayate returned to the notary to receive his freedom papers from Rodríguez. He paid her 10,000 mrv, perhaps completing an earlier down payment.[119]

Loans proved key to the way that the aljama and its individual Muslim members ransomed foreign Muslims. Muslims from Granada and Seville joined to finance the manumission of a family of Muslims from Málaga from their owner, a member of Seville's concejo. The manumission required the coordination of the Muslim communities in order to free the family in Seville and collect their repayment of the debt (and associated taxes) in Málaga.[120] There could have been a close relationship between the lenders and the manumitted family, but such practices more generally reflect the practice of charitable ransoming.

There is no evidence that Seville's alcalde de los negros organized funds to ransom West African captives in the city, though it is possible that such a function was carried out by the city's Black and mulato confraternities. This was the case in Valencia, where the bylaws of the Casa dels Negres explicitly called for sheltering, defending, and collecting alms to free Black slaves.[121] The Dominican confraternity of the Rosary, which had branches around the Spanish and Portuguese world, also took up manumission. In 1526 its confraternity in São Tomé set out a charter based on one in use in Lisbon, which claimed that its brothers could demand that masters free any Black slaves who were members of the organization. They also actively sought to enact testamentary manumissions of members that were delayed. Later charters suggest they continued to involve themselves in freeing members.[122] It is likely that Seville's Black institutions played a small part in manumissions as well.

The aljama was a living institution that reproduced Jewish and Muslim practices, but also created a class of individuals who derived status from membership. The archives provide clear evidence that the communities were constantly adjusting to changing situations. The contemporary Christian treatment of Islam and Judaism as *leyes* (laws) recognized them as systems that regulated behavior according to traditional precepts. Circulating treatises, such as the *Leyes de Moros*, demonstrate that Muslim and Jewish communities continued to call upon their leaders to resolve moral as well as legal problems. But the aljamas were also collections of individuals who interacted with the majoritarian, Christian population. Living within one's law inevitably necessitated reorienting oneself toward other laws.

The archival materials do not open the aljama wide. Instead they reveal a narrow sector of the Muslim and Jewish populations of the city and almost nothing of the enslaved and free Black populations. Most residents likely never had their names recorded by a notary. Many Muslims and Jews may have had a more ambivalent relationship to their faith than their officers did, because to declare oneself publicly a Jew or Muslim was an invitation to taxation and prejudice as much as a statement of faith.

Despite these limitations, it is clear that the aljamas were complex institutions that divided up the tax burden; ritualized marriages, divorces, and property transfers; directed young men and women into occupations; and reproduced religious knowledge and literacy over generations. They were led by elected and appointed officials, but were also constantly brought into existence by people who acted within, through, and even outside them. Religions and laws as actually practiced were both dynamic and constrained, just like the lives of their practitioners.

5

Caciques and Local Governance in the Andes

DON GONZALO TAULICHUSCO, son of the kuraka ruling the Rimac Valley when the Spaniards arrived, wrote a will in 1562.[1] It was taken down in Spanish by a notary with the assistance of an interpreter, indicating that his Spanish was imperfect for the precisions of the task. The document opened with a lengthy Christian protestation and laid out meticulous preparations for funeral masses throughout greater Lima, and his burial at the church in Magdalena, where his subjects lived.

The cacique's legacy was complex, described through entangled legal forms that emerged from his personal engagement with Spaniards, his understanding of community politics, and his attempts to protect his subjects' patrimony into the future. The third cacique in the post-conquest Rimac Valley (succeeding his father Taulichusco and brother Guachinamo), he was the one to confront the undeniable repercussions of conquest. In litigation filed in the 1550s—an earlier attempt to redress colonial wrongs—he and his witnesses described how Spanish invaders had devastated the community, building their city on fertile orchards and farmlands. Subsequent wars between Spanish factions and between Spaniards and Inka resisters had taken an enormous toll as well. According to his accounting, don Gonzalo lost more than 90 percent of his subjects to death and flight and too much of the region's arable land to sustain those remaining.[2] He sought, via his will, to create enough wealth for them to feed themselves and meet tribute payments.

Don Gonzalo had struggled to compete on the conquistadors' terms. His father had negotiated away their lands, perhaps understanding the deal as a long-term rental in exchange for tribute, as he had previously arranged with other kurakas seeking temporary residence in the valley. Instead, the community was removed, first to his lands called Chuntay to the west of the urban core, and then

Republics of Difference. Karen B. Graubart, Oxford University Press. © Oxford University Press 2022.
DOI: 10.1093/oso/9780190233839.003.0006

permanently to the town of Magdalena to its southwest in 1557. In Magdalena, they were conjoined with other similarly displaced parcialidades. Franciscan friars required them to convert and build a church. By the time don Gonzalo inherited the *cacicazgo* (cacical office and privileges), Spaniards were crowding into Lima and its agricultural hinterlands, many hoping to get rich by controlling Indian labor that would produce crops to feed the hungry city.

Don Gonzalo entered into a variety of partnerships with Lima's new vecinos. Some of these were clearly attempts to manage his losses, as when he contracted with the Spaniards Juan Benítez and Andrés Machuca to grow wheat—a recently introduced crop—on his own land with his subjects' labor, but the Spaniards' capital, seed, and technical knowledge. In both cases he presented himself in control of the partnership, dismissing the Spaniards with payment for "whatever their labor deserved" and reserving the rest of the profits for his own estate. Other ventures were less successful. He noted that he had sold a piece of land to the city's treasurer, but he was swindled on the price and, in any case, the land was not fully his to sell. He asked his executors to return the 500 pesos to the official and half the land to the cacique of Aycayo, subject to him. The rest should remain "for whatever person succeeds me in the cacicazgo and for his descendants, but that they may not sell nor alienate them at any time." He attempted to annul other sales as well, noting that he had alienated lands that were not his on multiple occasions.

Don Gonzalo's will is a haunting portrait of the early colonial cacique as the leader of a diminished polity, maneuvering haltingly to dominate the increasingly unfavorable situation. But he presented a new strategy for his community, drawing upon forms of regional land tenancy that had existed prior to conquest, those introduced by the Spaniards, and some innovations.[3] He maintained that much of the land was not privately held but pertained to his cacicazgo, which would necessarily be designated to whoever succeeded him in the office. Other properties were personal inheritances from his father or were titled to him by Spanish officials to be disposed of as he liked. He chose to convert those personal properties into a community fund, leaving the better part of his herds of cattle, pigs, and mares, certain lands and houses, and some crops to his subjects "to pay the community's tribute."

This community fund resonates with an Andean practice known as *sapci*. In highland Quechua communities, sapci was "'that which belongs to all'... shared endowments characterized as common resources that ideally belonged to the community."[4] The term sapci does not appear in coastal legal documents from the sixteenth century, and don Gonzalo himself asserted in court papers filed in the 1550s that the lands of the valley were his own and not his community's. Given that coastal societies organized themselves and their resources differently than did those of the Quechua highlands, sapci might represent a borrowed concept that had useful implications after the Spanish conquest.[5]

Unlike most highland sapci, the new community funds created under don Gonzalo's will were not to be held as permanent endowment. He left instructions with his executor, Franciscan Fray Torixa, to auction off items as the priest saw fit. He was then to distribute those funds individually, "divided among all the said Indians without any favoritism nor one receiving more than the other, and do with them what best serves the benefit and utility of the said Indians." In other words, don Gonzalo created collective holdings in order to atomize them in the same way that collective tribute payments were individually imposed upon adult males.[6] The future cacique would still have to manage labor, tribute, joint ventures, and land grabs, but don Gonzalo believed that making his subjects into independent actors would ameliorate some of the crisis.

Don Gonzalo's will introduces the Indigenous jurisdictions of the New World. Native communities, either under cacicazgos or reduced into pueblos de indios, produced law and governance. Like the aljamas in Castile, they struggled to maintain their own character despite royal ordinances, municipal interventions, and the practices that surrounded them. They also had to deal with drastic declines in population and relocation processes. But they continued to function as self-governed bodies, producing their own forms of justice under increasingly difficult circumstances.

The Republics of the Spanish Americas

Historians commonly refer to the conceptual model of plural legal jurisdictions that Iberian Christians instituted in their American colonies as the "two republics": the *uso y costumbre* (customary law) of native communities, referred to as the *república de indios*, under the authority of their cacique or ethnic lord; and that of Spanish municipalities and officials, the *república de españoles*.[7] This terminology is often misunderstood—there was not a single republic of either Indians or of Spaniards, but many smaller republics or municipalities subject to their own custom, all of which were subject to the laws of the monarch and Catholic Church. However, the organization of law through republics underlines the continued importance of local jurisdiction under Iberian rule.

While this model developed from the Castilian legal framework it was modified, beginning in the middle of the fifteenth century, by contemporary theological and legal debates at the court as well as in practical struggles with communities across the Americas and in Africa. Portuguese and Castilian incursions on the African continent and its islands defined two distinct kinds of interactions: trade and political relations between African and European sovereigns, and European raids yielding African captives. The former, often ignored in Atlantic scholarship, recognized Africans' *dominium* or absolute right to property in persons and possessions, no matter their religion. The extensive diplomatic exchanges between Portugal, the papacy, and Kongo after 1483 are only the best known of these relationships. In contrast, the raids led to debates regarding the justification for invasion of sovereign land or trade in its captives.[8] By the time of Columbus' voyages west, papal bulls established self-defense as well as the promise of conversion as a justification for invading Muslim, Muslim-adjacent, and even pagan lands.[9]

Isabel and Fernando, receiving Columbus' report on the inhabitants of the Caribbean, turned to Pope Alexander VI to mediate their possession and occupation. Columbus had sailed farther south than a previous treaty with Portugal allowed, and the Portuguese and Castilians requested papal assistance in sorting out claims over the Canary and Caribbean islands. Pope Nicholas V's *Romanus Pontifex* (1545) had justified the Portuguese conquest of the Canaries as part of a universal mission to bring infidels to Christ, as a bulwark against Muslim expansion, and as an inevitable process. The 1479 Treaty of Alcaçovas temporarily settled conflict over Castilian and Portuguese expansions south toward the African continent by turning the Canaries over to Castile and drawing a line of demarcation to their south, where Castile recognized Portuguese jurisdiction. In 1493, Alexander VI extended this imaginary jurisdiction into the western Atlantic, accepting Castile's description of Caribbean inhabitants eager to accept the Christian faith. He directed the Castilian monarchs to carry out that mission on his behalf. The bulls assumed that Castile would have a monopoly on trade and dominium without explicitly invalidating infidel dominium.[10]

This ambivalence set up the terms of Spanish rule in the Americas. As the contemporary theologian and jurist Francisco de Vitoria noted, "unbelief does not destroy either natural law or human law; but ownership and dominium are based either on natural law or human law; therefore they are not destroyed by want of faith."[11] While native sovereignty did not supersede Christian sovereignty, Spanish vassalage did not dissolve indigenous political life. Once imperial rulers—which the Crown usually deemed to have been illegitimate tyrants—were removed, Spain recognized native nobles as the bearers of local authority and law. Thus "Indians" were to become Christian subjects of Spanish monarchs, yet they also would be subject to their own leaders and law.

In this sense, then, *indio*, often mistaken for a racial category, was more generally a legal sign.[12] It named people who were free vassals of the Spanish crown and bound to royal obligations and privileges (including the payment of tribute and the reception of Christian sacraments and education), but were socially and legally incorporated in their political community of origin.[13] The local law that Indigenous judges utilized within the community was not necessarily continuous with pre-conquest practices, and it might have to be negotiated through viceregal authorities. In effect, Indian law was whatever Indigenous authorities could use unhampered, could get viceregal authorities to legitimate, or had successfully imposed upon them by viceregal administrators. Like Seville's Muslims and Jews, not to mention its artisan guilds and municipalities, Indians were governed by their fueros as well as the other institutions placed over them by the Catholic Church and the Crown, resulting in multiple, though not autonomous, jurisdictions.

Indigenous local governance presented some political conflicts. The Crown feared empowered caciques, as it also worried about Spanish encomenderos and other powerful citizens who demanded the unfettered right to native labor, the autonomous exercise of law, and aristocratic privileges. The Crown attempted to curtail the authority of Indigenous nobles on a number of fronts: by instituting cabildos, rotating governments of plebeian officials to challenge caciques within pueblos; by making Christianization a qualification for holding any office; and by revising the standards for cacicazgo succession, allowing viceroys to challenge and replace those caciques they considered tyrannical, non-Christian, or illegitimate. These interventions were significant and created new Indian leadership tied to colonial rule in powerful ways. But local governance survived and even thrived in its new forms.

With the removal of imperial rulers like the Inka, local and provincial elites formed a key level of the plural jurisdictions of the New World. But their position was shaped by a number of other lines of authority in the sixteenth century, including royal *audiencias* (appeals courts) and corregidores, Spanish cabildos that competed for control of native labor and resources, and representatives of various arms of the Catholic church. Their republics, like the aljamas, changed over time, as did their governance. Leaders, whether hereditary nobility or new political actors, strategically reinvented customary law by intermingling older ways with ideas emerging from Spanish contact. The republics of the New World offered multiple fronts for inventing Indian political practices.

Conquering with Caciques

The native nobility proved crucial to Spanish colonization. They led armies that enabled conquest and brokered alliances to facilitate Spanish settlement, often expecting to rule jointly.[14] The Crown explicitly demanded that conquistadors honor caciques' jurisdiction over their own subjects in the early Caribbean. The model was articulated in 1516, when, after Fernando's death, the interim regent Archbishop Cisneros sent three Jeronymite friars to enact a commission's reforms to Caribbean settlements thrown into chaos by royal mismanagement and a

spiraling mortality rate. The plan insisted that native communities be autonomous units located nearby Spanish settlements,

> and those caciques must take care with their Indians in ruling them and
> governing them as will be stated below . . . that each place will have juris-
> diction for itself within its limits, and that the said cacique will have
> jurisdiction to punish the Indians who misbehave in the place where he
> is superior.[15]

By 1517, the commissioners had overturned their own plan and declared the
Indians incapable of self-rule, but caciques remained the legally responsible party
in the relationship between community, Crown, and Church.

The very term cacique summarized the emergent relationship. Local political
cultures had their own language of authority. Spanish conquistadors were less
interested in learning and deploying new vocabulary than they were in finding
tyrannical rulers to displace at the top and units of laborers who could produce a
steady stream of income. The Taíno term cacique became a generic category for
the legitimate local ruler (called a "natural lord") of such a unit, a middleman
tasked with delivering his subjects' wealth to a Spaniard.[16]

Indigenous nobles learned to use the term when making claims in the viceregal legal system, but it usually floated alongside regional political language. In
much of the Andean highlands, this meant that below the "Inka," the head of the
Cusco-based, Quechua-speaking ethnic group that dominated the empire they
called Tawantinsuyu, there were a variety of kurakas who were responsible for different numbers of subjects at different political levels, all existing in complicated
relationships to one another.[17] Inka census-takers had a precise vocabulary to dis-
tinguish different levels of political organization, with 100 subjects said to form
a guaranga, and 1,000 a panaca. Each level would have a kuraka, as well as lesser
nobles or principales, sometimes paired in parallel moieties with superior and
lesser leaders.[18] Outside the highland centers of Inka control or influence, different political formations existed at the local level. Coastal polities were paired in
ranked moieties with dual leaders that were embedded in complex hierarchies.
Their paramount lords functioned as a council rather than as autocrats. These
more decentralized regions had been temporarily knit together under Inka domination but, with the Spanish conquest, local political systems often re-emerged,
with important consequences for governance.[19]

The preexisting political units could not remain as they were, since the Crown
required units of labor that could deliver a certain amount of tribute to recipients
and be easily served by one of a small number of available priests. Larger units

were subdivided, or smaller ones patched together, to form those encomiendas. Both reformulations necessitated redrawing lines of authority, theoretically layering caciques within some newly imposed hierarchy but in reality creating multiple paths for future individuals to claim the office.[20]

Encomienda was contracted in a ritual that involved encomendero and cacique joining hands in a ceremony of possession in front of a representative of the municipality and a notary. When in 1539 the cacique Chayavilca (head of the Rimac Valley polity of Maranga) was assigned to encomendero Nicolás de Ribera, the *alcalde ordinario* (municipal judge) Francisco Núñez clasped Chayavilca's hand "in his own name and on behalf of the other caciques and *principales* [nobles] and Indians" and placed it in Ribera's. The notary reported that Chayavilca stated that "he was taking and took it in recognition of the said possession in his own name and on behalf of the other principales and Indians and the said alcalde ordered the said cacique to serve the said Nicolás de Ribera."[21] Performing such ritual acts in front of a notary implied consent for the Spaniards, although it is always possible that caciques understood the terms somewhat differently than did the Spanish participants. Their willingness to complain and litigate when encomenderos violated those terms suggests that they eventually understood well enough.

Not all native officials accepted these conditions. In addition to outright rebellion, many demanded greater autonomy through the legal system, and, on at least one occasion, at the royal court. In 1528, a delegation of members of the Tlaxcalan (central Mexican) nobility traveled to Spain to negotiate their status with Charles V. They had served as key allies to Hernando Cortés during the conquest of Tenochtitlán under the expectation that they would rule an autonomous empire. Using Spanish political rhetoric that emphasized their loyalty and service, they requested that their subjects be excluded from encomienda and that they remain *señores naturales* (legitimate natural lords, the equivalent of Spanish nobility) with jurisdiction over their people.[22]

In recognition of their role in the conquest and their political skill at court, the Crown granted this request, as well as a subsequent petition that requested he confer on Tlaxcala the privileged status of *leal ciudad*, or loyal city. The Tlaxcalans were not autonomous, and a corregidor was imposed upon them to mediate their relationship to the viceroy and king. The Tlaxcalan nobility retained jurisdiction over the region on behalf of the king, collecting his tribute (from their own subjects as well as from Spaniards living within their jurisdiction) and admitting priests to evangelize their subjects. This victory did not undermine the system that was being developed to administer the Americas, but simply changed the position of Tlaxcalan elites within it.[23]

Claiming Jurisdictions

What jurisdiction did caciques have? Political changes on both sides of the Atlantic over the course of the sixteenth century played a role in determining its limits. Habsburg monarchs Charles V and Philip II increased their royal power on the peninsula by multiplying local units of self-government. They did so by selling charters, liberating new towns from existing cities in exchange for cash and loyalty.[24] The new small towns and villages elected their own concejos as well as judges and other officers, and they received fueros from the king. Royal appellate judges who heard appeals of municipally rendered sentences or intrajurisdictional complaints became known as *audiencias*. The monarchs transformed the temporary position of corregidor into a standing royal officer who would interact with the municipal regidores. The limits of his jurisdiction coincided with those of the concejo.[25]

None of these measures centralized political power, which was dispersed into a variety of institutions and communities symbolically gathered under the monarch's "head."[26] The cortes, meetings of procurators or representatives of Iberian cities, became even more powerful as they allocated revenue to the Crown and thereby limited its autonomy. But the turn toward towns and their government, along with bureaucratization, set the cornerstone of rule in the Atlantic colonies.

There, the Crown was intent on preventing another aristocratic crisis. Charles V and Philip II kept most jurisdiction in the royal domain, or within municipalities overseen by their corregidores. Only Columbus and Cortés received seigneurial jurisdiction over towns.[27] The New Laws (1542) placed limits on the heritability of the encomienda, resulting in conspiracies in New Spain and outright rebellion in Peru. In the 1550s, the nearly bankrupt Philip II considered cash offers from both encomenderos and Andean caciques to change the rules regarding encomiendas. Encomenderos requested not only perpetuity and noble standing, but also civil and criminal jurisdiction over encomienda Indians. The caciques offered cash to be liberated from encomienda. Philip considered both offers before a bribery scandal ended the debate, but he explicitly rejected the encomenderos' demand for seigneurial jurisdiction.[28] While resigned to establishing some hereditary privileges in order to resolve his fiscal problems, Philip was not willing to devolve political jurisdiction over native subjects to Spanish settlers.

Instead, Philip extended the Castilian program of town governance. Conquering Spaniards founded towns and cities with elected governments (here known as cabildos), and the Crown placed royal officials in proximity. Lima's cabildo notoriously rejected its corregidor, arguing that it already hosted a viceroy and an audiencia that duplicated his function, but the office was installed elsewhere in the Spanish Americas. Initially corregidors even had jurisdiction over encomienda Indians, "in order to be aware of everything that happens in their districts, both civil and criminal, among Spaniards as between Spaniards and Indians, and between Indians and Indians, and the grievances they have from their encomenderos."[29]

This extension of jurisdiction was also part of an attack on cacical autonomy in the 1550s and 1560s. The Crown began by denying caciques jurisdiction over criminal offenses that called for severe physical penalties, as had happened to Castilian aljamas in the previous century.[30] Viceregal officials began enforcing this ban as a way to rein in caciques perceived as too powerful or too autonomous. The most infamous intervention came in Peru in 1566, when the administrator Dr. Gregorio González de Cuenca executed north-coast cacique don Juan Collique for putting his own subjects to death for a crime. While González de Cuenca was chided for overstepping his own jurisdiction in the case, it was clear that Indian justice was no longer autonomous.[31]

In 1565, Philip II inserted a specialized *corregidor de los naturales* at the provincial level, tasked with collecting tribute from Indigenous subjects and ensuring their Christian education and protection. These officials would oversee a juridical structure whose expressed intention was not to undermine Indigenous customary law. Instead it was to prevent the tyranny of caciques, curb abuses by Spanish priests and encomenderos, and dampen the rampant lawsuits by native litigants in the courts.[32]

The final key to governance came in 1573, when Philip II announced the end of conquest and the beginning of a reorganization of the Indies along the lines of republics, particularly linking Catholic reform (and specifically the objectives of the Council of Trent, 1545–1563) to the creation of well-designed cities and towns. Drawing upon conversations with advisors (including the incoming viceroy of Peru, Francisco de Toledo), Philip II issued a series of ordinances on "discoveries, new settlements and pacification in the Indies."[33] These set a template for the establishment of towns, which should have at least thirty vecinos (defined as the male settler, who would also bring his immediate family, including parents and other relatives who might live separately in the town). Physically the town would center on a four-square-league rectangle or square that would be subdivided into residential units, municipal commons and pasturage, and agricultural lands for each family. These small political units would be governed by elected and appointed officers drawn from the homogeneous community of vecinos who would work for the republic's common good.[34] The vecinos of large urban centers would mostly be Spaniards; in rural pueblos, they would be Indians.

Philip also undermined the encomenderos by turning them into salaried employees of the Crown with no authority over Indians. He similarly limited the power of caciques, to whom he also issued salaries in exchange for managing labor and collecting tribute. While caciques were still designated as natural lords they were stripped of most jurisdiction. Their subjects were turned into vecinos of *pueblos de indios* or Indian republics, to be governed by an annually elected cabildo alongside their hereditary caciques, much as Castilian nobles were required to govern their municipalities alongside a council of *pecheros* or commoners.[35]

Pueblos de indios became the means for transforming native communities into Christian tributaries under Christian leaders. Each town was required to build a church and receive a priest who was assigned to catechize and give sacraments. The Church's Third Council of Lima, held in 1583, further articulated the priests' duties to native communities, and ecclesiastic authorities created Indian church officers.[36] Beginning in the 1570s, the sons of caciques and other nobles were sent to boarding schools. El Colegio del Príncipe, the royal boarding school in Lima for the sons of the native nobility, was founded in 1610.[37] The education they received prepared them for their roles as monitors of their subjects' moral lives and also produced a literate elite class capable of acting in defense of its communities.

These reforms were intended to restructure Spanish American governance. Drawing upon nearly a century of debates and models, by no means fully implemented, the reforms telegraphed the Crown's intentions: to limit the heritability of the encomienda to three lifetimes, gradually abolishing the model; to gather native parcialidades into rural republics that would be governed by Indian alcaldes much as in cities and towns; and to attack the privileges of the caciques, who would be sidelined as functionaries who collected tribute and delivered labor.[38]

However, the ordinances were too optimistic about the ease of carrying out such impositions. Corregidores de los naturales dominated provincial authority, pueblos emerged as the major urban spatial form, even in the vertical Andes, and elected Indian leaders like alcaldes took office. But caciques were far from marginalized. Contemporaneous critics recognized that pushing hereditary authorities aside could be dangerous for the colonial project. One voice was that of Licenciado Francisco Falcón, the *Protector de Indios* (a Spaniard who served as legal advocate for Indians), who left critical commentary in the margins of a copy of Governor García de Castro's 1565 ordinances for corregidores. Falcón worried about the ramifications of restricting caciques too much, writing, "it ought to state what caciques are in charge of ordering and doing, and how all the Indians should respect and obey them as subjects, because to do otherwise would do them harm and turn the parcialidades into *behetrias* (communities governed by ad hoc military leaders, a synonym for disorder)."[39]

Whether because of hesitation from viceregal authorities or simply due to the impossibility of enforcement, the reforms did not end but rather reshaped Indigenous local rule. Caciques continued to exercise authority, particularly through their ability to claim property and litigate on their own and their communities' behalf. While they lost their standing as paramount lords, they strategized to retain their relevance. They did so alongside a widened vein of nobles and commoners seeking access to their limited power.

Jurisdictional Interventions

The holdings of Peruvian archives demonstrate that caciques were not sidelined. Caciques brought torrents of litigation on behalf of their subjects (and themselves), so much so that viceroys sought ways to "protect" them from lawyers and notaries. They allied and fought with encomenderos in their own battles for continued relevance, and they served as key informants for viceroys. Caciques stood, in the words of recent scholarship, among colonial "Indigenous intellectuals."[40] They were at the forefront of making Spanish legal practices intelligible in order to promote community interests.[41]

They often received their legal education in contests over cacicazgo succession, which were galvanized by the reshaping of native polities into pueblos de indios. The Crown declined direct jurisdiction over Indigenous succession practices. Philip III's 1614 explicit assertion that "customary law must be kept in the succession of cacicazgos" restated principles established by Philip II in 1557 and actions by others before him.[42] But the Crown retained the right to discern that customary law. In the pre-Hispanic Andes, kurakazgo succession was not formulaic, neither across regions nor over time. In many cases, a slate of candidates could stand for the office, and the kuraka, a council, or a paramount lord and his advisors determined the successor by taking into account political circumstances and candidates' abilities. Direct father-to-son inheritance could take place but was not presumed. This kind of contestation led to violence, with kurakas removed or murdered when their subjects or overlords considered them unjust or dangerous.[43]

While the Crown asserted its respect for local practices, in practice it favored direct father-to-son succession. The monarch and his representatives also reserved the right to intervene when royal officials deemed candidates inadequately Christian or temperamentally unsound, and when one candidate brought suit against another and requested intervention. The latter became a common phenomenon, and candidates and their legal representatives regularly presented petitions to receive the office to the corregidor. If he was unable to resolve the conflict, he took testimony and brought it to the Real Audiencia for a decision.[44]

These drawn-out experiences—often taking years of litigation—taught nobles the finer points of the legal system.

There were many claims to be pursued, particularly because encomienda and reducción divided or combined polities, transforming complex embedded hierarchies and diarchies into singular lineages. Older conflicts also returned. Inka rulers had previously removed and replaced local authorities whom they did not trust, and their descendants brought suit for a return to power.[45] High mortality rates and the ban on multiple wives for noblemen meant that, in many cases, there was no direct male heir from a recognizably married couple, making it difficult to present a simple narrative that pleased officials. As a result, men and women across the Andes consulted with legal agents and presented their candidacy, often arguing (truthfully) that it was continuous with pre-conquest practice. Many of these struggles reached the courts, where successful candidates learned to narrate a story that met the expectations and needs of the viceregal authorities, but also could be corroborated by the testimony of community elders.[46]

In the early years of contact, succession in parcialidades—the units formed of *ayllus* or kin groups, often in diarchies—functioned much as it had previously, barring direct interventions. In the Rimac Valley (likely ruled by dual kurakas before conquest), don Gonzalo Taulichusco left no direct heirs, but was grooming two nephews to succeed him.[47] Instead, he was succeeded by don Cristóbal Huacay, perhaps because the community deemed him more competent or because they were alternating lineages to accommodate both of the former diarchies. Either would have been consistent with pre-conquest practices.[48] But in the late sixteenth century, Viceroy Toledo formulated a more dependable process for designating successors. While he championed direct father-to-son succession, Toledo recognized the dissonance emerging over competing lineages with legitimate claims. The viceroy had his administrators conduct inquiries into the organization of highland Andean communities in the distant past, and into the changes brought by the Inka and Spanish conquests. They spoke with members of Inka lineages and other highland elites. This ethnography was foundational to a highly politicized program for reforming Andean polities.[49]

The narratives that Andean nobles passed to his colleagues, coupled with his own expectations about what constituted legitimate succession, underpinned the emerging rules Toledo shaped for cacicazgo succession. Building upon the work of contemporary legal scholar Juan de Matienzo, Toledo outlined three stages of Andean history: a first stage "without much order" characterized by a variety of forms associated with *behetría*, or governance without institutionalized succession; a middle stage of Inka tyranny, which provided order but under an illegitimate government; and Spanish rule, which provided both legitimacy and order.[50] The viceroy asked informants to describe the Inka conquest of their polity and how the Inka created local chieftainships: did he ratify kurakas already in office, or did he choose those leaders he wished to reward?[51] While Inka rule was deemed illegitimate, it could produce legitimate kurakas, those men wisely chosen by the Inka to rule for the good of their republics, and, in particular, those chosen by Topa Inka Yupanqui, whom Toledo understood to have created the modern system of "kurakas, caciques and principales."[52]

Candidates learned to engage with that language in their claims.[53] Where earlier postulants referred to a spectrum of local practices, by the late sixteenth century claimants had shifted toward a fairly narrow template, articulating an Indigenous "tradition" that resonated in Spanish ears. For example, when don Gabriel Martín fought for his cacicazgo in north coastal San Martín de Reque in 1595, he noted that his pre-Hispanic ancestor Zapque Zula appointed his son, Efquen Zula, "born to his wife who was legitimate in his law." This became a common, if obfuscating, way of turning the custom among Andean nobles to have many unranked female partners into a legitimate primary wife among a passel of secondary ones.[54] Sometimes this had surprising outcomes. The case of female *cacicas*, a somewhat unique feature of Peru's north coast, pushed out narratives of multiple unrelated male candidates in favor of a single, direct heir, who could be female in the absence of males.[55] Noble women successfully claimed the role of cacica across the colonial Andes, even where it had not previously existed. All sorts of pre-Hispanic practices continued to play a vital role in producing a legitimate present, but did so through translation into a mutually intelligible language of succession.[56]

Litigation from 1574 in Ichocchonta, in Recuay (Huaylas), demonstrates the learning process for Andean litigants.[57] The Huaylas-Recuay region was one of the great prizes of the conquest because of its dense and highly organized population, and the wealth of resources they managed. Pizarro kept the largest encomienda of Huaylas for himself, dividing Recuay between his two closest allies, Jerónimo de Aliaga and Sebastián de Torres, in 1538. In 1572, Viceroy Toledo sent Alonso de Santoyo to reduce Huaylas into fewer, larger units, creating new caciques out of the older pyramidal power structure.[58] He divided the thousand tributaries of Ichocchonta, a *guaranga* (large political unit of multiple ayllus) within the encomienda of Recuay, between two interim caciques, one a commoner named Martín Jurado and the other the nobleman don Juan Caxaguaraz, neither of whom was a direct descendant of the most recent caciques of the guaranga. These two fought with two other candidates, don Pablo Curas and don Gonzalo Roque Pariar, in a long and contentious litigation that came before the Real Audiencia in Lima in 1574. Jurado and Caxaguaraz eventually fell out of the suit, leaving Curas and Roque Pariar to debate succession.

Don Gonzalo laid out his case for succession through Chinchiraque, kuraka when Topa Inka conquered the region. Topa Inka "made no innovations but on the contrary validated [those already in office]." The Inka also presented Chinchiraque with a wife, Mallao Cuyor. This pair's son, Tarapacoy, succeeded him in the office, followed by his own son, Alachava, who was kuraka when Pizarro and the Spaniards entered Cajamarca. At the end of his long reign, Alachava was succeeded by his son don Lorenzo Malqui Yanar, don Gonzalo's father, who "possessed the cacicazgo for many years, and as its lord was in charge of collecting tribute for his encomendero."[59] Unfortunately for don Gonzalo, at his father's death he was too young to succeed in the position. Upon reaching adulthood, he presented himself as the legitimate cacique.

Don Gonzalo's narrative embraced the clear father-to-son descent that generically appealed to the viceroy and the courts. He (and his legal advisors) tied that simplified genealogy to key historical markers to assert his antecedents' willing and competent participation in Inka and encomienda life. It was a concise and transparent solution to the cacicazgo dilemma.

Yet it was not compelling. Don Gonzalo was bested by don Pablo Curas, who offered two different accounts of the history of the cacicazgo, an initial unsuccessful version, and then a second that he honed through the experience of litigation. The first account reveals the tensions that had long existed within the guaranga. When Chinchiraque was kuraka "at the time of Topa Inka," Ichocchonta was divided into two moieties, the second headed by Xulcapoma, and "they did not recognize that one was primary over the other, but were equal in degree."[60] Chinchiraque and Xulcapoma ruled together and were succeeded jointly by their respective sons, Tarapacoy and Caruarimango. But when Tarapacoy died his line was not replaced, leaving Caruarimango to govern alone. The dual cacicazgo ended.

Caruarimango died without living sons, leaving just an underage grandson (don Pablo Curas) who could not yet serve. Caruarimango's brother briefly held the cacicazgo. Malqui Poma then took office; don Pablo Curas coyly stated that this was "because he said that his ancestors were caciques," a point clarified by one of his witnesses as meaning that he was a relative of Chinchiraque, from the other side of the dual cacicazgo.[61] After Malqui Poma's death, don Lorenzo Malqui Yanar claimed the cacicazgo as Tarapacoy's grandson. Having erased the descendants of the second moiety, don Pablo Curas claimed that with Tarapacoy's death, the cacicazgo should be his.

These two narratives indicate different strategies. Don Gonzalo embraced a simplified genealogical approach designed to appeal to Spanish notions of descent. Don Pablo Curas' story revealed historical aspects of local politics, but he refused to link it either to Inka or Spanish administrations. Curas' choice probably reflected the Huaraz peoples' ardent resistance to Inka conquest, and connected the present to the more ancient past, bypassing the Inka and Spanish conquests.[62] While he revived the workings of the dual moiety to explain his own claim, he just as quickly discarded it when it might suggest power-sharing.

The Council of the Indies apparently wished to investigate don Pablo Curas' thread. Philip II wrote to Alonso de Santoyo in July 1574, requesting more testimony from nobles and elderly men in the neighboring communities in order to verify the "customary" form of succession in Ichocchonta "since the time of the Inkas and since the Spaniards entered into this land and by what order and reason it was, and the sons and brothers they had, and their descendants, and to whom at present [the cacicazgo] pertains and why."[63]

Don Pablo Curas and his advisors became aware that they had played the game wrong—their position was apparently stronger than the other candidates' but their discourse did not line up with the emerging Toledan consensus about succession. Don Pablo's legal team left no room for misunderstanding in their next set of interrogatory questions. They asked witnesses "do they know that after the death of Xulcapoma, Caruarimango, his firstborn son, succeeded in the said guaranga of Ichocchonta, which he had held and possessed in the time of the Inka, and when the Spaniards entered into the land and long after that, until he died?" And

> Did the witness know that at the time when the Marqués don Francisco Pizarro, governor of these kingdoms, gave the Indians of Chuquirraguay, where the guaranga of Ychocchonta is located, in encomienda to captain Juan de Aliaga, he gave him three guarangas, whose lords were Apocalla, the other Marcaoma, and of the third guaranga, of Ychocchonta, the lord was the said Caruarimango, grandfather of the said don Pablo Curas?[64]

Seven new elderly witnesses spoke in favor of this narrative, none bearing the title don and all requiring Quechua-Spanish interpreters.[65] Don Pablo Curas' ability to change gears and absorb the new language enabled the court to find in his favor. If don Gonzalo was initially more adept with the conquerors' legal discourses, don Pablo's revision offered both a sense of complex truth and the necessary rhetoric.

The suit over the cacicazgo of Ichocchonta demonstrates one way that caciques and other Indigenous actors learned to litigate in the sixteenth century. They presented narratives to the courts and their subjects that wove together aspects of their collective history with what they understood as colonial modes of legitimacy. Viceregal authorities were required to respect cacical jurisdiction when they found it intelligibly legitimate. Men and women who wished to be recognized as caciques and cacicas could only protect their jurisdiction by working through such a template. The caciques emerging from this crucible proved to be savvy at litigation far beyond protecting their own offices.

Litigating for the Community

Caciques also went to court on behalf of their subjects. They litigated tribute rates in the sixteenth century, arguing that respect for "use and custom" entailed paying a tribute rate no higher than that previously assessed by the Inkas. They contested population counts and sued when natural disasters destroyed their harvests. Cacical success in delaying or lowering tribute payments was one of the things that most irked encomenderos and officials, who sought to keep them away from lawyers and notaries and out of the courts. It also bound their subjects to them.

As Andean populations declined due to high mortality, migration, and concealment, caciques requested that the authorities re-inspect their communities and establish a new population count and *tasa*, or tribute schedule. Inspections could be excruciating for the communities that requested them. In addition to the usual costs of litigation, communities had to host the inspection team and suffer the loss of work time.[66] Nonetheless, many caciques demanded these interventions in order to lower tribute burdens.

In some cases, they claimed temporary extenuating circumstances due to natural disasters. After terrible rains and floods lasted more than a month in 1578, the native communities of the north coast sued to have their tribute refunded. Floods were not uncommon, especially during El Niño and La Niña cycles, but those inundations caused the rivers to overflow their banks, wiping out the year's harvest and damaging the irrigation system, which had to be repaired by labor mobilizations. According to their lawsuit, the communities lost significant resources: corn, beans, and sweet potatoes rotted in the fields and in storehouses; chickens and ducks starved to death; their homes and their church collapsed; and the canals were overwhelmed.[67] Laborers spoke of eating grass for three months while cleaning out the irrigation system. Nonetheless, the parcialidades continued to pay tribute in full during the deluge, though the encomenderos accepted cash in lieu of scarce commodities. The caciques accused encomenderos of converting the tribute rate to coin at market prices that were grossly inflated by the shortages. Some caciques took out loans or sold their own possessions in order to pay, and others were imprisoned for default. In compensation, they asked for the year's tribute to be returned to them. Their encomenderos opposed them, including doña Luisa de Mendoza, who responded that their losses were limited, that the "lazy Indians are enemies of work," and that the only hardship they suffered was drinking less *chicha* (corn beer) that year.[68]

More commonly, however, communities requested new population counts to prove their human losses. In 1594, the caciques of Huamachuco (in the northern highlands) demanded a reassessment after an epidemic of measles and smallpox. The viceroy took the radical measures of pausing tribute collection entirely until the new count could be made and of commuting much of the tribute in woven cloth to less labor-intensive wheat and corn. The new census showed a loss of nearly 20 percent in the tributary population over the decades, and the tasa was permanently lowered, to the indignation of the encomendera, doña Florencia de Mora y Escobar, who accused the caciques of hiding tributaries.[69] While some historians have argued that the dramatically high mortality rates that appear in some accounts are exaggerated, there is no doubt that epidemic disease and migration placed pressure on populations, and caciques took advantage of this fact—as well as their ability to conceal adult men—to bargain tribute rates downward.[70]

Caciques, then, went to court to protect and extend community rights. Collective interests could also coincide with or be entwined with personal interests. When don Gonzalo Taulichusco went to court between 1555 and 1559, he testified to his family's great service to the Crown: giving up their lands to build the city of Lima, fighting on the side of the king during the various uprisings that shook early Spanish rule, and diverting labor to build and sustain the new urban center. He concluded that he and his people "are exhausted and spent," his community having dwindled from 4,000 to some 200 Indian men "and because they cannot stand the said work many of my Indians have fled and left their houses, wives, and children." Given their exemplary service to the Crown and their inability to support themselves, he asked for a personal *merced* or financial recognition of his service, and his community's exemption from tribute.[71]

Property Regimes in the Courts

Caciques also exercised jurisdiction over the management and defense of property and resource rights, which included protecting claims against outsiders (Spaniards but also native competitors) and adjudicating use and distribution within their communities. In the century after conquest, lands and embedded resources were being expropriated in stunning ways, from outright seizure to onerous titling requirements to occupations and unauthorized sales.[72] Practices within the community also shifted, as subjects redefined their relationship to property. Both kinds of jurisdiction, internal and external, brought caciques to courts as plaintiffs and defendants, transforming land tenure and property law in the Americas.

When structuring its relationship to populated American territories, the Crown asserted control over vacant land while recognizing Indigenous dominium over the lands they put to productive use for their sustenance and for payment of an agricultural tribute. But that dominium had to be defended. Collective holdings had to be regularized by royal authorities who assessed the land's history and size and sold the community a title.[73] The Crown reserved the right to expropriate and sell lands it considered under- or unused. While native communities retained theoretical land rights, defending those rights in practice was expensive and restrictive.

Colonization also transformed Andean property regimes. Pre-conquest land tenure was not homogeneous, particularly differing between coast and highland, and is still not well understood.[74] While the coastal regions were nucleated and their leaders appear to have claimed land rights, distributing or renting them to community members and to outsiders, in the highlands members of an ayllu were often dispersed over large, non-contiguous territories at differing altitudes and ecological niches. Access to many productive zones allowed for raising a variety of commodities and animals that could be distributed within the ayllu rather than through a market. By some accounts, ayllus rotated plots assigned for individual and communal use depending upon family and community needs, productivity of lands, and environmental or weather patterns. In those cases, kurakas might be responsible for reassigning or recharacterizing plots, moving them between collective and individual use. And if some land was held collectively or rotated through families, the nobility seem to have had permanent possession of territories that were associated with status or office. Inka elites, for example, cleared residents from land they wished cultivated for themselves and created systems of permanent royal estates associated with lineage in the Cusco Valley.[75]

Spaniards tended to ignore this diversity, characterizing Andean approaches to land tenure as exotically communal. But their own practices in Castile were not radically different, though its settlements were far more nucleated. There the monarch claimed eminent domain over the kingdom, and municipalities held vast commons that their leaders assigned periodically among vecinos according to a variety of methods.[76] Nonetheless many Spanish commentators in the sixteenth century presented a simplistic dichotomy between civilized Spaniards, who embraced private property, and primitive Andeans, who were victimized by rapacious leaders.[77] The process of nucleation and relocation associated with reducción enabled both Andeans and Spaniards to reimagine land tenure, and gave royal officials a way to justify dispossessing caciques of their territories.

As the guardians of both territory and property relations, caciques found themselves challenged on many fronts. They faced pressure from their communities, which made historical arguments for the just management of resources but also saw opportunities for individual and group advancement by embracing innovations. They were surrounded by colonists who invaded their lands, offered desperately needed cash, or simply crowded them and usurped resources, making their holdings less productive. Royal officials responded with protective legislation, prohibiting them beginning in 1562 from selling any lands to any individual without specific license.[78] It is no surprise that leaders like don Gonzalo Taulichusco took dubious opportunities that ended up undermining his own community and his status.

The reducción movement of the late sixteenth century relocated communities and reassigned resources. In its wake, viceroys sent royal inspectors to carry out a process called *composiciones de tierras*. In conversation with caciques, local priests, and community members, these officials determined which lands were held collectively or individually or attached to the cacicazgo. They sold legal titles to those who could prove ownership or long-standing use, including community lands, and auctioned off any they determined unused. The funds raised by the sales went to the Crown, and the lands most often ended in Spanish hands. These meetings were notoriously contentious and some inspectors were accused of corruption. Composiciones not only altered property relations in communities but they gave caciques and commoners a legal language to argue about differences between private ownership and unalienable patrimony, as well as documentation that could stand up in court.

They also produced conflict, which brought communities into the courts to assert claims about tenure and ownership that could not be resolved internally. A case involving the community of Collique, reduced near Lima, is representative. In the 1590s, don Fernando Nacar, cacique of Collique, asked the Real Audiencia for title to a group of lands near Carabayllo, where his community had been resettled jointly with a rival ethnic group, the Huancayos. He claimed that an inspector had adjudicated the lands in his father's favor twenty years earlier, and that he had simply rented them to a number of Huancayo men to cultivate. Don Fernando's community, however, joined with the cacique of Huancayo in 1605 to argue that these were actually their commons: in practice, "if he sometimes rents or cultivates [them] he does so as cacique, not because they were his or he had right to them."[79]

The Audiencia found for don Fernando and against the community's definition, perhaps convinced by the documentation or by testimony from Spaniards and the cacique of Carabayllo that don Fernando had been cultivating the land for generations, and his usufruct rendered him permanent owner. If, as seems likely, the inspector had recategorized community lands as the cacique's private holdings decades earlier, the courts had little interest in overturning the ruling, particularly given the small size of the community. The court was far more comfortable with a privatization that placed the lands into a vibrant rental market.

Caciques were among the first Andeans to explore the opportunities of the new property regimes. They stood to gain wealth or power if they could convince officials that lands attached to their office or community were their own personal inheritance, or if they could sell off property to eager Spaniards under the table. But in their role as community leaders they also had to push back against processes like composiciones that threatened their self-sufficiency and turned Indigenous farmers to itinerant wage laborers or, worse, migrants. The numerous resettlements and titling inspections turned what should have been internal problems into issues for the courts, which were invested in commons only insofar as they were used in approved ways. Caciques had to defend themselves as supporters of their communities but also savvy investors. As they honed the legal language to make these cases, they participated in creating a body of law that governed property and resource management.

Unwritten Governance

Cacical jurisdiction around succession, tribute allocation, and certain kinds of property is well known because conflicts in those practices could end up in court. Other forms of jurisdiction are harder to identify. Titles issued to caciques and governors generally characterized their office as a model of Christian virtue and a curb on Indian vice. For example, when a cacica's husband was named governor in Jauja in 1629, his title stated, "nor should he allow [his subjects] to have other vices, punishing whatever they might be in the appropriate form."[80] In 1597, the guardian of the young cacique of Guaripampa (Jauja) received a title stating:

> I order that the caciques and principales of said repartimiento consider you and hold you as governor of the said pueblo and ayllu and the Indians that make it up, that they obey you and respect and revere and comply with your orders insofar as they do not contradict our holy Catholic faith and that all attend Christian catechism, forcing them to do so if necessary.[81]

Most important, caciques were responsible for collecting tribute and distributing labor, stopping idolatrous practices, and bringing their subjects to church.[82] Civil justice, conflict between members of a community, and minor criminal matters were ascribed to the Indian alcalde or judge, a position theoretically prohibited to caciques, but were likely handled by either.

Caciques' political jurisdiction was not a fiction nor was it under wholesale attack from Spanish or Andean political institutions. Viceregal authorities occasionally stepped aside, establishing the limits of cacical positive jurisdiction over their own communities. In the following case, the Real Audiencia did just that, demarcating cacical jurisdiction through its refusal to intervene.

In 1558, Andean nobleman don Francisco Tomabilca brought murder charges against his cacique, don Alonso Pariasca. The men lived in Piscas, near Cuenca.[83] Tomabilca made his complaint to Viceroy Hurtado, who created a commission to investigate the charges. Tomabilca was angry because don Alonso had stolen some lands from him—a field planted with coca—and had placed his mares in another of don Francisco's fields where they ate all his crops. Don Alonso had also, according to the complaint, stolen two pieces of clothing, his Indian servants, and three or four baskets of coca leaves, the last of these taken and destroyed "to irritate him." Don Francisco concluded with the statement that he raised the complaint because don Alonso had threatened to murder him, as he had previously murdered don Francisco's brother, Carbayana, in a drunken rage.

The viceroy's commission snapped into action at the final charge, interviewing witnesses who gave disturbing testimony about the violent, drunk cacique who whipped and burned a young boy, and then beat him to death with his co-conspirators. This would have been an egregious violation of the cacique's jurisdiction, which excluded corporal punishment of his subjects. But the witnesses also wished to discuss the complex civil charges, which had to do with changes to don Francisco's status within the community, and only two Andean men claimed to have been present at the purported murder. Don Alonso defended himself on the murder charges—the boy died from a mare's kick, he said—and ignored the claims regarding property. The courts cleared don Alonso due to the lack of evidence that Carbayana was murdered, and nothing else was the business of the royal court.

Don Francisco's other charges, clearly the reason for the false accusation of murder, bear examining. He stated that his father had enjoyed noble privileges under the regime of don Alonso's father, the former cacique. Those included the use of a coca field, servants, and some tribute in cloth. When don Alonso succeeded to the cacicazgo, he failed to extend those privileges to don Francisco. Don Alonso and the community more broadly interpreted this as a question of office: the cacique had the right to distribute privileges. In contrast, and with the courts in mind, don Francisco utilized the language of hereditary property, claiming that the field and servants were possessions he had inherited from his father. Had the courts had jurisdiction, they might have found favor with this slippage between office and individual, but it was not their issue to decide.

Plaintiffs often dangled bait before the high courts in this fashion as an adjunct to venue-shopping. Violence, idolatry, and immoral behavior were waved as red flags to get the attention of viceroys and judges to intervene in more quotidian problems. In 1569, two ayllus near the town of Anta in the Jauja Valley similarly turned an argument over resource allocation into a charge of torture and violence.[84] The Angaraes and Hananguancas had long had hostile relations, most recently stemming from a crisis over control of salt marshes. Don Diego Pucumucha, the cacique of the Angaraes, complained to the Real Audiencia that his community had been mistreated by don Pedro Chuquillanguy, cacique of the Hananguancas. The complaint, which referred to don Pedro by his Quechua name, Pucua Chuquillanqui (ignoring both his baptismal name and the Spanish honorific "don"), stated that the cacique, accompanied by "nearly one hundred" men from his ayllu and an unnamed mestizo man, had stormed onto Angarae fields seeking don Diego. When they did not find him, don Pedro seized and tortured an Angarae named Gonzalo Myche "in the way the Inkas used to do." Don Pedro and his entourage proceeded to the Angarae lands, where they stole potatoes, salt, and the tuber oca, and then burned the granaries.

Don Pedro's version of events was slightly different. He had recently won a lawsuit against the Angaraes for ownership of the salt marshes, and he and a Spanish judge named Martín Alonso were bringing the order issued by the corregidor of Huamanga to take possession of the lands. The two were accompanied by ten Hananguanca men and a mestizo translator. Don Pedro claimed that the Angaraes refused to allow him entry into the marshes, so he stood at the fence with Martín Alonso and made his official notification from there. Subsequently the Angaraes attacked, beat, and robbed don Pedro at his own home.

Most of the testimony concerned the cacique's illicit torture of Gonzalo Myche, supposedly tied up with a knotted hemp cord so tightly that it cut through his flesh to the bone. The charges depicted the cacique as an old-style tyrant overstepping his legal boundaries, even to the point of calling his torture method "Inkaic." Once again this seems to have been a ruse to get the courts to undermine the cacique. The Spanish judge and mestizo translator who were present could not corroborate the torture. Another man from a different ayllu testified that he had not seen or heard anything like torture at the site, but he had noticed one of the Angarae women adding fuel to the granary fire.[85]

Don Pedro countered that this was calling for interference in local problems. The Angaraes' case was built on perjury and false associations; they brought the charges "maliciously, as a pretext and to express grievances, and with their habitual cunning."[86] They invented their case "to obscure justice" and because they were accustomed "at any little problem to complain to the next Spaniard they pass."[87]

But the Angaraes also had a jurisdictional argument to make. Don Pedro had gone to royal authorities to resolve his dispute with them and then had walked the cedula onto their territory while bearing his staff of office, a violation of their jurisdiction. Don Pedro defended himself, noting that the Angaraes were under the corregidor's jurisdiction, and he was simply bringing his order to the community. The staff belonged to the Spanish judge, he said, not the cacique. That very corregidor, perhaps because of a relationship with the encomendero of the ayllus and the local priest, both supporters of the Angaraes, ruled against don Pedro, requiring him to pay restitution for the burned crops and exiling him for nine months. However, the Real Audiencia overturned this verdict, on the grounds that there was no clear witness testimony that torture took place. Once again, the highest court refused to intervene in matters they considered to fall within the cacique's jurisdiction.

These cases, while few, are important for establishing that jurisdictional limits were quite well known, enough so that enterprising litigants and their attorneys had to muddy the lines to gain attention. The cases often began with disagreements about hierarchy and the distribution of obligations, benefits, and resources. These clearly were civil matters for internal adjudication. Instead, complainants interspersed real and fictitious claims in the hopes of attracting the ear of a royal judge. The judges' refusal to intervene in local civil conflicts supports the argument that cacical jurisdiction was significantly more than collecting tribute and ensuring attendance at church.

The Castilian practice of multiplying republics as an instrument against aristocratic privilege provides the template for understanding native self-governance in its viceroyalties. The internal struggles over power in Castile helped create the multi-jurisdictional foundations for colonial rule in the Americas. In this sense, the 1570s, with Viceroy Francisco de Toledo's reforms and Philip II's ordinances on towns, was a pivotal conceptual moment that generalized the form of pueblos de indios, the Christian Indian republics that were staffed by elected officials with a jurisdictional as well as evangelical imperative.

But that is far from the whole picture. The caciques, hereditary elites of the Andes, were not sidelined. The most important local facilitators of the economic project of encomienda, they managed, along with other leaders, the needs of their communities. They also served themselves, earning the opprobrium of many colonial critics and their own subjects. Viceroy Conde de Nieva put the criticism succinctly in 1563: Indians had to be protected from their own caciques and nobles, for "these will rob them and not even leave them the wax in their ears."[88] But what they did so well was learn to represent themselves and their subjects in ways that their new overlords might find convincing and unthreatening.

Ironically, this massive effort of translation by caciques, who learned the new legal languages and markers and found ways to speak of their own past and present through them, hides their work from view. The entanglement of laws and customs erodes an insider's view of post-conquest society, although ethnohistorians struggle optimistically to disentangle the narratives. Unlike Iberian Muslims and Jews, native leaders could look to no external body of knowledge or network of believers. Even worse, caciques' ability to master the legal language of colonial administrators renders them invisible as community leaders, who distributed not only labor and resources but also privileges and sanctions. Only by reading the archival materials for silences and refusals—true markers of Andean jurisdiction—can some of their roles be recovered.

6

Entangled Authority in the Lima Valley

IN 1582, CATALINA GUALCUM was an elderly resident of Santiago del Cercado, not far from the ayllu of Sivillay (reduced into Carabayllo in 1573) where she had been born. She still owned four agricultural properties in Sivillay, inherited from her parents forty years earlier, or roughly a decade after Spaniards had entered the region. These were rented to Spanish tenants, but she worried that with her death they might drift permanently into their hands. She approached the city's alcalde ordinario, Garci Pérez de Salinas, to express these concerns. Her notarized statement, which served in lieu of a will, called upon the city's authorities to make sure that, on the occasion of her death, the lands would be turned over to the Jesuits at the Cercado, who would use them to pay for her funeral and other good works.[1]

Catalina Gualcum was worried about two increasingly common problems in the Lima Valley. First, Spanish individuals and Catholic institutions were rapidly amassing agricultural property by purchasing it from owners or at auctions or by simply expropriating it opportunistically. By the turn of the seventeenth century, much of the valley would be in non-Indigenous hands, increasingly concentrated into haciendas and worked with enslaved African or waged native labor. Her second fear likely came from within Sivillay; with her death, its cacique and Indian cabildo might absorb the land, or some distant relative could claim it according to local inheritance practices. She no longer wished to be subject to whatever mechanism her pueblo utilized for redistributing the property of its dead. Rather than trusting to the enforcement of a will, she called directly upon Lima's alcalde to ensure that the lands would be transferred to the Jesuits, one of the biggest landholders in the region. In effect, she asked the city's power brokers to enter her pueblo's jurisdiction in order to aid her soul's progress through purgatory, to undermine her natal authorities, to gratify an institution that had supported her, or all of these.

Republics of Difference. Karen B. Graubart, Oxford University Press. © Oxford University Press 2022.
DOI: 10.1093/oso/9780190233839.003.0007

The late sixteenth century was a transformative period in the valleys surrounding Lima. In the 1570s, under Viceroy Toledo, polities were relocated and placed under new governance. Caciques continued to hold their offices and exercise power in more limited ways, but they were joined by new leaders, often commoners, who represented the changing face of the pueblos. Required to represent their interests before Spanish authorities, the leaders of pueblos, whether caciques or Indian alcaldes, invoked customary law to engage with new political realities.

On many fronts, pueblos did what ayllus and parcialidades had done before the Spanish conquest: they organized mass labor as well as individual tasks, they supported those in need, they divided up resources and defended them from outsiders, they practiced reciprocity in various forms, they cared for orphans and widows, and they oversaw the distribution of inheritances. They differentiated among members through privileges, defining the basic social structure of the community. They managed their natural environment, from choosing crops and plowing fields to maintaining the acequias that irrigated them. They did all these things in a way that accorded with and regenerated their sense of justice. But they did so using new mechanisms, institutions, and vocabularies that allowed them to describe and defend their world to their conquerors.

This chapter shows how the reorganization of the Lima Valley into pueblos de indios created new polities that continued to make meaningful individual and collective decisions in the face of Spanish expropriation and hegemony. The introduction of new Spanish authorities, particularly Lima's corregidor de los naturales del Cercado, did not undermine their jurisdictions, although these became more curtailed and contested than in the immediate past. Cabildos, caciques, and individuals made both strategic and desperate attempts to assert justice under colonial rule. This brought them into conflict with migrants like Catalina Gualcum, intent upon using Spanish power to define her family land as private property she could transfer to the Jesuits, as well as with Spanish invaders and administrators. While there is little direct documentation of these struggles, the archives offers glimpses of those struggles to define relationships to resources, property, and power.

The Lima Valley at the Spanish Conquest

The establishment of Lima as a center of Spanish governance and commerce required the relocation of numerous communities, the seizure or reassignment of a great deal of labor, and the negotiation of many political relationships.[2] The small encomiendas of the valley were redirected to provisioning the city, especially with new crops like wheat and European domestic animals.[3] Native laborers constructed the city's buildings and infrastructure, connecting it with the port of Callao and the wealth of the Andes. They maintained and expanded the system of acequias and they turned Inka *tambos* (way stations) into inns to support masses of regional travelers. They did this in the company of Lima's new inhabitants, Spaniards and their Black slaves and servants, who arrived as word of Peru's wealth spread.

As communities shrank, they lost control of their resources. Spanish entrepreneurs, including religious orders, hit upon the strategy of capturing land in the coastal valleys and requisitioning, buying, or hiring native and Black labor. This resulted in the early development of massive *haciendas* and *estancias*, plantations and ranches. The loss of the Andean señoríos, the confederations that had coordinated resource use among the many parcialidades of the three valleys, left numerous small and dislocated cacicazgos. Lima's most powerful vecinos demanded labor, land, and access from local caciques, who now operated as isolated powerbrokers with limited resources.

By 1549 the polities of the valley were already vulnerable. A tributary census carried out that year noted that Taulichusco's parcialidad, granted in encomienda to doña Francisca Pizarro (the daughter of Francisco Pizarro and Inés Huaylas Yupanqui) had only ninety tributaries, annually required to provide 30 pesos in cash, 400 *fanegas* (600 bushels) each of corn and wheat, 5 fanegas (7.5 bushels) of beans, 420 fowl, and regular deliveries of fish and eggs.[4] They also supplied eight persons to serve in the encomendera's household and guard her cattle. While encomienda did not legally entitle holders to anything beyond labor, doña Francisca's assignment suggested that tribute was not the most robust aspect of the grant. The document noted that "should the encomendero [*sic*] desire to plant more wheat or corn in the said valley using oxen, he [*sic*] may do so without damaging the Indians and their lands and water sources." Conflicts over territory

Table 6.1 Tributary Populations
of Valley Encomiendas, 1575

Encomienda	Tributaries (Adult Males)
Surco	479
Magdalena	246
Carabayllo	184
Maranga	133
Late	86
Lurigancho	83
Pachacamac	162

Source: Keith, *Conquest and Agrarian Change*, 34; Sánchez-Albornoz, "La mita de Lima."

and resource use were already beginning to surface, and royal administrators took notice.

In 1573, Viceroy Toledo ordered the many small parcialidades reduced into six colonial pueblos de indios: Magdalena, Surco, Late, Lurigancho, Carabayllo, and Pachacamac.[5] In accordance with Philip II's ordinances, these were set out in imitation of Spanish towns to encourage policía in their inhabitants. Their populations were also counted to set tribute rates and establish the number of laborers who would be sent to the city for the mita each year.

No written acts of foundation remain from the pueblos de indios of the Lima Valley, but the archives provide evidence of the particularities of these sites and especially the ways that specific communities addressed their changing needs through acts of governance. If the founding of the Christian town was intended to erase old practices embedded in the landscape, the struggle to maintain local control left an imprint.[6]

Table 6.2 The Reorganization of the Lima Valley

Cacicazgo	Ayllu	Reducción (1573)
Lima	Maranga	Santa María de Magdalena
	Guadca	
	Amancaes	
	Huala	
Surco	Calla	Santiago del Surco
	Centualli	
	Ydcay	
	Cucham	
Ate	Guancho Guaylas	Santa Cruz de Late
	Pocorucha	
Lurigancho	Huachipa	Lurigancho
	Tantacaxa	
Carabayllo	Colli	San Pedro de Carabayllo
	Chiquitanta	
	Huancayo	
	Sivillay	
Pachacamac	Sutca	Pachacamac
	Manchay	
	Caringas	

Sources: Rostworowski de Diez Canseco, Señoríos indígenas; Charney, Indian Society, 33.

The Reorganization of Space and Status

Pueblos were founded through a ritual act of physical disruption, often a symbolic act of possession (the pulling of grass, moving of rocks, or slashing of trees with swords) marking out the limits of the municipality, laying a cross or stone on the site of the future church and other key buildings, establishing justice by erecting a pillory for the public punishment of criminals, and recording the names of the founding citizens.[7] The site would be divided or gridded, with lots designated for particular citizens' homes and lands as well as commons and pastures.[8]

Creating the pueblo de indios required choosing a proper site with adequate water, fertile land, pastures, and woodlands for the size of the target population. Once that was accomplished, Toledo ordered, the inspectors

> will give orders to plan the said towns according to their wide and straight streets and blocks, indicating the number [of blocks] for the plaza and a place for the church, if there is not already one, and for a house for the priests, and a plot for the community meeting space, and cabildo, and the tribunal for the alcaldes that they must have, and a jail with separate cells for men and women, and yards for the service of the jail, and a chamber for the jail keeper.[9]

They would lay out a large house for the cacique and smaller, detached homes with doors on the street for commoners. Houses could have a small garden but, for health reasons, humid agricultural lands were to be located a distance from the town. Officials were instructed to seize any community lands that were too far from the reducción to be easily maintained. Those could be distributed to anyone who could prove, with a title, that their lands had been seized to create the town. The new pueblos de indios would not only bring together scattered native populations to create efficient labor forces and accomplished converts, but would be a spatial reminder of Spanish domination and governance.

Juan de Matienzo, a judge of the audiencia of Valladolid and Charcas, best articulated the juridical bases for this reorganization in 1567. He believed that the former lords of the land had been tyrants, and their aristocratic descendants were corrupt and lazy, but he understood that their legitimacy could be harnessed for Spanish purposes. Rather than entirely undermined, caciques should be left in their señorío to collect tribute, to "be lazy, and drink, and tell stories," and "govern in general but not command in particular."[10] New experts would command, trained in modern policía, and particularly in reading, writing, and Christian devotion. In a sketch, he showed how these men and Spanish authorities would

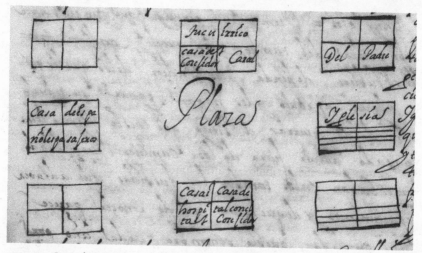

FIG. 6.1 Juan de Matienzo's Schematic Layout of Pueblos de Indios. From Juan de Matienzo, *Gobierno de Perú* [1567] Reprinted with permission of Obadiah Rich collection. Manuscripts and Archives Division. The New York Public Library. Astor, Lenox, and Tilden Foundations.

anchor the town with buildings to house the priest, the corregidor, a *tambo* or inn, a hospital, a jail, a cabildo, and a *tucurico* or manager of Indian labor.

Andeans would carry out the physical organization and construction. In terms of the distribution of plots, Spanish administrators recognized that they were not the best able to judge "the qualities of the persons," in the words of one founding act, beyond the obvious.[11] When Viceroy Toledo personally reduced highland Huamanga in 1570, he required consultation with "the caciques and nobles and Indians of the district" along with the "provisor and inspector of the bishopric and the priests and religious of the parish, and the corregidores of the Indians and their encomenderos." Once the plan was agreed upon, the viceroy turned the project over to the parish priest, but community members constructed their houses together under the direction of their caciques and nobles.[12] In the residential cores of these towns, they could occupy the space according to their own rules.[13]

New Politics for New Towns

New political leaders would oversee this landscape. Instead of a single (or dual) hereditary leader, a group of men would have to compete for annually elected terms, cycling through the prestigious offices over their adult careers. According to Toledo's instructions, each year on New Year's Day, following mass, the previous year's elected alcaldes and regidores would join the corregidor at the cabildo offices and elect a slate of two alcaldes, four regidores, one alguacil, a procurador, and a mayordomo. A notary "or *quipucamayo*" would be appointed as well; the special skills needed for this office made it a permanent rather than elected job. In some locations, a native procurator or attorney would also be elected, a person with enough legal knowledge to represent the community in court.[14] The persons receiving the most votes from the slate of sitting officers would swiftly be sworn in and begin their terms. Unbaptized Indians were ineligible for any office, and caciques were theoretically ineligible for the offices of alcalde and regidor. Nobles were ordered "not to interfere in the elections of the alcaldes, regidores, and other offices of the republic, nor to campaign for any candidates." Other restrictions attempted to keep close relatives and members of the same ayllu from dominating the slate.[15]

Despite wishing to sideline caciques, Andean administrators did not favor raising up commoners. Francisco Falcón, the legal advocate for Indians, noted that candidates for cabildo offices should be noblemen, *indios principales*, "because beside the fact that the other Indians are quite poor and very uneducated, the change would be great if the *hatun runas* [Quechua, commoners], who have and have had so much respect for the caciques, suddenly came to dominate the caciques."[16] Since alcaldes were to be first-instance judges, they required a lettered education and legitimate authority. Even so, that first-instance jurisdiction came to be defined as acting "solely to make inquiries, take into custody, and bring delinquents to the jail of the district's Spanish town, though they may punish any Indian who misses mass on a feast day or gets drunk or a similar fault, with a day in prison or six or eight lashes of the whip."[17]

But the bright line that Spanish viceroys sought between caciques and cabildos was largely flouted. In areas with small populations, there were rarely enough eligible adult men to staff so many positions each year. Coastal nobles successfully sought offices in their cabildos and confraternities precisely because they had so few other routes to power and wealth compared to caciques of the highlands.[18] Even if the office paid little, it offered exemption from tribute and service, an important status marker at a time when elite privileges were diminishing. The son of a cacique from the nearby highlands of Guamachuco applied to be alguacil mayor in 1581; the position allowed him to bear the symbolic staff of office as well as enjoy exemptions that a member of a noble family would have enjoyed automatically in earlier times.[19] And cabildo members worked in concert with caciques to accomplish various community tasks. In 1602, the cacique, principales, and alcaldes of Surco jointly signed paperwork ordering a cedar and gold altarpiece for its church, likely drawing on the holdings of their community treasury.[20]

Setting Cabildo Limits

Indian cabildos were the first-instance courts for civil matters within communities. Above them sat a royal appointee, the corregidor de los naturales. Part of an apparatus intended to protect native people from both Spanish and cacical rapaciousness, the corregidor was a confirmation of and check upon Indian officeholders. Given the size of the provinces corregidores were assigned to supervise, they probably left most communities alone. Lima's corregidor was intended to physically visit each of the thirteen valley repartimientos on the first day of every January to confirm elections, a long journey in desert heat that seems unlikely.[21] His larger purview was to enforce restrictions on Indians, such as those on the sale of land and the purchase of African slaves, as well as to adjudicate local issues that crossed or sat between Indigenous jurisdictions. The two sets of extant records from his office in the late sixteenth and early seventeenth centuries, notebooks left by the notaries Rodrigo Castillejo (who held the office at least between 1596 and 1602) and Cristóval de Piñeda (1612–1613), demonstrate the evolution of the office over its first forty years, but also hint at its limits.[22] Their silences indicate the spaces that must still have been reserved for caciques and Indian cabildos.

The corregidor's tribunal was distinct from Mexico City's contemporary Juzgado General de Indios, the General Indian Court, created by Viceroy Luis de Velasco in 1591 to adjudicate native claims across New Spain.[23] Men and women across Mexico used the court energetically to seek protection and justice, presenting their cases to the viceroy and his legal assistant. Velasco, upon becoming viceroy of Peru at the turn of the seventeenth century, requested a similar tribunal for the Andes.[24] The court was enacted in Lima under the auspices of the newly created corregidor de los naturales del Cercado, but its scope was far more limited. Its geographic reach was not all of the Andes, but only greater Lima. Nor did he exercise a broad judicial mandate, either because he was not intended to do so, or because Indigenous clients did not trust him. There is some evidence it was the latter case. In 1657, don Felipe Carguamango, a sergeant in the Indian infantry company, wrote to the king requesting to be named alcalde mayor "with exclusive jurisdiction" over Lima and its rural environs within five leagues of the city. He claimed that the position was needed "for the support of the Indians, and for many who are outside this city, who do not dare to enter it to request (resolution for) their harms."[25] Instead, the corregidor initially focused on controlling vagrancy and informal employment, and then moved to manage the flow of resources (especially property) between communities and outside of cabildo jurisdiction.

In the beginning, the corregidor oversaw the kinds of urban labor contracts that the city's Indian alcaldes had previously managed, placing native children and the underemployed into jobs and apprenticeships. In 1596–1597, corregidor Alonso de Mendoza Ponce de León wrote labor contracts for 115 native adults and children, twenty-five of them for apprenticeships and the rest for a variety of arrangements including domestic service, short-term farm labor, and work contracts between artisans. The placements were most often with Spaniards, but also included native and Black masters.[26] Notary Castillejo also drew up paperwork allowing thirty-two Indigenous individuals and communities to rent agricultural lands to others, again mostly to Spaniards. The corregidor issued a small number of manumission papers for enslaved men and women freed by Spanish owners, licensed sales contracts of Black slaves to Spanish and (in one case) free Black purchasers, arranged legal tutelage for native minors, oversaw the will of a cacique, and wrote up powers of attorney for Andean plaintiffs in litigation. His main charge in this period was overseeing anti-vagrancy employment policy and licensing the sale of Indian lands.

With the opening of the tribunal, the corregidor's purpose became more complex. In 1603, Viceroy Velasco named the sitting corregidor of the Cercado, Josephe de Ribera, to be the city's first *juez* (judge) *de los naturales*.[27] Thereafter, every corregidor attached to the Cercado also served as judge, assisted by an Indian alcalde mayor.[28] The first Indian alcalde mayor was Andrés Ramírez Inga, named in 1602.[29] His job description called upon him to help the corregidor move Indians into the Cercado from informal housing around the city and collect their tribute, much like a regular alcalde, but he was also invited to provide legal assistance to resolve conflicts extrajudicially. In other locations, alcaldes mayores acted as pro bono defenders for Indians.[30] Ramírez Inga might well have done so, too, although his position was officially intended to deflect lawsuits away from the courts.

Over the course of sixteen months in 1612–1613, corregidor de Ribera's notary drew up numerous documents, of which 107 are legible and intact. Twelve of these were contracts between Spaniards, especially royal officials. In March 1612, he drew up a contract between the viceroy and a silversmith to make a variety of objects, including silver pillars for the viceroy's bed.[31] Fourteen contracts were written between two or more Indigenous parties or for a single Indigenous individual, such as a will. But the vast majority, eighty-one, were contracts between one Andean and one Spanish party. The corregidor's docket in 1612–1613 was dominated by situations wherein native residents of the valley's pueblos left the jurisdiction of their cacique or Indian alcalde, and required Spanish authority to approve or legitimate that act, such as contracting for work in the city or renting property to someone outside their community.[32] Far from undermining pueblo authority, the corregidor simply managed cases where a single pueblo lacked jurisdiction.

Although less frequently than before, the corregidor still oversaw apprenticeships and labor contracts. These included placing an Andean lute-maker in
Potosí for a year, an "Indian" (Filipino) butcher from Manila hired by a Spaniard
to slaughter animals for the Easter season, and two native men from coastal
Lunaguaná who went into partnership with the Spaniard Antonio de Clavijo to
farm his lands in Late.[33] The corregidor's focus shifted to activities that were prohibited to, or restricted for, Indigenous subjects, especially the management of
land. His work accompanied the first wave of *composiciones de tierras*, the royal
process for assessing, expropriating, and titling land to native individuals and
communities.

The viceroy carried out the first composición in the Lima Valley in 1590. Each
community had to present proof of ownership of lands and defend its need for
them. Individuals also could present proof of their private ownership of plots. An
inspector adjudicated each case, issuing titles for a fee to some, and setting aside
what he judged excess land to be auctioned. With title in hand, communities
and individuals could enforce sales, gifts, and inheritances in court.[34] Catalina
Gualcum, writing eight years before the first composición, likely did not have
the title to the four fields she wished to donate to the Jesuits, or she would have
simply made that arrangement without the alcalde's help. But titles did not confer
legitimacy in everyone's eyes. In 1596, when Constança Ticlla willed a small field
to one of Surco's Indian officers to compensate some unstated debt, she noted
that she had inherited the lot from her late father and had her ownership confirmed by the land inspector, but still urged "may neither my heirs nor anyone
else impede [the gift]."[35] A land title might be valid evidence in civil or ecclesiastic
court, but could still be contested within the community.

The corregidor de los naturales enforced the restrictions on the use of Indian
lands, which a royal order had clarified in 1609. Any lands distributed to individuals or the community as a collective could not be sold or rented to a Spaniard
without the viceroy's approval.[36] The corregidor's records authorize no sales during this period, though informal and illegal arrangements were common. Instead,
his records indicate that a rental market was flourishing. In 1611–1612, members
of the pueblos of Magdalena, Lurigancho, Surco, Late, Pachacamac, and Guadca
all appeared before the corregidor to rent lands to Spaniards. Coastal communities needed cash more than they needed land, which required scarce labor and
other inputs to be productive. These rentals, as much as sales and seizures, transformed the valley's economy.

Rentals could be quite extensive, as when Antonio de Clavijo rented twenty
fanegadas from the community holdings of Pucurucho, a tiny ayllu that was
reduced into the pueblo of Late.[37] Clavijo owned lands in the valley and rented
many more. He occasionally rented land back to Andean workers, as he did to

Diego Cancha Sacsa of Late, who rented twelve fanegadas from Clavijo in his own town.[38] Individuals like Clavijo, as well as representatives of the religious orders, were strategically buying or renting all the land they could as they began the process of building the haciendas and vineyards that would soon dominate the landscape and commercialize agriculture.[39]

Viceregal officials worried about Spanish landowners and renters strangling coastal pueblos' ability to sustain themselves. But many native individuals as well as communities chose this strategy, and not only under duress. For widows, rents were a source of secure income from lands they could not work. Magdalena Picona of Late declared in 1630 that she had purchased lands from an encomendero, but "I can no longer cultivate the eleven fanegadas of land as I am single and widowed," and had long rented them to Jorge Márquez, a Spaniard. Márquez paid her in advance and offered small loans to cover the costs of her "necessities in illness and to feed and dress myself."[40] Similarly doña Ana Collon of Magdalena owned eight fanegadas in the Guatca Valley, which she rented for many years to the Spaniard Pedro Ximenez Menacho. The tenant paid in advance and above the agreed-upon price. She gratefully left him a small piece of the land in her will.[41]

Most of the pairs who came to the corregidor to write up these rental contracts consisted of a Spanish man and an Indigenous man or woman, seeking enforceable contracts with the dominant authorities. Rentals between members of the same pueblo would have been contracted before native authorities or arranged informally. But when parties from different communities contracted, they also chose to approach the corregidor. One illustrative contract also provides evidence that pre-conquest political organization continued to have valence long after reducción. Francisco de Sálazar and don Esteban Guaca, both residents of Magdalena, asked the corregidor to notarize a rental agreement. Each man was a member of a different ayllu reduced into Magdalena, and they were governed by distinct caciques even if they lived in the same pueblo.[42] The corregidor was the sole person with jurisdiction in this case.

Finally, two cases demonstrate that the corregidor might have exercised more jurisdiction than is evident in the notarial records. Both of these were attempts to keep Indigenous civil and criminal litigation out of the courts. On one occasion in 1612, Ribera's notary drew up a property donation from Pedro Alonso, originally of Lurigancho, to his sister Madalena Pazña. It turned out to be the resolution of a painful argument between the siblings over their parents' estate. Pedro Alonso had moved to Lima and lost touch with his family, and when their parents died, his sister had claimed the estate. Pedro Alonso eventually approached the Protector de Indios to begin litigation over his share of the inheritance. Instead, the corregidor helped the parties work out an agreement. He wrote up the property donation such that Pedro Alonso received his share of the inheritance, but then donated it to Madalena in exchange for her agreement to care for him in his current illness.[43]

The second was a criminal case later the same year. Juan Bañol, an African-born enslaved man owned by the Spaniard Juan Pérez de Cometa, was accused of murdering Pedro Llanpen, one of a group of native men who had spent the night in their fields in Guancho Guaylas to protect their crops from theft. Around midnight they got into a fight with Juan Bañol, accusing him of stealing from them. In the conflict, Juan Bañol punched Pedro Llanpen in the throat, choking him to death. Juan Bañol sought sanctuary in the monastery of San Francisco, and the farmers demanded justice. In collaboration with the corregidor, Juan Bañol's master offered the men a settlement of 70 pesos, for which they agreed to drop the case and avoid a lengthy trial.[44]

The jurisdiction of the corregidor de los naturales reflects the ongoing concerns of royal authorities about native peoples. His office was intended to keep them from being exploited by greedy leaders or outsiders, and to promote notions of policía including work discipline and wage labor. He also raised revenues, redistributed land, and tried to curb Indigenous litigation. But his jurisdiction did not enter into the internal civil affairs of the pueblos. There, instead, caciques and cabildos maintained their own systems, however narrow and relatively impoverished.

Property Regimes in the Lima Valley

The new authorities who emerged to guide the pueblos managed all manner of resources, distributed tribute obligations, organized collective businesses, and facilitated litigation. They also oversaw changing property regimes. In part this reflected physical changes: dispersed coastal communities, organized around fictive kin units, were concentrated and nucleated, and their many cacicazgos were edited to produce singular lines of authority. In addition to removing distant agricultural properties, viceregal authorities introduced urban towns whose lands were not associated with a community's historical forms of social organization. Their occupants, however, relied upon local memories and knowledge to govern their use.

The new town of Santiago del Surco, for example, drew upon its customs to manage physical resources. Surco's urban private residences were constructed around 1573, and they began to appear in Indigenous wills by the 1590s. Three wills produced in 1596 alluded to houses within the town and burial in its church, evidence that the urban nucleus was functioning as intended.[45] But litigation from 1603 offers a rare glimpse of the process by which these lots had been distributed. Surco was the largest reducción in the valley, composed by bringing together four ayllus, each headed by its own cacique. The litigation was prompted by the death of Juan Cuchi, who left no children. His nephew Domingo Yucana went to court to get possession of Juan Cuchi's house in the town, but he was challenged by a female relative, Ynes Nacay. Testimony from seventy-year-old Pedro Hucho clarified the claims. When Toledo was viceroy, don Diego Tabel, governor of the pueblo, had "indicated and given solares to each parcialidad and ayllu, and a site in which they might build houses in the said pueblo of Surco."[46]

In keeping with the distribution, Cuchi and his brother received a plot "in the site where the Indians of their said parcialidad were and lived."[47] Ynes Nacay likewise lived on that solar, but she married Martín Pacal, who was subject to another cacique. Custom required her to give up her relationship to her ayllu and move to that of her husband. Domingo Yucana, son of the brother who resided with Juan Cuchi, demanded possession of the solar, accusing Ynes Nacay of attempting to evade paying tribute to her new ayllu. The town's Indian alcaldes decided the lawsuit in Yucana's favor. Ynes Cuchi appealed the finding to the corregidor and the Real Audiencia, and both upheld the alcaldes' position.

The resolution reveals three key facts. First, the original act of foundation and distribution was carried out through ayllus and parcialidades, whose relationships were reinforced even as the compound community was being reorganized by viceregal authorities. Second, the political structure of Surco was transforming because of reducción and urbanization, but this process overlaid new roles (alcaldes, regidores) on still-existing older ones (caciques, governors).[48] Third, the internal compound ayllu structure continued to matter three decades later despite population loss and the embrace of new forms of property. While Juan Cuchi's house had become heritable property, it remained subject to the customary law that had created it and Spanish authorities stood ready to enforce this particular definition.

The resettlement of ayllus into pueblos de indios was intended—as it also was in Spanish towns—to allow for certain kinds of local practices to continue within and alongside the structures. Because of Spain's commitment to customary law, communities managed resources according to these beliefs. Migrants like Catalina Gualcum might prefer different outcomes, leading them to invoke urban authorities against the Indian leaders of their towns. More generally, native residents along the coast uneasily adapted their relationships to property, land, people, and resources by entangling their beliefs with those of their conquerors.

Community Property Strategies

Not all post-conquest collective strategies hewed to some older practice, nor did they necessarily represent interests that were clearly opposed to those of Spaniards, themselves a diverse lot. The treatment of property in documents from the late sixteenth and early seventeenth centuries demonstrates a tendency to mix heterogeneous strategies, drawing upon a variety of knowledges and interests. The array of descriptions of land tenure and use that appear in colonial documentation reflects how colonized subjects interacted with their new legal environment. Some of these changes were forced upon them, and ultimately all post-conquest property rights depended upon a relationship with Spain's institutions.[49] But the entanglement between Spanish and Indigenous conceptions of property also represents collective attempts to assert self-governance and control over resources.

Don Gonzalo Taulichusco's will offers a rich early example of such an eclectic approach to property as a response to crisis. He had claimed in documents placed before the courts in the 1550s that he, as cacique, owned much if not all of the land in the Rimac River Valley prior to the Spanish conquest. Many witnesses supported this claim, which he put forward as grounds for a grant rewarding his services to the Crown as well as for compensating his losses.[50] His will tells a much more complex story.

Don Gonzalo described his most valuable assets using the following categories: lands he received as a grant (merced) from the Real Audiencia; those he inherited from his father Taulichusco; those he owned without clarification; those he owned collectively with other subject parcialidades; land that belonged solely to his Indian subjects; land that his father left to minors, naming him as guardian until they reached adulthood; enslaved Black men and women purchased with his own money; herds of animals that might be his personal property or might belong to the community; crops that were sown with the labor of his subjects in a business arrangement with a Spaniard; and houses built with his subjects' labor.

In brief, he claimed personal ownership only of lands granted directly to him by Spanish authorities or those he inherited individually from his father, and of enslaved humans whom he had purchased. An entire category of land was not listed in his will, namely, those parcels attached to the cacique's office, which would automatically go to his successor. He also made clear that some of the lands over which he claimed authority actually belonged to other collectives, such as the parcialidades subject to him as paramount lord but under their own caciques. The will suggests a real struggle over definitions. Don Gonzalo had violated his community's understanding of land tenure, but he also took care to transform some of his unqualifiedly personal holdings into community wealth.

He was also careful to recognize that labor produced ownership in certain cases. For example, his brother Guachinamo's subjects had constructed his home in Lima. He ordered the value of the house to be split between his nephew and the men who had built it. He similarly left the crops resulting from joint agricultural projects with Spaniards to be divided among the Spanish owners and the Indians who labored in the fields.

Don Gonzalo made a few individual legacies, including a gift of a mare to his *criado* Diego, who had "served him since he was a child." The Spanish term criado implied a form of fictive kin and the cacique might have been using the concept to explain an older relationship between Andean nobles and the subjects assigned to care for them.[51] Don Gonzalo left Diego's service to his widow doña Juana, with the admonishment that no other cacique should demand his labor "because the said Diego is and has been his criado" and that Diego was exempt from tribute payments. At a time when caciques were increasingly criticized for their demands of personal service from their subjects, don Gonzalo asserted Diego's position within the pyramidal structure of the macroethnicity, attached not only to the office but to the family. Although the gendered aspects of coastal property inheritance are not well known, don Gonzalo took care to leave his personal merced to his wife, doña Juana. He did not do so in the manner of a Spanish legacy, which might have established what property had been hers prior to marriage and what community property was gained during the marriage to parse out her share, but as a pure gift.[52] He left a share of the corn being grown on his land to doña Juana and to Diego, and left the rest to the community.

Don Gonzalo transformed most of his property into a community resource, a kind of sapci. He expected that his houses, his slaves, and some of his lands would be sold at auction and the funds distributed to his subjects "so that they may pay the tribute or do with it whatever seems best to the executors." This liquidation, which represents a true break with the ways that property was dealt with in the pre-Hispanic valley, was a desperate measure, a call to rethink strategies. By tossing much of his herds, his lands, his houses, and his slaves into a pot to be redistributed as community wealth, and potentially as individual wealth, don Gonzalo was acknowledging his inability to protect his community. That he left the decision-making to a Catholic priest and the cacique of the largest surviving community as his executors was a testament to his belief that the answer would have to come from shared knowledge and separate interests.

Don Gonzalo was not alone in collectivizing resources as a kind of sapci, a practice with resonances in Spanish as well as Andean law. Indigenous leaders were using liens known as *censos* to raise collective funds for their communities.[53] The cacique of Late, don Cristoval Xutu Chumbi, was forced to sell lands in order to settle a debt with a Spaniard in the middle of the sixteenth century. When he did so, he attached a censo whereby any owner or renter of the property paid annual fees into the community's treasury, assigned toward each of its three ayllus.[54] In 1584, the community petitioned for, and received, permission to withdraw funds to restore and improve their church, and to purchase eighteen scythes and four plows for their wheat harvest. The cacique's family also requested personal withdrawals from the funds to support them after his death. Similar censos benefited numerous communities, creating stopgap flows of income as populations became smaller and poorer.[55] But communities had to couch their petitions in acceptable language to gain access to the funds, making them less fungible than don Gonzalo's transformation of his collective property into individual grants. Native peoples had limited control over these new forms of sapci.

Competition over Resources

Pueblos de indios defined and then collectively defended or managed other resources still under their administration. Two particular cases are clarifying, those of the acequias or canals that kept the desert coast irrigated and the tambos, or inns, that housed the streams of travelers passing through Lima. In both cases, pueblos de indios faced crises over resources and had to articulate their common good and imagine how to strategize against the demands of other parties.

Water was arguably the valley's most valuable resource. For generations, coastal Andeans had made desert lands productive through complex irrigation projects that channeled melted snow from the mountains down to their arid fields. Four acequias carried water from the Rimac River to private and collective holdings. Prior to the Spanish conquest these systems likely defined political communities, each taking responsibility for maintaining and repairing the canal that fed their fields. They also established reciprocal bonds within or across communities, which continued into the early years of Spanish occupation.[56] Don Gonzalo Taulichusco assigned lands to the Cañari, Indigenous soldiers who settled in Lima after they assisted Pizarro in the conquest. In exchange he required their help maintaining the canals under his jurisdiction.[57] As late as 1566, the cacique of Mala offered land to the nearby community of Coayllo in exchange for similar assistance.[58]

Conquistadores had strategically planned Lima so that its highest-status residents would draw water from two principal acequias, giving its cabildo control over and responsibility for the city's water supply.[59] Spaniards acquired more rural lands and placed thirsty domestic animals in the valley, demands that stressed the old system for adjudicating use and organizing maintenance. Spaniards enlarged and covered the canals, and Lima's cabildo declared that water conflicts came under its own jurisdiction, creating the position of water judge in 1556.[60] The monarch, who considered all water his own dominion, charged the protector de indios and the corregidor de los naturales with ensuring that the pueblos de indios retain access to water. Conflicts were common, but usually resolved by sending a city official to adjudicate what had long been the realm of Indigenous señoríos.

In the seventeenth century, the competition over water became desperate. The same canals served both native and Spanish properties, leading the water judge to establish a schedule to regulate the flow of the acequias. In theory, each night, all weekend, and all day on holy days, the intakes to Spanish properties would be blocked to direct water toward community use. But practice differed. In 1630, the protector de indios registered a complaint on behalf of the pueblo of Surco. He declared that although "the Indians are lords over all the water of the large acequia of that town," Spanish farmers and the Mercedarian order were refusing to block their intakes, stealing Indians' water. In response, the community of Surco had sent a dozen young men to swim up the canal at night and redirect the water toward the town and fields. They were met by Spaniards who reopened the hatches. The protector reported that the town periodically went dry for ten or twenty days at a time, and the community fields were endangered. The case was ultimately resolved when the Jesuits rented Surco's community lands and took control over the canal. They widened it and placed armed guards, allowing their hacienda as well as the town of Surco to receive regular irrigation.[61] The irony of Catholic clerics shielding Indigenous communities by taking over their lands should not be lost.

Indian cabildos also collectively managed their tambos. These inns had punctuated the Inka road system, providing lodgings and storage for a variety of imperial and local needs including mail service, moving tribute payments, and military action. Before the Spanish conquest, communities largely staffed them as part of the mit'a labor owed to the Inka.[62] Spanish authorities called for their maintenance and expansion, turning them into something more like the medieval European *fondaco* or hostel/storage/trading post, but also a public space to serve the community.[63] The tambo was central not only to travel but to governance. Indeed, Matienzo's 1567 plan for the spatial organization of pueblos de indios included a "house for Spanish travelers" to sit right on the plaza. Because existing structures were not placed conveniently for new purposes, communities were required to raise buildings and to staff and supply them to accommodate travelers who included priests, inspectors and other officials, merchants, soldiers, and their pack animals.

Tambos played a central role as public spaces. When Governor Vaca de Castro went to Huarochirí in 1544 to expand Nicolás de Ribera's encomienda, he met with Ribera's procurator and a group of Indigenous representatives before a notary at the town's tambo.[64] The 1549 inspection of Maranga for the purpose of establishing tribute rates also used a local tambo. After mass, a working group gathered at the tambo of Mayacatama that included two Spanish inspectors, a

Black man named Antonio who acted as Quechua interpreter, the cacique don Antonio, and three nobles representing different ayllus. Together, these men heard the royal instructions and swore to uphold them.[65] Natives in these communities fed and cared for these officials, their staffs, and animals.

Caciques and their subjects complained that managing tambos was one of the most onerous of their requirements.[66] The Lima Valley was especially taxed due to the commercial traffic from the Spanish fleets that periodically flooded the region with merchants, muleteers, and their retinues. Population decline left pueblos with limited ability to divert labor toward staffing and running the tambos.

The communities of Surco, Late, Carabayllo, and Pachacamac alighted on the solution of subcontracting management of their tambos to Spaniards for an annual fee. In 1612–1613, the communities asked the corregidor de indios to auction off tambo management, each receiving about 300 pesos for a three-year contract.[67] They would continue to supply some mita labor for the inns, but did not have to supply or maintain them, and oversight of the mitayos would be transferred from the cacique to the corregidor's office. There was not a great deal of interest from Spanish entrepreneurs, but when they succeeded, communities welcomed the flow of revenue into their treasuries as well as the lessening of labor burdens.[68]

New strategies for managing resources are perhaps the clearest lens for seeing how reorganized polities assessed their positions and approached a collective future. Cabildos and caciques faced their losses in populations and resources, and moved between defensive mechanisms (such as suing for ostensible rights), acts of rebellion or confrontation (with armies of swimmers shutting the irrigation outlets), or innovations within the colonial vocabulary (subcontracting their obligations to outsiders). In the long run, none of these would hold back the transformation of the valley into Spanish haciendas and estancias, but the communities, through their collective leaderships, did not go down without a fight.

Entangled Economies

By the turn of the seventeenth century, valley caciques no longer used their wills to create community wealth. Andean norms became interwoven with Spanish practices, turning most property into legacies to individuals, families, or institutions of the Catholic Church.[69] Nonetheless, some wills indicate ongoing group strategies. The collectivization of chicha brewing in Surco provides an example of innovation. The fermented corn beer has a long history in the Andes, dating back to at least AD 600–1000, and has long been understood as part of the reciprocal economy of the Andean world.[70] Brewing supplies were commonly mentioned in early Andean women's wills. The beverage has generally been understood to be a product made by an individual woman or perhaps by slaves and servants working for such an entrepreneur. It was a lucrative if slightly disreputable business.[71]

Andean women living in the areas surrounding Lima trekked into the city to sell their wares daily. Rather than individual vendors, the women appear to have been part of large business chains. María Capan of Surco, who left a will in 1596, asked her executors to collect a debt from the Spaniard Diego de Carbajal for a large amount of chicha purchased on credit, perhaps for resale.[72] In the same year, again in Surco, Costanza Ticlla's will lists as part of her estate "a large pot in which chicha is made, holding three *arrobas*, which is in this town's tavern, and also two small pots, one of which holds two arrobas and the other one arroba, also in the tavern." She stored even larger containers in her home, as well as seven small bottles scattered across the homes of her clients.[73]

Constanza Ticlla's business was clearly more than a domestic or even small commercial operation. It was part of the community's larger project of supporting a collectively run tavern associated with her ayllu, Ydca, and founded on its land.[74] The privatization, in a sense, of the chicha industry—formerly mass-produced at imperial administrative sites or by specialists within communities, as well as within the household for domestic consumption—and its association with street vendors as well as tambos and taverns, shifted both the symbolic meaning of the drink and its role as a source of wealth. It was stripped of its ability to act as a symbol of reciprocal diplomatic relations or to fulfill its spiritual function of feeding the ancestors. While viceregal authorities sought to stop caciques from distributing chicha to workers and from brewing chicha for ritual use, they simultaneously regulated its mass production and sale from vendors to a multi-ethnic urban population.[75]

Given the scale of chicha consumption, with its requisite raw materials, labor, space for production, and a means of distributing heavy containers, the business could take on political dimensions in the colonial world. In Lima's Cercado, the Jesuits taxed a town tavern to pay the priests' salaries. The corregidor de los naturales Hernán Vázquez ran a chicha operation in Carabayllo, delivering raw corn to one group of native workers under his jurisdiction to produce the drink, which he used to compensate a second group required to cultivate wheat for him.[76] Surco proposes another possibility: a gendered community chichería, whose profits might be allocated toward tribute payment or other community functions, and whose management might be collective rather than private. If the overall movement of early colonial society was toward the atomization of labor, chicha production offers an argument that collective strategies still mattered and could succeed.

The policy of reducción created pueblos de indios. These patchwork units were promoted as republics that could advance policía and give rise to new hispanized and Christian Indian leadership. Indian alcaldes and cabildos, alongside caciques and governors, carried out acts of translation and conversion, rearticulating community justice through a colonial grammar that guaranteed tribute payment, labor provision, and attendance at church.

The intersection between physical relocation, colonial demands, and native practices was a violent and creative space. Diminished communities evaluated their remaining resources and strategized. That creativity is only visible by recognizing the ways that Indigenous leadership improvised responses that were legitimated and strengthened by their communities' practices. Some acts, like litigating in court, required lots of resources including money, knowledge, and time. But quieter acts, like choosing where family groups would build homes on the new grid of the pueblo, were also political, setting terms for how the core units of native society would reproduce themselves. The existence of multiple layers of authorities protected the ability of communities to respond in ways that they could at least partially control.

Those responses were neither culturally conservative nor were they genuflections to a new order. Three wills written by native women (Elvira Coyti, María Capán, and Costança Ticlla) living in Surco in 1596 illustrate this tension, reflecting the language of the reducción alongside that of the community's response.[77]

The documents all refer to town authorities, ignoring the paramount cacique, most likely don Francisco Tantachumbi who served with his wife, doña María Miñan. Instead, the town's two alcaldes, "by authority of the King Our Lord," as the documents put it, coordinated the women's acts. Alcalde Juan Sallac signed three of the four testaments. Also present as witnesses were Surco's two regidores and its alguazil. The notary in all three cases, don Lorenzo, was Surco's *segunda persona*, a nobleman, perhaps from a competing ayllu from the cacique's in the power-sharing arrangement typical after reducción.[78] The Church also created new authorities, like the town's *fiscal* (who served the local priest and compelled community attendance at mass and catechism). These were the officials most likely to appear in a will, an explicitly Christian instrument that drew upon Spanish inheritance law, and whose writing was prompted by religious bequests and funerary requirements. Surco already had a full complement of colonial authorities by the turn of the sixteenth century, and they were definitively structuring important aspects of town life.

The wills indicate the effects of reducción and composición on property. Costanza Ticlla and Elvira Coyti both owned houses presumably built on sites distributed at the pueblo's founding, and passed them on to their grandchildren. Royal law also intervened in their lives: Costança Ticlla had a plot of pacay trees that she ordered cut down and sold as firewood, leaving forked prop and shoots, "as is required in the ordinance," presumably referring to anti-deforestation laws. In keeping with the restrictions on the sale of lands, none of the women liquidated their property holdings, but instead made gifts and donations to family, friends, and the Catholic Church.

The wills also demonstrate some resistance to change. Ayllu membership continued to color the distribution of obligations and rights, and it was one of the first identifying phrases after the testator's name, usually absent in wills in Lima or the Cercado. The women refer to chicha sales, both individual and through the community tavern. While the new economy introduced goats, they were now pastured collectively like camelids, and the increasingly ubiquitous chickens—which one testator donated to the church to pay for her funeral masses—were left to a variety of friends and family members to help them pay tribute. The wills reflect not a cash economy but a system of obligation and pawnage that was informed by Spanish monetary practices. María Capán stated in a clause that Diego Mita owed her "a new shirt made of two *varas* of red taffeta, and seventy bells that I loaned him for dancing." She required them returned without stains or missing bells, or else their cash value. The wills reveal a world of collective struggle and reinvention.

Because they govern the disposition of individual property, wills rarely discuss collective activity explicitly. In the absence of the records of town authorities, there is little certainty about the ways collective obligations were met. The acts of forming a government, of electing officers and carving out their social roles, and of using these institutions to manage resources and funds were inherently political, producing not only citizens but also everyday contemplations of the common good. There is no doubt that Spanish authorities seized jurisdiction where they liked and controlled important community resources both implicitly and explicitly. But only by claiming that these other aspects of daily life did not matter, that they were entirely overshadowed by jurisdiction over criminal acts or the management of conflicts that moved outside the community, can the role of local community practices be overlooked.

PART III

Order and Disorder

The subordinated republics of religious minorities in Castile and colonized subjects in the Americas were solutions to problems: how to incorporate outsiders into a system that could make efficient use of their political and economic systems? Two final cases, one a colonial failure and one a colonial success, show how the production of difference within the institution mattered. Atlantic slavery introduced a substantial population of free Black residents into Seville and Lima, but only in Seville were they granted an official form of self-governance. In the Americas, the idea of a Black republic circulated sporadically, but only as a penalty or disciplinary measure or a way to seize labor from unwilling free people. In contrast, royal authorities built an urban pueblo de indios to manage ungoverned Indigenous people in Lima. It did not gather all the city's natives under the aegis of the Jesuits, but it became an experiment in colonial self-governance. By participating in these contests over jurisdiction and rule, the ungoverned Black populations and the self-governed Indian town also contributed to hegemonic ideas about them as racialized subjects.

7

The Specters of Black Self-Governance

IN 1475, JUAN DE VALLADOLID, a royal servant of African descent, was named *mayoral* and judge of Seville's Black population by the monarchs Isabel and Fernando. The order appointing him noted the office was a reward for "the many good and loyal and notable services that you have done for us" as well as because of his "aptitude" and his "noble lineage among the said Black men and women." He was not called a slave in that documentation; he might have been a free servant in the royal household. The community he was to govern would be both free and enslaved.

The royal order appointing Juan de Valladolid describes his tasks in some detail:

> We make you *mayoral* and judge of all the Black men and women, mulato [*loro*] men and women, free and enslaved, who are captive or free in the very noble and very loyal city of Sevilla and in all of its archbishopric. And [We order] that the said Black men and women, mulato men and women may not hold any festivals or courts among themselves, except in your presence. . . . And We order that you be knowledgeable of the conflicts and lawsuits and marriages and other issues that might arise among them, and only you, insofar as you are an apt person for this, or whatever person has your power of attorney, and you should know the laws and ordinances that ought to hold sway.[1]

Juan de Valladolid had a dual charge, to act as magistrate for his community's internal conflicts and to manage their public festivals. The first is a function already familiar in a variety of similar circumstances. Just like the officials of *aljamas* of Muslims or Jews, or leaders of pueblos de indios, the mayoral would enforce a constrained form of customary law within the group, though its

Republics of Difference. Karen B. Graubart, Oxford University Press. © Oxford University Press 2022.
DOI: 10.1093/oso/9780190233839.003.0008

content is currently opaque.[2] The second charge speaks to other familiar conflicts. He was to manage the public expression of a community deemed consequentially different from the dominant group. Significantly, the monarchs called upon the authorities of other republics, including the concejos of Seville and nearby towns, to accept him as the representative of enslaved and free Black men and women.[3] While his jurisdiction was limited, that power was to be respected.

Seville had a *república de negros*, a corporate framework intended to represent the jurisdiction and political leadership of the city's non-Muslim Africans. The institution only appeared in a weak form in the New World, as occasional attempts to collectivize Black people for particular ends. Lima never had a Black alcalde or any secular organization of its enslaved or free Black residents. The absence of that republic had ramifications for managing the city's large Black population.

Other intermediate political forms emerged in the Americas to fulfill the needs of Black subjects and Spanish officials. But the framework of the república de negros continued to affect public imaginations, even in its absence. Authorities sometimes envisioned it as a disciplinary measure, and Black communities sometimes claimed it as a space of freedom. The failure to constitute the free Black population of the Spanish Americas through republics meant not only that Black subjects had no internal authority to produce justice for them, but also that there were no Black authorities with whom other officials could negotiate. This lack caused administrative inefficiencies and exacerbated discourses about social disorder and crime. But it also provided useful cover for men and women of African descent who preferred not to negotiate with authorities over fiscal and labor demands. Like Lima's Indians, they could be elusive.

Blackness in Andalucía

If the office of alcalde was established at the end of the fourteenth century as later documentation claims, it would have been under the monarch Enrique III, perhaps in conjunction with a hospital (perhaps a chapel in San Anton Abad) and confraternity (Nuestra Señora de los Ángeles) founded by the archbishop of Seville, Gonzalo de Mena, to serve the city's slaves.[4] Bishops often created hospitals to provide mutual support for the poor as well as the infirm, and they were used for pastoral care as well as other forms of instruction.[5] They could be places of *recogimiento* or seclusion for the poor, widowed women, and orphans. A contemporary hospital in Seville, dedicated to orphaned children, offered room and board, shoes and clothing, Catholic doctrine, and medical assistance, and also taught them to read, write, and count.[6] But many were not physical structures at all, but forms of mutual support attached to Catholic confraternities, and vehicles for fundraising,

The date of 1390 for an institution solely dedicated to Black slaves in Andalucía seems early, although West Africans had been present in the city at least since it was under Muslim control. Historian Alfonso Franco Silva scoured relevant notarial protocols for information about Seville's enslaved populations in the fifteenth and sixteenth centuries. The protocols—largely bills of sale—say more about slave markets than the city's resident demography, but they illustrate the changing ethnic and religious face of slavery over the fifteenth and sixteenth centuries.

While much of Eastern Iberia drew slaves from the Mediterranean trade, which brought Eastern Europeans and Orthodox Christian Greeks to the crown of Aragón, in Castile the majority of slaves sold were the result of war and the raiding of Muslim territories.[7] In the fourteenth century, Castilians invaded the Canary Islands, captured and enslaved its inhabitants, and replaced them with imported West African, Muslim, and *morisco* slaves. West Africans arrived on the peninsula throughout the Muslim occupation and after Christian conquest, though not in large numbers until the fifteenth century. After 1492, men and women native to the Americas, *indios*, entered the slave trade. Though Isabel declared them her free vassals in 1493, the enslavement of Indigenous people was common until Charles V began the formal process of prohibiting it with the New Laws of 1542. Even so, Indian slavery remained legal in some cases until 1679.[8]

Fifteenth-century sales contracts identify slaves in a variety of ways, but mostly used the adjective *negro* (Black) to indicate Africans from the non-Muslim, western mainland. Muslim slaves could be called "moro," "berberisco," or "blanco."[9]

Table 7.1 Ethno-racial Descriptions of Enslaved People in Notarial Protocols, 1450–1525

	Canary Islanders	Indians	Negros	Moros	Loros
1450s–1470	0	0	4	1	0
1471–1480	1	0	21	17	5
1481–1490	1	0	19	9	3
1491–1500	65	2	206	74	27
1501–1510	55	14	627	272	131
1511–1520	25	13	1819	628	202
1521–1525	8	10	609	515	162

Source: Franco Silva, *Regesto*, 140–46.

While men and women labeled "guineos" (those who entered the Atlantic from the coasts of Upper Guinea and Senegambia) came to be the most numerous newcomers in the sixteenth century, they continued to live among a variety of other enslaved people.[10] Enslaved Muslims were initially exempt from the expulsion edicts, and newly enslaved Muslims continued to arrive in Spanish kingdoms from conflicts in Granada and North Africa.[11] In the fifteenth century, religion was a greater fault line than pigmentation on the peninsula.

From this picture, it is not impossible but unlikely that a confraternity, hospital, and mayoral were instituted to support Black slaves in 1390, because they would have been relatively few and constituted a very small subset of the enslaved population. Indeed, the earliest mention of racial identity in the confraternity's documentation appears in regulations written in the 1550s: "we order that free mulatos, indios, and negros enter into our Brotherhood; if some enslaved person wishes to enter it must be with license from their master." By this time West and West Central Africans had a sizable presence in the city, and the office of mayoral had long existed.[12]

It is possible that the confraternity and hospital were opened in 1390 for Christian slaves—men and women of various origins who had accepted baptism or were born into Christianity—rather than dedicated to West Africans in particular. Enslaved Muslims could turn to aljamas and mosques for religious, economic, and social support. Slaves born into or converted to Christianity would have had no affinity group.[13] By the fifteenth century, Christian slaves were most commonly moriscos (converts from Islam), baptized New World Indians, or new converts from West Africa, and thus the origin was muddled.

Alternatively, the institutions may have been founded specifically for Black Africans because they were overrepresented as victims of the crises of the late fourteenth century. Those years saw multiple epidemics of the Black Plague (1349–1350, 1361, 1374, 1384) as well as other infectious diseases, high mortality, a long economic crisis, an earthquake in 1386, and the pogrom of 1391.[14] Slave ownership in Seville was not only for elites. Artisans and families of moderate means might have one or two slaves or servants.[15] As they experienced the economic downturn, owners might have abandoned older or infirm slaves rather than pay for their upkeep and medical care. Cast-off Muslim slaves might have received support from the city's aljama and even secured freedom through *alfaqueques*, the officials who helped ransom captive Muslims. But impoverished and enslaved Christians would have lacked such supports, and the Archbishop might well have stepped in to offer structures for mutual aid and spiritual guidance.

The archbishop's hospital-confraternity and the office of the mayoral provided support and leadership for a small but destitute group of enslaved Black men and women that no one else claimed. Over the course of the fifteenth century, the Black population increased and made these institutions more viable and dynamic, linking their histories to Blackness rather than enslavement. When the archbishop's body was moved from its original burial site to the Monastery of La Cartuja in 1594, Seville's chronicler Ortiz de Zúñiga reported that the city's Black population "accompanied the procession, made joyful noises, as for their Patron and benefactor."[16] The confraternity became deeply connected to the experience of being Black in Seville.

By the middle of the fifteenth century, Seville's Black population was certainly large enough to warrant institutional support. In addition to those who resided there, large numbers of enslaved people passed through its market en route to other regions. Free people of African descent also lived there; Alfonso Franco Silva has located some 1,153 statements of manumission in fifteenth-century archives, as a lower limit.[17] Institutions and regulations intended to guide and curb them followed, setting apart cultural practices that could be perceived as foreign or disruptive. Ortiz de Zúñiga wrote retrospectively that Enrique III had treated Seville's Blacks "with great benevolence . . . allowing them to come together for their dances and parties on holidays, for which reason they attended to their work with joy and better tolerated their captivity."[18] Enrique or his successors restricted those festivities to a zone facing the church of Santa María la Blanca.

Confraternities were key to the integration of Black slaves into Iberian cities.[19] They were collectives that enabled devotees to worship together, but they also served to articulate a group's social presence in the urban landscape. Many were founded to serve a particular occupation, neighborhood, or advocation, and the Church extended them for the purposes of evangelization of new Christian populations. Baptized slaves, for example, were encouraged to participate in lay activities, often alongside freedmen and their masters. Some orders began to organize confraternities dedicated to Black worshippers in particular, such as the popular Dominican Confraternity of the Rosary. Lisbon's Black Rosary claimed in its 1565 founding statement to have been in existence since 1460, though that account is questioned.[20] As confraternities shifted from being created for the purpose of evangelizing Black people to being founded by Black devotees, they often embraced Black saints, such as Elesban and Efigenía of Ethiopia, or Benedict of Palermo.[21] Black catechists often interpreted or preached for priests who did not speak African languages, producing new theologies.[22]

Confraternities institutionalized the ways that Black parishioners had long been active in public expressions of Catholicism. A Black confraternity was founded in Barcelona in 1455, although the city's Black Christians had already been participating in its Corpus Christi celebrations. Valencia formed its first Black cofradía in 1472, at the petition of those who noted their custom of making pilgrimage to the monastery of San Agustín.[23] Seville's large and diverse population of African descent gave rise to four confraternities in the early modern period—Rosario, Los Ángeles, Preciosa Sangre, and San Ildefonso—the last dedicated for mulato, or mixed-race, cofrades. Black worshippers might also have belonged to confraternities that did not claim a Black identity.

Free Black men and women joined confraternities for a variety of reasons, among them piety, of course, but also cultural fellowship, and financial and material support. Their diverse provenance and the history of enslavement made it difficult to call upon familial or cultural networks, making shared ritual experiences more profound.[24] They also found their ways to confraternities though practices associated with their enslavement. Manumission terms often required annual religious obligations in memoriam of the former owner, for example.[25] Linking freedom to religious practice could encourage other forms of devotion, and the obligatory relationship with a priest could turn into a closer tie or a channel for pressure.

In this environment, much of Seville's enslaved Black population embraced Christianity in some form. Initially, many were seen as successful converts, particularly those born into slavery (that is, within an Old Christian household). The Church and Crown did not consider non-Muslim Africans enemies of the faith and welcomed them with less suspicion than they did converts from Islam and Judaism.[26] In 1501, Isabel and Fernando instructed the new governor of Hispaniola, Nicolás de Ovando, not to bring to the island "Moors or Jews or heretics or reconciled heretics or persons recently converted to Our Faith, unless they are Black slaves or other slaves born in Christian hands, our subjects and native to our kingdom."[27] At least briefly, Seville's African-descent converts were considered trustworthy members of the religious fold.

Festivals and Processions

The first confraternity to explicitly serve Seville's Black population was established under the advocacy of Nuestra Señora de los Ángeles, but it became popularly known as the *cofradía de los negritos*, where the diminutive "little Blacks" suggested the public's casual deprecation of the participants. This familiarity was an important aspect of the ways that Blackness was perceived in the city, where it was not necessarily associated with violence or fugitivity. Black characters appeared in fictional texts and onstage because of a persistent fascination on the part of authors and audiences, and while they reflect some of the diversity of Black experiences in Iberia, they also tended to be portrayed broadly, sometimes with buffoonery, and with a certain contained menace or sense of inappropriateness.[28] Black subjects were expected to participate collectively in public ceremonies. When Queen Isabel entered Seville during Corpus Christi celebrations in 1477 and 1497, the concejo ordered all "the Blacks who might be in the city" to join in her reception, but the line between performing an entertaining exoticism and creating disruption could be ambiguous.[29]

Confraternities, like the alcalde de los negros (who was likely a confraternity member if not a mayordomo), were intended to discipline public and private behavior. This role is explicit in Los Ángeles' founding rules, which ordered that a new member be proposed by a sitting member and discussed in a secret meeting of its cabildo, which would research him or her for evidence of "drunkenness, thievery, concubinage, blasphemy." Lesser bad habits could be "corrected lovingly" but after two such corrections a member would be ejected.[30]

African-descent Christians, like conversos and moriscos, could be suspected of false conversion. Public concerns about these groups' behavior were also linked. Francisco Núñez Muley, a morisco who attempted to mediate the forced assimilation of Muslims in Granada in 1567, complained that, while the morisco community was being stripped of cultural practices not inherently linked to Islam, non-Muslim Africans were under no such prohibition. Drawing upon popular anti-African sentiment in his defense of moriscos, he asked, "Can we say that there is a lower race than the Black slaves of Guinea? Why are they allowed to sing and dance to their instruments and songs, and in the languages in which they normally sing them? In order to give them pleasure and consolation in terms that they understand."[31]

African arrivals to Seville were likely re-enacting West and Central African practices in their festive performances and in their confraternities. This integration had already begun in West Central Africa. Kongolese elites embraced Catholicism by adapting it to their own practices, requiring Catholic bishops to proclaim the legitimacy of Kongolese kings, and reinterpreting their own ceremonial processions with Portuguese instruments and Catholic ritual. While not all enslaved Africans in Iberia came from places or social classes that had already embraced Christianity, their public festival performances in cities like Seville were infused with their own experiences.[32]

Competitors for public space and the ecclesiastic authorities would accuse members of Los Ángeles of inappropriate and even violent behavior at religious processions. In 1604, the (non-Black) confraternities of La Antigua and Siete Dolores charged Los Ángeles' Black cofrades with outrageous behavior during the 1603 Holy Week.[33] The argument began as a disagreement about procession order—a common conflict because position in the procession signaled urban social and political status—but turned violent, according to a witness from a rival confraternity:

And my cofradía, being closer to the beginning of the street than [Los Ángeles] and being such an established cofradía, made up of illustrious and calm people, but the Black cofradía, with bellicosity . . . came running through the confectioner's shop below, scandalously, they ran at and broke through the ranks of the cofradía of La Antigua by force, and against their will, throwing rocks and hitting the female cofrades with sticks and with weapons, and they wounded some of the cofrades and did other things of notable injury, as I have offered testimony, the said Black cofradía commonly acts like barbarians and every year that their cofradía processes during Holy Week they have quarrels, sometimes with cofradías of illustrious persons that process the same night, and other times with people [in the streets] who make fun of them.[34]

Another member from La Antigua said, "the Blacks in question had taken out swords and bucklers and cutlasses and threw rocks at the cofrades of La Antigua and tried to kill them," leading to the arrest of eleven members of Los Ángeles.[35] Others testified that the confraternity used its statue of Christ as a battering ram and set its garments on fire.

While arguments over procession order were not uncommon during Holy Week and occasionally turned into fights, the non-Black witnesses took care to paint members of Los Ángeles as predators and aggressors. The language of weaponry and bellicosity, the refusal to call the confraternity by its name but only as that "of the Blacks," and the use of the word "barbarian" were all part of an emerging critical discourse that would also flourish in the New World. It is not difficult to imagine that Isabel and Fernando had appointed the venerable Juan de Valladolid as the mayoral and judge of the Black republic with an eye to keeping those nascent forces in check.

The establishment, then, of a weak republic for the growing Black population of Seville made sense. If it was not a coherent group in terms of historical origins—speaking a multitude of languages and emerging from heterogeneous political and cultural communities—it did occupy a uniquely visible space in the city. Most Black residents were enslaved and would have welcomed a political organization that could translate for them, speak on their behalf, and offer material and emotional support.[36] Municipal and royal authorities could call upon its officers to enforce discipline and disseminate information. Seville's archbishop saw these institutions as supports for conversion and a model for Catholic integration, and he likely saw ample opportunities for charitable contributions from the public.

Exactly what the mayoral did, other than report to other officials and organize public gatherings, is unknown. There is no documentation of his acts as judge. He does not appear even in the rare cases where he might presumably be needed. In 1495, a forty-five-year-old Black slave named Búcar fell sick of consumption while in the possession of a Sevillano man named Francisco Gomez Prieto.[37] His owner was in Huelva, and Gómez Prieto, for unstated reasons, asked a glassmaker named Rodríguez Álvarez, also in Seville, to take him in. Búcar died while in Álvarez's power, and Álvarez and another witness approached two of the city's notaries to produce a sworn statement about the man's condition, presumably so that the master did not blame Álvarez for the loss of his property. While the mayoral's absence from this scene is not proof of anything, it is suggestive of the limits of his authority outside his own small republic.

"Prejudicial to the Republic"

By the time of Lima's settlement, discourses about a Black propensity for violence were more hegemonic among Spaniards. Lima's city ordinances in the 1550s singled out Black Limeños as predators, vagrants, and bad influences on native communities.[38] They were also attacked for their refusal to contribute to the common good, even when free. On the other hand, Spanish law sometimes took the position that enslaved Africans could not be integrated into the community because they arrived in the kingdom involuntarily, and thus had not sworn allegiance to the Spanish monarch. The Crown would, at times, continue to characterize their descendants, collectively, as foreigners, although individuals who had performed meritorious service could petition to be naturalized.[39]

Despite their legal exclusion at the level of the kingdom, free Blacks often acted and were received as householders with obligations within their cities and towns. In Lima, this meant that the city council accused them of failing in their obligatory contributions to the commonwealth by way of getting them to perform labor that no vecino would consider. In December 1555, Lima's cabildo claimed that free Black men and women "who enjoy the benefits of their residence (*vecindad*) along with whatever other vecinos receive, are very prejudicial to the Republic and are of no utility to it."[40] To remedy their situation, the cabildo demanded that Black residents clean, at their own cost, "all the streets and plazas of this city," scrubbing manure and removing trash, which were considered to produce miasmas that threatened public health. The cabildo named a free Black man, Francisco Hernández, as acting inspector to round up the Black cleaning crew, because "he is elderly and known to be married and a property-owner in this city." Hernández was given the authority to seize and imprison anyone who refused to work.[41] Not surprisingly, this move against the free Black community was unsuccessful and the inspectors quit, complaining that their office paid no salary or benefits.[42]

Even without the assistance of a Black inspector, the cabildo returned to the free Black population when it needed extra labor for distasteful, servile tasks. When the Rímac River overflowed its banks in 1572 and 1578, free Black and mulato residents were called upon to build dykes.[43] In May 1589, during a small-pox epidemic, cabildo officers assigned deputies to assess need in the city's parishes. At the meeting's end, they contemplated what to do with the very poor Spaniards, Blacks, and mulatos who might be sick and had no access to a doctor, and decided to "compel" healthy free Blacks in the city to care for them.[44] There is no evidence of their success in mustering that labor in any of these cases.

This discourse of laziness, crudeness, and refusal to attend to the common-wealth of the places that made their liberty possible shared roots with discourses about the character of Indian and mestizo populations. It also drew upon the larger charges raised against the poor as rootless and vagrant, in need of a trade and a master. But in the case of men and women of African descent, these con-verged with issues about *cimarrones* (runaway slaves) and slave revolts.

Cimarrón Communities

The most important form of self-governance that Black people exercised in the Atlantic world took place in fugitivity. Enslaved people fled servitude from the first years in the Caribbean, in protest against unbearable working conditions, violence, and untempered authority over their lives and movements. As early as 1503, Hispaniola's governor Ovando had complained of Black slaves' flights into Taíno territory, and in 1513 the royal treasurer unsuccessfully advised the king to stop granting licenses to bring slaves to the island.[45] The flight of individuals or small groups often resulted in new and even permanent forms of community.[46] Persistent cimarrón settlements, sometimes called *palenques*, gave rise to the Crown's use of Black republics to manage unruly governance and to direct labor toward colonial goals.[47]

In the 1520s, a community of fugitive Taínos in Hispaniola was joined by cimarrones fleeing an uprising on Governor Diego Colón's sugar plantation and mill. The community grew to several hundred men, women, and children, who fought off armed patrols. Spaniards finally negotiated peace between 1528 and 1533, ultimately granting the group the status of a free town or republic, on land of their choosing, their start-up subsidized by some material aid. In exchange, the community agreed to police the area for subsequent fugitives. Their cacique Enrique demonstrated his good faith by turning in "six Blacks that he had," per-haps recent arrivals.[48] Some Black members of the community may have refused the terms that Enrique accepted, remaining in the mountains. The negotiations produced two important outcomes: the recognition of a pueblo de indios under its own cacique, the model that would be extended throughout the Spanish empire; and the demand that pacified cimarrones capture fugitive slaves. Black self-governance would often be predicated upon policing others.[49]

Communities forged out of bands of fugitives, often in conjunction with native groups and rural Spanish farmers, could persist for long periods. The royal treasury or local vecinos and merchants might finance raids against them for some time, but fugitives could often wait them out.[50] Weary governors, viceroys, and cabildo members would agree to terms that included manumission for the runaways and constrained political autonomy along the model of the reducción, with the requirement that the community pay tribute and capture any new runaways in the region.

This governance model was developed in Castilla del Oro (modern Panamá).[51] The rivers and mountain roads across its isthmus carried silver from Potosí, enslaved cargo, and all manner of wealth and imported goods between the royal fleet in the Caribbean and South American settlers. There were ample places in the mountains and jungle for escaped slaves to hide, relatively unhampered, for long periods. Fugitives provisioned themselves by intercepting merchant caravans and trading with, or stealing from, local communities. The relatively few permanent Spanish settlers in the region made it possible for palenques to cluster even near to cities like Portobello and Panamá.

Spanish officials found it nearly impossible to roust these palenques and often preferred a tense coexistence. Local cabildos—made up of slave owners and merchants whose income was threatened—tended to be less complacent and financed attacks with forces of "trusted Black slaves bought for this purpose, to whom freedom was promised in exchange for their loyal services," as Governor Alvaro de Sosa told the king in 1555.[52] While the military incursions had periodic successes, by 1549 as many as 1,200 men, women, and children continued to live free of their masters in small groups, coming down from the mountains to trade with locals, raid supplies, free slaves, and intercept commercial traffic. It was only in the 1570s, as French and English pirates began to ally with cimarrones against Spanish merchant caravans, that the Crown offered lasting peace in the form of a handful of free pueblos de negros.[53] Thereafter, pueblos de negros were offered in a variety of places as a solution to stubborn Black fugitivity.

Black Lords of the Land

The framework of self-governance occasionally proffered by Spanish authorities was adapted from the Indian reducción and the Spanish town, in expectation that such jurisdictions could produce concrete expressions of loyalty and generate efficient rule for Black subjects. But Spanish administrators theorized

key differences between Black and native subjects: Africans and their descendants were involuntary immigrants, they might retain loyalty to African rulers,
and they did not live among their own leaders and judges in the Americas. In
some cases commentators claimed that successful palenques were led by African
royalty, much as Juan de Valladolid had supposedly descended from kings and
caciques were the descendants of pre-Hispanic natural lords. Pedro de Aguado, a
Franciscan priest who took part in the Panamanian negotiations, reacted to these
discourses, condemning the palenque leader Bayano as a false king, ridiculing his
expectations to be treated in the manner of caciques, and calling his desire to rule
his own territory an act of treachery against his true sovereign.[54]

It is worth contemplating briefly the meaning of such kingship. It is easy
to dismiss the notion that African royals were enslaved, brought to the New
World, and coincidentally emerged as palenque leaders.[55] But enslaved Black
people recognized the power of such a narrative because they lived surrounded
by Indigenous governance. If caciques were addressed as "don" and given noble
privileges, Black leaders should want no less. Palenques were also spaces where
participants recreated African political models, derived from a synergy of
diverse traditions.[56] By the eighteenth century, Black confraternities elected
kings and sometimes queens to govern and represent them, borrowing the
trappings of European as well as African royalty.[57] These productions of self-
governance drew upon a complex set of possibilities from across the Atlantic
world. The archives only offer external representations of such acts, from the
perspectives of Spanish and Portuguese observers, making it difficult to draw
larger conclusions.

These explanations did little to assuage official concerns about Black governance, and the offer of pueblos de negros was often accompanied by punitive
measures. Philip II described the procedure in 1573.[58] He empowered audiencias and cabildos to dispatch soldiers, carrying his royal order in their hands,
and approach cimarrones, informing them that they could cease their hostilities
and accept reducción, or be taken as prisoners, with a bounty of forty pesos for
a decapitated head, or ten pesos alive. Those brought in alive would be hung or
returned to their masters, mutilated. The brutality, along with the brandishing of
the order as evidence that this was no trick, were intended to move cimarrones to
the option of peace within a stated deadline.

Upon acceptance, local officials would issue palenqueros freedom papers, par-
doning them for any crimes they might have committed, and would designate
a place for them to resettle under a priest and a Spanish judge. The free Black
townspeople would act as slave catchers, empowered to keep their captives or sell
them to new masters. As loyal vassals of the king, they would keep the roads safe,
and they would labor and make good use of the land.

Despite the challenging terms, many new pueblos de negros were founded in Castilla del Oro. City leaders petitioned the audiencia in 1579 to execute Philip's order locally after a costly war with cimarrones and corsairs ended in 1577.[59] The audiencia extended their initial offer to the cimarrones of Portobello, sending an enslaved messenger to inform them.[60] In 1579, don Luis Mozambique, whom the Spaniards termed "king of the cimarrones of Portobelo" but who called himself its "principal caudillo," responded. He submitted a petition "of my own and spontaneous will" to accept the terms "that [he and his palenque] be free and not enslaved ... that [the Audiencia] receive them at the said reducción so that from then on they be accepted as His Majesty's loyal vassals."[61] The act transformed them from enslaved enemies of the kingdom to a community of "good and loyal vassals," who would join in the defense against corsairs and interact horizontally with other towns and cities. Don Luis was installed as governor and judge.

The transition to reducción was not entirely smooth but it was effective. The Spaniard installed to supervise their pacification complained that Governor don Luis' subjects continued to refer him as king.[62] The resettled subjects objected to the initial site offered, too far from the city where they had been selling their crops, and were moved to a location near Nombre de Dios and by the Francisca River.[63] The act of foundation, as of any other town or city, implied that don Luis' subjects received jurisdiction under him as first-instance judge in civil and minor criminal matters "in the form and manner and with the qualities and prerogatives that the other cities and towns of Spaniards have in this kingdom."[64] The former cimarrones also successfully rebuffed an attempt by the cabildo of Nombre de Dios to assimilate one of the towns to its political jurisdiction in 1590.[65] They required their own republic to discern and protect their own common good.

In the last quarter of the sixteenth century, royal authorities introduced the pueblo de negros as a way to coopt more organic forms of Black governance that were emerging in fugitivity. It was modeled on the reducción, a solution to the challenge of gathering Indigenous laborers and parishioners, but it had punitive features stemming from its origins in cimarronaje. The form would spread, turning palenques into Black towns in Mexico, Ecuador, Colombia, and many other places.[66] Even so, they were rare. Only under extraordinary circumstances and in the wake of stubborn persistence would cimarrones be granted self-governance. Spaniards, however, came to see the model as a solution to problems of labor discipline.

Pueblos de Negros for Policía

Lima had occasional problems with cimarrones, but never resolved them by establishing pueblos de negros. Peruvian officials did propose similar institutions for a different purpose: as extensions of slavery toward collective labor ends, particularly in mining. Proponents argued they would take a population that was lazy, criminal, and unskilled, and turn them into men and women who could contribute to the common good.[67]

In 1557, Viceroy Marqués de Cañete proposed that gold fields recently discovered in Carabaya (Puno) could be worked by a mining reducción made up of free people of African descent from across the viceroyalty. At least sixteen free Black persons were transported there, to be governed by a Spaniard.[68] The reducción collapsed, in part because the gold fields were unproductive. But similar ideas resurfaced from time to time. Viceroy Toledo in 1570 suggested to the king that all free people of African descent be sent to labor in mining, "paid at a different rate than that given to the Indians." Lima's cabildo in 1574 sent a representative to Spain to petition the Crown to resettle all of the region's free Black people in "remote valleys where they may receive governance and support themselves from their labor and live in decency."[69] Neither plan was enacted, but they show that Spanish officials in Lima, which had a large and growing free Black population, saw the Black reducción as a viable solution to labor shortages.

Two more schemes, both well-developed but not executed, illustrate how this idea was taking hold. In 1592, Francisco de Auncibay, judge of Quito's Real Audiencia, proposed to provide enslaved labor to regional gold fields and mercury mines going untapped because of the dissipation of native communities. He called for the Crown to purchase up to 2,000 enslaved men and women from Africa and offer them on mortgage to Spanish residents of Cali, Popayán, Almaguer, and Pasto at 400 gold pesos each.[70] Over eight years, the owners would make payments to the Crown totaling 400,000 pesos drawn from the gold extracted by the slaves. In addition, the Crown would collect its accustomed *quinto* or 20 percent tax on the gold, reaping another 200,000 pesos.

Auncibay framed his scheme as a moral and civilizing act, one that would transform barbaric Africans into people of policía. He noted that slavery was a shameful practice, but "this business has been so reformed" by Spanish law "and the equality of Castilian justice, that to be a slave is akin to being a child and like being a companion and relative," that is, one who receives tutelage. "The blacks themselves would receive no affront," he claimed, "because for them it would be a great service to be taken from Guinea, from that fire and tyranny and barbarity and brutality where without law and without God they live as savage brutes, carried to a better land, healthier for them, and fertile, they would be happy at their salvation."[71]

Civilizing "brutes" through work carried risks. Work gangs would be assigned to mines and transferred to new sites when the ore was depleted. Workers were not to leave the towns, and owners were warned not to take Black women or children into their homes as servants lest they become acculturated and desire a life beyond mining. But self-governance—within the family and the community—would encourage growth, "because the evil that attends the servile condition is perfected and purged by the possession or quasi-possession of oneself, and of one's woman, and of one's little house and plot and little ones, and the aptitude for [holding] the said office." A Black alcalde and other officers would be responsible for rounding up fugitives. A Spanish corregidor or his lieutenant would visit the camps and limit owners' abuse of their slaves.

In Auncibay's mining scheme enslaved people would have no exit. Even if they purchased their freedom (once the owner's mortgage was paid off) they would be required to remain in the mining towns and pay tribute as day-workers, because "[they must understand] that the mine is not theirs." Like Quiroga's hospital-pueblos, these were fantasies that legitimated slavery and dispossession as the foundation of imperial governing practices.[72]

A second proposal came from Dominican friar Miguel de Monsalve a few years later. His policy memo to the king raised an important objection: how could the model for Indian governance, the reducción, be imposed on people with a dissimilar legal existence? In part this distinction came from a moral defect: Black subjects required supervision, "as people who do not recognize dominion they live within the law of their choice, they hear mass if it pleases them, they confess when it serves them." As a result of their free will (*albedrio*), they added nothing to the "utility of the republic," avoiding work and marriage because of their preference for criminality and concubinage.[73] In contrast, Indigenous communities lived freely under their own law and Catholic discipline, and because they obeyed hereditary leaders, contributed to the common good through both labor and tribute.

Because he had so little trust in the ability of free people of African heritage to exhibit policía, Monsalve argued for direct Spanish control, including a governor who would not only stand as judge but would make rounds at night to make sure that unmarried couples were not sleeping together. He supported appointing minor Black officials under the governor's watch. This worry even reached to the duty to police cimarrones. Monsalve feared giving them weapons "because of the danger that Republics risk if Blacks have arms, as they are our capital enemies." He advised that the Spanish governor could issue bows and arrows from a locked deposit as needed. But he also turned their potential enmity to the kingdom's own good, giving them the right to use whatever violence necessary to bring in fugitives who resisted capture.

Perhaps the most crucial distinction with Indian governance was the fact that free Black subjects had no native right to land in the Americas, which Monsalve considered the justification for Indian tribute. Monsalve resolved this quandary by associating the payment with Black gratitude for access to Christianity and Spanish law:

> Because they have your Majesty and your Justice for their defense and support, it is a certainty that they owe Your Majesty tribute, even more so as they are administered sacraments, taught the law of God, and finally, they enjoy goods and liberty of a kind they would not exercise in their lands [in Guinea] where before they always had perpetual fear of losing them, with their children and wives, and even [fear of] dying, which here they not only do not have this fear, but they possess their wives and children securely and they are masters of slaves and property, as many whom I know have today, and they have many possessions and rents and slaves and many other riches.

Monsalve's tortured logic—that former slaves should be grateful for their enslavement, because it saved them from an ongoing fear of enslavement—encapsulates the contradictions that pervade these resettlement schemes. Free and enslaved Blacks were simultaneously outsiders, without authentic claims to land and governance, and also loyal vassals, who should pay tribute in acknowledgment of the justice and peace they received from their monarch. They were the terrifying enemies of Spaniards and yet their best defense for controlling the chaos caused by runaway slaves and corsairs. Like Indians, they required instruction to improve their piety and their work discipline, but they could not graduate from that education, except the few who acquired the trappings of colonial wealth: real estate, luxury goods, rents, and slaves. The separation and self-governance schemes proposed to extract wealth and work from free and enslaved Blacks were, in the end, impossible to deploy. Only the Marqués de Cañete's 1557 plan for Carabaya was enacted at all, and that failed.

Conscripting Tributaries

As the Atlantic slave trade to Latin America increased, so did the free Black population of its cities. By the seventeenth century, nearly a quarter of Lima's large African-descent population was free.[74] Most had become free through self-manumission, saving wages (*jornales*) until they had enough to compensate a master at a price either mutually agreed-upon or asserted by the owner.[75] Their ability to save at all was often indebted to a system of hiring out: in cities, slave-owners were often artisans and rarely had more than one or two slaves. When they did not require labor themselves, they rented their slaves to others who did and the daily wage was distributed unevenly between master and laborer. Masters kept accounts of enslaved persons' accumulated savings, which could be supplemented with loans from relatives, acquaintances, or a confraternity.[76] Thus Lima, like most large Spanish American cities, also had a sector of wage-earning Black and mulato men and women who existed in the interstices between slavery and freedom.

The Crown understood the free African-descent population as a revenue challenge: why did these men and women not pay tribute? While most of the city's Black residents were exceptionally poor, some were well-compensated artisans and entrepreneurs. Some appeared in the 1613 Indian census as homeowners, landlords, and employers of native workers. In 1601, Pedro Gallego, a free Black man, worked as a construction laborer in the monastery of San Agustín at a respectable annual salary of 500 pesos. A free mulato carpenter in 1639 received 525 pesos a year, while a domestic servant or apprentice would receive less than half of that amount.[77] Some free Black women were themselves slave owners, using their human capital to create an income stream that stabilized their precarious existence.[78]

In the 1570s, royal officials pushed to extract wealth and labor from Indigenous communities still recovering from the trauma of conquest and colonization. Enslaved and free people of African descent offered another opportunity to expand taxation. In 1574, just as he was creating policy for using pueblos de negros as an incentive to pacify cimarrones, King Philip II issued an order regarding the opportunities posed by the viceroyalties' free African-descent population:

> Insofar as we are informed that many of the male and female slaves, both Black and mulato, who have come to our Indies and resided there with its great wealth, have come to free themselves, and that these [persons] have many profits and riches, thus, for many just reasons, and especially because they live in our lands and are maintained in peace and justice in them, and have left slavery and are now free in them. Additionally, because in their native lands they had the custom of paying tribute, in great quantities, to their kings and lords, with just and right law they may be asked to pay it to us, and that it should be a silver mark every year.[79]

Tribute marked the subjugated status of colonized subjects within the Spanish empire. Indigenous communities paid collectively, an amount decided by counting healthy adult men at some moment and multiplying by the head tax. Spaniards and their descendants residing in the colonies understood their exemption from tribute as a birthright. Mestizos were largely exempted from tribute in the sixteenth century because of their potential attachment to elite Spanish society; many of the first generations of Spanish creoles were the children of

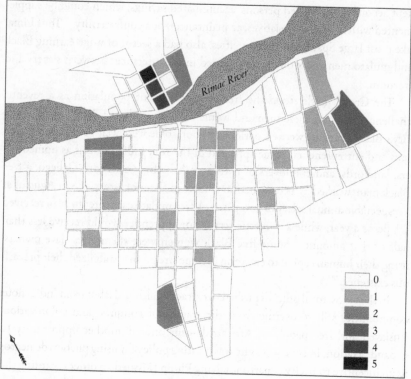

FIG. 7.1 Distribution of Black Residents Named in 1613 Census of Lima.

Source: Contreras, *Padrón de los indios de Lima*; Bromley and Barbagelata, *Evolución urbana de Lima*, 8. Map by Matthew Sisk, Navari Family Center for Digital Scholarship, University of Notre Dame.

native mothers raised by Spanish fathers.[80] As well, native communities balked at including mestizos on their tribute registers, as they had little power over them. Enslaved men and women paid no tribute because it would have been a tax on their masters.[81] And the category of *zambo* or *zambaigo* was appearing in records by the 1570s to mark the children of mixed Indigenous and Black parentage. Following the logic of *partus sequitur ventrem*, the law that enslaved any child born from the womb of an enslaved woman, the mother's status was determinant of the child's freedom.[82] The question of tribute, however, was less clear. In 1572, the king declared in a letter to the Audiencia of Guatemala that, if the mother was free and native but the father enslaved, the child was free but had to pay tribute "like the Indians."[83] That statement did not use the term zambaigo, which began to appear in orders in 1573, suggesting that the status question was essentially creating the new category.[84] Nonetheless, there is little evidence that people placed into this category paid tribute until the 1574 order.

That law was likely a response to the growth of the free African-descent population, and the sense that at least some were meeting with economic success. While most were quite poor, the existence in cities like Lima of small numbers of free Black and mulato men and women who owned houses, land, finery, and slaves of their own was presumably jarring to tax-hungry officials. Philip II, at least, received word that those subjects could pay.

But Philip's order posed difficulties: who had the legitimacy or power to collect such a tax, and how would he know from whom to collect? Panamá was one of the first cities to attempt a census and collection. Some very poor and elderly Black residents requested personal exemptions from the Audiencia and received them. Mulata and Black women married to Spanish men were exempted, after petitioning, on the basis that it was unacceptable for a Spaniard to pay tribute.[85] The city's procurator, representing a large contingent of free Black men and women, challenged the assessment altogether. He claimed the king was misled about the region's economic health: "Not only do the said Black and mulato men and women have no such enterprises and wealth but the [Spanish] citizens of this city and kingdom themselves do not have them either," he argued, noting the general shortage of arable land.[86] He argued that demanding payment from impoverished Black residents would disturb the commonwealth, because they would flee or turn to theft and rebellion. He was granted a stay, though records show collections in at least 1595 and 1596.[87] The existence of pueblos de negros, with their officials, surely facilitated the process.

Peru proved a different case. While the king's order was read in Lima in 1574, there was no immediate move to create such a census or demand payments.[88] In 1577, the viceroys of Peru and New Spain ordered that all free Blacks and mulatos live with employers, so that a full census could be taken and tribute could be deducted from their salaries.[89] These orders were not implemented. When he took office in 1596, Viceroy Velasco made tribute collection more of a priority than his predecessors, but his first target was the smaller city of Arequipa, which registered and collected sums from forty African-descent men and women. An alcalde de los mulatos carried out that collection, creating at least an ad hoc republican framework. Small amounts were also collected in Trujillo until its cabildo noticed that many Blacks were fleeing to other cities to avoid payment.[90]

Because of continuing ambivalence on the part of local and regional governments towards the laws and the absence of legitimate Black political leaders to facilitate their implementation, Lima found it nearly impossible to collect payments. After a census in 1595, the city banked a mere seventy-five pesos from free Blacks and mulatos.[91] No further contributions were logged for eight years. In 1604, Viceroy Velasco ordered all African-descent men and women between the ages of eighteen and fifty to pay at the rate of four pesos for men and two for women. The corregidor de los naturales del Cercado, don Joséph de Rivera, was appointed collector. Rivera claimed to have collected funds between 1604 and 1606, but failed to deposit them with the treasury. Moreover, he created a situation of enormous hostility with potential taxpayers, who met his agents at the door armed with weapons. The subsequent corregidor, Domingo de Luna, refused to attempt collection at all.[92]

In 1610, Viceroy Montesclaros ordered a new census for Lima, which identified 410 eligible tributaries (of a total free Black population of 630) and successfully farmed out collection for two years. Tax farming benefited the treasury, as the collector had to pay the amount no matter what he collected, but apparently it was not attractive to subsequent candidates for the office, who could not be found until 1619. After 1621 the office disappeared.

Proposals were entertained for using other Black and mulato institutions, like confraternities, to bring in voluntary contributions. Most effectively, a mulato guild was founded to collect tribute, organize its militia, and fundraise for special events and festivals. The guild made efforts to do all of these, including policing the citizenry in search of delinquent contributors.[93]

In 1632, Pedro Martín Leguisamo, a silversmith who had moved from Panamá to Lima, complained to the Real Audiencia that he had been serially harassed by the mulato guild. He repeatedly refused membership in the guild—and the various obligations that accompanied it—on the grounds that he was the legitimate son of "Juan Martines de Leguizamo and of María García his legitimate wife, and that his said father was a [Basque] nobleman and an hidalgo." He argued that the privileges of nobility exempted him from the category, no matter his mother's status. He was a paying member of the silversmith's guild and claimed the right to "carry arms as the Spaniards do, and to enjoy all the privileges that Castilians have" as an active member of the Spanish militia. He adamantly refused the category of mulato for himself, and the city and royal courts repeatedly found on his behalf, although they seemed unable to stop the mulato guild and militia from attempting to sign him up.[94]

After 1574, Crown officials learned that it was not enough to demand financial contributions from the Black community, but that they needed to provide institutional structures—republics—that could extract tribute via legitimate leadership. Indian tribute functioned when legitimate governance models that provided important material benefits to subjects—including local Spaniards who could be called upon to enforce collection—were in place. The almost total absence of effective Black self-governance, not to mention the refusal to grant Black communities resources, left a vacuum for taxation. Castilla del Oro, with its tiny and impoverished pueblos de negros, was only somewhat more effective than wealthy Lima.

Confraternities as Republics in Lima

The main vehicles that Limeños of African descent used to make semi-autonomous political and organizational decisions were their Catholic confraternities. By the late sixteenth century, Black participation in sodalities was extensive. The archbishop enumerated fifteen confraternities for worshippers of African descent in a 1619 report.[95] These were mostly small and poor, and many likely dissolved after a few years, but there was no doubt in Lima of the dedication of many enslaved and free people of African descent to confraternity life.[96] Their festive performances and meetings were enthusiastic, and Spanish Limeños, like their Sevillano counterparts, had a penchant for describing them as rowdy, featuring drunken or criminal behavior.[97]

As in Spain, the sodalities also collected membership fees and alms, redistributing them to their own needy as well as to support and comfort the sick, dying, and dead of the city. They were organized in a variety of ways. Early Lima was ethnically diverse, with an enslaved population that initially drew from Senegambia and then broadly West Central Africa. Unlike the better-known cases of African-descent peoples in late colonial Brazil and Cuba, Lima's Black subjects did not necessarily organize their confraternities around ethnic origins, known as *casta* or *nación*. Some embraced heterogeneous communities, while others broke off into splinter groups reflecting shared experiences and desires.

The cofradía of Nuestra Señora de La Antigua, for example, in its beginnings appealed broadly to free and enslaved Blacks and mulatos.[98] Their sixteenth-century records rarely even noted members' casta origins. But by the 1630s, the membership had split into two factions, "creoles of this city" and "creoles of Cabo Verde," both of which drew upon their birthplace in a new environment after their ancestors' forcible removal from the African continent. This factionalization, which led to the election of a mayordomo from each group, suggests that the experience of self-determination within New World slavery could at times be more unifying than reference to ancestral African origins.[99]

Other confraternities suffered worse internal schisms; the cofradía of San Juan Buenaventura, founded by free Blacks from Guinea-Bissau in 1604, fell apart three years later when the members born in Guinea-Bissau (*casta Biohoes*, in their words) tried to expel the members who were born or creolized in Panama before moving to Lima.[100] The African-born cofrades cast aspersions on the Panamanian creoles, calling them "consumed by sin and drunkenness," and accusing them of stealing the community's alms for their own devices. The vicario general of the archbishopric, on the basis of reports by the Franciscan priest who oversaw the confraternity, allowed the expulsion, leaving the confraternity at least temporarily unified around an African ethnic moniker.

These documents reveal Black men and women working out ways to construct community and political representation in Lima. These lines of conflict could reflect stories of origin or the long experiences of movement across the Atlantic world. Two of the city's largest Black confraternities reorganized themselves in the seventeenth century to reflect changing cultural and linguistic alignments. Nuestra Señora del Rosario was founded by the Franciscans but in 1593 was moved to the Dominican church. Many cofrades were unhappy with the change and formed a new sodality within San Francisco called Nuestra Señora de Los Reyes. Both flourished in the seventeenth century, but each created its own distinct political structure. By 1646, Los Reyes was referring to itself as the "cofradia of the eight *moreno castas*," and each casta elected its own representative to sit at the organization's cabildo or annual meeting.[101] A protracted lawsuit reveals the structure, with seats going to representatives of the Bran, Terranovo, Jolofo, Mandinga, Biafara, and three other mixed groups (those members called themselves Sape, Congo, Angola, Nalu, Balanta, Bañol, and Berbesi). The groups, called *bancos*, collected alms from their membership and distributed funds among themselves, delegating the confraternity's work along those ethnic lines.

But the suit also shows that the confraternity used its historical memory to define its structure. The order by which these representatives were seated at its cabildo in 1646 reflected the identities of the men and women who had left Rosario in 1593 to found the new cofradía. According to this memory, the first founder was Lorenzo Bran, and thus the Bran representative received the first chair; the second was a Terranova, and thus those cofrades were entitled to the second chair, and so on. Ironically a document dated 1589 tells the story of the foundation somewhat differently, giving credit for foundation to one Antonio Rodríguez, "free moreno," and likely a creole. By the middle of the seventeenth century, cultural origins mattered enough to rewrite that history.

The remaining members of Rosario also came to organize themselves (after 1608) by bancos, headed by a *caporal*, or officer who collected their fees and alms. The combined membership was presided over by a single mayordomo. By the 1620s, Rosario had eleven distinct bancos. In 1639, the extreme decentralization framed a crisis, as the election within a poorly attended cabildo meeting was denied legitimacy ostensibly because not all of the castas were represented.[102] The complainants also argued that the elected mayordomo was incompetent, unused to governing, and a debtor to the organization. Their insistence that the problem was procedural led Church authorities to deny their request for a new election, on the grounds that the bancos were a recent innovation and not essential.

Toward the end of the seventeenth century, Rosario was again in conflict. The Sape caporal complained that he was illegitimately seated behind his Cocolí counterpart. Like Los Reyes, Rosario had moved to assigning seating order by place in the historical foundation of the cofradía, and the Sapes and Cocolíes produced distinct memories of those events. In the end, the Cocolíes produced a paper title to their primacy, issued in a previous litigation, which won over Church officials, whatever the local memory.[103]

If Lima had no pueblo de negros or republic that could effectively roust labor and pay taxes, it did have powerful African-descent confraternities that organized themselves according to their own shifting needs and experiences, a reflection of where they had come from and where they found themselves. They raised significant funds that they could use, within reason, to follow their own interests. The Church made great use of these organizations to integrate and discipline their African-descent members, and the cofrades were proud and active participants in the city's many festivities and processions, but there were limits to their utility to Spanish authorities. As voluntary organizations under the umbrella of the Church, they could not be pushed too hard or they would dissolve. With this protection, they remained important sites for Black self-governance as the centuries went on.

In 1475, Juan de Valladolid took office in Seville as mayoral and judge of that city's Black community. The office had resonances with the ways that leaders of aljamas and guilds functioned: he managed petty disputes, kept track of marriages, illnesses, and deaths, and enforced regulations about the ways that free and enslaved people of African descent could participate in public life. The record is silent on the kind of law he invoked for the men and women who might have looked to him for support. But, like the leaders of Muslim and Jewish aljamas, he managed the public reputation of a community that was asserted to have a significantly different common good from the society around them. The Black republic created governance and material support for a community that largely lacked resources. Enslaved Muslims, by contrast, could appeal to the Muslim aljama for support; enslaved non-Muslim Africans had no such community of interest prior to the creation of the mayoral.

In the New World, this paradigm faltered. Enslaved and free people of African descent were not empowered to establish republics, except for the rare occasions when Spanish monarchs and viceroys saw the pueblo de negros as a solution to a larger problem, like stubborn palenques or a lack of laborers in mining. Instead men and women of African descent, free and enslaved, sought status and mutual aid through institutions like confraternities, guilds, and militias. Spanish authorities could use these as mechanisms for making certain kinds of demands, but they largely functioned without onerous oversight. Like the pueblos de indios, Black towns and other Black institutions produced a loyal citizenry, a way to gather tribute and organize labor, they simplified missionary activity, and they devolved less appealing aspects of governance onto the subjects. Little is known of the kind of governing they did, or the laws they invoked. They survived in part because they were unobserved.

Free Black towns have sometimes been viewed as products of agentive acts by former slaves, who demanded to be respected in republics on the order of the Spanish and Indigenous dual legal system.[104] Particularly celebrated are cases such as that of Yanga (Ñanga), who founded a palenque in San Lorenzo (Mexico) in the seventeenth century and then negotiated for the status of republic. Yanga's case is important because a Spanish contemporary recorded a version of those negotiations. According to the document, his terms included freedom for those already in the settlement; the appointment of Yanga himself, supposedly of royal birth, as magistrate; and the appointment of an external magistrate "who is nei-ther mestizo nor creole nor man of letters but is a man of cape and sword," perhaps a demand that the Spanish official sent to oversee them be a peninsular soldier rather than a local creole enemy. They requested partial segregation, asking that Spaniards stay out of the town except for market days, although Franciscan friars would minister to their religious needs. Finally, they agreed to pay tribute and raise an army to defend the king, as well as return future runaway slaves to their masters.[105]

These ambivalent conditions, which led to the founding of San Lorenzo in 1608, reproduce nearly exactly those granted to Castilla del Oro's palenques in the late sixteenth century. It takes nothing away from Yanga's followers' extraor-dinary success at evading conquest, at maintaining political unity, and at ensuring economic survival to note that these negotiations led to an outcome that pleased Spanish authorities at least as much as the former cimarrones. They allowed scarce Spanish military resources to be dedicated to other concerns, and raised the possibility of more revenue, more food in the markets, peace on the highways, and militia reinforcements.

The ambivalences become visible when measured against other histories—those of the reducciones, but also of corporate governance in Iberia for religious minorities as well as sub-Saharan African Christians. Africans' "foreignness" within the Spanish kingdoms was not universal, and indeed it had to be con-structed. While people of African descent were counted as foreign at the end of the colonial period when full citizenship was on the table, their status was more ambivalent in the fifteenth, sixteenth, and seventeenth centuries. The contradic-tion between foreigner and vassal was elided in the attempts to collect tribute for the monarch, where their vassalage to the Spanish monarch was recognized as parallel to, and substituting for, the customs of their homeland. African-descent peoples were integrated neither into the república de españoles, nor into a formalized república de negros through which they might negotiate their relationship with the Crown. This republicless limbo left most free people of African descent only able to claim rights on an ad hoc and individual basis, rather than as members of a corporate group. But in the first centuries of conquest, Spanish officials saw republics as an occasionally useful measure for governing certain free people of African descent, and these were a testament to the frustration royal officials experienced at governing their unruly territories.

8

Walls and Law in Lima and Its Cercado

YSABEL CAXAYLLA APPEARED before the Indian alcalde of her adopted home of Santiago del Cercado, the walled Indian town built on the outskirts of Lima, in September 1611.[1] She stated that she was about ninety years old, from the ayllu of Guancho Guaylas in the Late Valley, and had been abandoned by her husband Martín Potosí a decade earlier. She wished, as part of her testamentary arrangements, to donate land she owned in Late to the Jesuit church in the Cercado. Under Spanish inheritance law, her absent husband might have a claim on those fields as community property. She asked Juan Mateo, the Cercado's Indian alcalde, to conduct an investigation and approve the legacy.

Juan Mateo and his Indian scribe, don Francisco de Fuentes, carried out the investigation. Juan Mateo interviewed four elderly Indigenous men who hailed from the towns around Lima or from Trujillo and Cajamarca, near Martín Potosí's hometown. They were established, permanent residents of the Cercado, described as having "house and family" in the walled town, and one currently served as its regidor or alderman. They coincided in their testimony that Potosí had disappeared and never returned, failing to "make a life with her." They failed to report how she had come to own the properties; if purchased by the married couple, Potosí would have had joint ownership. Instead they argued that Caxaylla had been abandoned and had no legally compulsory heirs, and thus she was at liberty to dispose of any property as she pleased. They painted a picture of an isolated, lonely, unwell elderly woman with no children or heirs; moreover, "she had no hope of having any, given that she is an older woman and debilitated and quite old."

At the end of the testimony the alcalde Juan Mateo issued his finding that the case be advanced to the Spanish magistrate, the corregidor de los naturales don Josephe de Ribera, so that he might render a decision. Don Francisco de Fuentes

Republics of Difference. Karen B. Graubart, Oxford University Press. © Oxford University Press 2022.
DOI: 10.1093/oso/9780190233839.003.0009

drew up the documents, and Juan Mateo signed them. The file moved to Ribera's court, where he acknowledged the hearings, conceded the request, and had his own scribe, Cristóbal de Piñeda, write up his order, inserting Juan Mateo's original documents within.

These pages offer one answer to a mystery: what did the Indian leaders of the Cercado do? Unlike their counterparts in Mexico, Peru's Indian cabildos left few records, a fact often explained by Viceroy Toledo's order that they produce summary judgment and the lack of a pre-Hispanic tradition of narrative writing in the Andes.[2] Those answers have never been fully satisfying, because Indigenous scribes drew up wills and other contracts, so writing was neither disallowed nor uncomfortable. These pages, tucked within the corregidor's notary's own papers, show that Peru's native cabildos upheld justice and kept some records. The Cercado's Indian alcalde prepared cases for higher authorities when he could not resolve them independently. Andean communities self-governed, but they did so embedded within a hierarchy that often hid their labor.

The document also demonstrates that officials in the Cercado, in particular, had to articulate law as an intervention between the practices of the rural pueblos de indios and those of the city. This was not a simple matter of imposing "Spanish" law on colonized people. Juan Mateo's investigation centered the experiences of urban Indians, whose intentions often diverged from those of their rural kin, but were not reducible to a Spanish worldview. The alcalde's work was also steeped in the rhetoric of protection. While colonial and ecclesiastic officials imagined the Cercado as a reducción for the formation of Christian subjects who could serve the city's common good, in reality it was a site of contestation over what that common good should look like and who could assure its health.

As the home to more than a thousand men, women, and children from across the Andean region, Santiago del Cercado represented the city's largest and most

FIG. 8.1 Signature of Indian Alcalde Juan Mateo (left) at end of document drawn up by his scribe don Francisco de Fuentes (signature and rubric, right) for the corregidor of the Cercado. With permission from Archivo General de la Nación, Lima, Peru, Protocolos Notariales 1532 Piñeda 1610–1611, ff. 539r.

powerful institution of Indigenous self-governance. It gave life to a sense of collectivity among people of diverse origins and transmitted those cultural and political values to the highest viceregal authorities and the Catholic church. In the absence of shared traditions, its legal and political practices had to be invented and then translated for the approval of authorities. The law produced in the Cercado emerged from the politics of constructing a sense of Indianness and, as such, it signaled Indian difference to Spanish administrators.

The Cercado had an outsize effect on colonial relations. As one of the Jesuits' early programs, and directly under the jurisdiction of royal officials in the viceregal capital, the law that emerged there shaped broader Spanish ideas about Indians. As a locus for temporary migrants who returned to their pueblos after their labor turn, it disseminated ideas across much of the Andean world. The legal structure that naturalized Indian subjects as inherently different and lesser—sometimes to the immediate benefit of those subjects—had repercussions beyond the Cercado's walls. Property law, as called upon by Isabel Caxaylla, is an excellent proxy for seeing how individual and collective notions of the common good could be a site of tension and a transmitter of racial ideas far beyond one small, self-governed Indian town.

Urban Self-Governance

While rural self-governance, drawing upon the memories of pre-conquest polities, was key to Spanish administration of the wealth of the Americas, urban native governance was an afterthought. In the early years, the Crown intended converted, hispanized Indians to join cabildos alongside Spaniards. In 1530, Charles V issued draft edicts to the Audiencia of New Spain with blank spaces where officials could write in the names of native men invited to join the cabildo "so that the Indians get along better with Spaniards and come to appreciate their form of government." Few were invited.[3] Instead, the Spanish founders of cities formed cabildos and, as they gained power, imposed barriers to entry, cutting out non-elites of all kinds.[4]

Occasionally, Spanish city councils did recognize Indigenous and Black residents as vecinos, a term that increasingly (although inconsistently) signaled a permanent resident's participation in urban politics. But use of the term did not necessarily mean that they could participate as equals. One of Lima's founding vecinos, according to Father Bernabé Cobo, was don Martín, a Quechua translator during the conquest, who received a solar during the city's act of foundation but disappeared as a public figure.[5] The cabildo of the north coastal city of Trujillo officially affirmed the status of vecino for an Indigenous tailor named Rodrigo Xuarez when it issued him a solar in 1553 "given that he is a Spanish-speaker and married and a tailor by trade and has children whom he [educates] as Christians. And . . . so that others take him as example and do the same as him."[6] Most of Trujillo's upwardly mobile native population was denied the status of vecino and all were excluded from its cabildo. They coined their own term for an urban property owner, *solarero* (owner of or resident in a solar), which they asserted in notarial documents.[7] But despite their numerical power—in 1604, Indians made up 36 percent of its 3,500 residents—they did not have a seat at the municipal governing table.[8]

Indigenous and African-descent men and women sometimes called themselves vecinos in documents. A notary in 1651 described Juana Barba as a "free Black woman, vecina of this city [Lima] and native of it" in 1651.[9] She was a slave-owner with a substantial estate featuring the kind of jewelry that sumptuary law prohibited Black women from wearing. She had no ability to exercise the political privileges of vecindad in Lima, but she was wealthy and the notary accepted the language of vecina, though he did not call her doña. While some free Black men and women were able to accumulate wealth in seventeenth-century Lima, their access to political power was not similarly transformed.

In the absence of access to municipal office, urban Indians often formed their own governments. These often developed out of parish or barrio organizations. Mexico City contained four Indigenous parishes in the sixteenth century, which rotated offices among them.[10] Cusco, where a large Indigenous population included many members of the Inka nobility as well as competing ethnic groups, was divided into eight dynamic Indigenous parishes with their own cabildos and notaries.[11] Mining centers such as Potosí and Zacatecas also developed urban Indigenous governments specific to their neighborhoods.[12]

Lima did not have Indian parishes, though Santa Ana, San Sebastián, and San Lázaro had large native and free Black populations scattered among less affluent Spaniards. With the brief exception of the Indians of San Lázaro, these did not form secular Indian cabildos; confraternities abounded and a few would become powerful in the seventeenth century.[13] As a city composed mostly of migrants who settled among the Spanish founders and lived within their compounds, it had no magnetic center for Indian authority. This turned out to be a challenge for Spanish administration.

Labor Governance

Self-governance was not a favor to the colonized, but an instrument for ruling them and extracting their labor. The absence was felt in Lima. Enslaved laborers helped build the city, kept its streets clean, and worked on the coastal haciendas, but at a prohibitive cost for many would-be entrepreneurs. Indigenous labor was more abundant and the cost could be modest for those who could command it. Lima's encomenderos staffed their city homes with Indigenous servants and demanded that the caciques of their encomiendas bring groups of laborers in for larger projects. In 1539 the caciques were assigned solares in the city to house their subjects.[14]

The majority of Lima's vecinos, who did not have encomiendas, resented their lack of access to cheap labor. While Andean men, women, and children were also migrating to Lima independently for work, they tended to find jobs as servants and artisans and could not easily be mustered for labor drafts. Food production was an early crisis point. Faced with shortages, the Audiencia in 1550 passed an ordinance allowing any Spaniard with an imminent need for agricultural labor to seize Indians from non-agricultural employment, even against their employers' will.[15] That same year, the cabildo penned a letter to the monarch requesting, among other concessions, the grant of an encomienda, as they had had in Jauja, "to repair the bridges and acequias of the said city, because it is very necessary and beneficial to the natives."[16] The monarch, who was attempting to curtail encomienda, denied the request, leaving the city dependent on encomenderos' willingness to share their own contingents.

The influx of temporary and permanent Indigenous residents raised concerns in the cabildo. The city ordinances of 1550–1551 took three main approaches to establishing control.[17] First, they required that all temporary workers live alongside their caciques on the assigned solares, facilitating care for the sick and attendance at church. Second, they ordered permanent migrants to live with a Spanish master to learn a trade or work as domestic servants. Finally, they expanded the jurisdictions of don Antonio and don Gonzalo Taulichusco, the caciques of nearby Huarochirí and Magdalena, to include ungoverned Indians in the city. The two caciques were named regidores and instructed to resolve civil complaints, keep Indians sober, and enforce churchgoing. In the ceremony marking their confirmation, the Audiencia's judges gave don Antonio and don Gonzalo staffs of office topped with a silver weight, and all the accompanying honors. Apart from the impressive ceremony, they did not leave much documentation of their acts.

Governance remained a struggle. The Crown named a Spaniard to the office of corregidor de los naturales in 1565, to provide justice for urban as well as rural Indians, and Lima's cabildo selected Indian alcaldes to collect tribute and to act as civil judges. While tribute revenues did not noticeably increase, litigation did. One of Lima's regidores, Captain Juan Cortés, complained to the Crown in 1568 that the Indian alcaldes were too successful at working the legal system, having "begun to bring claims from the natives to the corregidor and [alcaldes] ordinarios, the said Indian alcaldes search for cases and invent them in order to harass and mistreat [Spanish officials] for naming Spanish-speaking caciques as judges."[18] By the 1570s, the alcalde's role was reduced to placing apprentices and servants.[19]

City officials made other feeble attempts to force free Black and native residents to work by creating paid offices. In 1555, the cabildo hired a free Black man to round up Black men and women to scrub the city's streets of manure. In 1558, it charged the city's Spanish regidor with hiring twenty Indigenous men and a Spanish supervisor to open the irrigation system so that clean water could enter the city.[20] An Indigenous man, identified only as Martín, was hired in 1562–1563 to serve as the city's executioner and to wash down the central plaza every Saturday "and those times when it may be necessary," for an annual salary of twenty pesos.[21] And in 1567, the cabildo named an Indigenous "constable for Indian affairs" because the natives "received such aggravation in working for people who do not pay them, taking them by force . . . as well as the bad treatment that the blacks give them." The constable was supposed to receive a salary of one hundred pesos a year to intercede in such conflicts. The city's general procurator challenged the use of public funds for the mandate, but the office was created. By 1580, that office was downgraded into leader of a paid cleaning squad, supervised by a Spanish market inspector.[22] By 1602, when Pablo Cusqui Giton held the office of constable, his job largely consisted of "clearing the tables of the tribunal of the (Spanish) alcaldes and sweeping the floor."[23]

While not overtly powerful, these offices became part of a larger framework that Indigenous men might use for their social mobility. The 1613 census reported men bearing the titles of *alcalde de los naturales*, *alcalde de los oficiales*, *alguacil mayor*, and *alguacil*. Four men held ranks in Lima's Indian infantry unit (three *capitanes de indios* and one *sargento mayor*), an institution that included some 500 soldiers in ten infantry squadrons.[24] Twenty-seven men held positions within the Church, leading confraternities as elected *mayordomos* and *mayorales*, or working in parishes as priest-appointed *sacristanes* and *fiscales*.[25] By the turn of the seventeenth century, Lima had many Indigenous leaders with extremely limited jurisdictions. No single official could call upon the city's Indians to pay their tribute or to labor collectively. Despite all the ways that Black and native inhabitants could organize themselves, Lima remained a place where most easily evaded fiscal and labor demands.

The Invention of the Mita

A general solution to the labor crisis appeared in 1573 when Viceroy Toledo standardized the mita. As his predecessors had done on an emergency basis, Toledo adapted an Andean labor practice; his innovation was to turn it into an annual requirement that would last for centuries. The Quechua term mit'a named a reciprocal obligation of one community member to another, or of a community as a whole toward a leader in exchange for services or protections. Toledo's colonial mita instead required each community to send 15 percent of its adult male tributary population for a period of six months annually to the mines, agriculture, or public works in exchange for a minimal wage.[26] Toledo explicitly designed the mita program to wrest control of labor from individual encomenderos and reassign it to public ends, predominantly in extractive mining.[27] Lima was designated as a recipient of the mita "of the plaza," which brought over 1,300 laborers each year from coastal and highland communities to build and maintain its infrastructure and work on local farms.[28]

The expansion of the mita dovetailed with the creation of the reducción of Santiago del Cercado on a site about two miles east of the city center, between 1568 and 1571. The Cercado was an unusual reducción because it was attached to a major city and surrounded by an adobe wall. Intended to facilitate labor provision and promote religious education for the contingents of mitayos who arrived each year, it also claimed to shield rustics from the urban dangers that surrounded them. The town placed additional layers of governance around the mitayos and other residents: they lived within the overlapping jurisdictions of their own caciques, an Indian cabildo and its officers, the corregidor de los naturales, and the Jesuits.

FIG. 8.2 Santiago del Cercado and its walls in 1923.
Source: Variedades (Lima), No. 796, June 2, 1923.

While Peruvian viceroys had come to accept that caciques could not be pushed entirely aside within reducciones, urban centers like Lima offered the possibility of a clean slate. If its inhabitants could dodge their old caciques to avoid tribute payment, they could also be remade in the political image of the subordinate Indian republic. Even their physical organization on the site might be unfettered from previous modes of holding property. The Cercado was proposed as a site that would create a productive, Christian, Indian republic.

An Urban Reducción

In 1568, Governor Lope García de Castro, serving in the interim after the death of Viceroy Conde de Nieva, initiated the construction of Santiago del Cercado, where he hoped to place not only the permanent urban Indian residents and the temporary mita workers, but also the populations of the nearby pueblos de indios Santiago del Surco, San Juan de Lurigancho, and Magdalena. This town was to be set on lands called Cacahuasi, part of the encomienda assigned to Rodrigo Niño, where a group of *yanaconas*, or former Indian auxiliaries to Pizarro, resided.[29] García de Castro expanded the plan to include lands expropriated from other Spanish grandees as well, raising funds for their purchase by auctioning the solares that the cabildo had assigned to the region's caciques. He soon abandoned the idea of incorporating the valley's pueblos and instead focused upon residents of the city itself.

As he seized the solares, paying their owners what the documents characterized as a "just price," alcalde Antonio López described the social problem that he sought to resolve:

> [I]n this said city and its hinterlands there are many dispersed rancherías of Indian men and women, where they live such that, being divided and dispersed, it has not been possible to keep accounts of them so that they can be catechized and taught the elements of our holy Catholic faith.[30]

They "live at large and at their own discretion and will," he charged, without restraint on their "vices, laziness, and drunkenness." The solution, put in motion by López's evictions, was to "bring them together and reduce them to towns." Construction on the wall began, most likely using labor from mitayos alongside enslaved and free Black men and women.[31] Corregidor Alonso Manuel de Anaya and Father Diego de Porres Sagredo managed the project.[32]

The town had a small plaza headed by a church dedicated to Santiago. In 1570, Viceroy Toledo asked the newly arrived Jesuit order to minister to the parish, along with the nearby highland province of Huarochirí. A new order founded in

1534, the Jesuits approached their work in Lima as a way to establish their place in the New World, symbolized by their divergent choices of a walled urban parish and a dispersed, rural sector of the sierra.[33] They selected Huarochirí, they claimed, over the coastal town Lunaguaná, because the highland was "more difficult and nearly inaccessible . . . the Indians then lived according to their ancient customs and their ancestors, which was not to live in towns but divided and separated by parcialidades, living but three or four families in any place and that many more in another, one, two, or more leagues away."[34] The Cercado, in turn, served a key aspect of Jesuit method, which was to instruct the most apt pupils and move on.[35] By ministering to mitayos who could take their knowledge back to their home parishes, they could be both centered in Lima and mobile throughout the region. This also established the new order prominently in the viceregal capital. As Padre Diego Bracamonte reported, the Provincial's first sermon in the church of Santo Domingo was announced with a temblor. Though the earth shook, the full audience remained present "with the desire to hear the Padre."[36]

Santiago del Cercado would house hundreds of mitayos from across the region each year. Adult men, sometimes accompanied by their families, walked up to 200 miles to be distributed as agricultural, construction, or occasionally household laborers. The Jesuits provided them with religious guidance and

FIG. 8.3 Church of Santiago del Cercado. Photograph by Karen Graubart.

education, contributing two priests, and a coadjutor paid 500 pesos every year out of tribute revenues.[37] This stipend was at least briefly supplemented by a tax on every bottle of chicha sold in the Cercado's tavern.[38]

The Jesuit project in Lima concretized their critique of the city's religious practices, which they considered inadequate in both form and content. According to Father Giovanni Anello Oliva, the Jesuits would increase and improve the delivery of sermons, provide sacraments more regularly, and inculcate in parishioners a life of contemplation and reflection on their Christian duties through home visits and other personal interactions.[39] The creation of a walled Indian town centered on a church, as well as an eventual school for the sons of caciques, a cemetery, a hospital, and a jail for idolators, was a strike at the reform of ritual as well as space. It was to solve the problem that Viceroy Toledo laid out in a letter to the monarch in early 1570, namely, to have the Indians "who are already conquered and brought to the gospel and to your majesty's royal obedience, live tranquil and with firmness and contentment in the Christian faith that they have received."[40]

Tranquility was an ongoing concern. The 1560s had been marked not only by evidence of inadequate conversion, but by Indigenous uprisings and violent resistance. Lima's Spanish residents also worried about runaway slaves and the possibility of slave revolts. In response, the cabildo issued ordinances in 1570 restricting the movement of people of African descent, free or enslaved. The Jesuits claimed a unique ability to calm these waters. Padre maestro Luis López claimed that he, with the help of three or four brothers, brought together 2,000 Black Christians in the streets of Lima on Sundays and holy days in Christian processions, and

> up til now neither religious nor police could stop their heathen dances nor the drunken festivities, where they kill one another in the plazas and streets, nor the running away from their masters to the mountains; and after the Company arrived and took this on, God has been served that they have changed their ways, that there are no dances nor is the atabal [drum] heard, nor murder committed, nor does a Black man flee to the mountain.[41]

The Cercado's walls set the parish of Indians apart from a world its authors characterized as full of predatory Spaniards, unconverted and uncontrolled Indians, and rebellious and violent Blacks.[42]

Despite the grand plans, the Cercado ended up limited in its practice. Not only did the reducción policy imposed on the valley's populations eliminate the need to gather them into the walled town, but the "at-large" laborers and migrants in the city mostly remained where they were, too. Two moments were foundational in establishing that Indians had the right to live where they chose. The first was when fishermen, who lived on the bank of the Rimac River in San Lázaro, were violently relocated to the Cercado one night in 1590. The valuable land beneath some of their homes was sold to wealthy Limeños and their confraternity was removed to the Jesuit neighborhood.[43] They were not forced to remain in the Cercado; a royal order of 1595 allowed them to live where they chose.[44] Instead, the viceroy attempted to induce relocation by exempting permanent residents of the Cercado from mita.[45]

The second attempt came in 1603, when the Jesuits lobbied the corregidor de los naturales of the Cercado to move all Indigenous inhabitants of Lima to their care. In support of this strategy, Viceroy Velasco promoted Andrés Ramírez Inga, the former Indian alcalde of the Cercado, to the position of alcalde mayor. The appointment letter specifically charged him with settling "the Indians who might be in this city and in the rancherías of San Lázaro and in houses and *corrales*" in the Cercado, due to the "great damage that follows from . . . living among people who drink excessively, from which result deaths and other terrible injuries." Ramírez Inga would receive, in addition to his salary of 250 pesos, a peso for every Indian certified to have relocated for a full year.[46]

It is unclear how many urban residents were removed, but a collective represented by ten men who identified themselves as "Indians from San Lázaro" petitioned in 1604 for their right to freedom of movement and residence.[47] The group presented themselves as well-off artisans and laborers, possessors of agricultural properties and stores, and members of confraternities. They claimed to have been deprived not only of their property but also of their political and religious autonomy, and of their marriages, as women were being held apart from their husbands.

Archbishop Toribio de Mogrovejo and some municipal authorities also challenged the removals. The city's alguacil mayor appeared before the cabildo to argue that the demand to move "all the Indians, craftsmen of all kinds, who own their own stores and houses where they live and work" would be damaging because "these were very useful and beneficial Indians . . . because they produce the city's manufactures in those trades, and the trades could not be sustained without them," leaving the city with fewer commodities and services at far higher prices.[48]

After sixteen frustrating years of litigation, royal rulings in their favor, and the viceroy's insistence that he could not safely implement their dispersal, Lima's Indigenous residents were ultimately confirmed in their freedom. Phillip III's 1606 order ensured that they could not be forced to move to the Cercado, although they could be made to labor in particular ways and their lands could still be expropriated for the city's needs.[49]

Even so, the Cercado became a bustling town. Encircled by a solid wall with two doors that opened to the city and a third to the countryside, it contained thirty-five blocks, each divided into four solares. Every pueblo sending mitayos to Lima was required to purchase lots to shelter their members.[50] The solares came to be designated by the names of their collective owners—the solar of Huarochirí, or of Cajatambo—reminiscent of the toponyms Andeans customarily used to demarcate their agricultural plots. The transient and permanent population can only be estimated. A document from 1571 states that the pueblos of the Lima Valley sent 193 mitayos that year. Most came from much farther afield. The Jesuit José de Arriaga reported in 1594 that the Cercado regularly contained some 1,300 baptized men and women over the age of twelve, most of whom were seasonal mita laborers.[51]

The Cercado became more than a way station for temporary workers, nor was it a ghetto housing marginal individuals displaced from the city center.[52] Instead, it grew into a neighborhood where some Indigenous men and women might build careers and lives. Its shared practices emerged through the crucible of cultural diversity. Most reducciones gathered peoples with similar histories, even if they were reorganized for colonial purposes. The Cercado's residents came from the coast and the highlands, as well as the distant north and south. Some were enslaved people of African heritage. They spoke a variety of languages and had distinct histories. They would have to negotiate those differences along with the expectations of the Spaniards who surrounded them.

Walls and Barriers

The example of medieval Castile provides a reminder that minority or subordinate communities sometimes found separation desirable. Walls could preserve community coherence, though they occasionally had far more devastating effects. But they were not very central to colonization in the Spanish Americas, where they were considered unnecessary and prohibitively expensive to build.[53] One exception was military: Spaniards erected walls, presidios, and garrisons to fortify settlements against attacks from hostile native populations or European competitors for conquest and treasure.[54] Those walls conveniently contained the slaves and prisoners who were building them. *Atarazanas*, fortified docks, were used in Mexico City to ward off Indigenous attacks that never came. In many cities, wealthy and powerful settlers turned their own compounds into personal fortresses, *casas fuertes*. But despite constant talk of threats, few cities erected walls.[55] English Dominican friar Thomas Gage noted their absence during his travels in Oaxaca in 1625, which "lieth open without walls, bulwarks, forts, towers, or any castle, ordnance, or ammunition to defend it."[56]

The religious founders of convents and missions, however, did embrace walls. In Oaxaca, Gage pointed to the example of the city's Dominican convent, with walls thick enough that horses could pull carts across them.[57] The seventeenth-century Jesuit missions of Paraguay were enclosed cities for the religious as well as small groups of refugees who came to be protected from enslavement and encomienda and to receive Christian doctrine while living under native governance.[58] Across the Spanish Americas, walls were central to female enclosure in convents and housing for women seeking divorce, to maintain safe distance between the worldly and the sacred.[59] Ironically, the religious opted for fortification while their secular compatriots placed their faith in "spiritual walls," a reliance upon faith and piety to protect the cities they constructed as islands of policía.[60]

In this context, Santiago del Cercado in Lima appears unique. Its walls did not so much protect Indian souls or bodies—its residents came and went freely to work in the valleys and the city—as set them apart and control access to their possessions and livelihoods. As Viceroy Velasco noted to the king in 1598, the Cercado was

> a good site, and near the city and populated by many Indians, and where adobe houses have been built for many more than there are today, with an abundance of water, being at the head [of the river], with space for their gardens of legumes and raising fowl and other husbandry that they are accustomed to have for their sustenance; and all is surrounded by an adobe wall so that the Blacks and mestizos may not rob them nor assault them by night as they often do in other places, where there is no protection.[61]

Protection served as the watchword for the project. Toledo worried about placing Christian Indians in proximity to unconverted ones, for example, just as Castilians wished to separate Jews from conversos. He also feared that people of African descent and, most important, Spaniards would prey upon Indians. In a 1572 letter to Philip II, Toledo noted that he generally wished "encomenderos and Spaniards, mestizos, and blacks not to live among Indians nor do business with them because of the poor treatment they give them" but also called for licensing trusted individuals to interact or live with Indians, such as "married mestizos who, with their wives, wish to live among Indians . . . and some married Spanish men who wish to live in Indian locales that are along roads."[62]

Nonetheless, men and women of African descent lived in the Cercado, mostly enslaved people purchased by Indian inhabitants or the Jesuit order.[63] Their presence was perceived as the culmination of the Indians' process of hispanization. As Father Cobo put it, "The Cercado is a neighborhood where only Indians live . . . they are all so hispanized, men and women alike, they understand and speak our language; in the way they dress and decorate their homes they look like Spaniards, and it is enough to say to prove this that, among them, they have more than eighty Black slaves who serve them."[64]

The Cercado's walls, then, were not to prevent attacks or contagion, as all manner of urban residents walked through the gates regularly. The walls were intended to help produce policía and to buttress Andean inhabitants as part of a plan for human development that would enable them eventually to participate fully in Iberian society, as a Christian republic providing labor for the city. But that plan would have limits; Indians were never to be received as fully hispanized.

Customary Law within the Walls

The Cercado, like any reducción, had its own native leadership: alcaldes, constables, and a cabildo on the model of a Spanish town. It also had an Indian alcalde mayor, whose office was attached to that of the corregidor de los naturales. The Cercado had no inherent nobility, although caciques from many regions lived there while pursuing litigation or supervising their mitayos. Its early elected leaders appear to have come from plebeian lineages, rising to power through skilled trades, membership in the infantry company, and service to the Catholic Church. There were possible exceptions, like Andrés Ramírez Inga, whose surname suggests that he was associated with the Cusco elite (though he did not use the don as would be expected).[65] But on the whole, its officials were permanent residents who earned moderate incomes in the city and parlayed that success into political office.

The Indian leaders of the Cercado were subject to multiple higher authorities. The absence of a kingdom-wide native advisor to the monarch—such as the alcalde mayor de las aljamas in Castile—meant there was no singular coordination above them. Instead, there were many lines of command and influence, including the Jesuits who controlled the religious life of the parish and the corregidor de los naturales, as the town's de facto judge. They also interacted with Lima's cabildo, though the Crown explicitly denied that body any power over them because their interests so often conflicted. Because Lima was the seat of governance for the viceroyalty of Peru, the Cercado's leaders had ready access to the Real Audiencia and the Archbishop. When the Cercado's first Indian constable, Diego Ticayo, had not received payment for his first two years on the job—which required bringing Indians to church and keeping them sober, "among other things"—he took his complaint to the Audiencia, which issued him the thirty pesos.[66] The archival record suggests that Cercado officials cultivated relationships with all of these institutions, and residents creatively explored many venues for righting their wrongs.

All these leaders and venues claimed to keep them safe from predations, but in practice—or at least in the archival record—this often manifested as a concern with property. At times they sought to protect native subjects from adopting certain forms of property tenancy and ownership that might, theoretically, worsen their situation. Indigenous residents of Lima were already restricted in the kinds of property transactions they could engage in, and they had access to a legal Protector to keep the ignorant from being connived. In 1594, Juana Sánchez successfully sued, with a court-appointed lawyer, because she purchased an over-priced lot from a Spaniard due to her ignorance. The seller argued that she was "a Spanish-speaking woman, of good understanding, knowledgeable about business like any Spanish man" but in the end had to refund the price. Sánchez's status as a member of the class of miserables overruled her particular characteristics.[67]

Polo Ondegardo, the Spanish corregidor of Cusco in the mid-sixteenth century, argued strongly that these novices should embrace certain institutions from Spain, but not give up all of their own practices. In protecting their fueros or customary law, they should avoid all "evil and reprobate innovations."[68] From this perspective, the role of the town's walls shifts slightly. The predations that the Jesuits and corregidor were refusing included those that invited certain definitions of property. The slim caseload of surviving petitions from the office of the corregidor of the Cercado reveals that conditions of property ownership were of great importance to the Crown and its representatives. In particular, they sought to manage the ways that natives came to engage with property law, routing it through their difference.

This concern can be seen through the transformation of the Cercado's solares, the lots that communities purchased collectively to house mitayos. A handful of wills written between 1605 and 1610, twenty-five or thirty years after the gates opened, illustrate the changes.[69] Four Indigenous testators called themselves owners of houses on solares associated with the communities of Pisco, Chincha, and Huarochirí, though none hailed from these places; they lived in the Cercado as permanent residents and not as mitayos or even descendants of mitayos.

How did these men and women come to think of themselves as homeowners in a collective site? Some of the houses may have been retired community structures, like the house don Diego Flores purchased at a later date in the solar of the Olleros, "previously its tavern."[70] But in the first Cercado generation, the transformation of collective into private property seems to have come into being through acts of individual improvement, both to structures and to land, either by mitayos or by permanent residents living on bits of available solares. Magdalena Yauri Chumbi noted obliquely that she had purchased her house and garden for twenty-nine pesos from another Indigenous man named Juan Cabilca.[71] Diego Sedeño's will added more information. He had originally purchased his house from Juan Paichucama for twenty-four pesos in cash. Since then he had added a bedroom and living room with draperies and an unfinished roof, a locked door to the street, and many fruit trees. These improvements, then, marked the residence as his own even if he had no title to the solar on which it was constructed. And Maria Llacsa ordered that her house and garden in the Cercado be sold in a public auction to the highest bidder, raising the question of whether this was an open real estate market, and whether someone who was not Indigenous could purchase his or her way into residence in the Cercado.[72] The will was composed by the town's notary, suggesting that he, at least, believed the request was legal.

These were not common experiences in those first decades. Even permanent Cercado residents, when drawing up a will, listed assets like domestic animals, or inexpensive clothing, perhaps some furnishings or a small amount of jewelry or coins. They might name agricultural lands back in their towns of origin that they wished distributed in a certain way. But they did not call themselves vecinos nor did they attempt to transfer ownership of their places of residence to another. Pedro Xulca, for example, lived in a house on the solar of Chincha, where he had installed two doors costing him four pesos. He did not claim to own the site or the house, but only the doors.[73]

Where did these residents derive the belief that improving a property gave them ownership over it? Spaniards certainly understood that improving or erecting structures was inherent to the process of "taking possession," which largely involved acting unimpededly on and occupying untitled land.[74] They enacted a version of this ritual whenever a piece of property changed hands: breaking sticks, throwing grass, calling out "possession, possession" unhampered in front of an audience. But that act was generally prologue to the production of a written title and the issuance of boundary markers. And while this might have worked on rural frontiers, it did not play out in Lima. In 1574, a native man named Juan told the following story in his will: "Francisco Martín, a tanner, had given me a solar next to San Lázaro (church) for myself and my wife, and I possessed this solar as my own, and built on it a house and corral for cattle, and afterwards, Francisco Martin sold it to an Indian for 150 pesos." Juan demanded one hundred pesos of the price for himself, leaving the other fifty as a fee to Martín. He learned to his dismay that Lima's officials did not consider improvement to a property to constitute ownership of the structure or the land beneath it. Since he had not ceded title to Juan, Francisco Martín had retained the right to his solar no matter what the temporary occupant had done.[75]

More likely, Cercado residents brought this belief that property could be redefined from their experiences in pueblos de indios, where communities had worked out the details of planning and distributing lots and building structures together. Communities often incorporated flexibility and the possibility of

redefinition into their use of lands, whether drawing upon pre-conquest practices or inventing new methods. The Yauyos, a highland community to Lima's
east, for example, seem to have understood land tenure as having fluid, rather
than fixed, boundaries in this period. Plots could transition in and out of collective and individual use, depending upon the needs of the decision-making collective.[76] This ran counter to the process of boundary marking and titling that
Spanish authorities enforced, but could prevail quietly within the realm of the
community. At the same time, rural communities experienced having their lands
captured and redefined by outsiders and insiders alike, and they must have had
quick and elastic responses to the ongoing threats. They also came to understand
the close relationship between property ownership and colonial power. Mitayos
and migrants brought versions of this knowledge to the Cercado.

By the seventeenth century, some permanent residents of the Cercado were
converting space on collectively owned solares into private homes and gardens,
and attempting to pass them to their heirs or sell them in a developing real estate
market. Cercado leaders participated in some of these actions. In 1691, the corregidor de los naturales received a petition from the Cercado's procurator requesting
that Matheo Felipe, described as an Indian vecino, be assigned a vacant solar as a
meritorious gesture.[77] Matheo Felipe had for many years been *mayoral* of the solar
of Huaylas, an office designating either the person who supervised the mitayos
from Huaylas, or someone who acted as a local arbitrator or representative for
the residents on that solar. He had, for unstated reasons, been dispossessed of his
own home and "thrown outside the walls" where he and his family were living in
a field. The procurator requested that a vacant site in the solar of Quiquis be reassigned to Matheo Felipe. The corregidor investigated, learned that the plot was
described as "ownerless," suggesting that it was neither privately nor collectively
titled, and so ordered. In the final ceremony, Matheo Felipe held the Indian alcalde's hand and they carried out rituals of possession together before they signed
the documents that would establish his enduring title to the site.

The cooperation between officials at different levels here is notable. While
Spanish corregidores made law, they depended upon Indian notaries and alcaldes to witness, draw up, and legitimate the process. Indian officials worked out
the details between parties informally as well, often sidestepping higher-level
interventions. They also performed official acts independently, as when in 1687
Francisco de Contreras and doña Juana Josefa de Contreras appealed to alcalde
Hernando de Rivera to have a solar and house they inherited from their late parents in the Cercado legally divided in two.[78] The community's officials gathered
at the solar, measured out two equal sectors, and had their notary document the
acts for posterity; Rivera kept the papers in a locked box in the town for safety.

The parish's authorities were occasionally called in to resolve confusion between property regimes. In 1686, the alcalde was asked to decide upon the ownership of a solar by Diego Tobar and his wife Ynes Lázaro.[79] Lázaro claimed to have inherited the solar, in the site called *Olleros* (Potters), from her late father Captain Gerónimo Cansinos, but had no papers to prove her case. Their witnesses, some of whom titled themselves vecinos of the Cercado, testified to Captain Cansinos' long occupation of the site, with a period of rental to a third party after his death, before his son "displaced" the renter and moved in with his own family. The Indian cabildo found Ynes Lázaro and her husband to have legitimate possession of the solar by virtue of being Captain Cansinos' heirs. The renter's potential claim was pushed aside because of the legitimacy of the original claim and the inheritance.

But what might be unique about the Cercado is that these distinct regimes—collective solares for temporary community housing, privately owned homes and gardens, and rentals or convertible housing for non-mitayos who also did not own property—all coexisted in tension. These were not simply different rules about managing property but distinct philosophies about the best way for Indians to live: were they inherently associated with collective property, or were they to be encouraged to invest money and labor to improve and transfer land? Officials approached the problem from a variety of perspectives as well. The tensions were often resolved by drawing upon a colonialist caricature of Andean frailty and ignorance rather than an expectation that they should act like urban Spaniards. That caricature was as casually rendered by Andean parties as by Spaniards; it became fundamental legal rhetoric for litigants.

Juana Ñusta and the Yauyos' Solar

One final case demonstrates how this tension could be resolved through the insistence on Indian difference. In 1652, two noblemen, on behalf of the community of the Yauyos, filed a complaint with the viceroy to evict the widow Juana de Ávalos from their assigned solar in the Cercado.[80] The Yauyos had lost control of the site they had purchased nearly a century earlier, leaving them without a place to live while they tended to fields they were renting in the Late Valley.

Through their procurator, the Yauyos argued that the loss of their solar caused them to have difficulties meeting required tribute and mita obligations. Drawing upon the rhetoric of royal protection, they noted that their children "lacked Christian doctrine and were being raised like barbarians" outside the Jesuit town's walls.[81] They asked the king's representative to "shield these poor ones." They also identified themselves as *forasteros* (outsiders) rather than permanent residents, highlighting their transitory occupation of the site for the sole purpose of paying the community's tribute.

The rector of the Cercado, Father Luis de Teruel, gave testimony that

> the Yauyos have a site of two or three blocks, purchased with their community's funds, which, because it was unused, some have planted with gardens, but this is done with the knowledge of the caciques of said province and thus whenever they have wished to establish residence in it, it must be restored to them as their own property.[82]

These phrases suggest that the Yauyos had consented to a temporary change in the use of the field. They had transformed it from commons to private holding for a period, but wished to return it to commons because it was now in their best interest. This resonates with what is known about their practices in the sierra, where they treated land tenure fluidly.[83] In the priest Teruel's worldview, though, it looked more like a short-term loan or a generous decision not to remove squatters until the land was needed. In his eyes the land had an inviolable character as a collective holding. While they differed in reasoning, both the Yauyos and the priest wished for the same outcome.

The corregidor, don Joseph de Carbajal Marroquín, under direction of the viceroy, restored the property to the Yauyos in August 1653 in a ceremony. Together with Father Teruel they publicly walked the boundaries, performing various rituals including stating that the garden on it was "called that of Domingo Francisco," a recitation of the plot's genealogy that memorialized its alternative history and the ongoing claim. These practices, too, might have had different meanings for participants. At the end they declared that the act of possession had taken place "quietly and peacefully without contradiction, and in this the said corregidor gave them protection."[84]

But in September, the parties returned to court. A lawyer representing the family and heirs of the late Captain Domingo Francisco asked the corregidor to assert their ownership of the solar. According to their account, Domingo Francisco, a commander in the Indian infantry company, had spent 6,000 pesos improving the site, which he had left to his widow and children. The couple had occupied the site for more than fifty years continuously, and the story the Yauyos had presented just months before was a sinister, if convincing, fiction. Juana Ñusta, deploying a Quechua title of nobility rather than her family name of de Ávalos and calling herself vecina, presented her late husband's will into evidence.[85]

The will illuminates Captain Domingo Francisco's path to colonial prosperity. Born in the Cercado to a man who used the honorific don, Francisco had acquired a large portfolio of lands in the Late Valley, most of which he rented to

Indigenous tenants. Some he had purchased, others were inherited from family members, and he claimed to have received titles to them all from the king.

Captain Francisco indicated that he had already resolved a lawsuit over the contentious property with the Yauyos. He explained why it was his in familiar terms:

> Item, I declare as my property a *huerta* (cultivated land) that I have in this pueblo of the Cercado, with its house, which is bounded at the top by a solar of Yaucha and on a side by the huerta of San Agustin, and on the other side with the solares of the Indians of Jauja and below by the solares of the Yauyos; that I cultivated this huerta myself and it was purchased from different persons and because of the right that the Indians of San Cristobal [de los Yauyos] claimed to it, I have brought a lawsuit in this Real Audiencia and the judges found on my behalf, for myself and my heirs, and I made this huerta because it originally was an uncultivated field and it is entirely completed . . . which I have fenced in, and so I declare it as my property.

Here again, a Cercado resident claimed that the act of improvement granted him a form of possession that could be passed down to his heirs. His will went much farther in demonstrating his individual success, as the owner of five Black slaves, four saddled horses, two muskets, a sword and dagger, a helmet and buckler, and other pieces of a military uniform, as well as luxurious clothing.

Captain Domingo Francisco, in other words, represented a success for the colonial project. He requested burial in the Cercado's church wearing the habit of San Francisco and left bequests to numerous confraternities. He had risen to a position of status within the spaces available to native men, becoming captain of the Indian infantry unit and gaining the attendant privileges. He owned enslaved Black men and women, the most potent symbol of colonial authority available to him. He had bought the lands that desperate communities were placing on the market and was provisioning the city by renting them back to now-landless farmers. He had had these lands officially titled by the Crown, removing them from native patrimony, and he had sued to defend his property. Now he wished to pass on his individual success to his widow and children. But he came into conflict with the tensions around property and Indians in the Cercado.

The viceroy and the corregidor de los naturales ruled against him, affirming the Yauyos' collective ownership of the solar. The corregidor's decision, read alongside other cases over land rights, reveals the Cercado's status as a space where Indians were protected—and arrested—on their path to becoming colonial subjects. The Crown was concerned about the encroachments on native communities in the valleys surrounding the city. Royal officials acted aggressively to monopolize the privatization of their lands, leaving collective holdings as a community's main defense against expropriation. While some Cercado residents had transformed their temporary spaces into small private residences—through the act of building shacks and planting gardens on slices of sites—the Crown reserved its preference for collective use of the land in support of the legal definition of its Indian subjects as tributaries and mitayos. The viceroy's final word on the subject in August had been to tell the corregidor to "demand that the alcaldes of the Cercado turn the solares over to [the Yauyos], wherein they can have a house and from there take care of their fields, where they find lands for rent, and charge the Jesuits to admit them and enroll them, like others, in the said town."[86]

In short, the leaders of the Yauyos understood themselves to be able to assign usufruct on property flexibly and likely projected that onto the solar they purchased in the Cercado. That belief came into conflict with the actions of Domingo Francisco, who understood property as a means to generate long-term wealth to protect his family. He had also learned that possession could be asserted through improving land or adding structures, as well as by acts of titling that could be completed after the fact. Overseeing all of this were a Jesuit priest with sympathy for the Yauyos—his putative flock—refracted through his own beliefs about Indian abilities; and the corregidor, viceroy, and audiencia judges, all with their eyes on the universal implications of this moment and assuredly with far less experience of the ways of the rural republics.

That all this took place in the Cercado mattered. By setting out a walled town dedicated to conserving the ability of rural communities to supply labor and financial support to the city, royal officials had the opportunity to shape property regimes. But claims worked through layers of jurisdiction, so the Yauyos might have first called upon the Indian alcalde and the Jesuits, then formally taken their complaint to the corregidor and the viceroy. Royal officials considered the laws regarding possession, but they also contemplated the effects of their ruling on tribute payments and Catholic instruction. The emergent strategy to collect royal funds—to favor the Yauyos as a collective even while the rest of the Cercado was transforming around them—was also part of a definition of colonial indigeneity.

———

Santiago del Cercado was founded to solve an urban problem. The need for cheap labor led to the imposition of a universal labor draft, the mita, which brought over a thousand Andean workers to Lima each year. There they were joined by permanent migrants, mostly artisans and laborers who spread across the city in ways that concerned Spanish authorities. They settled into the rhythm of the city and invented their own institutions. They also lived in inconvenient and unsanitary places, and they lacked the kind of oversight that made Spaniards feel safe. The Cercado was a double solution: they built a walled town to house those laborers, and they imposed layers of governance upon them, from Indian officials who could manage day-to-day issues to royal appointees who could issue summary judgment.

The Cercado's walls were permeable in terms of human access. There is plenty of evidence that outsiders broke in to disrupt its life, and that its residents came and went freely. But they did present a clarity about jurisdiction and a space wherein law could be made by all those layers of authorities. Caciques, alcaldes, fiscales, and other men and women defined the ways that their subjects approached colonial officials. They invented new enterprises, borrowed from the laws and customs of others, partnered with them, and fought against them. There should be no doubt that in the Andes, as in New Spain and other regions, local autonomy mattered a great deal to everyday life, and played a key part in producing Indigenous ways of being, even in the coastal regions so numerically and economically dominated by Spanish rule.

In the Cercado, native authorities like alcalde Juan Mateo carried out actions within their jurisdiction, managing the welfare of transient and permanent immigrants, distributing resources, collecting taxes, and keeping the peace. The alcalde was embedded within a larger web of jurisdictions, of the corregidor and the Jesuits as well as within layers of procurators and bureaucrats. He was also responsible to the changing forms of justice that were being brought to the city from rural pueblos.

But the case of the Cercado shows another side of that story. Indigenous ways of being were determined in conversation with Spanish beliefs and acts. The concept of policía that was promoted within reducción policy imagined an Indian subject who was inherently different from a Spaniard. The legal category of Indian also came to imply cultural characteristics, rendering the colonized Indian never fully modern, urban, or civilized.

The role of the kuraka and the law he or she enforced within the ayllu became productively entangled with Spanish notions of lordship and jurisdiction over a republic, enabling the emergence of a multiplicity of legal forms and beliefs. But Andean understandings of what was happening had to be translated through a Castilian grammar, which ultimately empowered the monarch and his legal system to fix meanings upon Andean subjects. Even while both Spaniards and Andeans lived with a variety of ways to recognize, use, and alienate property, Spaniards required that Andeans be simplified and reduced. The Cercado's wall serves as a metaphor for the way law was naturalized and instrumentalized as persistent difference.

Conclusion: Republics Producing Difference

ON DECEMBER 28, 1591, the statue of the Virgin of Copacabana with her infant Jesus sweated or wept for forty-five minutes within their small, straw-roofed chapel in Santiago del Cercado. Cloths used to wipe the tears away smelled of rosemary or some "celestial" scent. The event punctuated both the conflict over the shrimpers' earlier removal from San Pedro to the Cercado and Archbishop Mogrovejo's pursuit of a reputation for holiness. It provided evidence of the shrimpers' Christianity and was one of the miracles that eventually led to Mogrovejo's canonization.[1] The story is well known within the histories of Lima and of colonial religion. The Virgin of Copacabana's roots were in the Lake Titicaca region where native celebrants associated her with older Andean practices. Her veneration spread rapidly across the region through the Marian cult of Candelaria, eventually arriving in San Lázaro, Lima.[2] In the seventeenth century, the miracle would assist in the emergence of a powerful system of Indigenous self-governance in that neighborhood.[3]

While the miracle had extensive repercussions, it was a deeply local event that reshaped the Indian republic at its center. The chapel where it took place was a humble structure that Mogrovejo had had erected directly after the fishermen's removal from San Pedro in 1590. It was to replace the chapel of Nuestra Señora del Reposo, an Indigenous confraternity housed in the leper hospital of San Lázaro. The confraternity had, in 1588, sponsored the fabrication of a statue of the Virgin by two Spanish artists, a sculptor and a painter, which drew upon European artistic traditions.[4] When the Indians were removed to the Cercado, they brought the sculpture with them and renamed her, and their confraternity, Nuestra Señora de Copacabana. In doing so they connected themselves to the cult in Lake Titicaca and the statue produced there by the Quechua artist Francisco Tito Yupanqui.[5]

Republics of Difference. Karen B. Graubart, Oxford University Press. © Oxford University Press 2022.
DOI: 10.1093/oso/9780190233839.003.0010

According to later documentation, the parishioners present at nine in the morning of December 28, the Feast of the Holy Innocents, included a Spaniard from the Hospital of Espíritu Santo, accompanying a very ill enslaved woman named Esperanza, and four Spanish women who said they attended regularly on Sundays. The regular priest, Quechua specialist Alonso de Huerta, asked Juan de Pineda to say mass for him. Pineda was reportedly unenthusiastic because of the heat and the distance he had to travel from Lima.

Pineda called in the Andean parishioners and the Spanish and Black visitors. A Spanish woman first noticed the tears. One of the Jesuits at the church of Santiago heard the uproar and arrived to announce his skepticism. Archbishop Mogrovejo opened a file that very day to investigate the miracle. He took testimony from the Spaniards and Blacks present, but not from the Indians, no doubt thinking that church officials would not have considered his native parishioners and co-litigants to be impartial witnesses.[6] The official story of the Andean Virgin appearing to a displaced indigenous parish became authorized through the words of non-Indians. The Catholic Church removed the statue itself to a chapel in the cathedral, away from the care of the parishioners who had dressed and tended to for her for decades.

Even more profoundly for the residents, the miracle led to a Spanish takeover of their confraternity and provoked conflict within and against their leadership. By 1604, the fishermen of San Pedro de los Camaroneros had been pushed aside within the confraternity by a group of Indigenous master artisans. This was the group that litigated, with Mogrovejo, for their freedom of movement and ended the forced removals to the Cercado. Between 1604 and 1607, the confraternity of Copacabana, led by those artisans, fought against the mismanagement of their funds. Miguel Sánchez, the cofradía's former mayordomo and a tailor and signatory of the 1604 complaint, was arrested when he refused to turn the financial books over to the new mayordomo, Hernando Quispe, also a tailor.[7] The following year, Quispe and the second mayordomo, shoemaker Sebastián Francisco, charged the chaplains Alonso de Huerta and Francisco Gambarana with financial mismanagement.[8] Such conflicts were common within cofradías, whose leaders were not always competent treasurers or stewards, but these tensions were magnified by the onslaught of fame and money.

After the Virgin wept, wealth flooded into the confraternity. Members collected thousands of pesos in alms from the public each year, along with jewelry for the statue and income-generating gifts of houses, haciendas, and domestic animals.[9] Funds also came in from new members, who included some of the city's most elevated citizens; Mogrovejo had opened the confraternity up to non-Indians against the express wishes of the cofrades.[10] The Spanish chaplains kept their accounts separate from those of the Indigenous mayordomos, maintaining a secret log of the gifts from Spanish cofrades. They utilized the cofradía's own statue to fundraise without the mayordomos' permission and diverted funds illegally to their own projects. Huerta had also mixed his own sheep in with those belonging to the cofradía on a ranch in Huamantanga, making custody of the growing flock ambiguous.

In 1606, an ecclesiastic judge ruled in favor of the Indian mayordomos, requiring Huerta and Gambarana to repay the confraternity more than 14,000 pesos and ordering that all the institution's funds be kept in one single account from then on (and its animals separate from personal property). New chaplains would be named. But the conflicts did not end. An earthquake later that year destroyed the Virgin's new chapel at the cathedral, and the rescued statue was placed on the main altar, turning it into a public object of worship. The cofradía begged to remove it to a new chapel they were building in San Lázaro, but the cathedral's dean refused, arguing that it was an inappropriate site for such an exalted image. He also prohibited them from burying their members in the cathedral's chapel, a privilege that Mogrovejo had previously granted and a prestigious honor that recognized the deceased as true Christians and prominent citizens. Instead they were reduced to the status of questionable converts as well as being denied a connection to their own miraculous Virgin.[11]

The Indians of San Lázaro would rebuild, and eventually they became the center of Indigenous political life in Lima. But the events of 1604–1607 revealed how their jurisdiction could shrink when wealth and power were involved. Church officials, especially the archbishop, were content to use the small Indian confraternity as a symbol of the miraculous status of creole belief in Peru. They were eager to fundraise through an association with an institution built by the city's beleaguered Indians. They sided with the Indians against bad stewards, replacing them with priests who would be marginally more transparent while they managed the cult's substantial resources. But they also were suspicious of the fame that accompanied the miracle and of the ability of the confraternity to manage its excesses. The republic became the mechanism through which all of these ambivalences were expressed—both the embrace of native collectivity and the lack of confidence in its ability to command.

The republic was a malleable political and corporate form. It could be called into being by citizens or imposed by the Crown, and in either case would coevally produce law, jurisdiction, a sense of identity among its members, and a distinct characterization of that identity for outsiders. When it served no purpose for its members—like Lima's absent Black republic—the form could dissolve. When it surpassed authorities' expectations of appropriate wealth and power, they might co-opt or overtake it. But most of the republics examined here had more complicated lifespans, expanding and contracting over time. The Muslim and Jewish aljamas of Seville diminished every decade, eventually corresponding to a small number of leading families that found it a source of comfort or prestige. Even in the face of expulsion, perhaps most important at that juncture, the aljamas continued to pay their taxes and meet in their cabildos. The republics that survived were meaningful to their members, however reduced, as well as useful to authorities.

The Crown and other authorities often wished to mark republics associated with subordinated peoples by space as well as law. At times, members of the republics embraced the promise of a shared place. In the words recorded from Axataf's negotiation with Fernando III in the thirteenth century, the Muslims desired a wall "so that everyone would be safe."[12] As the residents of Seville's judería understood in 1391, walls themselves did not provide protection, though many preferred collective living in some form. The Jewish cabildo returned to the former judería as a source of status, Muslim artisans were more dispersed yet gravitated toward locations shared by coworkers, and many Andean immigrants moved to Lima's Cercado where they could proclaim their status as vecinos and demonstrate their status as owners of real estate and enslaved humans. Even more radically, rural polities had ambivalent relationships with their reduced pueblos, which required that they reconstruct their economic and social practices but guaranteed them some autonomy and limited property rights. The survival of Indigenous languages, cultural practices, and political systems across the Americas results from that restructuring. These are not scattered remnants or relics of the pre-Hispanic past, but contingent ways that communities have reimagined themselves up to the present.

The very fragility of the republic demonstrates its utility, particularly in moments of instability and threat. At some point after 1391, well-off Jews returned to reclaim spaces in the former judería. It mattered to them to be near one another, alongside their synagogues and sites of collective memory. Indigenous cofrades recognized the removal of the Virgin of Copacabana to Lima's Cathedral as an attack on their sovereignty despite the more prestigious location, which signaled the importance of a native cult to the city. While all of these disempowered individuals were deeply integrated into their urban societies, they recognized that integration did not guarantee security. The Muslim artisans who watched Christian authorities carry off their few valuables because of debt to Christian lenders are a bleak reminder; if coreligionist lenders also pursued arrears callously, they did so without the public humiliation that raised feelings of inferiority and abandonment. This analysis offers a different perspective on the old debate on medieval convivencia or punctuated equilibrium: even the equilibria were tense, and subordinate peoples had a pervasive knowledge of their precariousness.

Not everyone participated in the republic. Peoples who did not live within marked spaces—urban Indians, people of African descent, Muslim and Jewish residents who remained outside aljama politics and group practices—also honed identities but they did so in ways that are more complicated to evaluate.[13] They might appear in the historical record more often than those who worked out their problems within their republics, but they do so within a hegemonic legal language that erases intention and particularity. The Indigenous-language cabildo records that have survived for centuries in Mesoamerica provide isolated examples of what might have been in the files of Seville's aljamas, Andean cabildos, or the Castilian mayoral de los negros. The Mesoamerican records show communities struggling to locate their own justice in a changing world, even as they borrow or adapt the terms placed upon or encircling them.[14]

The particular forms that archives take have been central to this analysis. In unfortunate contrast to Mesoamerica, none of the major archives for late medieval Seville or early Lima contains anything more than a handful of documents internal to these republics: the author's delight in encountering Juan Mateo's signature buried within a massive and unindexed notarial register signaled its rarity. Remembering those republics has required imagination and new methods of interpretation, inventing a kind of historical negative space by contemplating what records do exist and imagining what is missing. Mapping the imagined archive onto urban space revealed the connections that held communities together even when their borders proved entirely permeable.

Moreover, not only were the republics different across the Atlantic, but notarial methods changed over time and space, requiring a flexibility of analysis. The notarial records that provide data for understanding fifteenth-century Seville were often just a few spare sentences long, though they indicated unexpected information such as the client's residential parish. In Lima, in contrast, notarial archives contain Indigenous and Black residents' wills and more detailed records of property transfer than are found in Seville, though notaries rarely indicated where their clients resided beyond town or city. Censuses in the Andes could be more ethnographic than those in Castile because colonial administrators needed to understand native peoples to better extract their wealth and govern them; they believed they already understood enough of the social worlds of Jews and Muslims. And, as viceregal administrators complained, Indigenous men and women were tireless litigators, leaving extraordinary documentation of intentions and strategies. Writing social histories of both locations produced rich anecdotes and ample data points that demonstrated how different similarly organized juridical boundaries could look across the Atlantic world. As a result, *Republics of Difference* necessarily tells distinct kinds of stories in each location. But the stories from each location provoked questions for the other: what does it mean that a particular kind of document does not exist in a location? What details might we know if we had the same kinds of materials in both? Thinking through two locations with superficially similar archives has been provocative and sometimes revelatory.

Finally, while the legal form of the republic did not cause race to come into existence, the effects of race thinking are revealed through their institutional productions of law and culture. The Cercado's rise demonstrates how the association of space, law, and subordination led to the invention of new practices that entangled the expectations of both insiders and outsiders. The forced concentration of migratory laborers, joined by voluntary permanent settlers as well as the people they enslaved, created multiple layers of jurisdiction and a number of property regimes in tension. While rural pueblos could largely act autonomously because their politics were considered irrelevant by Spanish authorities, in the Cercado close access to the king's representatives, his highest court, and the Jesuits led to more meddling in everyday affairs. There, colonial forces could promote certain notions of indigeneity that would travel across the empire with Spaniards and Indians alike. The result was an increasing belief that Indians' difference was rooted in their law as well as their bodies, even as many adopted Spanish attitudes. In contrast, if the internal records of Seville's judería could be found, they might show more autonomy of law and less disagreement in property relations since Jews, Muslims, and Christians largely agreed about the ways that commodities, including land, changed hands, outside of small differences regarding inheritance practices. Many Christians wished Jews and Muslims to convert. They sometimes considered them monstrous and always believed they worshipped falsely, but they did not necessarily see them as lacking in urbanity. Viceregal authorities convinced themselves that Indians had to be compelled to embrace work discipline, develop their intellects, and leave behind primitive beliefs and practices.

It has been crucial to include Black republics in this analysis, despite the conclusion that they were mostly absent and always underdocumented. West and West Central Africans were present on both sides of the Atlantic, and the failure of viceregal officials to consistently produce republican structures to serve them in the Americas, and the rise of confraternities within that vacuum, reveals not only the power of the institutional structure; it further reveals how racialization emerged as an explanatory form in the early modern world. In Seville, the Black republic was mostly a loose form of discipline. It was intended initially to provide mutual aid to people without social networks. It developed to deflect Black subjects' minor conflicts away from the courts, the municipality, or masters and to assign responsibility for containing their public acts, which non-Blacks sometimes characterized as disruptive. Had any records survived, they would doubtless demonstrate how people from dispersed origins, many under conditions of enslavement, imagined justice and mutual support, possibly in ways scholars have not previously imagined. Confraternity records of the period mostly indicate how others perceived them, and reflect the experience of individuals who found the Catholic Church an attractive outlet for their faith and ritual practices.

But even this fragile republican structure did not survive the Atlantic passage. Instead, two distinct but interrelated practices emerged—fugitivity and reducción. Enslaved men and women chose freedom in the form of fugitivity to repair their lives, although it came at great cost. Even those who were not murdered, captured, or returned to the slave market faced lives of insecurity and fear of invasion. Some found community, others remained isolated in their freedom. The offer, then, of the pueblo de negros, with all of its burdens and subordinate offense, might have spelled relief. The state-authorized pueblo de negros was a facsimile of freedom. It arrived with the insistence that Blackness embodied an inherent tendency to laziness and criminality, and a suspicion that people of African descent might always be in the wrong place. It required its members to police enslaved people, and to define themselves against them. It is not difficult to trace the connections between this official colonial narrative and modern anti-Black racism.

The Castilian and then Spanish dependence upon jurisdictional pluralism to delegate certain types of authority to subordinate corporate groups created physical and intellectual spaces for the production of law. But the spaces were animated by inhabitants who insisted (not always with one voice) that they understood their own common good. If the dominant powers asserted their ability to characterize and caricature subordinate groups, historical sources provide glimpses of how members of those groups responded. They resisted interventions, borrowed liberally from what surrounded them, constituted and disciplined their communities, and invented their practices over long periods. The Iberian republics could be strong or weak instruments. They contained difference, but they also produced difference.

Notes

INTRODUCTION

1. Archivo de Protocolos de Sevilla (hereafter APS) Oficio 4, Pedro Alvarez, signatura 2154, folios (ff) 220–21r. (October 8, 1475). The title Raby could indicate an ordained rabbi or a Talmudic scholar.

2. Córdoba, possibly a *converso* or convert from Judaism, worked for Pedro de Astúñiga, the son of the Christian nobleman who had been awarded all of Seville's remaining synagogues after the 1391 pogrom.

3. On this concept, see Benton, *Law and Colonial Cultures*; Benton and Ross, *Legal Pluralism and Empires*; Owensby, *Empire of Law*.

4. Spanish historians have debated the language used to characterize the interactions of the three religions in the medieval period, which has always had political overtones. *Convivencia*, a term coined by Américo Castro in 1948 to emphasize Muslim and Jewish contributions to Spanish culture, has been rightly criticized for underplaying coexistence's violence, though it still carries weight as a counter to the ideological position that Spain's roots are solely European and Christian. For the historiography and an argument that *convivencia* lacks nuance for understanding the power dynamics of medieval Iberia—perhaps less unique in Europe than the debate has implied—see Soifer Irish, "Beyond Convivencia." For another term, *conveniencia*, see Catlos, *Muslims of Medieval Christendom*, 508–14.

5. A burgeoning literature on race and racialization in the medieval and early modern periods informs my analysis throughout. Scholars of race, especially in the United States, have at times declined to use the term to describe phenomena in the premodern world. But biology and culture generally collapse into one another, undermining arguments that race could not exist before genetics emerged to explain it. Barbara Fields's insight that race is an ideology rather than an idea or element of biology may be the best frame for understanding how racialization took place before race

science; see Fields, "Slavery, Race and Ideology." For useful examples of the debate over the term in the early modern European world see Burns, "Unfixing Race"; Feros, *Speaking of Spain*; Fracchia, *"Black but Human"*; Hall, *Things of Darkness*; Heng, *The Invention of Race in the European Middle Ages*; Jordan, "Why 'Race'?"; Lipton, *Dark Mirror*; Mariscal, "The Role of Spain in Contemporary Race Theory"; Martínez, Nirenberg, and Hering Torres, *Race and Blood in the Iberian World*; Martínez, *Genealogical Fictions*; Nirenberg, "Was There Race before Modernity"; Patton, *Envisioning Others*; Rappaport, *The Disappearing Mestizo;* Ruggles, "Mothers of a Hybrid Dynasty"; Schwartz, *Blood and Boundaries*; Whittaker, *Black Metaphors*.

6. Chira, *Patchwork Freedoms*, 3.

7. Berman, *Law and Revolution*; Herzog, *A Short History*; Velasco, *Dead Voice*.

8. On the use of the term in the Iberian world, see MacCormack, *On the Wings of Time*, chap. 4; Quijano Velasco, "Las repúblicas de la monarquía."

9. Najemy, "Guild Republicanism in Trecento Florence."

10. The medieval Iberian historiography largely studies Jews and Muslims separately, with the exception of thematic edited volumes that study religious minorities, such as those carried out by John Tolan's RELMIN project on law and religious minorities or Davis-Secord, Vicéns, and Vose, *Interfaith Relationships*. Some scholars, including Mercedes García-Arenal, Miguel Ángel Ladero Quesada, Mark Meyerson, Isabel Montes Romero-Camacho, and David Nirenberg, have produced studies of both Muslims and Jews, usually in distinct works or chapters. None, to my knowledge, incorporates the growing non-Muslim African population; Alfonso Franco Silva, who wrote the first great study of Black Seville, has also contributed studies of the region's nobility. The literature on Indigenous Peru is far more substantial than on its African-descent population, and rarely discusses them together. For an overview of the Afro-Andean experience, see Arrelucea Barrantes and Cosamalón Aguilar, *La presencia afrodescendiente*. Two foundational works introduce Indigenous and Black populations in conversation: a suggestive older work by Harth-Terré, *Negros e indios*; and the more recent O'Toole, *Bound Lives*. Sherwin Bryant makes the important argument that slavery was central to conquest even when the enslaved population was slight: Bryant, *Rivers of Gold*.

11. Echevarría Arsuaga, *The City of the Three Mosques*, 69; Soifer Irish, *Jews and Christians in Medieval Castile*, 44. Jews and Muslims in fifteenth-century Seville also used the generic term *aljama* when speaking to Christian notaries, e.g., APS Oficio 4, Andrés González, Libro de 1441–94, ff. 117v–118v (December 9, 1454); APS Oficio 9, Luis García de Celada, Libro de 1500–1501 sin fecha (hereafter sf).

12. On the conquest and repopulation of Seville, see González Jiménez, Borrero Fernández, and Montes Romero-Camacho, *Sevilla en tiempos de Alfonso X*; González Jiménez, *La repoblación*; Collantes de Terán Sánchez, *Una gran ciudad bajomedieval*; Ecker, "How to Administer a Conquered City"; González Jiménez, *Sevilla 1248*.

13. For a regional analysis of these events, see Pick, *Conflict and Coexistence*.

14. Ruiz, *Spanish Society 1400–1600*.

15. Elliott, *Spain, Europe, and the Wider World*; Haliczer, *The Comuneros of Castile*. For an overview of theories of early modern Spanish governance, see Amelang, "Peculiarities."

16. Amelang, "Peculiarities," 45.

17. The foundational study is Franco Silva, *La esclavitud en Sevilla*.

18. Gestoso y Pérez, *Curiosidades antiguas sevillanas*, 101. See also Fra Molinero, "Los negros"; Jones, *Staging Habla de Negros*.

19. Coleman, *Creating Christian Granada*.

20. Haliczer, *The Comuneros of Castile*.

21. Antonio Feros argues that the plurality of identities in the early modern Spanish kingdoms mattered (and continue to matter) a great deal, even as monarchs would begin to construct an emerging Spanish nation out of that plurality. Feros, *Speaking of Spain*, especially chapters 1 and 3.

22. Green, *Rise of the Trans-Atlantic Slave Trade*.

23. Puente Luna, *Andean Cosmopolitans*, chap. 1.

24. Not all Spaniards in the period endorsed the slave trade as just. See, e.g., Fray Bartolomé de las Casas's mordant critique of African slavery, not long after his explicit endorsement of it as a solution to Indigenous genocide: Las Casas, *Brevísima relación de la destrucción de África*.

25. Fromont, *Afro-Catholic Festivals in the Americas*; Jaque Hidalgo and Valerio, *Indigenous and Black Confraternities*; Valerio, *Sovereign Joy*; Germeten, *Black Blood Brothers*.

26. See Benton, *Law and Colonial Cultures*, 1. In contrast, however, see Miller, "Muslim Minorities"; Abou El Fadl, "Islamic Law and Muslim Minorities."

27. Ruiz, *Spanish Society 1400–1600*, 4; see also Rappaport, *The Disappearing Mestizo*.

28. Lee, *The Anxiety of Sameness*.

29. Mangan, *Transatlantic Obligations*.

30. Kuznesof, "Ethnic and Gender Influences." Indigenous noblewomen were, in contrast, valued as marriage partners: Guengerich, "Capac Women."

31. Martínez, *Genealogical Fictions*. See also Schwartz, *Blood and Boundaries*.

32. This manifested through prohibitions on holding ecclesiastic offices as well as the designation of all Indians as *miserables* or unfortunates requiring legal support. See Duvé, "Derecho canónico." On the incorporation of people of African descent into the church and secular law, see Bennett, *Colonial Blackness*; Brewer-García, *Beyond Babel*.

33. MacCormack, *On the Wings of Time*. My use of the concept of policía, especially with respect to space, also draws upon Abercrombie, *Pathways of Memory and Desire*; Fraser, *The Architecture of Conquest*; Escobar, "Francisco de Sotomayor"; Kagan, "Urbs and Civitas"; Nemser, *Infrastructures of Race*.

34. Puente Luna, *Andean Cosmopolitans*, 34–35.
35. Lohmann Villena, "Testamento del curaca."

CHAPTER 1

1. APS, Oficio 4, Segura, Libro de 1502, ff. 207v–9v (February 15, 1502).
2. Isabel extended the decree to all Jews in Castile in 1492. Fernando allowed the practice of Islam in his kingdom of Aragón until his death in 1516. In 1525, Charles V expelled all free *mudéjares* from what was now consolidated as Spain. Coleman, *Creating Christian Granada*, 6–7. This order did not affect enslaved Muslims, who were not required to convert until 1626–1629; Phillips, *Slavery*, 25.
3. Nader, *Liberty in Absolutist Spain*, 31. Monarchs would increasingly place limits on those considered foreigners (including Roma, Muslims, and Jews), particularly with the opening of travel to the Americas, which required formal licenses for travel and where New Christians and enslaved people born in Spain of African descent would face prohibitions. Cook, *Forbidden Passages*.
4. Salamanca, "Placing Mobile Identities," 15–17. On the anti-vagrancy question, see Martz, *Poverty and Welfare*.
5. On enclosure, see Van Deusen, *Between the Sacred and the Worldly*.
6. Alfonso X, *Primera crónica general*, 766.
7. The maneuvers are described in Ortiz de Zúñiga, *Anales eclesiásticos y seculares*, Vol. 1: 39-52.
8. Chroniclers claimed that Muslims left in large numbers, but post-conquest information makes this questionable. González Jiménez, Borrero Fernández, and Montes Romero-Camacho, *Sevilla en tiempos de Alfonso X*. For Arabic-language accounts of the siege, García Sanjuan, "La conquista de Sevilla," 28.
9. Ecker, "The Conversion of Mosques to Synagogues," 190–91.
10. González, *Repartimiento de Sevilla*, II:65–67, 326–28, 342.
11. His estate of fig and olive trees measured 1930 aranzadas (an aranzada was nearly an acre), among the largest endowments granted. González, *Repartimiento de Sevilla*, II:32, 515–16. On Abdelhaq el Baezy, see Ibn Khaldun, *Histoire*, I:401. After devastating conflicts, the king of Baeza had signed a pact of fealty with Fernando, making Baeza a "vassal kingdom": Catlos, *Muslims of Medieval Christendom*, 54–56.
12. González, *Repartimiento de Sevilla*, II:68, 98, 104.
13. Montes Romero-Camacho, "El Infante Don Felipe," 1628.
14. González Arce, "Cuadernos de ordenanzas," 113.
15. Tenorio Cerero, *El concejo de Sevilla*, 48; Ladero Quesada, *Los mudéjares de Castilla*, 37. These are the earliest surviving records; most are missing.
16. Catlos, *The Victors and the Vanquished*, 127; Echevarría Arsuaga, *The City of the Three Mosques*, chap. 4.

17. The high population estimate comes from Torres Balbás, *Ciudades hispanomusulmanas*, 106. The lower number (which excludes Triana) is from Bosch Vilá, *Historia de Sevilla*, 341. There are no reliable sources for determining the actual population.

18. The earliest extant (partial) census of the city was carried out in 1384 to fund Castile's war with Portugal. Alvarez, Ariza Viguera, and Mendoza, *Un padrón de Sevilla*.

19. Navarro Sainz, "Subordinación política"; Howell, "Continuity or Change."

20. Díaz Ceballos, "New World Civitas"; Gil, "Republican Politics in Early Modern Spain"; Nader, *Liberty in Absolutist Spain*.

21. Álvarez, *El libro de los privilegios*, 20–21. See also Pike, *Enterprise and Adventure*; Airaldi, *Genova e Siviglia*; González Gallego, "El libro de los privilegios."

22. Hernández-Múzquiz, "Economy and Society," 44–46.

23. Franco Silva, "Los negros libertos." One of the earliest wills that can be attributed to a free Black person in Seville identified Elena Rodríguez, *negra*, as vecina of the collación of San Juan, where she owned a house. APS Oficio 4, signatura 2167, legajo 2, ff. 278–79 (March 28, 1501).

24. Ortiz de Zúñiga, *Anales eclesiásticos y seculares*, Vol. 3: 79. See also Moreno, *La antigua hermandad de los negros*.

25. Soifer Irish, *Jews and Christians in Medieval Castile*, 5–6.

26. Tolan and Fierro, *The Legal Status of Dimmis*; Meyerson, *The Muslims of Valencia*, 2.

27. Constable, "Regulating Religious Noise."

28. Echevarría Arsuaga, *The City of the Three Mosques*, chap. 4; see also Matheson, "Muslims, Jews, and the Question of Municipal Membership." Rubin notes that contemporary legislators also struggled to define this urban relationship, sometimes using "concives" or co-citizens. Rubin, *Cities of Strangers*, 57.

29. For example, Muslim residents in Seville's Salvador parish were registered and required to pay taxes toward cleaning the local garbage tip in 1403: Collantes de Terán Sánchez, "La aljama mudéjar de Sevilla," 145; Echevarría Arsuaga, "Las aljamas mudéjares castellanas," 96.

30. On this relationship, see especially Boswell, *Royal Treasure*; Echevarría Arsuaga, *The City of the Three Mosques*; Fancy, *The Mercenary Mediterranean*, chap. 3; Meyerson, *Jews in an Iberian Frontier Kingdom*; Soifer Irish, *Jews and Christians in Medieval Castile*. On the distinction between Jewish royal tenancy and the Islamic practice of *dhimmi*, see Soifer Irish, 21.

31. Soifer Irish, *Jews and Christians in Medieval Castile*, 28.

32. González Jiménez, Borrero Fernández, and Montes Romero-Camacho, *Sevilla en tiempos de Alfonso X*, 92. According to Ortiz de Zúñiga, the fee was required of all persons over the age of sixteen and was distributed as three mrv per person. Ortiz de Zúñiga, *Anales eclesiásticos y seculares*, Vol. 2: 73-74. The tax was still collected in the fifteenth century by the archbishop's officials, APS Oficio 9, García de Celada,

Cuaderno de 1468, sf (May 24, 1468); APS Oficio 23, Sánchez, Libro de 1472, sf (June 8, 1472).

33. Soifer Irish, *Jews and Christians in Medieval Castile*, 31.

34. Muslims in Valencia were far more numerous than their counterparts in Castile, and they were represented by powerful families: Catlos, *The Victors and the Vanquished*; Miller, *Guardians of Islam*; Meyerson, *The Muslims of Valencia*.

35. Collantes de Terán Sánchez, "Los mudéjares sevillanos," 233–34. The poor could apply for exemptions: see the exemption authorization of 1497 for the Muslims of Burgos, in Ladero Quesada, *Los mudéjares de Castilla*, 214–15.

36. González Jiménez, "Fiscalidad regia," 230–33, 239.

37. Cómez, *Los constructores de la España medieval*, 71.

38. Archivo Municipal de Sevilla (hereafter AMS), Tumbo de los Reyes Católicos, III-141, (January 25, 1487, Salamanca). See also Echevarría Arsuaga, *The City of the Three Mosques*, 77–78.

39. The Fourth Lateran Council, called to reform Christian discipline, issued five canons concerning Jews and Muslims. They called upon secular rulers either to control Jews and Muslims or to limit their interactions with Christians. Champagne and Resnick, *Jews and Muslims under the Fourth Lateran Council*; Stow, "The Church and the Jews"; Wayno, "Rethinking the Fourth Lateran Council of 1215." Stow and Wayno note that most of these prohibitions were not innovations, and that communication and enforcement were uneven.

40. Soifer Irish, *Jews and Christians in Medieval Castile*, 33. The positions of the church, an amalgam of institutions with distinct interests, were nuanced. On Toledo, see Pick, *Conflict and Coexistence*.

41. Echevarría Arsuaga, "Marks of the Other," 183.

42. On Regent Catalina's ordinances of 1408, restating her husband Enrique III's earlier legislation, see Fernández y González, *Estado social y político*, 397–99. On differences in the application of insignia statutes to Muslims and Jews in Castile, see Echevarría Arsuaga, "Marks of the Other."

43. Constable, *To Live Like a Moor*, 34–38.

44. Ladero Quesada, *Los mudéjares de Castilla*, 372.

45. Cited in Constable, *To Live Like a Moor*, 41.

46. APS Oficio XI, González, escrituras del siglo XV, cuadernos de 1465, sf (March 21, 1465). For the toca or headdress, see Anderson, *Hispanic Costume 1480–1530*, 171.

47. APS Oficio 4, Segura, Libro de 1441–1494, ff. 775v–76 (August 5, 1494).

48. APS Oficio 9, García de Celada, Libro de 1493, f. 38v (March 20, 1493).

49. There may have been a fourth, referred to as "la mezquita de la judería" in documents, though its location and when it was built remain unclear. Ecker, "The Conversion of Mosques to Synagogues."

50. Miller, "Muslim Minorities," 266; see also Abou El Fadl, "Islamic Law and Muslim Minorities."

51. The Council of Vienne (1311) prohibited the Muslim call to prayer in Christian realms, as well as the practice of pilgrimages to Muslim shrines in Christian lands. See Constable, "Regulating Religious Noise."

52. Soifer Irish, "Toward 1391," 309–10.

53. Until recently little has been known of Martínez other than Lea, "Ferrand Martinez and the Massacres of 1391"; Lea, "Acta capitular del Cabildo de Sevilla." Recent work by Soifer Irish has updated Lea and offers important critical insights, particularly regarding the way that conflicts between local elites riled up popular support for Jewish persecution: Soifer Irish, "Toward 1391." She has published transcriptions and an English translation of some of the court documents that record his words in Soifer Irish, "Ferrán Martínez's Speech."

54. Soifer Irish, "Ferrán Martínez's Speech," 2.

55. See the recreation of the events in Soifer Irish, "Toward 1391."

56. Ladero Quesada, *Judíos y conversos de Castilla*, chap. 1.

57. Montes Romero-Camacho, "Las minorías étnicas-religiosas," 146–49.

58. The donation of the former synagogue in the parish of Santa Cruz to the church in 1391 is documented in the Cathedral's archives, see González Ferrín, "Estudio e inventario," 366.

59. MacKay, "Popular Movements and Pogroms," 38–40.

60. Soifer Irish, *Jews and Christians in Medieval Castile*, 224–25.

61. Ferrer was part of the first wave of Dominicans who shifted to external proselytizing, though hagiography has exaggerated his successes: Vose, *Dominicans, Muslims and Jews in the Medieval Crown of Aragon*, 258–59.

62. Quoted in Nirenberg, *Neighboring Faiths*, 105.

63. These laws are contextualized in Echevarría Arsuaga, "Catalina of Lancaster."

64. Collantes de Terán Sánchez, *Sevilla en la baja Edad Media*, 89. On Alvar García de Santa María's chronicle, see Carriazo, *Anecdotario sevillano*, 30–31.

65. In León Tello, *Judíos de Toledo*, 459–60.

66. AMS, Actas Capitulares, B-AC 1437, fol. 50 (July 1437).

67. AMS, Sección X, Actas Capitulares, B-AC 1437, sm. fol. 50 (September 28, 1437).

68. The existence of elite Christian homes in what was ostensibly a judería was not particular to Seville: Roger Martínez-Dávila has found that Plasencia's judería was also home to some of the city's most important Christians. Martínez, "Jews, Catholics, and Converts," 108.

69. AMS, Sección X, Actas Capitulares, A-AC 1437, nov–dic, f. 7. These neighborhoods were also less prominent, as suggested by the term "barrera," which, like "adarve" and "calleja" indicated narrow alleyways closed to the streets.

70. The register is Wagner, *Regesto*. The period spans from the earliest notarial registers that survive in Sevilla (1441) to the expulsion of Muslims in 1502. Wagner briefly described the documents; in most cases I double-checked his summaries against the originals, which can only be viewed on microfilm now (his initials appear in pencil

in the margin of most documents he consulted). Matthew Sisk of the University of Notre Dame generated the maps from my data.

71. The largest merchant houses would have formalized their own agreements and not used a public notary. For the merchant class, see Otte, *Sevilla y sus mercaderes*; Lacueva Muñoz, *Comerciantes de Sevilla*. For merchants and notarization in the period, see Trivellato, *The Promise and Peril of Credit*; Rojas García, "El comercio por escrito."

72. On the highly debated numbers of conversos, see Ladero Quesada, "Sevilla y los conversos." For a benchmark, thousands of conversos were punished by Seville's Inquisition in the late fifteenth century, but many conversos migrated to avoid stigma, making it difficult to estimate earlier Jewish populations.

73. Collantes de Terán Sánchez, *Sevilla en la baja Edad Media*, 206–11.

74. Domínguez Ortiz, "La esclavitud en Castilla," 378; González Jiménez, "El trabajo mudéjar," 40–41; Viñuales Ferreiro, "El repartimiento," 191. The records for Seville's Jewish aljama are incomplete, Viñuales Ferreiro, "Los repartimientos de los judíos."

75. These values come from Collantes de Terán Sánchez, *Una gran ciudad bajomedieval*, 110–11.

76. Cervantes Saavedra, *Varias obras inéditas*, 29.

77. Wunder, *Baroque Seville*, 49.

78. APS Oficio 15, Rodríguez de Vallecillo, Libro de 1470–1479, f. 118 (June 22, 1474).

79. Castillo held the contract but subcontracted to Jews in other localities to collect for the archbishop. APS Oficio 23, Sánchez, Libro de 1472 sf (June 8, 1472).

80. APS Oficio 15, Rodríguez de Vallecillo, Libro de 1480–1499, f. 16 (April 23, 1493).

81. APS Oficio 15, 9098, Rodríguez de Vallecillo, Libro de 1470–1479, ff. 113v–14 (June 20, 1474).

82. AMS B-AC sm fol. 10; MacKay, "Popular Movements and Pogroms," 42.

83. APS Oficio 15, 9098, Juan Rodríguez de Vallecillo, Libro de 1470–1479, ff. 113v–14 (June 20, 1474).

84. For cases in Valencia, see Meyerson, *A Jewish Renaissance*, 129–31.

85. Perhaps a relation of the fourteenth-century scholar Isaac Pollegar (Pulguer), about whom see Baer, *A History of the Jews in Christian Spain*, vol. I: 335ff.

86. APS Oficio XI, Bartolomé González, escrituras del siglo XV, cuadernos de 1465 (March 21, 1465); Oficio 15, Juan Rodríguez de Vallecillo, Libro de 1470–1479, ff. 116v–17 (June 22, 1474).

87. Ferrer-Chivite, "El factor Judeo-Converso"; Lee, *The Anxiety of Sameness*, chap. 1.

88. APS Oficio 15, Juan Rodríguez Vallecillo, Libro de 1470–1479, f. 126v (June 27, 1474).

89. Paz y Espeso, *Catálogo I: Diversos de Castilla*, 31.

90. APS Oficio 23, Francisco Sánchez, Libro de 1472, sf (October 2, 1472).

91. APS Oficio 23, Francisco Sánchez, Libro de 1472 (August 26, 1472); APS Oficio 11, Bartolomé González, Siglo XV sf (1466).

92. APS Oficio 23, Francisco Sánchez, Libro de 1472, sf (June 15, 1472).

93. Most of the Jewish men whose occupation is indicated in the notarial documentation worked as merchants or in textiles, silversmithing, and other artisan professions. A census taken of the converso population in the early sixteenth century suggests that this is a fair sample, though conversos also held some less common occupations like scribe, jeweler, and sellers of spices and olives. Similar conclusions can be drawn from lists of conversos reconciled by the Inquisition. For both lists, see Gil, *Los Conversos*, 2:319–444.

94. For an analysis of the residential dispersal of conversos from documents regarding their punishment by the Inquisition, see Ladero Quesada, "Sevilla y los conversos." Many of these data points come after expulsion, during periods of intense inquisitorial activity. Those who remained in the judería might have been more likely to be accused of judaizing, or might have feared this.

95. APS Oficio 23, Diego Fernández, Libro de 1472 sf (April 20, 1472). In another document, the block also appears to be home to property owned by the Jewish Briviesca brothers, and a prominent Christian, Alfon García de Soria. APS Oficio 23, Francisco Sánchez, Libro de 1472, sf (August 26, 1472).

96. González, *Repartimiento de Sevilla*, I:364–65.

97. Royal permission was required to build new mosques. Instead, Muslims most likely worshipped in repurposed homes or sites outside the city that could be reached on foot. The Muslims of Trujillo had one on the city's outskirts; see Ladero Quesada, *Los mudéjares de Castilla*, 90–91.

98. Echevarría Arsuaga, "Las aljamas mudéjares castellanas," 95. Don Abrahán Xarafi, "alfaqui and physician," was named alcalde mayor of the Muslims of Castile in 1475. Ladero Quesada, *Los mudéjares de Castilla*, 85–88.

99. Women often had more flexibility using honorifics than men did. For examples from Indigenous Peru, see Graubart, *With Our Labor and Sweat*.

100. On the buskin or borceguí, see Anderson, *Hispanic Costume 1480–1530*, 78–80.

101. Dodds, Menocal, and Krasner Balbale, *The Arts of Intimacy*. On ceramic arts, especially the azulejeros who produced geometrically adorned polychrome mosaics and painted tiles, see Gestoso, *Historia de los barros vidriados sevillanos*.

102. APS Oficio 11, Bartolome González, cuadernos de 1465, sf (March 21, 1465).

103. APS Oficio 12, Gonzalo Bernal, Escrituras del siglo XV, sf (August 28, 1492).

104. APS Oficio 15, Juan Rodríguez de Vallecillo, Libro de 1490–1499, ff. 23v–24 (April 12, 1493). The use of *"moro blanco"* or white Muslim might reflect the increasing numbers of Black Africans in Seville at the end of the century.

105. Despite legal prohibitions, Christians occasionally apprenticed to non-Christians. In 1499, the Duke of Medinasidonia brought Muslim master plasterer Yça of Málaga to Seville from Granada to design for the family's properties. Yça also

took on Christian apprentices during his stay. APS Oficio 21, Juan Ruiz de Porras, Libro de 1506 sf (December 6, 1499).

106. Cómez, *Los constructores de la España medieval*; González Arce, "Sobre el origen de los gremios sevillanos"; Tarifa Castilla, "Ordenanzas del gremio."

107. Sevilla [España], *Ordenanzas de Sevilla*, chap. 155. These are city ordinances rather than rules internal to the guild.

108. Gestoso y Pérez, Historia de los barros vidriados sevillanos, 101-2.

109. APS Oficio 15, Juan Rodríguez de Vallecillo, libro de 1480–1489, f. 378 (December 31, 1488).

110. APS Oficio 15, Juan Rodríguez de Vallecillo, libro de 1480–1489, f. 96v (March 27, 1484).

111. Prior to the late fourteenth century, Christians and Muslims in Seville both might use maestre; for examples, see Alvarez, Ariza Viguera, and Mendoza, *Un padrón de Sevilla*. The linguistic practices were regional. For an example from a fishing confraternity/guild in Asturias in 1486 see Suárez Alvarez, " 'Novilísimo gremio.' " On the likelihood of parallel corporate forms of artisan regulation, see Conte Cazcarro, "La composición laboral de la aljama de moros de Huesca," 139–40.

112. APS Oficio 23, sig. 9100, Diego Fernández, Libro de 1472 (April 20, 1472); APS Oficio 15, Juan Rodríguez Vallecillo, libro de 1474–1479, f. 180v (July 22, 1474); AHS B-AC, 1455, ago-oct, fol. 34.

113. APS Oficio 9, García de Celada, libro de 1500–1501 sf (April 22, 1501). On Recocho as taverner, see APS Oficio 9, Luis García de Celada, Libro de 1499, sf (August 10, 1499).

114. Women commonly worked alongside their husbands in trades including masonry. Cómez, *Los constructores de la España medieval*, 74. The wife of a prominent Christian ceramicist of the time was nicknamed "la loçana," the crockery-maker, Gestoso y Pérez, *Historia de los barros vidriados sevillanos*, 372.

115. APS Oficio 23, Francisco Sánchez, Libro de 1472, folio suelto (1472).

116. Viñuales Ferreiro, "El Repartimiento," 204.

117. All of these before the notary Juan Rodríguez Vallecillo, Oficio 15, in January and February 1484.

118. APS Oficio XV, Juan Rodríguez de Vallecillo, Libro de 1480–1489, f. 64 (February 11, 1484).

119. AMS, Privilegios, carpeta 1a, documento 5; also published in Tenorio Cerero, *El concejo de Sevilla*, 192–96.

120. From the Arabic ad-darb, *adarve* referred to a narrow road atop a fortress wall, or an alley between residences in Muslim cities, like *callejón*. The word suggests marginality and containment as well as a link to the Arabic language. See Covarrubias, 41; Real Academia Española, *Diccionario*, "adarve."

121. Carande and Carriazo, *El tumbo de los Reyes Católicos*, III:388–89. See also Pike, "An Urban Minority," 369.

122. There is no record of the creation of the mosque, but its existence is documented, and in other cities faced with similar relocations, the monarchs designated sites for worship. Ladero Quesada, *Los mudéjares de Castilla*, 91–93.

123. APS Oficio 7 Pedro González, Escrituras de 1504, f. 77v–78 (August 14, 1480).

124. APS Oficio 4, Andrés González, Libro de 1441–1494, f. 123 (December 13, 1454).

125. In the Castilian city of Aranda, Muslim artisans used workshops outside the morería to evade the 1480 separation order. When other Muslims turned them in (for placing their businesses closer to Christian clients), the Concejo ruled that they could have other properties, but could not sleep in them. See Cantera Montenegro, "El Apartamiento," 506.

126. APS Oficio 15, Juan Rodríguez de Vallecillo, Libro de 1490–1499, f. 15 (April 23, 1493); Gestoso y Pérez, *Historia del barro vidriado sevillano*, 371.

127. APS Oficio IX Luis García de Celada, Libro de 1499, sf (March 4, 1499).

128. APS Oficio 4, Luis Garcia de Celada, cuadernos de 1493, sf (July 11, 1493).

129. APS Oficio 9, Luis García de Celada Libro de 1493, ff. 199–200v (July 3, 1493).

130. The total number fluctuated between nine recorded in a census of 1430, to thirty-eight signing a collective petition in 1477. Collantes de Terán Sánchez, *Sevilla en la baja Edad Media*, 118–19.

131. Sevilla [España], *Ordenanzas de Sevilla*, chap. CLV.

132. At least one case of a Christian artisan sponsoring the conversion of a Muslim colleague is documented: when the ceramicist Abdalla de la Rosa converted in January 1502, taking the name Juan de Toledo, his padrino was the ceramicist Pedro Chaves. Gestoso y Pérez, *Historia de los barros vidriados sevillanos*, 384.

133. AMS Actas Capitulares A-AC 1472, doc. 2195 ago–dic, f. 12; A-AC 1472, doc 2202 ago–dic, f. 24; APS Oficio 23, Francisco Sánchez, libro de 1472 sf (September 20, 1472); Collantes de Terán Sánchez, *Sevilla en la baja Edad Media*, 118–21.

134. APS Oficio IV Pedro Alvarez, libro de 1441–1494, f. 231 (October 12, 1475). Ruth MacKay notes that Seville was one of the earliest Christian Castilian cities to have *gremios*, drawing upon its Muslim artisan heritage. Mackay, *Lazy, Improvident People*, 15. We know very little about these prior to the sixteenth century; see Romero Muñoz, "Recopilación de las ordenanzas."

135. APS Oficio 4, Luis García de Celada, cuadernos de 1493, sf (July 11, 1493); Oficio 4, Bernal Fernández, Libro de 1537, cuaderno de 1475, sf (March 30, 1475).

136. APS Oficio 15, Juan Rodríguez de Vallecillo, Libro de 1470, f. 285 (October 19, 1474).

137. For the international merchants, see Trivellato, *The Promise and Peril of Credit*.

138. APS Oficio 23, Francisco Sánchez, Libro de 1472 sf (1472); APS Oficio 3 Juan Ruiz de Porras, Cuadernos de 1483, sf (October 1, 1483).

139. The original loan information has not been located. The confiscated repayment is registered in APS Oficio 15, Juan Rodríguez de Vallecillo, Libro de 1480–1489, ff. 321–22 (March 12, 1488). Reconciliation could involve prison terms and participation in regular public processions and other acts of humiliation and penitence, as well as payment of a large fine: Ladero Quesada, "Sevilla y los conversos," 432–33; Gil, *Los Conversos*, vol. 2, chap. XII. Martínez's punishment likely took place in February 1488, Wagner, "La Inquisición en Sevilla," 7.

140. APS oficio 15, Gonzalo de Plasencia, 1470–1479, f. 325v (November 17, 1460) and f. 332 (November 26, 1460).

141. APS Oficio 4, Pedro Álvarez, libro de 1441–1494, f. 223v–24, 228v (October 9 and 10, 1475).

142. APS Oficio 23, Francisco Sánchez, Libro de 1472, sf (June 8, 1472).

143. APS Oficio 4, Juan García, libro de 1441–1494, f. 77 (December 11, 1450).

144. APS Oficio 11, Bartolomé González, escrituras del s. XV, sf (undated, 1454).

145. For a very rough comparison, an analysis of notarial contracts involving merchants in Seville in the same period (1441–1500) examined thirty-six registers (one register per year for one notary) that historian Enrique Otte used to compile his magisterial study and tallied 2,550 total documents. Jews and Muslims were involved in a tiny minority of these, which are a fraction of the total surviving registers, themselves a subset of what was originally produced. See Lacueva Muñoz, *Comerciantes de Sevilla*.

146. One absent group was Muslim traders from Granada and other regions, who did business in Seville when political conditions allowed. Their near-total invisibility suggests that they kept their own records, or at least avoided the city's Christian notaries.

147. Genoese merchants offered larger loans to Muslims than other Christians did. For example, Jerónimo de Grimaldo extended nearly 3,000 mrv of credit to Mayr Abensemerro and nearly 6,000 mrv to maestre Mahoma, a borceguinero and brother of one of the city's alfaquíes, both in 1472. APS Oficio 23, Francisco Sánchez, Legajo 15963, Libro de 1472 sf (June 3, 1472) and (November 17, 1472).

148. APS Oficio 9, Luis García de Celada, Libro de 1499, cuadernos de 1472 (January 29, 1472); APS Oficio 23, Francisco Sánchez, libro de 1472 (November 16, 1472)

149. The Mediterranean trade experienced a crisis in the 1460s that was precipitated by cyclical famine and plague. The increased activity in Seville could be a response to this return to relative health. Ladero Quesada, *La ciudad medieval*.

150. APS Oficio 10, Luis García de Celada, Libro de 1500–1501, cuaderno de 1468 (May 25, 1468).

151. APS Oficio 23, Francisco Sánchez, Libro de 1472, sf (July 18, 1472); Oficio 12, Gonzalo Bernal, Escrituras del siglo XV (August 6, 1473; September 13, 1473).

152. APS Oficio 4, Bernal Fernández, Libro de 1537, cuaderno de 1475, sf (June 30, 1475).

153. APS Oficio 9, Luis García de Celada, Libro de 1499, cuadernos de 1479 (September 9, 1479).

154. APS Oficio 15, Juan Rodríguez Vallecillo, Libro de 1470–1479, f. 285 (October 19, 1474).

155. Meyerson, *The Muslims of Valencia*, 31.

156. APS Oficio 12, Gonzalo Bernal, Libro de 1448–1568, sf (September 14, 1448).

157. The original contracts are mostly missing, another sign of the incompleteness of the archival record.

158. APS Oficio 5, Fernán Ruiz de Porres, Cuaderno de 1498, f. 125v (July 29, 1498).

159. For example, APS Oficio 9, Luis García de Celada, Libro de 1498, f. 60 (February 21, 1498); Libro de 1499 sf (January 19, 1499); sf (February 17, 1499).

CHAPTER 2

1. Egaña, *Monumenta peruana*, vol. VI: 658.

2. For the full history of this movement, see Vergara Ormeño, "The Copacabana Indigenous Elite." Other details about San Pedro and the Cercado come from Lowry, "Forging an Indian Nation"; Coello de la Rosa, *Espacios de exclusión*.

3. Vergara Ormeño, "The Copacabana Indigenous Elite," 84.

4. E.g., Lee et al., *Libros de cabildos de Lima*, VII:435, 442–43; X:47, 282.

5. Vergara Ormeño, "The Copacabana Indigenous Elite," 74.

6. On the legal argument for obedient noncompliance with law under such circumstances, see Frankl, "Hernán Cortés y la tradición de las siete partidas."

7. Don Luis de Velasco to Felipe II, 13 April 1598, Levillier, *Gobernantes del Perú*, XIV:83–88. On Philip II's concerns about vagrancy, to which Velaso alludes, see Fernández Álvarez, *Felipe II y su tiempo*, 201, 207-212.

8. For a sampling of studies of Indigenous and Black societies in the greater Lima region in the sixteenth and seventeenth centuries: Coello de la Rosa, *Espacios de exclusión*; Mills, *Idolatry and Its Enemies*; Spalding, *Huarochirí*; Charney, *Indian Society*; Cosamalón Aguilar, *Indios detrás de la muralla*; Dueñas, *Indians and Mestizos in the "Lettered City"*; Estenssoro Fuchs, *Del paganismo a la santidad*; Hunefeldt, *Paying the Price of Freedom*; Jouve Martín, *Esclavos de la ciudad letrada*; Lowry, "Forging an Indian Nation"; Osorio, *Inventing Lima*; Ramos, *Death and Conversion in the Andes*; Tardieu, "Le marronnage à Lima"; Van Deusen, "The 'Alienated' Body"; Vergara Ormeño, "The Copacabana Indigenous Elite."

9. Salinas y Córdoba, *Memorial*, 245. For lack of appropriate English cognates and for historical accuracy, I use racial categories like *mulato*, *mestizo*, and *zambaigo* when indicated in the documents. Whenever possible, I employ terms that the actors used themselves. For clear statements on the difficulties of projecting modern definitions onto historical categories (especially when writing in English about colonial Latin America), see Ferrer, *Insurgent Cuba*, 10–12; Walker, *Exquisite Slaves*, 13–15.

10. For the sake of clarity, I use *kuraka/kurakazgo* to refer to pre-Hispanic rulers and their office, and *cacique/cacicazgo* for the colonial institution.

11. Rostworowski de Diez Canseco, *Señoríos indígenas*, 57, 90–95.

12. On the valley kurakazgos, see Rostworowski de Diez Canseco, chap. 2; Cobo, *Monografías históricas*, 39.

13. For an overview of the Spanish conquest of Peru see Cahill, "The Long Conquest"; Covey, *Inca Apocalypse*; Heaney, "The Conquests of Peru"; Lamana, *Domination without Dominance*. Osorio, *Inventing Lima*, discusses the geopolitics over establishing Spanish-controlled centers in Jauja, Lima, and Cusco, and especially the battle between the two latter cities for the status of *cabecera* or head city.

14. Charney, *Indian Society*, 6–7.

15. See, e.g., the letter from the cabildo of Jauja in November 1534, published in Cobo, *Monografías históricas*, 9–12.

16. The term *vecino* shifted meaning in the colonies. While on the peninsula it largely referred to anyone who established unchallenged permanent residency in a town or city, in the Americas it became a marker of status, usually a propertied individual eligible to serve in municipal governance. Lima's vecinos were extremely powerful. See Herzog, *Defining Nations*, chap. 1.

17. The (now lost) founding document is summarized and quoted in Cobo, *Monografías históricas*, 18–21.

18. Cobo, *Monografías históricas*, 35–36.

19. Fraser, *The Architecture of Conquest*, 40–48; Kagan, "Urbs and Civitas"; Nemser, *Infrastructures of Race*, chap. 1; Osorio, *Inventing Lima*, 2–7.

20. Pagden, *Lords of All the World*, 29–40.

21. Konetzke, *Colección*, I:38–57.

22. Real provision, Sept. 6, 1521, in Konetzke, *Colección*, I:71–72.

23. Duve, "La condición jurídica"; Owensby, *Empire of Law*, 55ff.

24. Las Casas requested that the Church receive jurisdiction over Indigenous subjects in 1545. The Crown did not comply, but issued protective ordinances calling them *miserables* first in 1563 and then generally in the 1580s. Cunill, "El indio miserable," 232–33.

25. Wherever possible throughout the text I use "Indigenous" or "Andean" to refer to native peoples of the Andean region. I use "Indian" when referring to the colonial category of tributaries or the legal designation, often following usage in the documents.

26. The key cédulas are published in Konetzke, *Colección*, I:182–83, 186–87. They are discussed in Málaga Medina, "Las reducciones en el Perú," 144–45. On *reducción* policy, see Mumford, *Vertical Empire*; Nemser, *Infrastructures of Race*; Scott, "Mirage"; Saitō and Rosas Lauro, *Reducciones*; Zuloaga, *La conquista negociada*.

27. Quiroga, *Don Vasco de Quiroga*, 224.

28. Baptiste, *Bartolome de Las Casas and Thomas More's "Utopia,"* 8–9.

29. del Valle, "A New Moses"; Verastique, *Michoacan and Eden*; Quiroga, *La Utopia en America*.

30. Decoster, "La sangre que mancha"; Guengerich, "Inca Women under Spanish Rule"; Martínez, *Genealogical Fictions*, 107.

31. Quoted in Villella, *Indigenous Elites*, 244.

32. The classic studies include Pease G. Y., *Curacas, reciprocidad y riqueza*; Rostworowski de Diez Canseco, *Estructuras andinas del poder*; Murra, *Formaciones económicas y políticas del mundo andino*. For Inka urbanization, see Morris and Thompson, *Huánuco Pampa*.

33. For an example from the highlands near Lima, see Spalding, *Huarochirí*, chap. 1. Long-distance trade was known in the Andean world, but ethnohistorians continue to debate its place; see Larson, Harris, and Tandeter, *Ethnicity, Markets, and Migration*.

34. The number is cited in Penry, "Pleitos coloniales," 400. For tempered skepticism over the success of the program, see Mumford, *Vertical Empire*, chap. 8. Penry argues that the program was successful in reformulating pueblo life, but not necessarily along the lines that Spanish administrators proposed. See also the essays in Saitō and Rosas Lauro, *Reducciones*.

35. Fraser, *The Architecture of Conquest*.

36. Nemser, *Infrastructures of Race*, 35.

37. E.g., Konetzke, *Colección*, I:260–61, 267, 442–43. On changing policy regarding marriage between Spanish men and Indigenous women, see Mangan, *Transatlantic Obligations*, chaps. 1–2.

38. Spain [Consejo de Indias], *Recopilacion de leyes de Indias*, bk. VI titulo iii leyes 21–22.

39. Konetzke, *Colección*, I:513.

40. Owensby, *Empire of Law*, 24–25; Spain [Consejo de Indias], *Recopilacion de leyes de Indias*, bk. VI, titulo iii, leyes 21–22. See also Konetzke, *Colección*, I:213, 297, 321, 513.

41. On Lima's ascent to head city of the viceroyalty, see Osorio, *Inventing Lima*, chap. 1.

42. Rostworowski de Diez Canseco, *Costa peruana prehispánica*.

43. Keith, *Conquest and Agrarian Change*, 35–36.

44. Rostworowski de Diez Canseco, *Señoríos indígenas*, chap. 2.

45. Hampe Martínez, *Don Pedro de la Gasca*, 138.

46. Cushner, *Lords of the Land*, 27–29.

47. Sánchez-Albornoz, "La mita de Lima"; on Potosí see Bakewell, *Miners of the Red Mountain*.

48. On that normalization, see Bryant, *Rivers of Gold*; Bennett, *African Kings*.

49. These estimates, pulled from contemporary censuses and reports, can be found with their sources in Bowser, *African Slave*, 337–41.

50. Bowser, 40–41. The Transatlantic Slave Trade Database (slavevoyages.org) contains updated information. Actual places of origin would not be the same as port of embarkation, but the latter might suggest common language groups, practices, and experiences.

51. McKinley, *Fractional Freedoms*.

52. Durán Montero, "Lima en 1613," 177. On the ways the callejón produced cross-cultural relationships, see Osorio, "El callejón de la soledad."

53. The Real Audiencia compiled statutes issued between 1550 and 1552 (Archivo General de Indias [hereafter AGI] Patronato 187, Ramo [hereafter r.] 15) and Carlos V issued ordinances in 1551, published as an appendix in Lima [Peru]. Cabildo, *Libro primero de cabildos de Lima*.

54. In Spain, fifteenth century economic expansion displaced rural people into towns and cities, where they often ended up as part of a growing underclass. In the century that followed, cities petitioned the Crown to control immigration for the poor, and there were vigorous debates regarding poor relief, the identification of the legitimately poor, and the creation of institutions to serve them. Work, rather than charity, was seen as key to ending poverty and government was encouraged to be the instrument. See Martz, *Poverty and Welfare*, Fernández Álvarez, *Felipe II y su tiempo*, and Spicker, *The Origins of Modern Welfare*.

55. Ordenanzas para la ciudad de Lima (1550–1551), AGI Patronato 187 r. 14 f. 13.

56. "Reales ordenanzas sobre los negros que hay en la ciudad de Los Reyes (Reino del Perú)," in Konetzke, *Colección*, I:385. Restated in a letter from the king to Viceroy Francisco de Toledo in December 1571, AGI Lima, 569, Legajo [hereafter leg.] 13, f. 343.

57. Lee et al., *Libros de cabildos de Lima*, bk. XIV: 435.

58. There were numerous such laws. The 1535 ordinances can be found in Lima [Peru]. Cabildo, *Libro primero de cabildos de Lima*, 26–27. The 1551 ordinances are found at AGI Patronato Real, 187 r. 14 and published in "Ordenanzas," 10–20. The 1560 ordinances are in AGI Patronato Real 188 r. 16, and published in Konetzke, *Colección*, I:384–88.

59. Lee et al., *Libros de cabildos de Lima*, IV:55–56. For similar ordinances in Mexico, see Valerio, " 'That There Be No Black Brotherhood.' "

60. The census was transcribed and published as Contreras, *Padrón*. The original is at the Biblioteca Nacional de España, Madrid, Mss/3032. Generations of social historians have mined it for information, notably Charney, "El indio urbano"; Durán Montero, "Lima en 1613"; Lowry, "Forging an Indian Nation"; Vergara Ormeño, "The Copacabana Indigenous Elite."

61. Women's ages were marked in the opposite margin, without further information.

62. See Vergara Ormeño, "The Copacabana Indigenous Elite," 101.

63. Juan Bromley painstakingly mapped the census onto historic streets in 1945, published in Bromley and Barbagelata, *Evolución urbana de Lima*.

64. There is no equivalent to the 1613 census for the city's Black population, but Nancy van Deusen has gathered data from a variety of sources across the seventeenth century, and shows that free Black people most commonly lived in Santa Ana, San Lázaro, the Cercado, the "El Baratillo" neighborhood of La Barranca, and at the city gates that exited towards Callao. Van Deusen, "The 'Alienated' Body," 8.

65. Walker, *Exquisite Slaves*. The language of the "symbolic economy" comes from Hall, *Things of Darkness*.

66. For insight into service and slavery in convents and monasteries, see Van Deusen, *The Souls of Purgatory*.

67. Asiento de Agustin Quina, Archivo General de la Nación, Perú (hereafter AGN), Protocolos Notariales (hereafter PN) 20 Castillejo (1596), ff. 73v–74; Asiento de Alonso Liviac, AGN PN 20 Castillejo (1596), f. 259.

68. Asiento de Pablo Carpapumbi, AGN PN 20 Castillejo (1596), ff. 342v–43.

69. Contreras, *Padrón*, 229–34.

70. Contreras, *Padrón*, 309–10, 281–82, 297.

71. Contreras, *Padrón*, 120, 149, 185, 298–99.

72. Contreras, *Padrón*, 51.

73. Contreras, *Padrón*,1 30, 430–31.

74. Contreras, *Padrón*, 232, 320–21.

75. Contreras, *Padrón*, 405–6.

76. Contreras, *Padrón*, 432–33. This entry is partly mistranscribed, see original in Biblioteca Nacional de España, Madrid, Mss/3032, f. 194v.

77. Contreras, *Padrón*, 340.

78. Vergara Ormeño, "Growing Up Indian," 88; Contreras, *Padrón*, 423.

79. Asiento de Agustín Quina, AGN PN Castillejo 20 (1596), f. 73v–74.

80. Contreras, *Padrón*, 370, 385, 96, 263, 375, 261.

81. Graubart, *With Our Labor and Sweat*, 66–68; Johnson, *Wicked Flesh*; McKinley, *Fractional Freedoms*; Vergara Ormeño, "Growing Up Indian."

82. Asiento de Baltazar Cacuna, AGN PN 20 Castillejo (April 28, 1597), ff. 714–15; Asiento de Cristóval Guana Xulca, AGN PN 20 Castillejo (December 10, 1596), ff. 491v–492; Asiento de Diego Pérez mulato, AGN PN 86 (April 22, 1608), ff. 45v–46v, 1608.

83. Asiento de Juan Carhua, AGN PN 20 Castillejo (December 5, 1596), ff. 488–88v; Asiento de Diego Alonso, AGN PN 20 Castillejo (November 18, 1596), ff. 454–54v.

84. Asiento de Pedro Yasaima, AGN PN 20 Castillejo (February 4, 1597), ff. 632v–33.

85. Many of the apprenticeship and service contracts were for orphans (i.e., the fatherless) or for those officials identified as vagrant or "perdido," lost. Premo, *Children of the Father King*, 58. Charney notes that such contracts often "merely camouflaged signs of abandonment": Charney, "Much Too Worthy," 91.

86. Premo, *Children of the Father King*, 54–59.

87. Asientos, AGN PN 20 Castillejo (27 May 1596), ff. 201v–302. For cases when masters failed to pay contracted salaries, see Graubart, *With Our Labor and Sweat*, 64–65.

88. Contreras, *Padrón*, 143–44.

89. As well as in Quiroz's study of sixteenth-century notarial records, suggesting that the Indigenous placements reflected the professional structure of the economy rather than pushed Indians into particular sectors. Quiroz Chueca, *Artesanos y manufactureros*, 95.

90. Salinas y Córdova, cited in Quiroz Chueca, *Artesanos y manufactureros*, 81.

91. Quiroz Chueca, *Artesanos y manufactureros*, 94.

92. Salinas y Córdoba, *Memorial*, 247–51; Cobo, *Monografías históricas*, 51–53. For a description of the buildings and site, see Osorio, *Inventing Lima*, 13–16.

93. Cobo, *Monografías históricas*, 53.

94. Graubart, *With Our Labor and Sweat*, chap. 4.

95. Contreras, *Padrón*, 185–97.

96. Contreras, 162–71.

97. Bowser, *African Slave*, 143–44.

98. Contreras, *Padrón*, 122–23.

99. Contreras, *Padrón*, 116.

100. Contreras, *Padrón*, 137.

101. Quiroz Chueca, *Artesanos y manufactureros*, 94. In the same period, Quiroz located 413 Spanish maestros.

102. Vergara Ormeño, "The Copacabana Indigenous Elite."

103. Contreras, *Padrón*, 378.

104. Graubart, *With Our Labor and Sweat*, 209. AGN PN 1853 Tamayo (March 1631), f. 74, and (July 1631), 250v.

105. Contreras, *Padrón*, 356–58.

106. Contreras, *Padrón*, 366–67.

107. AGI Lima, 143. See Puente Luna, "The Interpreter Admonishes the Viceroy."

108. Contreras, *Padrón*, 459.

109. Contreras, *Padrón*, 314–15, also 151.

110. E.g., Contreras, *Padrón*, 266, 416. See also Graubart, "Hybrid Thinking." Rappaport has an excellent meditation on the category of "Indian dressed as a mestiza," and why dress style often confused colonial observers; Rappaport, *The Disappearing Mestizo*, 50-51. Contreras described but did not tally the few subjects he accepted as mestizos.

111. It may have been used this way in other cities as well. The alcalde of the Indian tailors of Lima, Miguel Sánchez, stated that his wife was a criolla of the city of Huánuco, "and the criollos have no cacique nor encomendero." Contreras, *Padrón*, 149. See also Graubart, "The Creolization of the New World"; Puente Luna, *Andean Cosmopolitans*, 115–16.

112. AGI Lima, 143 f. 3.

113. Contreras, *Padrón*, 538. On Tlaxcala, see Baber, "Empire."

114. Contreras, *Padrón*, 392.

115. Contreras, *Padrón*, 269–70.

116. Contreras, *Padrón*, 324.

117. Graubart, "The Creolization of the New World."

118. Contreras, *Padrón*, 149.

119. Guamán Poma de Ayala, *El primer nueva corónica*, 470.

120. Contreras, *Padrón*, 379–80, 58. Sara Vicuña Guengerich (personal communication, 2019) believes that Cusi was likely the daughter of Felipe Quispe, and granddaughter of Titu Cusi and Chimbo Oclla of Vilcabamba. See also Guengerich, "Inca Women under Spanish Rule."

121. Bromley and Barbagelata, *Evolución urbana de Lima*, 25; Contreras, *Padrón*, 253–59.

122. On Indigenous litigation, see Puente Luna, *Andean Cosmopolitans*, chap. 2.

123. Contreras, *Padrón*, 253–55.

124. Puente Luna, *Andean Cosmopolitans*, 113.

125. Contreras, *Padrón*, 336. Pizarro rewarded the Cañari for their military assistance, and their exemption from tribute in exchange for carrying out certain obligations was restated by Viceroy Toledo in 1572. Toledo, *Relaciones de los vireyes*, I:93–95. Most of the men who claimed to be Cañari were nonetheless listed as tributaries. Contreras, *Padrón*, 393–94, but see 336.

126. AGN PN 1533 Piñeda (December 19, 1612), ff. 351–52.

127. Some of these connections are laid out by Charney, *Indian Society*; see also Puente Luna, *Andean Cosmopolitans*, 114.

128. AGN PN 1533 Piñeda (December 19, 1612), ff. 351–52.

129. Contreras, *Padrón*, 370. AGN PN 306 Castillejo (1603–1604), f. 559r-561r; 308 Castillejo (1607), f. 148-149r.

130. Ramos, "Indigenous Intellectuals in Andean Colonial Cities," 26.

131. AGN PN Tamayo 1851 (March 1623), f. 75v. Contreras, *Padrón*, 23.

132. AGN PN 1854 Tamayo (1626), f. 799.

133. AGN PN 181 Cristoval de Barrientos (April 1606), ff. 166–68v.

134. AGN PN 33 Esquivel (August 1, 1575), ff. 509–10v.

135. Venta de un solar, AGN PN 267, Alonso de Carrión (June 10, 1609), f. 100-2r. Contreras, *Padrón*, 77; Graubart, "The Bonds of Inheritance."

136. Testamento de Beatriz de Padilla, Archivo Arzobispal de Lima (hereafter AAL) Testamentos 56:13 (1663); Testamento de María de Huancavelica, AAL Tribunal de Bienes de Difuntos 69:6 (1666); Testamento de Juana Barba, AAL Testamentos 31:39 (1651); Testamento de Mencia Lopes, AGN PN 130 Pérez reg. 9 (June 24, 1578), ff. 439–44. All are discussed in Graubart, "The Bonds of Inheritance."

137. AGN PN 20 Castillejo (January 26, 1596), ff. 21–23v.

138. Testamento de Mencia Lopes, AGN PN 130 Pérez reg. 9 (June 24, 1578), ff. 439–444.

139. Testamento de María de Vilbao, AGN PN 221 Quiroz (October 1625), ff. 1101r–2v.

140. Testamento de María de Huancavelica, AAL Testamentos 69:6 (1666).

141. Testamento de Ana Biafara, AGN PN 77 Gutiérrez (July 22, 1586), ff. 1257–58.

142. AAL Cofradías 31:2 (1608).

143. Germeten, *Black Blood Brothers*, 88. For an important example from medieval Valencia, see Blumenthal, "'La Casa dels Negres.'"

144. AGN PN 20 Castillejo (June 7, 1596), ff. 227–28.

145. Testamento de María Angola, AAL Testamentos 62:18 (1664).

CHAPTER 3

1. A facsimile and a transcription of this undated document appear in Sáez, *Colección diplomática*, 534–38. The concejo's original statement is missing.

2. Burns, *Siete partidas*, II:270. The *Partidas* were written by members of a workshop, but Alfonso himself understood authorship to lie less in the act of writing and more in the sense of directing and editing the workshop's output; in that spirit I ascribe authorship to Alfonso and other monarchs in what follows. See Velasco, *Dead Voice*, 166.

3. Toledo's fuero dated to around 1086, and was probably first issued to Seville by Fernando III. González Arce, *Documentos medievales de Sevilla*, 137–40, 143–46, 148–53.

4. For a critical revision of the historiography on the shaping of Fernando's and Alfonso's legislation regarding Jews, see Soifer Irish, *Jews and Christians in Medieval Castile*, 179–80.

5. González Arce, *Documentos medievales de Sevilla*, 163–70.

6. Ladero Quesada, "De Toledo a Sevilla."

7. Howell, "Continuity or Change," 42; González Arce, *Documentos medievales de Sevilla*, 137–40, 163–70; Clavero, *Ordenanzas*, 53–55. Another scholar argues that the monarch left the fuero vague in order to facilitate royal intervention in the offices. González Jiménez, *Alfonso X el Sabio*, 322.

8. González Arce, *Documentos medievales de Sevilla*, 168–69.

9. González Arce, *Documentos medievales de Sevilla*, 175.

10. The fatwās of Al-Wanšarīsī are the best known, but recent scholarship has examined a variety of opinions from Mālikism. See Miller, "Muslim Minorities"; van Koningsveld and Wiegers, "The Islamic Statute of the Mudejars."

11. Miller, "Muslim Minorities," 257.

12. In addition to leaving behind property, family, and social networks, Muslims faced dangerous conditions traveling through Christian territories, including the possibility of enslavement. Miller, "Muslim Minorities," 260.

13. Wiegers, *Islamic Literature in Spanish and Aljamiado*, 83. On alfaquís and some of their tasks in fifteenth century Castille see Echevarría, "La sucesión femenina," 42, 46.

14. Montes Romero-Camacho, "Notas para el estudio," 346–47.

15. Montes Romero-Camacho, "La aljama judia . . .," 25–29.

16. Montes Romero-Camacho has collected the names and titles of Jews associated with the city in its first Christian century from the extant documentation. Montes Romero-Camacho, "Notas para el estudio."

17. Montes Romero-Camacho, "Notas para el estudio," 347.

18. Montes Romero-Camacho, "Juan Sanchez de Sevilla," 1100–1.

19. Hinojosa Montalvo, *Los mudéjares*, 37. See also González, *Repartimiento de Sevilla*, I:70–71.

20. Alfonso X, *Fuero real*, 118.

21. Burns, *Siete partidas*, V:1433–34. See also Soifer Irish, *Jews and Christians in Medieval Castile*, 187.

22. Suárez Bilbao, *El fuero judiego*, 364.

23. Baer, *A History of the Jews in Christian Spain*, I:284.

24. Suárez Bilbao, *El fuero judiego*, 377; Echevarría Arsuaga, "De cadí a alcalde mayor (II)."

25. Miller, *Guardians of Islam*, 81.

26. León Tello, *Judíos de Toledo*, 446–47.

27. Herzog, "Comunidad y jurisdicción," 456.

28. In Isabel's words, "so mi seguro e so mi guarda, amparo e defendimiento real" for Seville's Jews and their property. Montes Romero-Camacho, "La aljama judía de Sevilla," 46.

29. Haliczer, *The Comuneros of Castile*, 33.

30. González Jiménez and Montes Romero-Camacho, "Los mudéjares andaluces," 541.

31. Wiegers, *Islamic Literature in Spanish and Aljamiado*, 58.

32. Miller, *Guardians of Islam*, 57.

33. Wiegers, *Islamic Literature in Spanish and Aljamiado*, 57–61.

34. Miller, *Guardians of Islam*, 57–60.

35. Alfonso's vision can be contrasted with that of Jaume I of Aragón, whose 1247 (unpromulgated) standardization of the fueros of Aragón argued explicitly that Jews and Muslims should appear before Christian alcaldes. Canellas, *Vidal mayor*, 182.

36. Soifer Irish, *Jews and Christians in Medieval Castile*, 171–72, 196-8.

37. Burns, *Siete partidas*, III:639–41. On the forms of the oaths, see Vicéns, "Swearing by God."

38. León (Kingdom), *Cortes de los antiguos reinos*, V. 2, p. 210.

39. APS Oficio 5, Bernal, Cuaderno de 1441 (reissue of order dated September 27, 1441), ff. 74–75.

40. APS oficio 23, Sánchez, libro de 1472 sf (June 15, 1472).

41. Stated, e.g., in the 1351 cortes of Valladolid. Suárez Bilbao, *El fuero judiego*, 364.

42. APS Oficio 15, Rodríguez de Vallecillo, libro de 1470–1479 (undated, 1484), f. 48v.

43. Nader, *Liberty in Absolutist Spain*, 28.

44. Muslims were also allowed to lend, but they rarely did so. Soifer Irish, *Jews and Christians in Medieval Castile*, 189. On the association of Jews with credit more broadly, see Trivellato, *The Promise and Peril of Credit*.

45. The Catholic Church itself became a major lender, despite its public stand against usury. This legislation was aimed at creating legitimate and illegitimate forms of credit rather than ending the practice of charging interest. See Kathryn Burns, *Colonial Habits*.

46. Soifer Irish, *Jews and Christians in Medieval Castile*, 175.

47. Seville's procurators, in their petition to the 1371 cortes in Toro, also clearly linked these arguments; Enrique detached them while establishing that Jewish finance was central to his support of Jewish communities. See Soifer Irish, *Jews and Christians in Medieval Castile* and León (Kingdom), *Cortes de los antiguos reinos*, V. 2, p. 210

48. González Gallego, "El libro de los privilegios," 287–88, 299–300. See also Nader, *Liberty in Absolutist Spain*, 30–31; Pike, *Enterprise and Adventure*.

49. Catlos, *Muslims of Medieval Christendom*, 193; Echevarría Arsuaga, "De cadí a alcalde mayor (II)," 275–79.

50. Crespo Álvarez, "El cargo del rab mayor," 158–61.

51. Echevarría Arsuaga, "De cadí a alcalde mayor (I)"; Echevarría Arsuaga, "De cadí a alcalde mayor (II)."

52. The classic studies of the colonial cacique in this vein include Ramírez, "The 'Dueño de Indios'"; Spalding, *De indio a campesino*.

53. The studies include Torres Fontes, "El alcalde mayor de las aljamas"; Echevarría Arsuaga, "De cadí a alcalde mayor (I)"; Echevarría Arsuaga, "De cadí a alcalde mayor (II)"; Castaño, "Las aljamas judías de Castilla"; Castaño, "Tensiones entre las comunidades"; Crespo Álvarez, "El cargo del rab mayor"; Suárez Bilbao, "La comunidad judía."

54. Burns, *Siete partidas*, vol. III, 772.

55. Suárez Bilbao, *El fuero judiego*, 408–9.

56. Ladero Quesada, *Los mudéjares de Castilla*; Ladero Quesada, "Las juderías de Castilla."

57. Suárez Bilbao, "La comunidad judía."

58. Miller, *Guardians of Islam*, 56–57.

59. Baer, *A History of the Jews in Christian Spain*, II:119.

60. Suárez Bilbao, *El fuero judiego*, 127.

61. León Tello, *Judíos de Toledo*, 455; see also Castaño, "Tensiones entre las comunidades," 12.

62. Torres Fontes, "El alcalde mayor de las aljamas," 149–53. Ana Echevarría has done remarkable detective work to demonstrate the importance of Muslim familial connections in the role, and the centrality of the city of Toledo, home to an important mudéjar community, as part of her argument that the alcalde mayor continued to be an office of prestige and power. Echevarría Arsuaga, "De cadí a alcalde mayor (I)."

63. Baer, *A History of the Jews in Christian Spain*, 250.

64. Crespo Álvarez, "El cargo del rab mayor"; Castaño, "Social Networks"; Castaño, "Las aljamas judías de Castilla"; Castaño, "Tensiones entre las comunidades."

65. He apparently did not; in 1489 the office was held by Abrahen Redomero of Toledo. The letter is transcribed in Torres Fontes, "El alcalde mayor de las aljamas," 175–80. See also Wiegers, *Islamic Literature in Spanish and Aljamiado*, 85.

66. Torres Fontes, "El alcalde mayor de las aljamas," 181–82.

67. Suárez Bilbao, *El fuero judiego*, 118; Hunt, *Spain, 1474–1598*, 16–17.

68. Moreno, *La antigua hermandad de los negros*, 25; Ortiz de Zúñiga, *Anales eclesiásticos y seculares*, Vol. 4: 260. The founding date of Mena's hospital is given as 1393, though there is no surviving documentation from that period.

69. On representations, see Fracchia, *"Black but Human"*; Fra Molinero, "Los negros"; Jones, *Staging Habla de Negros*.

70. Moreno, *La antigua hermandad de los negros*, 43; Ortiz de Zúñiga, *Anales eclesiásticos y seculares*, Vol. 3: 78-79. Ortiz de Zúñiga refers obliquely to Juan de Valladolid's "cautiverio y despreciado color," though it is possible that he was free.

71. Carande and Carriazo, *El tumbo de los Reyes Católicos*, II:58–59.

72. Carande and Carriazo, *El tumbo de los Reyes Católicos*, II:58–59.

73. San Lázaro was established by royal order soon after the Christian conquest of the city and served all leprosy patients, who were not permitted to enter other institutions, in the region. Carmona, *El sistema de hospitalidad pública en Sevilla*, 54.

74. Carande and Carriazo, *El tumbo de los Reyes Católicos*, III:332–36. Carmona believes that the mayoral was always a "caballero principal de la ciudad," though he does not discuss the conflict in the documentation. Carmona, *El sistema de hospitalidad pública en Sevilla*, 64.

CHAPTER 4

1. The scholarship on the treatise is discussed in Villaverde Amieva, "Un papel."

2. "Leyes de Moros," 85–92.

3. Echevarría notes that in Ávila (Castile), Muslims and Jews were explicitly included "in urban life with full rights" as vecinos, though they were unable to hold posts in the city council. Echevarría Arsuaga, *The City of the Three Mosques*, 71; see also Nader, *Liberty in Absolutist Spain*, 30.

4. AMS B-AC August–October 1455, f. 76. When Muslims and Jews converted to Christianity, they became vecinos of the collación where they resided.

5. Many transactions might not have been written down at all. As Nader shows for early modern Castile, agreements may have been verbal, possibly witnessed, and property law could have been well enough understood to allow communities to distribute inheritances or resolve conflicts without the use of written documentation. Nader, *Liberty in Absolutist Spain*, 22–23.

6. Echevarría Arsuaga, "Islamic Confraternities and Funerary Practices," 348.

7. The modern churches replaced the original structures at different historical moments, and few traces of the original mosques/synagogues remain. For Islamic and Jewish remnants in Santa María la Blanca, see Gil Delgado, "Una sinagoga desvelada."

8. Ortiz de Zúñiga suggests "vague opinion" in the city that another mosque was located in San Salvador, *Anales eclesiasticos y seculares*, I: 245-45. On the various possibilities, see Ecker, "How to Administer."

9. León Tello, *Judíos de Toledo*, 469.

10. Wagner, "Un padrón desconocido," 381.

11. A mikvah has been excavated in a restaurant basement across the street from Santa María la Blanca, site of a former synagogue. See Gil Delgado, "Una sinagoga desvelada."

12. Ortiz de Zúñiga, *Anales eclesiásticos y seculares*, I: 245–46. The mistranslation of the stone's inscription is discussed in Ecker, " 'Arab Stones.' " Teaching likely took place within mosques in Spain, as separate madrasa architecture did not develop there. Kaluzny, "From Islamic Ishbiliya," 121.

13. For a reconstruction of Islamic legal texts in circulation, see Miller, *Guardians of Islam*. On the continued existence of at least written Arabic in fifteenth-century Castile, see Villanueva Zubizarreta and Araus Ballesteros, "Identidad musulmana"; Echevarría Arsuaga, "Islamic Confraternities and Funerary Practices." Granadan merchants were a regular presence in Seville, as were enslaved captives from war, making it likely that Arabic continued to be spoken in the city.

14. Miller, *Guardians of Islam*, 7.

15. *Brevario sunni*, cited in Echevarría Arsuaga, "Islamic Confraternities and Funerary Practices," 351–52. The *Brevario* does require that female family members stand in the rear of the funeral procession.

16. Echevarría Arsuaga, "Islamic Confraternities and Funerary Practices."

17. Collantes de Terán Sánchez, *Sevilla en la baja Edad Media*, 99–100.

18. Another pre-conquest cemetery might have been located in Triana, but was not in use in the fifteenth century.

19. Echevarría Arsuaga, "Islamic Confraternities and Funerary Practices," 361.

20. Casanovas Miró, "Las necrópolis judías hispanas," 212. One coffin is preserved on site in a glass vitrine within a modern parking garage, accessible to the public.

21. While the title "rabí" might be used for a Talmudic scholar, these men seem to be indicated as leaders of the religious community, and are not associated with other occupations. See Nirenberg, "A Female Rabbi?"

22. See Meyerson, *A Jewish Renaissance*, 234–35.

23. APS Oficio 3, García de Celada, Libro de 1489, sf (February 22, 1489).

24. Pope Sixtus IV gave permission for Isabel and Fernando to set up a permanent Inquisition to deal with the *converso* problem in 1478. The first *auto-de-fé* took place in Seville in 1481, and burned six men—all wealthy converts from Judaism—at the stake. See Kamen, *Inquisition and Society in Spain*, 31. The records of Seville's Inquisition are missing, and little is known about the content of the 1489 tribunal.

25. APS Oficio 3, Garcia de Celada, Libro de 1489, f. 135 (July 28, 1489), f. 214 (October 23, 1489), f. 217v (October 24, 1489), f. 234 (November 4, 1489), f. 294 (December 4, 1489), etc.

26. On sacred violence and Holy Week riots, see Nirenberg, *Communities of Violence*, chap. 7.

27. Ladero Quesada, "Las juderías de Castilla."

28. APS Oficio 4, González, Libro de 1441–1494, ff. 117v–18v (December 9, 1454),

29. APS Oficio 11, González, Escrituras del siglo XV, cuadernos de 1465, sf (February 4 and 5, 1465); APS Oficio 23, Sánchez, Libro de 1472, sf (June 8, 1472).

30. APS Oficio 11, González, Escrituras del siglo XV, cuadernos de 1465, sf (March 22, 1465).

31. APS Oficio 9, García de Celada, cuadernos de 1450–1489, cuaderno de 1489, folio suelto (April 2, 1489). Jews were expelled only from Andalucía in 1483, so there would have been small Jewish aljamas in other parts of the kingdom.

32. APS Oficio 9, García de Celada, Libro de 1500–1501, sf (undated).

33. Ladero Quesada, *Los mudéjares de Castilla*, 104–5.

34. APS Oficio 4, González, Libro de 1441–1494, ff. 117v–18v (December 9, 1454)

35. APS Oficio 9, García de Celada, Libro de 1500–1501, sf (April 22, 1501).

36. APS Oficio 9, Luis García de Celada, Libro de 1500-1501, sf (April 22, 1501). See also Gestoso y Pérez, *Historia de los barros vidriados sevillanos*, 384.

37. Herzog, "Comunidad y jurisdicción."

38. For an example from Aragón, see Miller, *Guardians of Islam.*

39. Miller, *Guardians of Islam*, 76. Miller also notes that the Inquisition intensely focused on morisca women, perhaps reflecting their understanding of Muslim women's involvement in legal and religious affairs.

40. AMS doc. 1175 B-AC 1439-B sm fol. 11.

41. González Jiménez, *La repoblación*, 131.

42. Though some texts that circulated appear to be far more conservative than contemporary practice suggests. Fernández, *El legado material hispanojudío*; Wiegers, *Islamic Literature in Spanish and Aljamiado*; Miller, *Guardians of Islam.*

43. Powers, "On Judicial Review in Islamic Law," 318.

44. Powers, "On Judicial Review in Islamic Law," 318.
45. Soifer Irish, *Jews and Christians in Medieval Castile*, chap. 6; Meyerson, *Jews in an Iberian Frontier Kingdom*, 8.
46. APS Oficio 9, García de Celada, Libro de 1499, sf (October 8, 1499).
47. On Xarafi in Granada, see Ladero Quesada, "De nuevo sobre los judíos granadinos," 309, 311; and Porras Arboledas, "Documentos cristianos," 235–36.
48. AMS B-AC 1447, sm f. 50v.
49. *Sic*, likely Carmoní. AMS A-AC 1450, sm f. 94.
50. Wiegers, *Islamic Literature in Spanish and Aljamiado*, 83. See also Echevarría Arsuaga, "La sucesión femenina."
51. Wiegers, *Islamic Literature in Spanish and Aljamiado*, 83–84.
52. APS Oficio 4, García de Celada, Libro de 1537 con Cuaderno de 1492, sf (May 11, 1492).
53. Miller, *Guardians of Islam*, 82–83; Ladero Quesada, "De nuevo sobre los judíos granadinos," 311.
54. Miller, *Guardians of Islam*, 82–85.
55. Blasco Martínez, "Notarios mudéjares de Aragón," 118.
56. Wagner, "Un padrón desconocido," 376.
57. Echevarría Arsuaga, "Trujamanes and Scribes."
58. In Aragón, prior to 1360, Muslims were supposed to contract before a notary assigned by the Crown (who might have been Muslim or Christian), probably because this stream of income was part of the salary. A law in 1360 made this more flexible. Blasco Martínez, "Notarios mudéjares de Aragón," 112.
59. Quoted in Powers, *Law, Society, and Culture*, 141.
60. Porras Arboledas, "Documentos cristianos," 234.
61. Kagan, *Lawsuits and Litigants*, 22–32, is the best brief summary of the heterogeneous influences.
62. Ruiz, *From Heaven to Earth*, chap. 2.
63. Ruiz, *From Heaven to Earth*; Eire, *From Madrid to Purgatory*.
64. Powers, *Studies in Qur'an and Hadith*, 8. Powers considers the Islamic law of inheritance to have developed long after Muhammad's initial revelations; it is this later system that is relevant for a discussion of the post=1200 period.
65. Powers, *Studies in Qur'an and Hadith*, 9–10.
66. Powers, *Studies in Qur'an and Hadith*, 9–10; Powers, *Law, Society, and Culture*, chap. 4. This was one of many ways Muslims could use legal fictions to circumvent apparently strict inheritance laws.
67. APS Oficio 4, García de Celada, Libro de 1537, cuadernos de 1492 sf (May 9, 1492).
68. APS Oficio 3, Garcia de Celada, Libro de 1496, hojas sueltas (undated).
69. Some Jewish wills survive from fourteenth-century Valencia, written by Christian notaries and utilizing the Latinate model. Burns, *Jews in the Notarial Culture*, 22.
70. Burns, *Jews in the Notarial Culture*, 24.

71. Burns, *Jews in the Notarial Culture*, 25–27.

72. Burns, *Jews in the Notarial Culture*, 30. Burns interprets these as representing concerns by Aragonese Jews whose families were being divided by the massive conversions of the period.

73. The penalty for not using a notary at all could be drastic: according to legislation made in 1274, in Lérida (Aragón), if a Muslim died intestate, half of his or her estate went to the Crown, and the other half went to the mudéjar aljama. Burns, *Jews in the Notarial Culture*, 34.

74. APS Oficio 4, Garcia Celada, Libro de 1537, cuaderno de 1492, sf (April 4, 1492); APS Oficio 9, García de Celada, Libro de 1500–1501, sf (October 23, 1500).

75. APS Oficio 9, García de Celada, Libro de 1499, sf (January 25, 1499).

76. Burns, *Siete partidas*, Vol. 5: 1435.

77. On dowry and *arras*, see Arrom, *The Women of Mexico City*, 62.

78. APS Oficio 4, García, Libro de 1441–1494, f. 27 (December 11, 1450); Oficio 11, signatura 6676 rollo 231M, Bernal f. 15, imagen 41.

79. Echevarría Arsuaga, *The City of the Three Mosques*, 74–75.

80. Echevarría Arsuaga, *The City of the Three Mosques*, 137.

81. APS Oficio 15, Gonzalo de Plasencia, Libro de 1470–1479, ff. 321–22 (November 11, 1460).

82. Meyerson, *The Muslims of Valencia*, 249.

83. APS Oficio 15, Rodriguez de Vallecillo, Libro de 1470–1479, ff. 123v–124 (June 1474).

84. Examples of cross-confessional apprenticeship contracts include APS Oficio 11 González, Escrituras del siglo XV, Cuadernos de 1465, sf (March 21, 1465); and Oficio 23, Sánchez, Libro de 1472 sf (May 27, 1472).

85. López Martínez, "Los judaizantes castellanos y la Inquisición en tiempo de Isabel la Católica," 407–8. It is not clear whether Álvarez's family members were conversos from these documents, but that seems the most likely explanation.

86. APS Oficio 9, García de Celada, Libro de 1499, sf (October 10, 1499).

87. APS Oficio 3, de Muros, Libro de 1496, f. 99 (April 21, 1496).

88. Vassberg, *Land and Society*.

89. Vassberg, *Land and Society*, 6–7.

90. APS Oficio 3, García de Celada, Cuadernos de 1498, sf (May 10, 1498).

91. APS Oficio 11, González, Escrituras del siglo XV, cuadernos de 1466, sf (February 21, 1466). This was known as an emphyteutic lease (related to the religious *censo enfitéutico*). See Vassberg, *Land and Society*, 94–95.

92. AMS, A-AC 1450, sm (December 9, 1450), f. 133

93. AMS, A-AC 1455 (August–October), f. 51.

94. APS Oficio 15, Rodriguez de Vallecillo, Libro de 1470–1479, f. 48v (undated, 1484).

95. E.g.: APS Oficio 11, González, Escrituras del siglo XV, cuadernos de 1465, sf (January 26, 1465); APS Oficio 23, Sánchez, Libro de 1472, sf (August 28, 1472).

96. APS Oficio 23, Sanchez (November 23, 1472), three unfoliated documents.

97. APS Oficio 4, Alvarez, Libro de 1441–1494, f. 311 (June 19, 1480); see also Oficio 15, Rodríguez de Vallecillo, Libro de 1480–1489, f. 153v (January 22, 1484).

98. APS Oficio 15, Rodríguez de Vallecillo, Libro de 1480–1489, ff. 139v–140 (January 19, 1484).

99. APS Oficio 12, Bernal, Escrituras del siglo XV, Cuadernos de 1493, sf (March 5, 1493).

100. APS Oficio 9, García de Celada, Libro de 1493, f. 36v (March 20, 1493).

101. On some Jewish families' success in the fifteenth century, see Meyerson, *A Jewish Renaissance.*

102. Sánchez Saus, "Cádiz en la época medieval," 272.

103. Wagner, *Regesto* passim.

104. APS Oficio 15, Rodríguez de Vallecillo, Libro de 1480–1489, ff. 63v–84 (February 11, 1484).

105. AMS B-AC 1467, sm, f. 19 (October 19, 1467).

106. AMS B-AC 1460, January–April, f. 129.

107. AMS A-AC 1471, June–July, f. 65.

108. AMS B-AC 1450, sm, f. 4. copia simple.

109. AMS A-AC 1453, sm, f. 66.

110. AMS B-AC 1454, July–August, f. 62.

111. APS Oficio 4, Segura, Libro de 1495, ff. 401–3 (October 12, 1495). See also APS Oficio 3, de Muros, Libro de 1496, f. 61 (March 25, 1496).

112. APS Oficio 5, Ruiz de Porras, Cuadernos de 1498, f. 60 (June 2, 1498).

113. APS Oficio 9, Garcia de Celada, Cuadernos de 1450–1486, ff. 15v, 23, 24 (August–September 1486).

114. AMS B-AC 1470, May–August, f. 44. On high-stakes ransoms, see Echevarría Arsuaga, "Trujamanes and Scribes."

115. Martín Casares, *La esclavitud en Granada*; Blumenthal, *Enemies and Familiars.*

116. Occasionally wills indicate manumission. A Sevillano painter who freed his Black slave in his 1523 will, and left him tools of the trade and sample drawings, is discussed in Méndez Rodríguez, "Slavery and the Guild."

117. APS Oficio 12, Bernal, Cuadernos de 1496, sf (October 10, 1496), sf.

118. Catlos, *Muslims of Medieval Christendom,* 158.

119. APS Oficio 5, Bernal, Cuaderno de 1497 f. 32 (March 16, 1497); Oficio 5, Ruiz de Porras, cuaderno de 1497 f. 35v (March 19, 1497); Oficio 5, Ruiz de Porras, cuaderno de 1497 f. 59 (April 15, 1497). This last case is also important evidence that self-purchase was institutionally recognized long before enslaved African and African-descent individuals extended and even revolutionized the process in the Americas.

120. APS Oficio 4, Segura, Libro de 1502, f. 131v–132 (January 25, 1502).

121. Blumenthal, *Enemies and Familiars,* 202.

122. Saunders, *A Social History of Black Slaves*, 154–56.

CHAPTER 5

1. Lohmann Villena, "Testamento del curaca."
2. In litigation, don Gonzalo claimed that the valley's population at contact included 4,000 adult males, and in the 1550s was reduced to some 200. The numbers were supported by nearly all witnesses except the cacique of Pachacamac, who lowered the original number to 3,000 (and claimed jurisdiction over Taulichusco). Rostworowski de Diez Canseco, "Dos probanzas de don Gonzalo," 163.
3. The claim that invaders did not understand the land tenure system they were attempting to dominate was a common strategy of both elites and commoners (and occasionally true). See Cline, "Oztoticpac Lands Map"; Graubart, "Shifting Landscapes."
4. Puente Luna, "That Which Belongs to All," 22. Sapci might also include other forms of capital, for example a cacique's prowess in litigation.
5. Coastal peoples did not usually speak Quechua, but Taulichusco was a *yanacona* or political ally of the wife of Huayna Capac, the last ruling Inka. See Rostworowski de Diez Canseco, "Dos probanzas de don Gonzalo," 115; Charney, *Indian Society*, 6.
6. Lohmann Villena, "Testamento del curaca."
7. A good statement of this model with its inherent failures and complications is Owensby, *Empire of Law*, 25.
8. For some key interventions in a burgeoning field, see Bennett, *African Kings*, chap. 3; Fromont, *Art of Conversion*; Green, *Rise of the Trans-Atlantic Slave Trade*; Green, "Beyond an Imperial Atlantic"; More, "Necroeconomics"; Muldoon, *Popes, Lawyers, and Infidels*; Thornton, *Africa and Africans*.
9. On the question of dominium and conversion, see Muldoon, *Popes, Lawyers, and Infidels*, chap. 6; Quijano Velasco, "Las repúblicas de la monarquía." Adorno notes that "[o]therness, with respect to the Amerindian, does not exist," the foundation of Juan Ginés de Sepúlveda's argument for a Catholic "just war" against the Indians. Adorno, *The Polemics of Possession*, 5.
10. Muldoon notes that Alexander VI's lawyers avoided denying infidel dominium, having largely acquiesced to the reality of Castilian conquest. Muldoon, *Popes, Lawyers, and Infidels*, 134–38.
11. Quoted in Anghie, *Imperialism*, 18.
12. Baber, "Categories," 28–29.
13. Herzog, *Defining Nations*, chap. 1; Herzog, "The Appropriation of Native Status"; Martínez, *Genealogical Fictions*, chap. 4.
14. See Matthew, *Memories of Conquest*; Matthew and Oudijk, *Indian Conquistadors*.
15. Konetzke, *Colección*, I:63–67. This was the basis for the experiment founded by Bartolomé de las Casas in 1520 in Cumaná; Bataillon, "The Clérigo Casas."
16. Pagden, *Lords of All the World*.

17. On Inka terminology see Ramírez, *To Feed and Be Fed*.

18. For an introduction to the literature on Inka political systems (which were not hegemonic across the Andes), see Brian S. Bauer, *The Development of the Inca State*; Julien, *Hatunqolla*; Murra, *Economic Organization*. For the misunderstanding of the role of Inka, see Ramírez, *To Feed and Be Fed*. David Cahill summarizes the research for the southern Andes, which was the most closely tied to the Inka empire; Cahill, "The Long Conquest." In north Andean Cajamarca, the decimal terminology was used but did not indicate precise numbers. Albiez-Wieck, "Indigenous Migrants," 485–86.

19. This is especially true of the north coast, long hostile to the Inka and only brought into that empire a few decades before the Spanish conquest (see Rostworowski de Diez Canseco, *Curacas y sucesiones*; Netherly, "Local Level Lords") but also key to understanding other regions; see Salomon, *Native Lords of Quito*; Zuloaga, *La conquista negociada*; Rostworowski de Diez Canseco, *Conflicts over Coca Fields*.

20. For an example of the theory, see Konetzke, *Colección*, I:64.

21. Rostworowski de Diez Canseco, *Obras completas 3*, II:321–22.

22. Baber, "Categories," 27; Díaz Serrano, "Repúblicas de indios." Much of the Spanish conquest was carried out with or by Indigenous allies, though not all received compensation; Matthew and Oudijk, *Indian Conquistadors*; Matthew, *Memories of Conquest*.

23. Even this status did not go unchallenged; in 1556 the viceroy of New Spain attempted to unseat the Indigenous *governador* of Tlaxcala on corruption charges, causing its cabildo to debate whether the viceroy had such a power, and what it meant for local rule. Owensby, *Empire of Law*, 38–39.

24. Nader, *Liberty in Absolutist Spain*, 4.

25. Moore, *The Cabildo in Peru*, chap. 2; see also Lohmann Villena, *El corregidor de indios*; Nader, *Liberty in Absolutist Spain*, 144–45.

26. Cañeque, *The King's Living Image*.

27. Nader, *Liberty in Absolutist Spain*, 85–86. The Tlaxcalan nobles could be added to that list, though only with respect to their own subjects and under the supervision of a corregidor.

28. Mumford, *Vertical Empire*, 53–71.

29. Spain [Consejo de Indias], *Recopilacion de leyes de Indias*, bk. V, tit. II, ley iii.

30. AGI Lima 567, L. 7, 81ff.

31. See Ramírez, "Amores prohibidos."

32. Lohmann Villena, *El corregidor de indios*, 509–19.

33. Poole, *Juan de Ovando*, chap. 7.

34. Academia de la Historia, *Colección de documentos*, VIII:484–538.

35. Konetzke, *Colección*, I:471–78.

36. Charles, *Allies at Odds*, 5–6.

37. Charles, *Allies at Odds*, 21.

38. Abercrombie, *Pathways of Memory and Power*, 224–25. A lifetime was understood as literally that: once the original holder died, it passed to his or her spouse or child, for a total of three persons.

39. Lohmann Villena, *El corregidor de indios*, 509–19.

40. For example, Burns, *Into the Archive*; Charles, *Allies at Odds*; Dueñas, *Indians and Mestizos in the "Lettered City"*; Puente Luna, *Andean Cosmopolitans*; Ramos and Yannakakis, *Indigenous Intellectuals*; Rappaport and Cummins, *Beyond the Lettered City*.

41. See Puente Luna, "That Which Belongs to All."

42. Spain [Consejo de Indias], *Recopilacion de leyes de Indias*, bk. VI: VII: iii.

43. See Rostworowski de Diez Canseco, "Succession"; Ramírez, *The World Upside Down*, chap. 2; Díaz Rementería, "El cacique en el virreinato del Perú."

44. Honores, "Una sociedad legalista," 106–7.

45. An important case is that of Cajamarca. See Noack, "Caciques, escribanos." See also Espinoza Soriano, "El primer informe etnológico"; Ramírez, "Amores prohibidos."

46. An exceptional analysis of this phenomenon is Powers, "A Battle of Wills."

47. Rostworowski de Diez Canseco, *Señoríos indígenas*, 80–82, 180–81; Charney, *Indian Society*, 6, 81; Rostworowski de Diez Canseco, "Dos probanzas de don Gonzalo."

48. Lowry, "Forging an Indian Nation," 131–32.

49. Though Toledo demonstrated some flexibility, as shown by Mumford, "Litigation as Ethnography."

50. Matienzo argued that "this Kingdom of Peru was justly gained and His Majesty holds title most justly . . . it is the tyranny of the Incas . . . keeping oppressed the natural kings of the Indians, which are the caciques of each repartimiento and province," which gave the Spaniards license to invade and conquer. Matienzo, *Gobierno del Perú [1567]*, 11. In Toledo's restatement, before Topa Ynga, "los dichos naturales no tenian ni tuvieron ningun senor ni cacique que los mandase ny governasse en tiempo de paz ni a quien tuviesen ninguna subjection y heran como behetrias sin que ouiese entrellos ningun genero de gouierno sino que cada uno gozaua de lo que tenia y biuia como queria." Levillier, *Don Francisco de Toledo*, vol. II: 4. For a contemporary gloss of behetría, see Rostworowski de Diez Canseco, *Señoríos indígenas*, 25.

51. Levillier, *Don Francisco de Toledo*, II:16.

52. Levillier, *Don Francisco de Toledo*, II:5.

53. Mumford, "Litigation as Ethnography."

54. AGN Derecho Indígena (hereafter DI) leg. 43 cuad. 39 (1595), f. 59. Andean nobles did not have a formula for assessing which wife would be the mother of the successor, with an exception among the Inkas who had tired of internecine wars at every succession and briefly invented the practice of legitimating the child the ruler had with his full sister. Rostworowski de Diez Canseco, "Succession."

55. On innovation and custom in cacicazgo selection, including the case of the cacicas, see Graubart, *With Our Labor and Sweat*, chap. 5; Garrett, *Shadows of Empire*;
Rostworowski de Diez Canseco, *Curacas y sucesiones*. Cacicas proliferated across
the Spanish American world, as shown by Ochoa and Guengerich, *Cacicas*.

56. See also Powers, "A Battle of Wills."

57. AGN DI leg. 3, cuad. 19 (1574). On Huaylas and its *guarangas*, see Varón Gabai,
Curacas y encomenderos; Zuloaga, *La conquista negociada*.

58. For a close reading see Zuloaga, *La conquista negociada*, chap. 4.

59. AGN DI leg. 3, cuad. 19, ff. 15v–16v.

60. AGN DI leg. 3, cuad. 19, f. 24. Varón Gabai makes no mention of dual cacicazgos;
his main ethnographic source is a 1558 visita, by which time Ichocchonta was certainly singular again. Susan Ramírez (personal communication) notes that there
were originally three guarangas and perhaps at one time three caciques rather than
a duality, the third erased by the emergence of the narrative of one and two caciques. Varón Gabai, *Curacas y encomenderos*.

61. AGN DI leg. 3, cuad. 19, ff. 24v, 29v.

62. Varón Gabai, *Curacas y encomenderos*, 38.

63. AGN DI leg. 3, cuad. 19, ff. 38v–39.

64. AGN DI leg. 3, cuad. 19, f. 40v.

65. The witness questionnaire added more color by asserting that Caruarimango
and his son Yaroquispe were murdered in warfare with their local enemies, the
Conchucos, leaving don Pablo Curas too young to take their place. This allowed
don Juan Caxaguaraz and Martin Jurado to usurp his seat, the child being unable
to speak out against them "from fear that they might kill him." The allusion to
violence also was a call for royal intervention, as will be discussed below.

66. For the effects on communities, see Guevara-Gil and Salomon, "A 'Personal Visit'";
Stern, *Peru's Indian Peoples*, 123–24.

67. The extant papers from these extensive litigations are dispersed over a variety of
archives and cases including Biblioteca Nacional del Perú (hereafter BNP) A 534
and AGN DI leg. 3 cuad. 26 (1580).

68. AGN DI leg. 3 cuad. 28 (1580) f. 400.

69. AGN DI leg. 3 cuad. 37 (1594) f. 7.

70. While some classic works exaggerate the effects of population decline (notably
Wachtel, *The Vision of the Vanquished*), most communities experienced deep contractions. Migration was also a common result, with important effects, as shown
in Powers, *Andean Journeys*. Spalding notes that the crisis was not so much demographic as it was "the squeeze between falling Indian population and the rapidly
growing numbers of Spaniards in the new kingdom"; Spalding, *Huarochirí*, 137–38.
For a comprehensive assessment of the tribute programs for north coastal communities, see Ramírez, *The World Upside Down*, chap. 4.

71. Rostworowski de Diez Canseco, "Dos probanzas de don Gonzalo," 111–13. The *probanzas* appear to have been unsuccessful. See Varón Gabai, *Francisco Pizarro and His Brothers*, 187–89.

72. Early colonial land-grabbing in Peru has been the topic of important studies: see Cushner, *Lords of the Land*; Glave Testino and Remy, *Estructura agraria*; Glave Testino, "Propiedad de la tierra"; Guevara Gil, *Propiedad agraria y derecho colonial*; Keith, *Conquest and Agrarian Change*; Lockhart, "Encomienda and Hacienda"; Ramírez, *Provincial Patriarchs*; Spalding, *Huarochirí*; Vergara Ormeño, "Hombres, tierras y productos."

73. Herzog, "Colonial Law and Native Customs," 309.

74. Key critical analyses include Puente Luna, "Of Widows, Furrows, and Seed"; Ramírez, *The World Upside Down*, chap. 3; Graubart, "Shifting Landscapes." The classic study is Murra, "Waman Puma"; on Inka practices, see Pease G. Y., "La noción de propiedad." Studies of the Cusco region include Burns, *Colonial Habits*, chap. 2; Glave Testino and Remy, *Estructura agraria*, chap. 2. Alternative theories for the coast are laid out by Rostworowski de Diez Canseco, *Costa peruana prehispánica*; Charney, *Indian Society*, chap. 2; Ramírez, *The World Upside Down*, 74–86.

75. Niles, *The Shape of Inca History*, 13–15.

76. Vassberg, *Land and Society*.

77. For example, Acosta, *Natural and Moral History*, 396; see also Ondegardo, "Informaciones acerca de la religión," 70. Betanzos hints at this but notes that, with conquest, "By grace of the Inca [the conquered] were to receive women and land," suggesting that the Inka's direct control over land was more of a threat than a reality. Betanzos, *Narrative of the Incas*, 111.

78. Esquivel y Navia et al., *Noticias cronológicas*, vol. I:208.

79. AGN Títulos de Propiedad, cuad. 745 (1605), ff. 11–12. See also Charney, *Indian Society*, 48–49.

80. BNP B1087 (1629). When women were appointed to the office of cacica, their husbands were sometimes named governor, often empowering them to collect tribute, with the expectation that the couple would rule together. Graubart, *With Our Labor and Sweat*, chap. 5.

81. AGN DI leg. 31 cuad. 622 (1597).

82. For early versions of these responsibilities, see Matienzo, *Gobierno del Perú [1567]*; Rostworowski de Diez Canseco, "Algunos comentarios"; Ramírez, *The World Upside Down*.

83. AGN DI leg. 1, cuad. 2 (1558). The case is discussed in greater detail in Graubart, "Learning from the Qadi."

84. BNP A440 (1569), f. 2.

85. BNP A440, ff. 8, 30v.

86. BNP A440, f. 27.

87. BNP A440, ff. 26v–27.

88. Levillier, *Gobernantes del Perú*, I:529–30.

CHAPTER 6

1. "Exclamación de Catalina Gualcum," AGN PN 10 Arias Cortez f. 267 (August 7, 1582).
2. On the valleys, see Flores-Zúñiga, *Haciendas y pueblos de Lima*, vol. 1, chap. 2. On Rimac's pre-Hispanic footprint, see Morgado Maurtua, "Reshaping Rimac."
3. Hampe Martínez, *Don Pedro de la Gasca*, 138.
4. Rostworowski de Diez Canseco, *Ensayos de historia andina*, 331. See also Rostworowski de Diez Canseco, *Doña Francisca Pizarro*, 36–39.
5. Rostworowski de Diez Canseco, *Señoríos indígenas*, chap. 2.
6. Abercrombie, *Pathways of Memory and Power*, 240.
7. On acts of foundation and their meanings, see Díaz Ceballos, *Poder compartido*, chap. 1; Fraser, *The Architecture of Conquest*, chap. 2; Seed, *Ceremonies of Possession*. On the relationship between architecture, public space, and morality see Escobar, "Francisco de Sotomayor."
8. The precise formula for this, written in 1573, long after most foundings had already taken place, is given in Philip II, "Ordenanzas sobre descubrimiento nuevo y población," in Academia de la Historia, *Colección de documentos*, 514–15.
9. Romero, "Libro de la visita general," 164.
10. Matienzo, *Gobierno del Perú [1567]*, 16.
11. Castillero Calvo, *Fundación y orígenes de Natá*, 60.
12. "Ordenanza para la reducción de los indios de Huamanga (1570)," in Toledo, *Francisco de Toledo*, I:5. On Toledo's visita and the transformations it brought forth, see Abercrombie, *Pathways of Memory and Power*, 237–51.
13. Such internal community maps are extant in parts of Mexico. Mundy, *The Mapping of New Spain*, 118–26.
14. Puente Luna, *Andean Cosmopolitans*, 44–45.
15. "Ordenanzas para los indios de todos los departamentos y pueblos de este reino," in Toledo, *Relaciones de los vireyes*, I:156–57.
16. Lohmann Villena, *El corregidor de indios*, 564–65.
17. Spain [Consejo de Indias], *Recopilación de leyes de los reynos de las Indias*, bk. VI, tit. III, ley xvi.
18. Charney, *Indian Society*, 79.
19. AGI Lima, 579 leg. 6, ff. 60v–61r (1581).
20. "Obligación," AGN PN 22 Castillejo (1599–1602) ff. 1472–74.
21. Novoa, *The Protectors of Indians*, 109.
22. They are AGN PN 20 Castillejo (1596); PN 22 Castillejo (1600); 1533 Piñeda (1612–1613).
23. On the Mexican *Juzgado*, see Owensby, *Empire of Law*; on the Peruvian case, see Borah, "Juzgado general."

24. AGN, Superior Gobierno, leg 6, cuad 93 (1685) includes copies of these orders.

25. AGI Lima, leg. 169 (1657); see also Puente Luna, *Andean Cosmopolitans*, 122–24.

26. Viz. AGN PN 22 Castillejo 1602, ff. 1624–1625 (December 10, 1602); AGN PN 20 Castillejo 1596 ff. 427v–428 (October 22, 1596); AGN PN 20 Castillejo ff. 342v–343 (August 10, 1596). He occasionally also placed Spanish apprentices with other Spaniards, though the vast majority of the clients were Indigenous.

27. Toledo established a *juez de los naturales* (with a vote in the city's *cabildo*) in Cusco in 1572, but not for Lima. Toledo, *Francisco de Toledo*, 179.

28. See Cobo, *Monografías históricas*, 121.

29. "Título de Andrés Ramírez Inga," AGN Libro donde se toma razon ... (1602) ff. 134r–35.

30. Puente Luna, *Andean Cosmopolitans*, 121.

31. AGN PN 1533 Piñeda 1612–1618, f. 34 (March 13, 1612).

32. For a more expansive reading of that docket, see Graubart, "Ynuvaciones Malas e Rreprovadas."

33. AGN PN 1533 Piñeda (1612–1618), f. 50 (April 10, 1612); f. 236 (August 2, 1612); f. 286v (September 10, 1612).

34. Ramírez, *Provincial Patriarchs*, 104–5; Abercrombie, *Pathways of Memory and Power*, 282–91.

35. AGN Testamentos de Indios (hereafter TI), leg. 1 (1596).

36. Konetzke, *Colección*, II:157.

37. "Arrendamiento," AGN PN 1533 Piñeda f. 43 (March 29, 1612). A *fanega de sembradura* (also called a *fanega* or *fanegada* in this period) was the area of land that could be planted with 1.5 bushels (a *fanega*) of seed; see Ramírez, *Provincial Patriarchs*, 279.

38. "Arrendamiento," AGN PN 1533 Piñeda, f. 40v (March 28, 1612). Clavijo previously served as a royal official in charge of reducciones in the northern Andes, giving him direct insight into the process.

39. On the development of haciendas see Keith, *Conquest and Agrarian Change*. On Clavijo, see Corr and Powers, "Ethnogenesis, Ethnicity and 'Cultural Refusal.'"

40. "Testamento de Magdalena Picona," AGN PN 1853 Tamayo, ff. 833–35v (September 11, 1630).

41. "Testamento de Doña Ana Collon," AGN PN 1856 Tamayo, ff. 635–37 (July 7, 1635).

42. "Arrendamiento," AGN PN 1533 Piñeda (1612–1618), f. 13 (January 1613). "Arrendamiento," AGN PN 1533 Piñeda (1612–1618), f. 39v (January 2, 1613).

43. AGN PN 1533 Piñeda (1612–1618), ff. 217v–220 (July 20, 1612).

44. AGN PN 1533 Piñeda (1612–1618), ff. 302–2v (October 24, 1612). Juan Bañol's owner also avoided the risk of having his human property punished by authorities.

45. "Testamento de Constança Ticlla," AGN TI, leg. 1, 1596; "Testamento de Elvira Coyti," AGN TI leg. 1, 1596; "Testamento de María Capan," AGN TI leg. 1, 1596.

46. AGN DI leg. 4 cuad. 47 (1603) f. 7v.

47. AGN DI leg. 4 cuad. 47 (1603) f. 7v.

48. The nested hierarchy of ayllus suggests a hierarchy of caciques, with one called the *cacique principal*, as described in testimony at Don Gonzalo Taulichusco's litigation in the 1550s; Rostworowski de Diez Canseco, "Dos probanzas de don Gonzalo," 113.

49. Herzog, "Colonial Law and Native Customs."

50. Don Juan, cacique of Surco, disagreed with this claim, presumably believing that some of the land was his own. Rostworowski de Diez Canseco, "Dos probanzas de don Gonzalo," 114–16.

51. Rappaport, *The Disappearing Mestizo*, 126. See also the discussion of don Francisco Tomabilca's anger at losing his father's *indios de servicio* in the previous chapter.

52. For gender and inheritance law, see Graubart, *With Our Labor and Sweat*, chap. 3.

53. On censos, most often associated with the Church, see Burns, *Colonial Habits*, 63-7.

54. "Recaudos tocantes al repartimiento de Lati," BNP A 164 (September 1584), f. 15ff.

55. See also "Reconocimiento del censo," BNP A 489 (July 1576), f. 10ff, for examples from Maranga and Guadca.

56. Netherly, "Management of Late Andean Irrigation Systems"; Rostworowski de Diez Canseco, *Señoríos indígenas*, 52–53.

57. "Probanza de los yanaconas de marqués don Francisco Pizarro," BNP, A15 (1550); Charney, *Indian Society*, 14.

58. Rostworowski de Diez Canseco, *Señoríos indígenas*, 191.

59. Morgado Maurtua, "Un palimpsesto urbano," 166; Kole de Peralta, "The Nature of Colonial Bodies," 33–36.

60. Lee et al., *Libros de cabildos de Lima*, VII:619. See also Barnes and Fleming, "Filtration-Gallery Irrigation," 50–52.

61. AGN Aguas leg. 1 cuad. 3.3.1.6 (1630); see also Cushner, *Lords of the Land*, 49–52.

62. Hyslop, *The Inka Road System*, 275.

63. Vaca de Castro wrote what appear to be the first colonial ordinances on *tambos* in 1543, Vaca de Castro, "Ordenanzas de tambos [1543]." On the fondaco, see Constable, *Housing the Stranger*.

64. Rostworowski de Diez Canseco, *Obras completas 3*, II:331.

65. Rostworowski de Diez Canseco, II:337.

66. E.g., Diez de San Miguel, *Visita a Chucuito [1567]*, 213.

67. For example, AGN PN 1533 Piñeda, f. 259 (September 24, 1612) and f. 132v (May 7, 1612).

68. In 1688, the income was used to pay the salaries of the cacique and priest, and to underwrite religious festivals. "Autos que a nombre de su comun siguió don Juan Tantachumbi." AGN DI cuad. 635 (1688); see also Charney, *Indian Society*, 93.

69. Charney, "For My Necessities," 333.

70. On chicha in the Andean world, see Weismantel, "Maize Beer and Andean Social Transformations"; Garofalo, "La bebida del inca"; Mangan, *Trading Roles*, chap. 3.

71. Mangan, *Trading Roles*, 84–92.

72. "Testamento de María Capan," AGN TI leg. 1 (1596).

73. "Testamento de Costança Ticlla," AGN TI leg. 1 (1596). An *arroba* was equivalent to about twenty-five pounds.

74. Surco's "town tavern" is also mentioned in litigation from 1603. AGN DI leg. 4 cuad. 47 f. 13v (1603).

75. Mangan, *Trading Roles*, 82.

76. "Expediente sobre el juicio de residencia," BNP A537 (1586). In Cuzco, caciques drew upon their personal resources as well as their traditional association with ritual reciprocity to dominate that city's chicha industry. See Garofalo, "La bebida del inca."

77. "Testamento de Elvira Coyti," "Testamento de María Capan," and "Testamento de Costança Ticlla," all AGN TI leg. 1.

78. The office of notary seems to have passed within the family. In 1635 the notary of Surco was don Lorenzo's brother, don Cristóval Yanchi Chumbi, also *segunda persona*. AGN PN 1854 Tamayo, f. 736 (August 1635).

CHAPTER 7

1. Carande and Carriazo, II:58–59. Loro was the contemporaneous way to describe people of mixed African-European heritage, later more commonly rendered as mulato.

2. Making a parallel with Black confraternities, it is reasonable to assume that the law involved practices remembered from diverse African experiences, as well as those learned in Europe: see Fromont, *Afro-Catholic Festivals in the Americas*; Soares, "Art and the History of African Slave Folias"; Valerio, "A Mexican Sangamento?"; Valerio, *Sovereign Joy*; Voigt, *Spectacular Wealth*.

3. "And We order the *concejo*, the *alcaldes*, the *alguacil*, the *veinte-cuatros*, the *caballeros*, the *jurados*, the other cities and towns and places of the archbishopric, to consent and to hold you as mayoral and judge of all the said *negros* and *negras* and *loros* and *loras*." Carande and Carriazo, *El tumbo de los Reyes Catolicos*, II:59.

4. Ortiz de Zúñiga, *Anales eclesiásticos y seculares*, Vol. 3: 79. See also Moreno, *La antigua hermandad de los negros*, 43.

5. Carmona García, *El sistema de hospitalidad pública*, 21.

6. Carmona García, *El sistema de hospitalidad pública*, 51.

7. Blumenthal, *Enemies and Familiars*; Hershenzon, *The Captive Sea*; Phillips, *Slavery*; Wheat, *Atlantic Africa*.

8. Isabel had declared the natives of the Americas to be her free vassals in 1493, but exceptions remained for those taken in "just war," rendering vast regions such as Nicaragua and Chile open for slaving. The New Laws (1542) set in motion a legal process through which those Indigenous slaves who could prove their provenance

might be freed. There was no blanket ban until Charles II issued law in 1679. Van Deusen, *Global Indios*; Reséndez, *The Other Slavery*.

9. See Franco Silva, *Regesto documental*; Martín Casares, "Evolution."

10. Toby Green identifies thirteen West African ethnic groups appearing in Atlantic records between 1547 and 1560, giving a sense of the geographic region from which these men and women were taken. After 1589 the trade moved south to West-Central Africa, a more culturally homogeneous region. Green, *Rise of the Trans-Atlantic Slave Trade*, 23, 27.

11. Jewish slaves who did not convert were subject to expulsion. Domínguez Ortiz, "La esclavitud en Castilla"; Martín Casares, *La esclavitud en Granada*.

12. This is the regla of the confraternity, copied into a seventeenth-century litigation. "La cofradía y hermandad de Nuestra Señora de la Antigua y Siete Dolores con la cofradía de Nuestra Señora de los Angeles y hermanos della," Institución Colombina (hereafter IC), Fondo Archivo Arzobispal (hereafter FAA), Sección Justicia: Serie Hermandades y Cofradías, leg 94 (1604).

13. Fernández Chaves and Pérez García argue that moriscos, who were a sizable part of the population of slaves in Seville, were unlikely to form affinity groups out of fear that their conversion would be questioned. Fernández Chaves and Pérez García, "The Morisco Problem and Seville."

14. Collantes de Terán Sánchez, *Sevilla en la baja Edad Media*, 433–34.

15. Some institutions (such as the Atarazanas Reales or Royal Shipyards) and great noble lineages possessed large numbers. The Duque de Medina Sidonia's enterprises held some 250 enslaved persons in 1507. Collantes de Terán Sánchez, 256–57; Ladero Quesada, *Andalucía a fines*, 185; Phillips Jr., *Slavery*, 108.

16. Ortiz de Zúñiga, *Anales eclesiásticos y seculares*, Vol. 3: 79.

17. Franco Silva, *La esclavitud en Sevilla*, 247. It is worth noting that only one record in the fifteenth-century notarial protocols refers to a free Black person (and that one is a much later copy of a fifteenth-century original), suggesting that freedom might have removed the need for describing Blackness in that kind of document. By the sixteenth century, the adjective is commonly attached to both free and unfree people in written materials.

18. Ortiz de Zúñiga, *Anales eclesiásticos y seculares*, Vol. 3: 78.

19. The literature on confraternities, evangelization, slavery, and Black devotees is large and growing. For a global introduction: Black and Gravestock, *Early Modern Confraternities*; Blumenthal, "'La casa dels negres'"; Brewer-García, *Beyond Babel*; Fromont, *Art of Conversion*, 202–6; Gual Camarena, *Una cofradía de negros libertos*; Jaque Hidalgo and Valerio, *Indigenous and Black Confraternities*; Kiddy, *Blacks of the Rosary*; Moreno, *La antigua hermandad de los negros*; Rowe, *Black Saints*, chap. 2; Soares, *People of Faith*; Valerio, "A Mexican Sangamento?"; Valerio, *Sovereign Joy*; Germeten, *Black Blood Brothers*; Walker, "Queen of Los Congos."

20. Saunders, *A Social History of Black Slaves*, 151.

21. Rowe, *Black Saints*, chap. 1.

22. Brewer-García, *Beyond Babel*.

23. Gual Camarena, *Una cofradía de negros libertos*.

24. On the Iberian re-creation of African ritual practices and cultural elements, see Valerio, "A Mexican Sangamento?"

25. Sánchez-Albornoz, "Los libertos," 23. See also McKinley, *Fractional Freedoms*, chap. 5.

26. Africans could be treated by royal authorities as Old Christians, at least until the middle of the seventeenth century, when *limpieza de sangre* designations became more systematized and restrictive. See Ireton, "They Are Blacks."

27. *Colección de Documentos*, XXXI:23.

28. Jones, *Staging Habla de Negros*.

29. On Isabel's entrance and the Africanness of festive performances, see Valerio, "Kings of the Kongo," 30.

30. "La cofradía y hermandad de Nuestra Señora de la Antigua y Siete Dolores con la cofradía de Nuestra Señora de los Angeles y hermanos della," IC, FAA, Sección Justicia: Hermandades y Cofradías, leg 94 (1604).

31. Núñez Muley, *A Memorandum [1566]*, 81.

32. Valerio, "Kings of the Kongo," chap. 1; Fromont, "Dancing for the King of Congo"; Heywood and Thornton, *Central Africans*.

33. "La cofradía y hermandad de Nuestra Señora de la Antigua . . .," IC, FAA, Justicia: Hermandades y Cofradías, leg 94 (1604).

34. "La cofradía y hermandad de Nuestra Señora de la Antigua . . ." IC, FAA, Justicia: Hermandades y Cofradías, leg 94 (1604), f. 1.

35. "La cofradía y hermandad de Nuestra Señora de la Antigua . . ." IC, FAA, Justicia: Hermandades y Cofradías, leg 94 (1604), f. 4.

36. For a crucial case of how this might have been done, see the study of African Christian translators in Cartagena in Brewer-García, *Beyond Babel*.

37. "Muerte de un esclavo," APS Oficio 15, legajo 9100, ff. 288r–288v (undated 1495).

38. Ordenanzas para la ciudad de Lima (1550–1551), AGI Patronato 187, r. 14.

39. Herzog, *Defining Nations*, chap. 7; Martínez, *Genealogical Fictions*, 159. This does not mean that local practices followed royal claims; indeed, they varied greatly. Chira, *Patchwork Freedoms*; Ireton, "They Are Blacks"; Wheat, *Atlantic Africa*.

40. Lee et al., *Libros de cabildos de Lima*, IV:356–57. On the role of work in the Castilian republic, see Mackay, *Lazy, Improvident People*, 46–71.

41. Lee et al., *Libros de cabildos de Lima*, IV:356–57. The cabildo also used the labor of the Indians of San Pedro de los Camaroneros to keep the river and city dumps clean before 1590, Lee et al., VIII:591; IX:322; X:130, 287. The association of free Blacks with sanitation might have to do with a belief that slave labor contributed to the problem. In Seville, in 1461, the *concejo* complained that the city was overrun

with piles of garbage and feces, dumped by "caballeros and escuderos who use their Black slaves to transport garbage" AMS, A-AC 1461 (August–December), f. 34.

42. Lee et al., *Libros de cabildos de Lima*, IV:516.

43. Lee et al., *Libros de cabildos de Lima*, VII:338–39; 9:174–75.

44. Lee et al., *Libros de cabildos de Lima*, XI:113–14.

45. *Colección de documentos*, V:43–45; Deive, *Los guerrilleros negros*, 24.

46. The literature on *cimarronaje* in the Caribbean is extensive. I draw here upon Altman, "The Revolt of Enriquillo"; Cáceres, *Negros, mulatos, esclavos y libertos*; Deive, *Los guerrilleros negros*; Landers, "La cultura material"; Landers, "Leadership and Authority"; Landers, "Cimarrón and Citizen"; Price, *Maroon Societies*; Rocha, "Maroons in the Montes"; Stone, "America's First Slave Revolt"; Tardieu, *Cimarrones de Panamá*; Wheat, *Atlantic Africa*.

47. Palenque may be taken from the wooden fences or *palos* that they used to surround and shroud their homes; see Covarrubias Horozco, *Tesoro*, 1336–37. The description of wooden palenques appears in Tardieu, *Cimarrones de Panamá*, 63–64.

48. AGI Santo Domingo 49, r. 4, n. 30. Quoted in Altman, "The Revolt of Enriquillo," 606. On linking the Indigenous and Black revolts, see Stone, "America's First Slave Revolt."

49. Altman, "The Revolt of Enriquillo," 602.

50. On the massive cost of fighting cimarrones, see Vila Vilar, "Cimarronaje en Panamá y Cartagena."

51. Panamá or Castilla del Oro is the subject of a number of important studies of cimarronaje. See Díaz Ceballos, "Cimarronaje"; Pike, "Black Rebels"; Tardieu, *Cimarrones de Panamá*; Vila Vilar, "Cimarronaje en Panamá y Cartagena." Also see Bethany Aram's interdisciplinary project, which includes a database of key documents, "An ARTery of Empire: Conquest, Commerce, Crisis, Culture and the Panamanian Junction (1513–1671)," https://www.upo.es/investigacion/artempire/.

52. AGI Panama 29, R. 6. n. 25, 1 (April 4, 1555). Transcribed in Tardieu, *Cimarrones de Panamá*, 69.

53. Díaz Ceballos, "Cimarronaje," 87–89; Pike, "Black Rebels," 258; Jopling, *Indios y negros en Panamá*, 368.

54. Aguado, *Historia de Venezuela*, chap. 11.

55. The most famous known case of enslaved royals is that of the two young members of an Old Calabar ruling family, slave traders themselves, who were captured by English slavers and removed to the Caribbean, eventually making their way back to Old Calabar and returning to slaving. See Sparks, *The Two Princes of Calabar*.

56. For an example, see Valerio, "A Mexican Sangamento?," 69.

57. On this literature see, e.g., Childs, " 'The Defects of Being a Black Creole' "; Fromont, "Dancing for the King of Congo"; Hunefeldt, *Paying the Price of Freedom*; Jouve Martín, "Public Ceremonies and Mulatto Identity"; Kiddy, "Who Is the King of Kongo?"; Lara, *Fragmentos setecentistas*; Mello e Souza, *Reis negros*

no Brasil escravista; Valerio, "Kings of the Kongo"; Voigt, *Spectacular Wealth*. The empire-wide interest in the idea of royalty is explored by Aram, "Three Kings."

58. Jopling, *Indios y negros en Panamá*, 368; see also Konetzke, *Colección*, I:489–90.
59. Hidalgo Pérez, "Una Historia Atlántica," 93.
60. AGI Patronato 234, r. 3 (1579), image 21.
61. AGI Patronato 234, r. 3 (1579). It is not clear what assistance the likely illiterate don Luis had in producing the petition.
62. "Relación de Antonio Salcedo," AGI Patronato 234, R. 3 (1579), image 6.
63. AGI Patronato 234, r. 3, image 12.
64. AGI Patronato 234 r. 3, image 10; Díaz Ceballos, "Cimarronaje," 91. Díaz Ceballos, *Poder compartido*, chap. 1.
65. Díaz Ceballos, "Cimarronaje," 95.
66. For an overview, see Landers, "Leadership and Authority."
67. For various royal orders of the 1550s calling upon authorities to place *mestizos* under supervision, and house them either in special *colegios* or (in New Spain) in *reducciones* with vagrant Spaniards, see Konetzke, *Colección*, I:298, 320, 328, 383–84.
68. Bowser, *African Slave*, 19.
69. AGI Lima, 108 (1574); AGI Lima 579, leg. 5 (1574); Levillier, *Gobernantes del Perú*, III:429; Bowser, *African Slave*, 158.
70. AGI Patronato 240, r. 6; transcribed in Ponce Leiva, *Relaciones histórico-geográficas*, vol. I: 518–26. On Auncibay and his scheme, see Lane, *Quito 1599*, 76–77; Bryant, *Rivers of Gold*, 1–5.
71. AGI Patronato 240, r. 6, translation courtesy of Kris Lane.
72. Bryant, *Rivers of Gold*, 3.
73. Undated memorial, Biblioteca Nacional de España (Madrid), Papeles varios de Perú y México, mss/2010.
74. Jouve Martín, *Esclavos de la ciudad letrada*, 41.
75. Eventually, courts would intervene as third parties to assess prices. De la Fuente, "Slaves and the Creation of Legal Rights." Even gracious or testamentary manumissions generally required self-purchase in some form; McKinley, *Fractional Freedoms*.
76. For examples, see Graubart, "The Bonds of Inheritance."
77. Harth-Terré and Márquez Abanto, "Perspectiva social y económico," 47.
78. Graubart, "The Bonds of Inheritance."
79. Jopling, *Indios y negros en Panamá*, 441.
80. Kuznesof, "Ethnic and Gender Influences."
81. In contrast, the English colony of Virginia taxed enslaved Black men and women who worked in productive industries in the seventeenth century, and masters paid. Brown, *Good Wives*, chap. 4.

82. On the relatively undiscussed strangeness of this proposition—that the children of free men were property rather than kin—see Brown, *Good Wives*, chap. 4; Morgan, "Partus Sequitur Ventrem."

83. Konetzke, *Colección*, I:467.

84. Konetzke, *Colección*, I:479.

85. For the cédula exempting the wives and children of Spaniards, see AGI Panamá, 40.

86. AGI Panamá 40, r. 191.

87. Jopling, *Indios y negros en Panamá*, 454–56.

88. Konetzke, *Colección*, I:482–83; Bowser, *African Slave*, 303.

89. Konetzke, *Colección*, I:502–3; Levillier, *Gobernantes del Perú*, 7:294; Bowser, *African Slave*, 303. The Cabildo had already called for such a policy in 1572, LCL 7:211.

90. Bowser, *African Slave*, 303–4.

91. AGI Contaduría 1700 (1595–1596), f. 98.

92. AGI Contaduría 1713 (1628–1629), f. 196.

93. Jouve Martín, "Public Ceremonies and Mulatto Identity."

94. AGI Escribanía, 1023B (1632). See also Bowser, *African Slave*, 306–7; on the mulato guild's festivals, see Jouve Martín, "Public Ceremonies and Mulatto Identity."

95. "Relación de las ciudades," in Lissón Chávez and Ballesteros Gaibrois, *La Iglesia de España en el Perú*, Vol. 5: 251-267.

96. Bowser, *African Slave*, chap. 9; Graubart, "So color de una cofradía"; Hunefeldt, *Paying the Price of Freedom*; Jouve Martín, "Public Ceremonies and Mulatto Identity."

97. Lee et al., *Libros de cabildos de Lima*, IV:55–56.

98. AAL Cofradías 64:1 (1574), 64:2 (1585). Much of what follows is developed in Graubart, "So color de una cofradía."

99. AAL Cofradías 64:11 (1630). On the ways that the mobile experience of New World enslavement produced profound knowledge and ties, see O'Toole, *Bound Lives*.

100. AAL Cofradías 51:1 (1607). Lima was one of the main destinations for cimarrones captured in Panamá, perhaps the source of some of this discourse of criminality.

101. AAL Cofradías 51:24 (1829), 51:2 (1608–1609).

102. AAL Cofradías 31:4 (1639).

103. AAL Cofradías 36:28 (1670–1671); but see also AAL Cofradías 64:1 (1574).

104. See the language of Landers, "Cimarrón and Citizen," 112; Price, *Maroon Societies*.

105. Landers, "Cimarrón and Citizen," 133–35. According to Daniel Nemser (personal communication), Yanga's son was later brought up on charges that he was not turning over runaways to Spanish authorities.

CHAPTER 8

1. "Ynformación," AGN PN 1532 Pineda 1610–1611, ff. 538–541 (1611).

2. For a rare and important counterexample, see Puente Luna and Honores, "Guardianes de la real justicia."

3. Historian Charles Gibson uncovered a single case in Puebla in 1561. Gibson, "Rotation of Alcaldes in the Indian Cabildo," 213.

4. Ramírez, *Provincial Patriarchs*, chap. 4.

5. Cobo, *Monografías históricas*, 45.

6. Trujillo (La Libertad). Concejo Provincial, *Actas*, I:127–28.

7. Graubart, "The Creolization of the New World."

8. Graubart, *With Our Labor and Sweat*, 16.

9. Juana Barba left her estate to the church and made a large donation to establish her younger sister as a religious servant (*donada*), which might have affected the notary's perception of her. "Testamento de Juana Barba," AAL Testamentos leg. 31:39 (Lima, 1651). For more examples across the Atlantic world, see Ireton, "They Are Blacks."

10. Gibson, "Rotation of Alcaldes in the Indian Cabildo," 215.

11. Burns, "Notaries, Truth, and Consequences."

12. On Zacatecas, see Velasco Murillo, "The Creation of Indigenous Leadership." On urban Indians more generally see Murillo, Lentz, and Ochoa, *City Indians in Spain's American Empire*.

13. Vergara Ormeño, "The Copacabana Indigenous Elite."

14. Lima [Peru]. Cabildo, *Libro primero de cabildos de Lima*, II:203.

15. "Ordenanzas para el buen gobierno," AGI Patronato 187, r. 14 (1550–1552), ff. 8–9.

16. "[P]ara los reparos de la dha ciudad puentes y acequias porque es muy necesario y provechoso a los naturales." Lee et al., *Libros de cabildos de Lima*, III:252–59.

17. Ordenanzas para la ciudad de Lima (1550–1551), AGI Patronato 187, r. 14, images 2, 10, 11.

18. "Real cédula sobre la jurisdicción de los alcaldes de indios," AGI Lima 578, leg. 2 ff. 140v–41r.

19. Lowry, "Forging an Indian Nation," 136–37. AGN PN 33 Esquivel (1569–1577) ff. 529, 536, 561, 647.

20. Lee et al., *Libros de cabildos de Lima*, V:27.

21. Lee et al., *Libros de cabildos de Lima*, VI:162, 465.

22. Lee et al., *Libros de cabildos de Lima*, IX:435; X:147, XII:45. The cleaners might have been the Indians of San Pedro, who were paid a sum equivalent to what they might have earned on mita. Lee et al., X:130, 287; Vergara Ormeño, "The Copacabana Indigenous Elite," 86.

23. Lee et al., *Libros de Cabildos de Lima*, VI:486–87, XIII:521, XIV:199.

24. A company already existed in 1589, when it welcomed the new Viceroy Marqués de Cañete to the city: Puente Luna, *Andean Cosmopolitans*, 113; Charney, *Indian Society*, chap. 3.

25. Contreras, *Padrón*. On church officials, see Charles, *Allies at Odds*. Women also served as confraternity mayordomas, but they were not registered as such in the census.

26. Spalding, *Huarochirí*, 164–66.

27. Spalding, *Huarochirí*, 26–27, 164–66.

28. Sánchez-Albornoz, "La mita de Lima."

29. In the Inka empire, yanaconas were personal retainers removed from ayllus and attached to nobles or to huacas. Pizarro used the term to refer to the regiment of Cañari soldiers that had assisted him in warfare, whom he assigned land and exempted from tribute payments. See Ramírez, *To Feed and Be Fed*, 27; Varón Gabai, *Francisco Pizarro and His Brothers*, 173–74.

30. "Foundation of Indian town of Cercado del Santiago [sic]," Library of Congress, Harkness Collection, document 866 (November 1, 1568).

31. The construction of the wall is not documented. The much larger and more expensive wall that encircled all of Lima in the late seventeenth century was constructed by the "mulatos, cuarterones, zambos and free blacks, Indians, and mestizos" of the city for very low pay, according to Burneo, *Las murallas coloniales*, 123. Free Black workers attempted to strike for higher wages and the viceroy threatened them with hard labor; Mugaburu and Mugaburu, *Chronicle of Colonial Lima*, 283. On the cost of Lima's wall, see also Bradley, *Spain and the Defence of Peru*, chap. 8. In contemporary port cities walls to keep out pirate attacks were often built by enslaved laborers. See AGI Santo Domingo 48, r. 9, n. 59 (1538) for one example.

32. Coello de la Rosa, "Resistencia e Integración," 117; Cárdenas Ayaipoma, "El pueblo de Santiago," 24.

33. For the Jesuit entry into Peru and the behind-the-scenes negotiations, see Torres Saldamando, "El primer y el último provincial." Hyland, "Conversion, Custom and 'Culture,'" 88.

34. Anello Oliva, *Historia del reino y provincias del Perú*, 253. The Jesuits abandoned the province within three years, claiming that they required a new challenge. Padre Oliva wrote that they also suffered significant losses to their numbers, two of six priests dying and one becoming quite ill due to the "great difficulties." On the Huarochirí parish, see Carcelén Reluz, "Los Jesuitas."

35. Hyland, "Conversion, Custom and 'Culture,'" 95.

36. Egaña, *Monumenta peruana*, vol. I: 247.

37. Torres Saldamando, "El primer y el último provincial," 452.

38. Philip II ordered an investigation into this tax in 1575; Egaña, *Monumenta peruana*, I: 740.

39. Osorio, *Inventing Lima*, 123–24.

40. Levillier, *Gobernantes del Perú*, 3:309.

41. Egaña, *Monumenta peruana*, I:257.

42. Coello de la Rosa, *Espacios de exclusión*.

43. Viceroy Hurtado de Mendoza sought to expand the city limits across the river, incorporating San Lázaro into the *traza*; he also ordered *composiciones de tierras* in the valleys in this period, to free up land and generate fees for the Crown. See Coello de la Rosa, *Espacios de exclusión*; Lowry, "Forging an Indian Nation"; and, most important, Vergara Ormeño, "The Copacabana Indigenous Elite."

44. The royal order is mentioned in many subsequent documents demanding that it be executed, though the original has not appeared. See Mogrovejo's letter to the king, April 18, 1603, in Lisson Chavez and Ballesteros Gaibrois, *La Iglesia de España en el Perú*, vol. IV, pt. 21, 491.

45. Archbishop Mogrovejo's 1591 letter to the king discussing the issue is published in Egaña, *Monumenta peruana*, IV:678–91. Viceroy García Hurtado de Mendoza made his case to the king in 1590, Egaña, IV:644–49. The Indigenous fishermen and women made their case in 1599, Egaña, VI: 657–60. For the king's order, see Levillier, *Gobernantes del Perú*, XIV:85–86, 186–87; Lowry, "Forging an Indian Nation," 47–48; Coello de la Rosa, *Espacios de exclusión*, 172.

46. "Título de alcalde mayor del Cercado," AGN, Libro de donde se toma razón (1602), ff. 134r–35r.

47. AGI, Patronato 248, r. 37 (1604). See the discussion in Vergara Ormeño, "The Copacabana Indigenous Elite," 119–23.

48. Lee et al., *Libros de cabildos de Lima*, XIV:435–36.

49. "Carta a Su Majestad del Virrey y Audiencia de Lima," Levillier, *Gobernantes del Perú*, XIV:83–88.

50. Each solar cost 109 pesos and 3 tomines. See Cobo, *Monografías históricas*, 352–53; Lima [Peru]. Cabildo, *Libro primero de cabildos de Lima*, II:204–5, contains the list of solares. Also AGN, Temporalidades, Cofradías legajo 323 cuad. 22.

51. Egaña, *Monumenta peruana*, vol. V: 378.

52. The language of ghetto come from Cárdenas Ayaipoma, "El pueblo de Santiago."

53. Kagan, "A World without Walls," 117.

54. Pollak ascribes the ubiquity of the walled and gridded European city to militarization and the appearance of military order. Pollak, *Cities at War*.

55. Kubler, *Mexican Architecture of the Sixteenth Century*, 77–80. Walls also presented limitations for expansion; Escobar, "Francisco de Sotomayor," 379–80. Lima would build a city wall, which ended up bisecting the Cercado, to protect it from sea attacks in 1684-87.

56. Kubler, *Mexican Architecture of the Sixteenth Century*, 81.

57. Kubler, *Mexican Architecture of the Sixteenth Century*, 81.

58. Livi-Bacci and Maeder, "The Missions of Paraguay"; Ganson, *The Guaraní*.

59. Van Deusen, *Between the Sacred and the Worldly*.

60. Kagan, "A World without Walls," 142–48.

61. Bromley and Barbagelata, *Evolución urbana de Lima*, 62; see also Cárdenas Ayaipoma, "El pueblo de Santiago," 27.

62. Levillier, *Gobernantes del Perú*, IV:230.

63. The earliest mention of slaves in parish records comes in 1582, Cárdenas Ayaipoma, "El pueblo de Santiago," 84.

64. Cobo, *Monografías históricas*, 126.

65. AGN, Libro dónde se toma razón (1602) ff. 134r–35r. The lack of the honorific "don" suggests the link was distant.

66. "Mandamiento y carta de pago," Library of Congress Harkness Collection, 874 (July 1570).

67. BNP A149 (1594), f. 28v.

68. Ondegardo, "Informaciones acerca de la religión," 47, 150.

69. Testamento de Diego Lastara, Testamento de Magdalena Yauri Chumbi, Testamento de Catalina Carguay Chumbi, all in AGN, TI leg 1A; Testamento de Diego Sedeño, AGN TI leg 1.

70. Perhaps the site of the collective brewing operation that had partly subsidized the Cercado's Jesuit governors. Testamento de don Diego Flores, AGN TI 1A, 1648.

71. A patacón was equivalent to a peso of eight reales.

72. Testamento de Maria Llacsa, AGN TI leg 1A, 1611.

73. Testamento de Pedro Xulca, AGN TI leg 1A, 1613. See also Testamento de Alonso de Paz, AGN TI leg 1, 1617.

74. Alfonso X, *Siete partidas*, Partida III, título XXX, laws 1, 2, 3, 6.

75. Testamento de Juan, AGN PN 33 Esquivel, 1569–1577.

76. Puente Luna, "Of Widows, Furrows, and Seed."

77. AGN Corregimiento del Santiago del Cercado (hereafter CSC) leg. 1 doc 6, 1691.

78. AGN CSC leg. 1, doc. 4, 1687.

79. AGN CSC leg. 1, doc. 3, 1686.

80. Autos que siguieron los indios Yauyos, AGN DI leg. 9, cuad. 130 (1653).

81. Autos que siguieron los indios Yauyos, f. 2v.

82. Autos que siguieron los indios Yauyos, f. 2v

83. Puente Luna, "Of Widows, Furrows, and Seed."

84. Autos que siguieron los indios Yauyos, f. 3v

85. Autos que siguieron los indios Yauyos, f. 4.

86. Autos que siguieron los indios Yauyos, f. 2.

CHAPTER 9

1. Vargas Ugarte, *Historia del culto de María*.

2. For some studies: MacCormack, "From the Sun of the Incas"; Ramos, "Nuestra Señora de Copacabana"; Amino, "Un milagro de La Virgen"; Angulo, "El barrio de San Lázaro de la Ciudad de Lima"; Estenssoro Fuchs, *Del paganismo a la santidad*.

3. On the politics of the cult see Vergara Ormeño, "The Copacabana Indigenous Elite."

4. Gómez, "Fashioning Lima's Virgin of Copacabana," 344.

5. AAL, Cofradías, leg. X, exp. 2, f. 252v. The cofradía later claimed that the Lima statue was a true copy of the one in Lake Titicaca, which remains a common belief to this day. Gómez, "Fashioning Lima's Virgin of Copacabana."

6. Vergara Ormeño, "The Copacabana Indigenous Elite," 104.

7. AAL Cofradías 10:1, 1604.

8. AAL Cofradías 10:2, 1605–1606.

9. According to Vergara, by the seventeenth century the cofradía owned houses and a tambo in San Lázaro as well as a tambo in the Cercado, and many houses and fields in the Lurigancho and Magdalena valleys. Vergara Ormeño, "The Copacabana Indigenous Elite," 139.

10. Vergara Ormeño, "The Copacabana Indigenous Elite," 139.

11. Ramos, "Nuestra Señora de Copacabana," 167; Vergara Ormeño, "The Copacabana Indigenous Elite," 143–44.

12. Alfonso X, *Primera crónica general*, 766.

13. Rappaport's reminder that the modern term race intersects with but is not coterminous with notions of individual and group identity in the early modern world bears repeating. Rappaport, *The Disappearing Mestizo*, 30.

14. See Premo and Yannakakis, "A Court of Sticks and Branches"; Terraciano, *The Mixtecs of Colonial Oaxaca*; Yannakakis, "Indigenous People and Legal Culture."

Glossary

acequia irrigation canal

albañil mason

alcalde (from Arabic, qādī) alcalde ordinario annually elected municipal judge

alcalde mayor provincial-level magistrate

alfaquí (from Arabic faqih) a student of Islamic law; sometimes the legal officer of a (Muslim or Jewish) aljama

alguacil constable

alguacil mayor chief constable

aljama (from Arabic, al-jamāʿa) term used in Castile to refer generically to Muslim or Jewish institutions of self-governance

almojarife tax collector

ayllu (Quechua) Andean kin group, before conquest often split into two parcialidades, each with their own ruler

borceguí buskin or soft leather boot, of Arab origin and in high fashion in the fifteenth century

borceguinero maker of borceguíes

cabildo municipal council; see also concejo

cacique (from Taíno) generic term used by Spanish colonists to refer to a hereditary, local-level Indigenous ruler; see also kuraka

cacicazgo the heritable office of the colonial cacique including its privileges and resources; see also kurakazgo

cédula royal order

censo a kind of mortgage permanently attached to a property, such that any subsequent owner would make annual payments to a third party

cimarrón (also maroon) escaped slave, often one who has formed community outside of Spanish control

cofradía Catholic sodality or confraternity organized around a shared worship practice, often engaged in public processions for feast days, and with a mutual-support component

collación parish

composición de tierras land inspection resulting in titling and/or expropriation

concejo   municipal council, see also cabildo

converso   name used to indicate a convert from Judaism to Christianity, or the direct descendent of a convert

corregidor   royally appointed magistrate, usually with jurisdiction over a province.

corregidor de indios or de naturales   magistrate in charge of Indigenous affairs and tribute collection in a province

dhimmī (Arabic)   the status given to resident Christians and Jews in an Islamic kingdom, wherein they had limited internal autonomy and the right to practice their faith, and paid a special tax.

diezmos   tithes to the Catholic Church

fatwās (Arabic)   legal rulings from Islamic jurists

fiqh (Arabic)   law

fuero   legal charter issued by a monarch to a municipality, usually confirming limited customary law

hidalgo   member of the lower nobility

judería   Jewish quarter or neighborhood

jurado   in Seville, one of the two nonvoting representatives of each parish to the concejo

kuraka (Quechua)   pre-Hispanic Andean local or regional ruler, often called cacique in Spanish documentation

kurakazgo (Quechua)   the heritable office of the pre-Hispanic kuraka including its privileges and resources

maestre   master craftsman, as used by Muslim artisans in Seville

maestro   master craftsman, usually given as a result of passing an examination in the trade

maravedí   smallest unit of account

mestizo/a   of mixed Spanish and Indigenous parentage

mita   forced labor requirement imposed on adult Indigenous men, also called repartimiento

mit'a (Quechua)   labor turn in pre-Hispanic Andes, usually with an expectation of reciprocity

morería   Muslim quarter or neighborhood

morisco/a   a convert from Islam to Christianity or the direct descendant of a convert

mudéjar   a Muslim living under Christian rule

mulato/a   of mixed Spanish and Black parentage

oidor   judge and member of the Audiencia

ollero/a   potter

padrón   enrollment or census, usually for taxation purposes

palenque   community created by escaped slaves

parcialidad   Spanish term for an Andean social or political division, often making up a diarchy within an ayllu

pecho   a head tax paid by non-nobles

peso (de a ocho)   silver coin worth between eight reales (272 maravedís)

policía   civic behavior or political life, implying Christianity, urbanization, and productive labor

qadi (Arabic)   judge of an Islamic community

qadi mayor   chief Muslim judicial official under the Crown of Castile

rab, raby, rabbi   Jewish ordained religious leader (rabbi) or Talmudic scholar

rab mayor   chief Jewish judicial official under the Crown of Castile

real   silver currency worth thirty-four maravedís

Real Audiencia   highest court of appeals in a province, with royally appointed judges

regidor   alderman

repartimiento   forced labor required of Indigenous adult men, often in mining. In the Andes, called mita.

sapci (Quechua)   that which belongs to all, a collective resource or fund for the community's use

señorío   lordships with jurisdiction over land and/or subjects

solar   standard piece of land or plot

tambo (from Quechua, tampu)   inn for travelers

toquero   maker of sheer headdresses (tocas) for women

vecino   a free person with obligations and privileges in a particular city or town

visita   extraordinary inspection

yesero   plasterer

zambo, zambaigo   a person with mixed Indigenous and Black parentage

Bibliography

ARCHIVES CONSULTED

In Spain

Archivo de Protocolos de Sevilla (APS)
Archivo General de Indias, Seville (AGI)
Archivo Histórico Municipal de Sevilla (AMS)
Archivo Histórico Nacional, Madrid (AHM)
Biblioteca Colombina, Sevilla (BC)
Biblioteca Nacional de España, Madrid (BNE)

In Peru

Archivo Arzobispal de Lima (AAL)
Archivo General de la Nación, Lima (AGN)
Biblioteca Nacional del Perú, Lima (BNP)

In the United States

New York Public Library, Manuscript and Archives Division (NYPL)
The Hispanic Society of America Library, New York City (HSA)

BIBLIOGRAPHY

Abercrombie, Thomas A. *Pathways of Memory and Power: Ethnography and History among an Andean People.* Madison: University of Wisconsin Press, 1998.
Abou El Fadl, Khaled. "Islamic Law and Muslim Minorities: The Juristic Discourse on Muslim Minorities from the Second/Eighth Century to the Eleventh/Seventeenth Century." *Islamic Law and Society* 1, no. 2 (1994): 141–87.
Academia de la Historia, ed. *Colección de documentos inéditos relativos al descubrimiento, conquista y colonización de las posesiones españolas en América y Oceania.* Madrid: Sucesores de Rivadeneyra, 1877.

Acosta, José de. *Natural and Moral History of the Indies*. Edited by Jane E Mangan. Durham, NC: Duke University Press, 2002.

Adorno, Rolena. *The Polemics of Possession in Spanish American Narrative*. New Haven, CT: Yale University Press, 2008.

Aguado, Pedro de. *Historia de Venezuela*. Edited by Jerónimo Bécker. Madrid: Est. tip. de J. Ratés, 1918.

Airaldi, Gabriella. *Genova e Siviglia, l'avventura dell'occidente: catalogo della mostra Genova, Loggia della Mercanzia—20 Maggio/19 Giugno 1988*. Genova: Sagep Ed., 1988.

Albiez-Wieck, Sarah. "Indigenous Migrants Negotiating Belonging: Peticiones de Cambio de Fuero in Cajamarca, Peru, 17–18 Centuries." *Colonial Latin American Review* 26, no. 4 (2018): 483–508.

Alfonso X. *Fuero real de Alfonso X el Sabio*. Edited by Antonio Pérez Martín. Madrid: Agencia Estatal Boletín Oficial del Estado, 2015.

Alfonso X. *Primera crónica general: Estoria de España que mandó componer Alfonso el Sabio y se continuaba bajo Sancho IV en 1289*. Nueva biblioteca de autores españoles 5. Madrid: Bailly-Bailliére é hijos, 1906.

Altman, Ida. "The Revolt of Enriquillo and the Historiography of Early Spanish America." *The Americas* 63, no. 4 (2007): 587–614.

Álvarez, Javier. *El libro de los privilegios concedidos a los mercaderes Genoveses establecidos en Sevilla (Siglos XIII–XVI)*. Madrid: Tabapress, 1991.

Álvarez, Manuel, Manuel Ariza Viguera, and Josefa Mendoza. *Un padrón de Sevilla del siglo XIV: estudio filológico y edición*. Sevilla: Ayuntamiento de Sevilla, Area de Cultura, 2001.

Amelang, James S. "The Peculiarities of the Spaniards: Historical Approaches to the Early Modern State." In *Public Power in Europe: Studies in Historical Transformations*, edited by James S. Amelang and Siegfried Beer, 39–56. Pisa: Edizioni Plus–Pisa University Press, 2006.

Amino, Tetsuya. "Un milagro de la Virgen y la libertad de los indios en Lima." In *Reducciones: La concentración forzada de las poblaciones indígenas en el virreinato del Perú*, edited by Akira Saitō and Claudia Rosas Lauro, 147–89. Lima: National Museum of Ethnology, Pontificia Universidad Católica del Perú, 2017.

Anderson, Ruth Matilda. *Hispanic Costume 1480–1530*. New York: Hispanic Society of America, 1979.

Anello Oliva, Giovanni. *Historia del reino y provincias del Perú y vidas de los varones insignes de la Compañía de Jesús*. Edited by Carlos M Gálvez Peña. Lima: Pontificia Universidad Católica del Perú, 1998.

Anghie, Antony. *Imperialism, Sovereignty and the Making of International Law*. Cambridge and New York: Cambridge University Press, 2007.

Angulo, Domingo. "El barrio de San Lázaro de la ciudad de Lima." In *Monografías históricas sobre la ciudad de Lima*, II, edited by Lima, Perú [Consejo Provincial], 89–168. Lima: Librería e imprenta Gil, 1935.

Aram, Bethany. "Three Kings between Europe, Africa and America, 1492–1788." *Jahrbuch für Geschichte Lateinamerikas*, 41–57. Köln: Böhlau Verlag, 2012.

Arrelucea Barrantes, Maribel, and Jesús Cosamalón Aguilar. *La presencia afrodescendiente en el Perú: Siglos XVI–XX*. Lima: Ministerio de Cultura, 2015.

Arrom, Silvia Marina. *The Women of Mexico City, 1790–1857*. Stanford, CA: Stanford University Press, 1985.

Baber, R. Jovita. "Categories, Self-Representation and the Construction of the Indios." *Journal of Spanish Cultural Studies* 10, no. 1 (2009): 27–41.

Baber, R. Jovita. "Empire, Indians, and the Negotiation for the Status of City in Tlaxcala, 1521–1550." In *Negotiation within Domination. New Spain's Indian Pueblos Confront the Spanish State*, edited by Ethelia Ruiz Medrano and Susan Kellogg, 19–44. Boulder: University Press of Colorado, 2010.

Baer, Yitzhak. *A History of the Jews in Christian Spain*. Philadelphia and Jerusalem: The Jewish Publication Society, 1966.

Bakewell, Peter J. *Miners of the Red Mountain*. Albuquerque: University of New Mexico Press, 1984.

Baptiste, Victor N. *Bartolome de Las Casas and Thomas More's "Utopia": Connections and Similarities: A Translation and Study*. Culver City, CA: Labyrinthos, 1990.

Barcia, María del Carmen. *Los ilustres apellidos: negros en La Habana colonial*. Ciudad de La Habana: Ediciones Boloña, 2009.

Barnes, Monica, and David Fleming. "Filtration-Gallery Irrigation in the Spanish New World." *Latin American Antiquity* 2, no. 1 (1991): 48–68.

Bataillon, Marcel. "The Clérigo Casas, Colonist and Reformer." In *Bartolomé de Las Casas in History: Toward an Understanding of the Man and His Work.*, edited by Juan Friede and Benjamin Keen, 353–440. DeKalb: Northern Illinois University Press, 1971.

Bauer, Brian S. *The Development of the Inca State*. Austin: University of Texas Press, 1992.

Bennett, Herman L. *African Kings and Black Slaves. Sovereignty and Dispossession in the Early Modern Atlantic*. Philadelphia: University of Pennsylvania Press, 2019.

Bennett, Herman L. *Colonial Blackness. A History of Afro-Mexico*. Bloomington: Indiana University Press, 2009.

Benton, Lauren. *Law and Colonial Cultures: Legal Regimes in World History, 1400–1900*. Cambridge: Cambridge University Press, 2001.

Benton, Lauren, and Richard J. Ross. *Legal Pluralism and Empires, 1500–1850*. New York: New York University Press, 2013.

Berman, Harold J. *Law and Revolution: The Formation of the Western Legal Tradition*. Cambridge, MA: Harvard University Press, 1983.

Betanzos, Juan de. *Narrative of the Incas*. Translated by Roland Hamilton and Dana Buchanan. Austin: University of Texas Press, 1996.

Black, Christopher, and Pamela Gravestock, eds. *Early Modern Confraternities in Europe and the Americas*. Burlington, VT: Ashgate, 2006.

Blasco Martínez, Asunción. "Notarios mudéjares de Aragón (siglos XIV–XV)." *Aragón en la edad media*, no. 10–11: 109–33. Zaragoza: Universidad de Zaragoza, 1993.

Blumenthal, Debra. "'La casa dels negres': Black African Solidarity in Late Medieval Valencia." In *Black Africans in Renaissance Europe*, edited by T. F. Earle and K. J. P. Lowe, 225–46. Cambridge: Cambridge University Press, 2005.

Blumenthal, Debra. *Enemies and Familiars. Slavery and Mastery in Fifteenth-Century Valencia*. Ithaca, NY: Cornell University Press, 2009.

Borah, Woodrow. "Juzgado general de indios del Perú o juzgado particular de indios de el Cercado de Lima." *Revista chilena de historia del derecho* 6 (1970): 129–42.

Bosch Vilá, Jacinto. *Historia de Sevilla: la Sevilla islámica, 712–1248*. Sevilla: Universidad de Sevilla, 1984.

Boswell, John. *Royal Treasure: Muslim Communities under the Crown of Aragon in the 14th Century*. New Haven, CT: Yale University Press, 1978.

Bowser, Frederick P. *The African Slave in Colonial Peru, 1524–1650*. Stanford, CA: Stanford University Press, 1974.

Bradley, Peter. *Spain and the Defence of Peru 1579–1700. Royal Reluctance and Colonial Self-Reliance*. Morrisville, NC: Lulu, 2009.

Brewer-García, Larissa. *Beyond Babel. Translations of Blackness in Colonial Peru and New Granada*. Cambridge: Cambridge University Press, 2020.

Bromley, Juan, and José Barbagelata. *Evolución urbana de Lima*. Lima: Talleres gráficos de la editorial Lumen, s. a., 1945.

Brown, Kathleen. *Good Wives, Nasty Wenches, and Anxious Patriarchs: Gender, Race, and Power in Colonial Virginia*. Chapel Hill: University of North Carolina Press and Omohundro Institute of Early American History and Culture, 1996.

Bryant, Sherwin K. *Rivers of Gold, Lives of Bondage: Governing through Slavery in Colonial Quito*. Chapel Hill: University of North Carolina Press, 2014.

Burneo, Reinhard Agustí. *Las murallas coloniales de Lima y el Callao: arquitectura defensiva y su influencia en la evolución urbana de la capital*. Lima: Universidad Ricardo Palma, 2012.

Burns, Kathryn. *Colonial Habits: Convents and the Spiritual Economy of Cuzco, Peru*. Durham, NC: Duke University Press, 1999.

Burns, Kathryn. *Into the Archive: Writing and Power in Colonial Peru*. Durham, NC: Duke University Press, 2010.

Burns, Kathryn. "Notaries, Truth, and Consequences." *American Historical Review* 110, no. 2 (April 2005): 350–79.

Burns, Kathryn. "Unfixing Race." In *Rereading the Black Legend. The Discourses of Religious and Racial Difference in the Renaissance Empires*, edited by Margaret Rich Greer, Walter Mignolo, and Maureen Quilligan, 188–202. Chicago: University of Chicago Press, 2007.

Burns, Robert I. *Jews in the Notarial Culture: Latinate Wills in Mediterranean Spain, 1250–1350*. Berkeley: University of California Press, 1996.

Burns, Robert I., ed. *Las siete partidas.* Translated by Samuel Parsons Scott. Philadelphia: University of Pennsylvania Press, 2000.

Cáceres, Rina. *Negros, mulatos, esclavos y libertos en la Costa Rica del siglo XVII.* Mexico City: Instituto Panamericano de Geografía e Historia, 2000.

Cahill, David. "The Long Conquest." In *Technology, Disease, and Colonial Conquests, Sixteenth to Eighteenth Centuries: Essays Reappraising the Guns and Germs Theories,* edited by George Raudzens, 85–126. Leiden: Brill, 2001.

Canellas, Vidal de. *Vidal mayor.* Edited by Antonio Ubieto Arteta. Huesca: Excma. Diputación Provincial. Instituto de Estudios Altoaragoneses, 1989.

Cañeque, Alejandro. *The King's Living Image: The Culture and Politics of Viceregal Power in Colonial Mexico.* New York: Routledge, 2004.

Cantera Montenegro, Enrique. "El apartamiento de judíos y mudéjares en las diócesis de Osma y Sigüenza a fines del siglo XV." *Anuario de estudios medievales* 17 (1987): 501–10.

Carande, Ramón, and Juan de Mata Carriazo. *El tumbo de los Reyes Católicos del Concejo de Sevilla.* Sevilla: Editorial Católica Española, 1968.

Carcelén Reluz, Carlos. "Los Jesuitas en su primera misión: Huarochirí, siglo XVI." *Anuario de Archivo y Biblioteca Nacionales de Bolivia* 2003: 111–33.

Cárdenas Ayaipoma, M. "El pueblo de Santiago. Un ghetto en Lima virreinal." *Boletín del Instituto Francés de Estudios Andinos* 9, no. 3–4 (1980): 19–48.

Carmona García, Juan Ignacio. *El sistema de hospitalidad pública en la Sevilla del antiguo regimen.* Sevilla: Excma. Diputación Provincial, 1979.

Carriazo, Juan de Mata. *Anecdotario sevillano.* Sevilla: Imprenta Municipal, 1988.

Casanovas Miró, Jordi. "Las necrópolis judías hispanas. nuevas aportaciones." In *Juderías y sinagogas de la Sefarad medieval: En memoria de José Luis Lacave,* edited by Curso de Cultura Hispano-Judía y Sefardí, 209–19. Cuenca: Ediciones de la Universidad de Castilla–La Mancha, 2003.

Castaño, Javier. "Las aljamas judías de Castilla a mediados del siglo XV: La Carta Real de 1450." *En la España medieval* 18 (1995): 181–203.

Castaño, Javier. "Social Networks in a Castilian Jewish Aljama and the Court Jews in the Fifteenth Century: A Preliminary Survey (Madrid 1440–1475)." *En la España medieval* 20 (1997): 379–92.

Castaño, Javier. "Tensiones entre las comunidades judías y la monarquía en Castilla, c. 1447–1474: El nombramiento del Juez Mayor de las Aljamas." In *Creencias y culturas,* edited by Carlos Carrete Parrondo and Alisa Meyuhas Ginio, 11–20. Salamanca: Universidad Pontificia de Salamanca, 1998.

Castillero Calvo, Alfredo. *Fundación y orígenes de Natá.* Panamá: Instituto Panameño de Turismo, 1972.

Catlos, Brian A. *Muslims of Medieval Latin Christendom c. 1050–1614.* Cambridge and New York: Cambridge University Press, 2014.

Catlos, Brian A. *The Victors and the Vanquished: Christians and Muslims of Catalonia and Aragon, 1050–1300.* Cambridge and New York: Cambridge University Press, 2007.

Cervantes Saavedra, Miguel de. *Varias obras inéditas de Cervantes, sacadas de códices de la Biblioteca colombina, con nuevas ilustraciones sobre la vida del autor y el Quijote.* Edited by Adolfo de Castro. Madrid: A. de Carlos é Hijo, 1874.

Champagne, Marie-Thérèse, and I. M. Resnick, eds. *Jews and Muslims under the Fourth Lateran Council: Papers Commemorating the Octocentenary of the Fourth Lateran Council (1215).* Belgium: Brepols, 2019.

Charles, John. *Allies at Odds. The Andean Church and Its Indigenous Agents, 1583–1671.* Albuquerque: University of New Mexico Press, 2010.

Charney, Paul. "'For My Necessities': The Wills of Andean Commoners and Nobles in the Valley of Lima, 1596–1607." *Ethnohistory* 59, no. 2 (Spring 2012): 323–51.

Charney, Paul. *Indian Society in the Valley of Lima, Peru, 1532–1824.* Lanham, MD: University Press of America, 2001.

Charney, Paul. "El indio urbano: Un análisis económico y social de la población india de Lima en 1613." *Histórica* 12, no. 1 (1988): 5–33.

Charney, Paul. "'Much Too Worthy': Indians in Seventeenth-Century Lima." In *City Indians in Spain's American Empire*, edited by Dana Velasco Murillo, Mark Lentz, and Margarita Ochoa, 87–103. Eastbourne, UK: Sussex Academic Press, 2012.

Childs, Matt D. *The 1812 Aponte Rebellion in Cuba and the Struggle against Atlantic Slavery.* Chapel Hill: University of North Carolina Press, 2006.

Childs, Matt D. "'The Defects of Being a Black Creole': The Degrees of African Identity in the Cuban Cabildos de Nación, 1790–1820." In *Slaves, Subjects, and Subversives. Blacks in Colonial Latin America*, edited by Jane G. Landers and Barry Robinson, 209–46. Albuquerque: University of New Mexico Press, 2006.

Chira, Adriana. *Patchwork Freedoms. Law, Slavery, and Race Beyond Cuba's Plantations.* Cambridge and New York: Cambridge University Press, 2022.

Clavero, Bartolomé. *Ordenanzas de la Real Audiencia de Sevilla.* Sevilla: Universidad de Sevilla, 1995.

Cline, Howard F. "The Oztoticpac Lands Map of Texcoco, 1540." *Quarterly Journal of the Library of Congress* 23, no. 2 (1966): 76–115.

Cobo, Bernabé. *Monografías históricas sobre la ciudad de Lima.* Lima: Librería e Imprenta Gil, 1935.

Coello de la Rosa, Alexandre. *Espacios de exclusión, espacios de poder: el Cercado de Lima colonial (1568–1606).* Lima: Instituto de Estudios Peruanos, Pontificia Universidad Católica del Perú, 2006.

Coello de la Rosa, Alexandre. "Resistencia e integración en la Lima colonial." *Revista andina* 35 (2002): 111–28.

Colección de documentos inéditos relativos al descubrimiento, conquista y organización de las antiguas posesiones españolas del ultramar. 2a Serie. Madrid: Rivadeynera, 1928.

Coleman, David. *Creating Christian Granada: Society and Religious Culture in an Old-World Frontier City, 1492–1600.* Ithaca, NY: Cornell University Press, 2003.

Collantes de Terán Sánchez, Antonio. "La aljama mudéjar de Sevilla." *Al-Andalus* 43, no. 1 (1978): 143–54.

Collantes de Terán Sánchez, Antonio. *Una gran ciudad bajomedieval: Sevilla.* Sevilla: Universidad de Sevilla, 2008.

Collantes de Terán Sánchez, Antonio. "Los mudéjares sevillanos." In *Actas del I Simposio de Mudejarismo.* 225–235. Madrid-Teruel: Diputación Provincial de Teruel y Consejo Superior de Investigaciones Científicas, 1981.

Collantes de Terán Sánchez, Antonio. *Sevilla en la baja Edad Media: la ciudad y sus hombres.* Sevilla: Sección de Publicaciones del Excmo. Ayuntamiento, 1977.

Cómez, Rafael. *Los constructores de la España medieval.* Sevilla: Universidad de Sevilla, 2006.

Constable, Olivia Remie. *Housing the Stranger in the Mediterranean World: Lodging, Trade, and Travel in Late Antiquity and the Middle Ages.* Cambridge and New York: Cambridge University Press, 2003.

Constable, Olivia Remie. "Regulating Religious Noise: The Council of Vienne, the Mosque Call and Muslim Pilgrimage in the Late Medieval Mediterranean World." *Medieval Encounters* 16 (2010): 64–95.

Constable, Olivia Remie. *To Live Like a Moor: Christian Perceptions of Muslim Identity in Medieval and Early Modern Spain.* Edited by Robin Vose. Philadelphia: University of Pennsylvania Press, 2017.

Conte Cazcarro, Anchel. "La composición laboral de la aljama de moros de Huesca." In *VI Simposio Internacional de Mudejarismo. Actas,* 137–42. Teruel: Centro de Estudios Mudéjares: Instituto de Estudios Turolenses, 1995.

Contreras, Miguel de. *Padrón de los índios de Lima en 1613.* Edited by Noble David Cook. Lima: Universidad Nacional Mayor de San Marcos, Seminario de Historia Rural Andina, 1968.

Cook, Karoline P. *Forbidden Passages. Muslims and Moriscos in Colonial Spanish America.* Philadelphia: University of Pennsylvania Press, 2016.

Corr, Rachel, and Karen Vieira Powers. "Ethnogenesis, Ethnicity and 'Cultural Refusal': The Case of the Salasacas in Highland Ecuador." *Latin American Research Review* 47 (2012): 5–30.

Cosamalón Aguilar, Jesús. *Indios detrás de la muralla.* Lima: Pontificia Universidad Católica del Perú, 1999.

Covarrubias Horozco, Sebastián de. *Tesoro de la lengua Castellana o Española [1611].* Madrid and Frankfurt am Main: Iberoamericana; Vervuert, 2006.

Covey, R. Alan. *Inca Apocalypse. The Spanish Conquest and the Transformation of the Andean World.* New York: Oxford University Press, 2020.

Crespo Álvarez, Macarena. "El cargo de Rab Mayor de la corte según un documento de Juan II." *Edad Media* 4 (2001): 157–98.

Cunill, Caroline. "El indio miserable: nacimiento de la teoría legal en la América colonial del siglo XVI." *Cuadernos intercambio* 8, no. 9 (2011): 229–48.

Cushner, Nicholas P. *Lords of the Land: Sugar, Wine, and Jesuit Estates of Coastal Peru, 1600–1767*. Albany: State University of New York Press, 1980.

Davis-Secord, Sarah, Belén Vicéns, and Robin Vose, eds. *Interfaith Relationships and Perceptions of the Other in the Medieval Mediterranean. Essays in Memory of Olivia Remie Constable*. Cham: Palgrave Macmillan, 2021.

De la Fuente, Alejandro. "Slaves and the Creation of Legal Rights in Cuba: Coartación and Papel." *Hispanic American Historical Review* 87, no. 4 (2007): 659–92.

Decoster, Jean-Jacques. "La sangre que mancha: la iglesia colonial temprano frente a indios, mestizos e ilegítimos." In *Incas e indios cristianos. Élites indígenas e identidades cristianas en los Andes coloniales*, edited by Jean-Jacques Decoster, 251–94. Cusco: Centro de Estudios Regionales Bartolomé de las Casas, 2002.

Deive, Carlos Esteban. *Los guerrilleros negros: esclavos fugitivos y cimarrones en Santo Domingo*. Santo Domingo, República Dominicana: Fundación Cultural Dominicana, 1997.

Díaz Ceballos, Jorge. "Cimarronaje, jurisdicción y lealtades híbridas en la monarquía hispánica." In *Dimensiones del conflicto: resistencia, violencia y policía en el mundo urbano*, edited by Tomás Mantecón Movellán, Marina Torres Arce, and Susana Truchuelo García, 79–102. Santander: Editorial de la Universidad de Cantabria, 2020.

Díaz Ceballos, Jorge. "New World Civitas, Contested Jurisdictions, and Inter-Cultural Conversation in the Construction of the Spanish Monarchy." *Colonial Latin American Review* 27, no. 1 (2018): 30–51.

Díaz Ceballos, Jorge. *Poder compartido. Repúblicas urbanas, monarquía y conversación en Castilla del Oro, 1508–1573*. Madrid: Marcial Pons, 2020.

Díaz Rementería, Carlos J. "El cacique en el virreinato del Perú: estudio histórico-jurídico." Sevilla: Universidad de Sevilla, 1977.

Díaz Serrano, Ana. "Repúblicas de indios en los reinos de Castilla: (Re)presentación de las periferias americanas en el siglo XVI." In *Comprendere le monarchie iberiche. Risorse materiali e rappresentazioni del potere*, edited by Gaetanos Sabatini, 343–64. Rome: Edizione Viella, 2010.

Diez de San Miguel, Garci. *Visita hecha a la provincia de Chucuito por Garci Diez de San Miguel en el año 1567*. Edited by Waldemar Espinoza Soriano and John V. Murra. Lima: Casa de la Cultura del Perú, 1964.

Dodds, Jerrilynn, Maria Rosa Menocal, and Abigail Krasner Balbale. *The Arts of Intimacy: Christians, Jews, and Muslims in the Making of Castilian Culture*. New Haven, CT: Yale University Press, 2008.

Domínguez Ortiz, Antonio. "La esclavitud en Castilla en la Edad Moderna y otros estudios de marginados." *Estudios de historia de España* 2 (1952): 369–428.

Dueñas, Alcira. *Indians and Mestizos in the "Lettered City": Reshaping Justice, Social Hierarchy, and Political Culture in Colonial Peru*. Boulder: University Press of Colorado, 2010.

Durán Montero, María Antonia. "Lima en 1613: aspectos urbanos." *Anuario de estudios americanos* 49 (1992): 171–88.

Duvé, Thomas. "La condición jurídica del indio y su consideración como persona miserabilis en derecho indiano." In *Un giudice e due leggi. Pluralismo normativo e conflitti agrari en Sud America*, edited by Mario Losano, 3–34. Milano: Giuffre Editore, 2004.

Duvé, Thomas. "Derecho canónico y la alteridad indígena: los indios como neófitos." In *Splendors and Miseries of the Evangelization of America: Antecedentes europeos y alteridad indígena*, edited by Wulf Oesterreicher and Roland Schmidt-Riese, 73–94. Berlin: DeGruyter, 2010.

Echevarría Arsuaga, Ana. "Las aljamas mudéjares castellanas en el siglo XV: redes de poder y conflictos internos." *Espacio, tiempo y forma* 14 (2001): 93–112.

Echevarría Arsuaga, Ana. "Catalina of Lancaster, the Castilian Monarchy and Coexistence." In *Medieval Spain. Culture, Conflict, and Coexistence. Studies in Honour of Angus MacKay*, edited by Roger Collins and Anthony Goodman, 79–122. Hampshire: Palgrave Macmillan, 2002.

Echevarría Arsuaga, Ana. *The City of the Three Mosques: Ávila and Its Muslims in the Middle Ages*. Wiesbaden: Reichert Verlag Wiesbaden, 2011.

Echevarría Arsuaga, Ana. "De cadí a alcalde mayor. La élite judicial mudéjar en el siglo XV (I)." *Al-Qantara* 24, no. 1 (2003): 139–68.

Echevarría Arsuaga, Ana. "De cadí a alcalde mayor. La élite judicial mudéjar en el siglo XV (II)." *Al-Qantara* 24, no. 2 (2003): 273–90.

Echevarría Arsuaga, Ana. "Islamic Confraternities and Funerary Practices: Hallmarks of Mudejar Identity in the Iberian Peninsula?" *Al-Masaq* 25, no. 3 (2013): 345–68.

Echevarría Arsuaga, Ana. "The Marks of the Other: The Impact of Lateran IV in the Regulations Governing Muslims in the Iberian Peninsula." In *Jews and Muslims under the Fourth Lateran Council*, edited by Marie-Thérèse Champagne and I. M. Resnick, 183–98. Turnhout: BREPOLS, 2018.

Echevarría Arsuaga, Ana. "La sucesión femenina en el contexto de los mudéjares castellanos," *eHumanista/Conversos* 8 (2020): 39-58.

Echevarría Arsuaga, Ana. "Trujamanes and Scribes: Interpreting Mediation in Iberian Royal Courts." In *Cultural Brokers at Mediterranean Courts in the Middle Ages*, edited by Marc von der Hoh, Nikolas Jaspert, and Jenny Rahel Oesterle, 73–94. Paderborn: Ferdinand Schoningh, 2013.

Ecker, Heather L. "'Arab Stones': Rodrigo Caro's Translations of Arabic Inscriptions in Seville (1634), Revisited." *Al-Qantara* 23, no. 2 (2002): 347–401.

Ecker, Heather L. "The Conversion of Mosques to Synagogues in Seville: The Case of the Mezquita de La Judería." *Gesta* 36, no. 2 (January 1997): 190–207.

Ecker, Heather L. "How to Administer a Conquered City in Al-Andalus: Mosques, Parish Churches and Parishes." In *Under the Influence: Questioning the Comparative in Medieval Castile*, edited by Cynthia Robinson and Leyla Rouhi, 45–66. Leiden: Brill, 2004.

Egaña, Antonio de, ed. *Monumenta peruana*. Monumenta Missionum Societatis Iesu. Rome: Monumenta Historica Soc. Iesu, 1954.

Eire, Carlos M. N. *From Madrid to Purgatory: The Art and Craft of Dying in Sixteenth-Century Spain*. Cambridge: Cambridge University Press, 2002.

Elliott, J. H. *Spain, Europe, and the Wider World, 1500–1800*. New Haven, CT: Yale University Press, 2009.

Escobar, Jesús. "Francisco de Sotomayor and Nascent Urbanism in Sixteenth Century Madrid." *Sixteenth Century Journal* 35:2 (2004): 357-82.

Espinoza Soriano, Waldemar. "El primer informe etnológico sobre Cajamarca, año de 1540." *Revista peruana de cultura* 11–12 (1967): 4–41.

Esquivel y Navia, Diego de, Félix Denegri Luna, Horacio Villanueva Urteaga, and César Gutiérrez Muñoz. *Noticias cronológicas de la gran ciudad del Cuzco*. Lima: Fundación Augusto N. Wiese: Banco Wiese, 1980.

Estenssoro Fuchs, Juan Carlos. *Del paganismo a la santidad. La incorporación de los indios del Perú al Catolicismo, 1532–1750*. Lima: Instituto Riva Aguero, 2003.

Fancy, Hussein. *The Mercenary Mediterranean: Sovereignty, Religion, and Violence in the Medieval Crown of Aragon*. Chicago: University of Chicago Press, 2016.

Fernández, Luis Suárez. *El legado material hispanojudío*. Cuenca: Universidad de Castilla La Mancha, 1998.

Fernández Chaves, Manuel, and Rafael M Pérez García. "The Morisco Problem and Seville (1480–1610)." In *Conversos and Moriscos in Late Medieval Spain and Beyond*, edited by Kevin Ingram, 75–102. Leiden: Brill, 2012.

Fernández y González, F. *Estado social y político de los mudéjares de Castilla, considerados en sí mismos y respecto de la civilización española*. Madrid: Impr. á cargo de J. Muñoz, 1866.

Feros, Antonio. *Speaking of Spain. The Evolution of Race and Nation in the Hispanic World*. Cambridge, MA: Harvard University Press, 2017.

Ferrer, Ada. *Insurgent Cuba: Race, Nation, and Revolution, 1868–1898*. Chapel Hill: University of North Carolina Press, 1999.

Ferrer-Chivite, Manuel. "El factor judeo-converso en el proceso de consolidación del título 'Don.'" *Sefarad* 45 (1985): 131–74.

Fields, Barbara. "Slavery, Race and Ideology in the United States of America." *New Left Review* 1, no. 181 (1990): 95–118.

Flores-Zúñiga, Fernando. *Haciendas y pueblos de Lima. Historia del Valle de Rímac*. Vol. 1. Lima: Fondo Editorial del Congreso del Perú, 2008.

Fra Molinero, Baltasar. "Los negros como figura de negación y diferencia en el teatro barroco." *Hipogrifo* 2, no. 2 (2014): 7–29.

Fracchia, Carmen. *"Black but Human": Slavery and Visual Arts in Hapsburg Spain, 1480–1700*. Oxford: Oxford University Press, 2019.

Franco Silva, Alfonso. *La esclavitud en Andalucía, 1450–1550*. Granada: Universidad de Granada, 1992.

Franco Silva, Alfonso. *La esclavitud en Sevilla y su tierra a fines de la edad media.* Sevilla: Excma. Diputación Provincial, 1979.

Franco Silva, Alfonso. "Los negros libertos en las sociedades andaluzas entre los siglos XV al XVI." in *Los marginados en el mundo medieval y moderno,* edited by M. T. Martínez Sanpedro, 50–64. Almería: IEA, 2000.

Franco Silva, Alfonso. *Regesto documental sobre la esclavitud sevillana (1453–1513).* Sevilla: Publicaciones de la Universidad de Sevilla, 1979.

Frankl, Víctor. "Hernán Cortés y la tradición de las siete partidas." *Revista de Historia de América* 53/54 (1962): 9–74.

Fraser, Valerie. *The Architecture of Conquest: Building in the Viceroyalty of Peru, 1535–1635.* Cambridge: Cambridge University Press, 2009.

Fromont, Cécile. *Afro-Catholic Festivals in the Americas: Performance, Representation, and the Making of Black Atlantic Tradition.* University Park: Pennsylvania State University Press, 2019.

Fromont, Cécile. *Art of Conversion: Christian Visual Culture in the Kingdom of Kongo.* Chapel Hill: University of North Carolina Press, 2014.

Fromont, Cécile. "Dancing for the King of Congo from Early Modern Central Africa to Slavery-Era Brazil." *Colonial Latin American Review* 22, no. 2 (2013): 184–208.

Ganson, Barbara Anne. *The Guaraní under Spanish Rule in the Río de La Plata.* Stanford, CA: Stanford University Press, 2006.

García Sanjuan, Alejandro. "La conquista de Sevilla por Fernando III (646 h/1248). Nuevas propuestas a través de la relectura de las fuentes árabes." *Hispania* 77, no. 255 (2017): 11–41.

Garofalo, Leo J. "La bebida del inca en copas coloniales: los curacas del mercado de chicha del Cuzco, 1640–1700." In *Elites indígenas en los Andes: nobles, caciques y cabildantes bajo el yugo colonial,* edited by David Cahill and Blanca Tovias, 175–212. Quito: ABYA YALA, 2003.

Garrett, David T. *Shadows of Empire: The Indian Nobility of Cusco, 1750–1825.* Cambridge and New York: Cambridge University Press, 2005.

Germeten, Nicole von. *Black Blood Brothers: Confraternities and Social Mobility for Afro-Mexicans.* Gainesville: University Press of Florida, 2006.

Gestoso y Pérez, José. *Curiosidades antiguas sevillanas.* Sevilla: El Correo de Andalucía, 1910.

Gestoso y Pérez, José. *Historia de los barros vidriados sevillanos desde sus orígenes hasta nuestros días.* Sevilla, Tipografía la Andalucía Moderna, 1903.

Gibson, Charles. "Rotation of Alcaldes in the Indian Cabildo of Mexico City." *Hispanic American Historical Review* 33, no. 2 (May 1953): 212–23.

Gil, Juan. *Los conversos y la Inquisición Sevillana.* Vol. 2. Sevilla: Universidad de Sevilla, 2000.

Gil, Xavier. "Republican Politics in Early Modern Spain: The Castilian and Catalano-Aragonese Traditions." In *Republicanism: A Shared European Heritage,* edited by

Martin Van Gelderen and Quentin Skinner, 1:263–88. Cambridge: Cambridge University Press, 2002.

Gil Delgado, Óscar. "Una sinagoga desvelada en Sevilla: estudio arquitectónico." *Sefarad* 73, no. 1 (2013): 69–96.

Glave Testino, Luis Miguel. "Propiedad de la tierra, agricultura y comercio, 1570–1700: El gran despojo." In *Compendio de historia económica del Perú*, edited by Carlos Contreras, II:313–446. Lima: Banco Central de Reserva del Perú, Instituto de Estudios Peruanos, 2009.

Glave Testino, Luis Miguel, and María Isabel Remy. *Estructura agraria y vida rural en una región andina: Ollantaytambo entre los siglos XVI–XIX*. Cusco, Perú: Centro de Estudios Rurales Andinos "Bartolomé de las Casas," 1983.

Gómez, Ximena. "Fashioning Lima's Virgin of Copacabana: Indigenous Strategies of Negotiation in the Colonial Capital." In *A Companion to Early Modern Lima*, edited by Emily Engel, 337–59. Boston: Brill, 2019.

González, Julio. *Repartimiento de Sevilla*. Madrid: Consejo Superior de Investigaciones Científicas, Escuela de Estudios Medievales, 1951.

González Arce, José Damián. "Cuadernos de ordenanzas y otros documentos sevillanos del reinado de Alfonso X." *Historia. Instituciones. Documentos* 16 (1989): 103–32.

González Arce, José Damián. *Documentos medievales de Sevilla en el archivo municipal de Murcia. Fueros, privilegios, ordenanzas, cartas, aranceles (siglos XIII–XV)*. Sevilla: Ayuntamiento de Sevilla, 2003.

González Arce, José Damián. "Sobre el origen de los gremios sevillanos." *En la España medieval* 14 (1991): 163–72.

González Ferrín, María Isabel. "Estudio e inventario de la documentación relativa a cuatro parroquias de Sevilla custodiada en el Archivo Capitular." *Memoria ecclesiae* 8 (1996): 363–67.

González Gallego, Ignacio. "El libro de los privilegios de la nación genovesa." *Historia instituciones documentos* 1 (1974): 275–358.

González Jiménez, Manuel. *Alfonso X el Sabio*. Barcelona: Ariel, 2004.

González Jiménez, Manuel. "Fiscalidad regia y señorial entre los mudéjares andaluces (siglos XIII–XV)." In *Actas del V Simposio Internacional de Mudejarismo*, 221–39. Teruel: Instituto de Estudios Turolenses, 1991.

González Jiménez, Manuel. *La repoblación de la zona de Sevilla durante el siglo XIV*. Sevilla: Secretariado de Publicaciones, 1993.

González Jiménez, Manuel. "El trabajo mudéjar en Andalucía. el caso de Sevilla (siglo XV)." In *VI Simposio Internacional de Mudejarismo (1993)*, 39–56. Zaragoza: Centro de Estudios Mudéjares: Instituto de Estudios Turolenses, 1995.

González Jiménez, Manuel, ed. *Sevilla 1248*. Madrid: Editorial Centro de Estudios Ramón Areces, 2000.

González Jiménez, Manuel, Mercedes Borrero Fernández, and Isabel Montes Romero-Camacho. *Sevilla en tiempos de Alfonso X*. Sevilla: Excmo. Ayuntamiento de Sevilla, 1987.

González Jiménez, Manuel, and Isabel Montes Romero-Camacho. "Los mudéjares andaluces (ss. XIII–XV)." In *Andalucía entre oriente y occidente (1236–1492): actas del V Coloquio Internacional de Historia Medieval de Andalucía*, edited by Emilio Cabrera, 537–50. Córdoba: Diputación Provincial, Área de Cultura, 1988.

Graubart, Karen B. "The Bonds of Inheritance: Afro-Peruvian Women's Legacies in a Slave-Holding World." In *Women's Negotiations and Textual Agency*, edited by Mónica Díaz and Rocío Quispe-Agnoli, 130–50. New York: Routledge, 2017.

Graubart, Karen B. "The Creolization of the New World: Local Forms of Identity in Urban Colonial Peru, 1560–1640." *Hispanic American Historical Review* 89, no. 3 (2009): 471–99.

Graubart, Karen B. "Hybrid Thinking: Bringing Postcolonial Theory to Colonial Latin American Economic History." In *Postcolonialism Meets Economics*, edited by Eiman Zein-Elabden and S. Charusheela, 215–34. London and New York: Routledge, 2004.

Graubart, Karen B. "Learning from the Qadi: The Jurisdiction of Local Rule in the Early Colonial Andes." *Hispanic American Historical Review* 95, no. 2 (May 2015): 195–228.

Graubart, Karen B. "Shifting Landscapes. Heterogeneous Conceptions of Land Use and Land Tenure in the Lima Valley." *Colonial Latin American Review* 26, no. 1 (2017): 62–84.

Graubart, Karen B. "'So color de una cofradía': Catholic Confraternities and the Development of Afro-Peruvian Ethnicities in Early Colonial Peru." *Slavery and Abolition* 33, no. 1 (March 2012): 43–64.

Graubart, Karen B. *With Our Labor and Sweat: Indigenous Women and the Formation of Colonial Society in Peru, 1550–1700*. Stanford, CA: Stanford University Press, 2007.

Graubart, Karen B. "'Ynuvaciones malas e rreprovadas': Justice and Jurisdiction in the Lima Valley." In *Justice in a New World. Negotiating Legal Intelligibility in British, Iberian, and Indigenous America*, edited by Brian Owensby and Richard J. Ross, 151–82. New York: New York University Press, 2018.

Green, Toby. "Beyond an Imperial Atlantic: Trajectories of Africans from Upper Guinea and West-Central Africa in the Early Atlantic World." *Past & Present* 230, no. 1 (2016): 91–122.

Green, Toby. *The Rise of the Trans-Atlantic Slave Trade in Western Africa, 1300–1589*. Cambridge and New York: Cambridge University Press, 2012.

Gual Camarena, Miguel. *Una cofradía de negros libertos en el siglo XV*. Zaragoza: C.S.I.C. Escuela de Estudios Medievales, 1952.

Guamán Poma de Ayala, Felipe. *El primer nueva corónica y buen gobierno*. Edited by John V. Murra and Rolena Adorno. Mexico City: Siglo Veintiuno, 1992.

Guengerich, Sara Vicuña. "Capac Women and the Politics of Marriage in Early Colonial Peru." *Colonial Latin American Review* 24, no. 2 (April 3, 2015): 147–67.

Guengerich, Sara Vicuña. "Inca Women under Spanish Rule: Probanzas and Informaciones of the Colonial Andean Elite." In *Women's Negotiations and Textual*

Agency in Latin America, 1500–1799, edited by Mónica Díaz and Rocío Quispe-Agnoli, 106–29. London and New York: Routledge, 2017.

Guevara Gil, Jorge Armando. *Propiedad agraria y derecho colonial: los documentos de la Hacienda Santotis, Cuzco (1543–1822)*. Lima: Pontificia Universidad Católica del Perú, Fondo Editorial, 1993.

Guevara Gil, Jorge Armando, and Frank Salomon. "A 'Personal Visit': Colonial Political Ritual and the Making of Indians in the Andes." *Colonial Latin American Review* 3, no. 1–2 (January 1994): 3–36.

Haliczer, Stephen. *The Comuneros of Castile.* Madison: University of Wisconsin Press, 1981.

Hall, Kim F. *Things of Darkness: Economies of Race and Gender in Early Modern England*. Ithaca, NY: Cornell University Press, 1995.

Hampe Martínez, Teodoro. *Don Pedro de la Gasca, 1493–1567: su obra política en España y América*. Lima: Pontificia Universidad Católica del Perú, Fondo Editorial, 1989.

Harth-Terré, Emilio. *Negros e indios; un estamento social ignorado del Perú colonial.* Lima: Librería-Editorial Juan Mejía Baca, 1973.

Harth-Terré, Emilio, and Alberto Márquez Abanto. "Perspectiva social y económica del artesano virreinal en Lima." *Revista del Archivo Nacional del Perú* 26:, no. 2 (1962): 1–96.

Heaney, Christopher. "The Conquests of Peru." In *Oxford Research Encyclopedia of Latin American History*, 29 Sep. 2016; Accessed 10 Jan. 2022. https://oxfordre. com/latinamericanhistory/view/10.1093/acrefore/9780199366439.001.0001/acref ore-9780199366439-e-61.

Heng, Geraldine. *The Invention of Race in the European Middle Ages*. New York: Cambridge University Press, 2018.

Hernández-Múzquiz, Rowena. "Economy and Society in Medieval and Early Modern Seville (1391–1506)." PhD diss., Columbia University, 2005.

Hershenzon, Daniel. *The Captive Sea: Slavery, Communication, and Commerce in Early Modern Spain and the Mediterranean*. Philadelphia: University of Pennsylvania Press, 2018.

Herzog, Tamar. "The Appropriation of Native Status: Forming and Reforming Insiders and Outsiders in the Spanish Colonial World." *Rechtsgeschichte–Legal History* 22 (2014): 140–49.

Herzog, Tamar. "Colonial Law and Native Customs: Indigenous Land Rights in Colonial Spanish America." *The Americas* 69, no. 3 (January 2013): 303–21.

Herzog, Tamar. "Comunidad y jurisidicción: Las aljamas judeo-castellanos (siglos XIII–XV)." In *Espacios y fueros en Castilla–La Mancha (siglos XI–XV)*, edited by Javier Alvarado Planas, 454–68. Madrid: Ediciones Polifemo, 1995.

Herzog, Tamar. *Defining Nations. Immigrants and Citizens in Early Modern Spain and Spanish America.* New Haven, CT: Yale University Press, 2003.

Herzog, Tamar. *A Short History of European Law: The Last Two and a Half Millennia.* Cambridge, MA: Harvard University Press, 2018.

Heywood, Linda M., and John K. Thornton. *Central Africans, Atlantic Creoles, and the Foundation of the Americas, 1585–1660.* New York: Cambridge University Press, 2007.

Hidalgo Pérez, Marta. "Una historia atlántica en el Panamá del siglo XVI: los 'negros de Portobelo' y la Villa del Santiago del Príncipe." PhD diss., Universitat de Barcelona, 2018.

Hinojosa Montalvo, José. *Los mudéjares. La voz del Islam en la España cristiana.* Teruel: Centro de Estudios Mudéjares: Instituto de Estudios Turolenses, 2002.

Honores, Renzo. "Una sociedad legalista: Abogados, procuradores de causas y la creación de una cultura legalista en Lima y Potosí, 1540–1670." PhD diss., Florida International University, 2007.

Howell, Ellen Douglas. "Continuity or Change: A Comparative Study of the Composition of the Cabildos in Seville, Tenerife, and Lima." *The Americas* 24, no. 2 (1967): 33–45.

Hünefeldt, Christine. *Paying the Price of Freedom: Family and Labor among Lima's Slaves, 1800–1854.* Oakland: University of California Press, 1995.

Hunt, Jocelyn. *Spain, 1474–1598.* New York: Routledge, 2001.

Hyland, Sabine Patricia. "Conversion, Custom and 'Culture': Jesuit Racial Policy in Sixteenth-Century Peru." PhD diss., Yale University, 1994.

Hyslop, John. *The Inka Road System.* Orlando: Academic Press, 1984.

Ibn Khaldun. *Histoire des Berberes et des dynasties musulmanes de l'Afrique septentrionale.* Translated by William McGuckin. Paris: P. Geuthner, 1925.

Ireton, Chloe. "'They Are Blacks of the Caste of Black Christians': Old Christian Black Blood in the Sixteenth- and Early Seventeenth-Century Iberian Atlantic." *Hispanic American Historical Review* 97, no. 4 (2017): 579–612.

Jaque Hidalgo, Javiera, and Miguel Valerio, eds. *Indigenous and Black Confraternities in Colonial Latin America: Negotiating Status through Religious Practices.* Amsterdam: Amsterdam University Press, 2022.

Johnson, Jessica Marie. *Wicked Flesh: Black Women, Intimacy, and Freedom in the Atlantic World.* Philadelphia: University of Pennsylvania Press, 2020.

Jones, Nicholas R. *Staging Habla de Negros: Radical Performances of the African Diaspora in Early Modern Spain.* University Park: Pennsylvania State University Press, 2019.

Jopling, Carol F. *Indios y negros en Panamá en los siglos XVI y XVII. Selecciones de los documentos del Archivo General de Indias.* Antigua, Guatemala, and South Woodstock, VT: Centro de Investigaciones Regionales de Mesoamérica and Plumsock Mesoamerican Studies, 1994.

Jordan, William Chester. "Why 'Race'?" *Journal of Medieval and Early Modern Studies* 31, no. 1 (2001): 165–73.

Jouve Martín, José Ramón. *Esclavos de la ciudad letrada*. Lima: Instituto de Estudios Peruanos, 2005.

Jouve Martín, José Ramón. "Public Ceremonies and Mulatto Identity in Viceregal Lima: A Colonial Reenactment of the Fall of Troy (1631)." *Colonial Latin American Review* 16, no. 2 (2007): 179–201.

Julien, Catherine J. *Hatunqolla, a View of Inca Rule from the Lake Titicaca Region*. Berkeley: University of California Press, 1983.

Kagan, Richard L. *Lawsuits and Litigants in Castile, 1500–1700*. Chapel Hill: University of North Carolina Press, 1981.

Kagan, Richard L. "Urbs and Civitas in Sixteenth- and Seventeenth-Century Spain." In *Envisioning the City. Six Studies in Urban Cartography*, edited by David Buisseret, 75–108. Chicago: University of Chicago Press, 1998.

Kagan, Richard L. "A World without Walls: City and Town in Colonial Spanish America." In *City Walls. The Urban Enceinte in Global Perspective*, edited by James D Tracy, 117–52. Cambridge: Cambridge University Press, 2000.

Kaluzny, Margaret. "From Islamic Ishbiliya to Christian Sevilla: Transformation and Continuity in a Multicultural City." PhD diss., University of Texas–Austin, 2004.

Kamen, Henry. *Inquisition and Society in Spain in the 16th and 17th Centuries*. Bloomington: Indiana University Press, 1985.

Keith, Robert G. *Conquest and Agrarian Change: The Emergence of the Hacienda System on the Peruvian Coast*. Cambridge, MA: Harvard University Press, 1976.

Kiddy, Elizabeth. *Blacks of the Rosary: Memory and History in Minas Gerais, Brazil*. University Park: Pennsylvania State University Press, 2005.

Kiddy, Elizabeth. "Who Is the King of Kongo? A New Look at African and Afro-Brazilian Kings in Brazil." In *Central Africans and Cultural Transformations in the American Diaspora*, edited by Linda M. Heywood, 153–82. Cambridge: Cambridge University Press, 2002.

Kole de Peralta, Kathleen M. "The Nature of Colonial Bodies: Public Health in Lima, Peru, 1535–1635." PhD diss., University of Notre Dame, 2015.

Konetzke, Richard, ed. *Colección de documentos para la historia de la formación social de hispanoamérica, 1493–1810*. Vol. I. Madrid: Consejo Superior de Investigaciones Científicas, 1953.

Konetzke, Richard, ed. *Colección de documentos para la historia de la formación social de hispanoamérica, 1493–1810*. Vol. II. Madrid: Consejo Superior de Investigaciones Científicas, 1958.

Koningsveld, P. S. van, and Gerald Wiegers. "The Islamic Statute of the Mudejars in the Light of a New Source." *Al-Qantara* 17 (1996): 19–58.

Kubler, George. *Mexican Architecture of the Sixteenth Century*. Westport, CT: Greenwood Press, 1972.

Kuznesof, Elizabeth. "Ethnic and Gender Influences on 'Spanish' Creole Society in Colonial Spanish America." *Colonial Latin American Review* 4 (1995): 153–76.

Lacueva Muñoz, Jaime. *Comerciantes de Sevilla. Regesto de documentos notariales del Fondo Enrique Otte.* Vol. 1. Valparaíso, Chile: Instituto de Historia y Ciencias Sociales Universidad de Valparaíso, 2016.

Ladero Quesada, Miguel Angel. *Andalucía a fines de la edad media.* Cádiz: Universidad de Cádiz, 1999.

Ladero Quesada, Miguel Angel. *La ciudad medieval.* Vol. 2. Historia de Sevilla. Sevilla: Universidad de Sevilla, 1976.

Ladero Quesada, Miguel Angel. "De nuevo sobre los judíos granadinos al tiempo de su expulsión." *En la España medieval* 30 (2007): 281–315.

Ladero Quesada, Miguel Angel. "De Toledo a Sevilla: sociedades nuevas y herencias del pasado." In *Sevilla 1248*, edited by Manuel González Jiménez, 451–66. Madrid: Centro de Estudios Ramón Areces, 2000.

Ladero Quesada, Miguel Angel. "Las Juderías de Castilla según 'servicios' fiscales del siglo XV." *Sefarad* 31 (1979): 249–64.

Ladero Quesada, Miguel Angel. *Judíos y conversos de Castilla en el Siglo V.* Madrid: Dykinson, 2006.

Ladero Quesada, Miguel Angel. *Los mudéjares de Castilla en tiempos de Isabel I.* Valladolid: Instituto "Isabel la Católica" de Historia Eclesiástica, 1969.

Ladero Quesada, Miguel Angel. "Sevilla y los conversos: los 'habilitados' en 1495." *Sefarad* 52:2 (1992): 429–47.

Lamana, Gonzalo. *Domination without Dominance: Inca-Spanish Encounters in Early Colonial Peru.* Durham, NC: Duke University Press, 2008.

Landers, Jane G. "Cimarrón and Citizen. African Ethnicity, Corporate Identity, and the Evolution of Free Black Towns in the Spanish Circum-Caribbean." In *Slaves, Subjects, and Subversives. Blacks in Colonial Latin America*, edited by Jane G. Landers and Barry Robinson, 111–45. Albuquerque: University of New Mexico Press, 2006.

Landers, Jane G. "La cultura material de los cimarrones: los casos de Ecuador, la Española, México y Colombia." In *Rutas de la esclavitud en África y América Latina*, edited by Rina Cáceres, 145–56. San José: Editorial de la Universidad de Costa Rica, 2001.

Landers, Jane G. "Leadership and Authority in Maroon Settlements in Spanish America and Brazil." In *Africa and the Americas: Interconnections during the Slave Trade*, edited by José Curto and Renée Soulodre-LaFrance, 173–84. Trenton, NJ: Africa World Press, 2005.

Lane, Kris. *Quito 1599: City and Colony in Transition.* Albuquerque: University of New Mexico Press, 2002.

Lara, Silvia Hunold. *Fragmentos setecentistas: escravidão, cultura e poder na América portuguesa.* São Paulo: Companhia das Letras, 2007.

Larson, Brooke, Olivia Harris, and Enrique Tandeter. *Ethnicity, Markets, and Migration in the Andes: At the Crossroads of History and Anthropology.* Durham, NC: Duke University Press, 1995.

Las Casas, Bartolomé de. *Brevísima relación de la destrucción de Africa.* Salamanca: Editorial San Esteban, 1989.

Lea, Henry Charles. "Acta capitular del Cabildo de Sevilla." *American Historical Review* 1, no. 2 (1896): 220–25.

Lea, Henry Charles. "Ferrand Martinez and the Massacres of 1391." *American Historical Review* 1, no. 2 (1896): 209–19.

Lee, Bertram T., Juan Bromley, Sophy E. Schofield, and Emilio Harth-Terré, eds. *Libros de cabildos de Lima.* Lima: Sanmartí Impresores, 1935.

Lee, Christina. *The Anxiety of Sameness in Early Modern Spain.* Manchester: Manchester University Press, 2016.

León Tello, Pilar. *Judíos de Toledo.* Madrid: Consejo Superior de Investigaciones Científicas, 1979.

León (Kingdom). *Cortes de los antiguos reinos de León y de Castilla.* Madrid: M. Rivadeneyra, 1861-66.

Levillier, Roberto. *Don Francisco de Toledo, Supremo organizador del Perú: Su vida, su obra [1515–1582].* Madrid: Espasa Calpe, 1955.

Levillier, Roberto. *Gobernantes del Perú, cartas y papeles, siglo XVI; documentos del Archivo de Indias.* Madrid: Sucesores de Rivadeneyra (s. a.), 1921.

"Leyes de Moros." In *Memorial histórico español: colección de documentos, opúsculos y antigüedades,* edited by Real Academia de la Historia [Spain]. 5:1–246. Madrid: La Real Academia de la Historia, 1853.

Lima [Peru]. Cabildo. *Libro primero de Cabildos de Lima.* Paris: Imprimerie PDupont, 1888.

Lipton, Sara. *Dark Mirror: The Medieval Origins of Anti-Jewish Iconography.* New York: Metropolitan Books, 2014.

Lissón Chávez, Emilio, and Manuel Ballesteros Gaibrois. *La Iglesia de España en el Perú: colección de documentos para la historia de la Iglesia en el Perú, que se encuentran en varios archivos.* Sevilla: Editorial Católica Española, 1943-56.

Livi-Bacci, Massimo, and Ernesto J. Maeder. "The Missions of Paraguay: The Demography of an Experiment." *Journal of Interdisciplinary History* 35, no. 2 (2004): 185–224.

Lockhart, James. "Encomienda and Hacienda: The Evolution of the Great Estate in the Spanish Indies." *Hispanic American Historical Review* 49, no. 3 (1969): 411–29.

Lohmann Villena, Guillermo. *El corregidor de indios en el Perú bajo los Austrias.* Madrid: Ediciones Cultura Hispánica, 1957.

Lohmann Villena, Guillermo. "Testamento del curaca don Gonzalo Taulichusco (1562)." *Revista del Archivo General de la Nación* 7 (1984): 267–75.

López Martínez, Nicolás. "Los judaizantes castellanos y la Inquisición en tiempo de Isabel la Católica." PhD diss., Pontificia Universidad Eclesiástica de Salamanca, Burgos, 1954.

Lovejoy, Henry B. *Prieto. Yorùbá Kingship in Colonial Cuba during the Age of Revolution.* Chapel Hill: University of North Carolina Press, 2018.

Lowry, Lyn Brandon. "Forging an Indian Nation: Urban Indians under Spanish Colonial Control, Lima, Peru 1535–1765." PhD diss., University of California, Berkeley, 1991.

MacCormack, Sabine. "From the Sun of the Incas to the Virgin of Copacabana." *Representations* 8 (1984): 30–60.

MacCormack, Sabine. *On the Wings of Time: Rome, the Incas, Spain, and Peru.* Princeton, NJ: Princeton University Press, 2007.

MacKay, Angus. "Popular Movements and Pogroms in Fifteenth Century Castile." *Past and Present* 55 (May 1972): 33–67.

Mackay, Ruth. *"Lazy, Improvident People": Myth and Reality in the Writing of Spanish History.* Ithaca, NY: Cornell University Press, 2006.

Málaga Medina, Alejandro. "Las reducciones en el Perú." *Historia y Cultura* 8 (1974): 141–72.

Mangan, Jane E. *Trading Roles: Gender, Ethnicity, and the Urban Economy in Colonial Potosí.* Durham, NC: Duke University Press, 2005.

Mangan, Jane E. *Transatlantic Obligations: Creating the Bonds of Family in Conquest-Era Peru and Spain.* New York: Oxford University Press, 2016.

Mariscal, George. "The Role of Spain in Contemporary Race Theory." *Arizona Journal of Hispanic Cultural Studies* 2 (1998): 7–22.

Martín Casares, Aurelia. *La esclavitud en Granada en el siglo XVI: Género, raza y religión.* Granada: Universidad de Granada, 2000.

Martín Casares, Aurelia. "Evolution of the Origin of Slaves Sold in Spain from the Late Middle Ages until the 18th Century." In *Serfdom and Slavery in the European Economy, 11–18th Centuries,* edited by Simonetta Cavaciocchi, 409–30. Firenze: Firenze University Press, 2014.

Martínez, María Elena. *Genealogical Fictions: Limpieza de Sangre, Religion, and Gender in Colonial Mexico.* Stanford, CA: Stanford University Press, 2011.

Martínez, María Elena, David Nirenberg, and Max-Sebastián Hering Torres. *Race and Blood in the Iberian World.* Berlin: Lit, 2012.

Martínez, Roger Louis. "Jews, Catholics, and Converts: Reassessing the Resilience of Convivencia in Fifteenth Century Plasencia, Spain." *Journal of Spanish, Portuguese, and Italian Crypto Jews* 1 (Spring 2009): 95–120.

Martz, Linda. *Poverty and Welfare in Habsburg Spain: the Example of Toledo.* Cambridge and New York: Cambridge University Press, 1983.

Matheson, Anna. "Muslims, Jews, and the Question of Municipal Membership in Twelfth- to Fifteenth-Century Portugal." In *Religious Minorities in Christian,*

Jews, and Muslim Law (5th to 15th Centuries), edited by Nora Berend, Youna Hameau-Masset, Capucine Nemo-Pekelman, and John Tolan, 191–215. Turnhout: BREPOLS, 2017.

Matienzo, Juan de. *Gobierno del Perú [1567]*. Buenos Aires: Compañía sud-americana de billetes de banco, 1910.

Matthew, Laura. *Memories of Conquest. Becoming Mexicano in Colonial Guatemala*. Chapel Hill: University of North Carolina Press, 2012.

Matthew, Laura, and Michel R. Oudijk. *Indian Conquistadors: Indigenous Allies in the Conquest of Mesoamerica*. Norman: University of Oklahoma Press, 2007.

McKinley, Michelle A. *Fractional Freedoms: Slavery, Intimacy, and Legal Mobilization in Colonial Lima, 1600–1700*. Cambridge and New York: Cambridge University Press, 2016.

Mello e Souza, Marina de. *Reis negros no Brasil escravista: história da festa de coroação de Rei Congo*. Belo Horizonte: Ed. UFMG, 2006.

Méndez Rodríguez, Luis. "Slavery and the Guild in Golden Age Painting in Seville." *Art in Translation* 7, no. 1 (2015): 123–40.

Meyerson, Mark D. *A Jewish Renaissance in Fifteenth Century Spain*. Princeton, NJ: Princeton University Press, 2004.

Meyerson, Mark D. *Jews in an Iberian Frontier Kingdom: Society, Economy, and Politics in Morvedre, 1248–1391*. Leiden: Brill, 2004.

Meyerson, Mark D. *The Muslims of Valencia in the Age of Fernando and Isabel: Between Coexistence and Crusade*. Berkeley: University of California Press, 1991.

Miller, Kathryn A. *Guardians of Islam: Religious Authority and Muslim Communities of Late Medieval Spain*. New York: Columbia University Press, 2008.

Miller, Kathryn A. "Muslim Minorities and the Obligation to Emigrate to Islamic Territory: Two Fatwas from Fifteenth-Century Granada." *Islamic Law and Society Islamic Law and Society* 7, no. 2 (2000): 256–77.

Mills, Kenneth. *Idolatry and Its Enemies: Colonial Andean Religion and Extirpation, 1640–1750*. Princeton, NJ: Princeton University Press, 1997.

Montes Romero-Camacho, Isabel. "La aljama judía de Sevilla en la baja edad media." In *El patrimonio hebreo en la España medieval*, I:25–52. Córdoba: Universidad de Córdoba, 2004.

Montes Romero-Camacho, Isabel. "El Infante Don Felipe, primer arzobispo electo de Sevilla (1248–1258): breve notas sobre un destino frustrado." In *Mundos medievales: Espacios, sociedades y poder*, edited by Beatriz Arízaga Bolumburu, II:1619–32. Cantabria: Universidad de Cantabria, 2012.

Montes Romero-Camacho, Isabel. "Las minorías étnicas-religiosas en la Sevilla del siglo XIV: mudéjares y judíos." In *Sevilla, siglo XIV*, edited by Rafael Valencia, 135–55. Sevilla: Fundación José Manuel Lara, 2006.

Montes Romero-Camacho, Isabel. "Notas para el estudio de la judería sevillana en la baja edad media (1248–1391)." *En la España medieval* 10 (1987): 343–65.

Moore, John Preston. *The Cabildo in Peru under the Hapsburgs; A Study in the Origins and Powers of the Town Council in the Viceroyalty of Peru, 1530–1700.* Durham, NC: Duke University Press, 1954.

More, Anna. "Necroeconomics, Originary Accumulation, and Racial Capitalism in the Early Iberian Slave Trade." *Journal for Early Modern Cultural Studies* 19, no. 2 (2019): 75–100.

Moreno, Isidoro. *La antigua hermandad de los negros de Sevilla: etnicidad, poder y sociedad en 600 años de historia.* Sevilla: Secretaría de Publicación de la Universidad de Sevilla, 1997.

Morgado Maurtua, Patricia. "Un palimpsesto urbano. Del asiento indígena de Lima a la ciudad española de Los Reyes." PhD diss., Universidad de Sevilla, 2007.

Morgado Maurtua, Patricia. "Reshaping Rimac into Ciudad de Los Reyes." Paper presented at Latin American Studies Association Congress, 2012.

Morgan, Jennifer L. "Partus Sequitur Ventrem: Law, Race, and Reproduction in Colonial Slavery." *Small Axe* 22, no. 1 (2018): 1–17.

Morris, Craig, and Donald E. Thompson. *Huánuco Pampa. An Inca City and Its Hinterland.* London: Thames and Hudson, 1985.

Mugaburu, Josephe de, and Francisco de Mugaburu. *Chronicle of Colonial Lima; the Diary of Josephe and Francisco Mugaburu, 1640–1694.* Norman: University of Oklahoma Press, 1975.

Muldoon, James. *Popes, Lawyers, and Infidels: The Church and the Non-Christian World, 1250–1550.* Philadelphia: University of Pennsylvania Press, 1979.

Mumford, Jeremy Ravi. "Litigation as Ethnography in Sixteenth-Century Peru." *Hispanic American Historical Review* 88, no. 1 (February 2008): 5–40.

Mumford, Jeremy Ravi. *Vertical Empire. The General Resettlement of Indians in the Colonial Andes.* Durham, NC: Duke University Press, 2012.

Mundy, Barbara E. *The Mapping of New Spain: Indigenous Cartography and the Maps of the Relaciones Geográficas.* Chicago: University of Chicago Press, 1996.

Murra, John V. *The Economic Organization of the Inka State.* Greenwich, CT: JAI Press, 1980.

Murra, John V. *Formaciones económicas y políticas del mundo andino.* Lima: Instituto de Estudios Peruanos, 1975.

Murra, John V. "Waman Puma, etnógrado del mundo andino." In *El primer nueva corónica y buen gobierno [1615],* by Felipe Guaman Poma de Ayala, edited by Rolena Adorno and John V Murra, xiii–xix. Mexico City: Siglo Veintiuno, 1980.

Nader, Helen. *Liberty in Absolutist Spain: The Habsburg Sale of Towns, 1516–1700.* Baltimore: Johns Hopkins University Press, 1990.

Najemy, John M. "Guild Republicanism in Trecento Florence: The Successes and Ultimate Failure of Corporate Politics." *American Historical Review* 84, no. 1 (February 1979): 53–71.

Navarro Sainz, José María. "La subordinación política de la tierra de Sevilla al concejo hispalense en el reinado de Isabel I." *Historia instituciones documentos* 38 (2011): 325–60.

Nemser, Daniel. *Infrastructures of Race: Concentration and Biopolitics in Colonial Mexico.* Austin: University of Texas Press, 2017.

Netherly, Patricia. "Local Level Lords on the North Coast of Perú." PhD diss., Cornell University, 1977.

Netherly, Patricia. "The Management of Late Andean Irrigation Systems on the North Coast of Peru." *Society for American Archaeology* 49, no. 2 (1984): 225–54.

Niles, Susan A. *The Shape of Inca History. Narrative and Archaeology in an Andean Empire.* Iowa City: University of Iowa Press, 1999.

Nirenberg, David. *Communities of Violence: Persecution of Minorities in the Middle Ages.* Princeton, NJ: Princeton University Press, 1996.

Nirenberg, David. "A Female Rabbi in Fourteenth Century Zaragoza?" *Sefarad* 51, no. 1 (1991): 179–82.

Nirenberg, David. *Neighboring Faiths: Christianity, Islam, and Judaism in the Middle Ages and Today.* Chicago: University of Chicago Press, 2014.

Nirenberg, David. "Was There Race before Modernity? The Example of 'Jewish' Blood in Late Medieval Spain." In *The Origins of Racism in the West*, edited by Miriam Eliav-Feldon, Benjamin Isaac, and Joseph Ziegler, 232–64. Cambridge and New York: Cambridge University Press, 2009.

Noack, Karoline. "Caciques, escribanos y las construcciones de historias. Cajamarca, Perú, siglo XVI." In *Elites indígenas en los Andes. Nobles, caciques y cabildantes bajo el yugo colonial*, edited by David Cahill and Blanca Tovias, 213–28. Quito: ABYA YALA, 2003.

Novoa, Mauricio. *The Protectors of Indians in the Royal Audience of Lima: History, Careers and Legal Culture, 1575–1775.* Leiden: Brill, 2016.

Núñez Muley, Francisco. *A Memorandum for the President of the Royal Audiencia and Chancery Court of the City and Kingdom of Granada.* Edited by Vincent Barletta. Chicago: University of Chicago Press, 2007.

Ochoa, Margarita R., and Sara V. Guengerich, eds. *Cacicas: The Indigenous Women Leaders of Spanish America, 1492–1825.* Norman: University of Oklahoma Press, 2021.

Ondegardo, Polo. "Informaciones acerca de la religión y gobierno de los Incas (1571)." Edited by Carlos A. Romero. *Colección de libros y documentos referentes a la historia del Perú* 3 (1916): 45–188.

"Ordenanzas para el gobierno de la Ciudad de Los Reyes, 1549 a 1624." *Revista de los Archivos y Bibliotecas Naciones* 5 (1900): 3–34.

Ortiz de Zúñiga, Diego. *Anales eclesiásticos y seculares de la muy noble y muy leal ciudad de Sevilla, metrópoli de la Andalucía.* Madrid: Imprenta Real, 1795-96.

Osorio, Alejandra B. "El callejón de la soledad: Vectors of Cultural Hybridity in Seventeenth-Century Lima." In *Spiritual Encounters. Interactions between Christianity and Native Religions in Colonial America*, edited by Nicholas Griffiths and Fernando Cervantes, 198–229. Lincoln: University of Nebraska Press, 1999.

Osorio, Alejandra B. *Inventing Lima: Baroque Modernity in Peru's South Sea Metropolis*. New York: Palgrave Macmillan, 2008.

O'Toole, Rachel Sarah. *Bound Lives: Africans, Indians, and the Making of Race in Colonial Peru*. Pittsburgh: University of Pittsburgh Press, 2012.

Otte, Enrique. *Sevilla y sus mercaderes a fines de la Edad Media*. Sevilla: Vicerrectorado de Relaciones Institucionales y Extensión Cultural, 1996.

Owensby, Brian. *Empire of Law and Indian Justice in Colonial Mexico*. Stanford, CA: Stanford University Press, 2011.

Pagden, Anthony. *Lords of All the World: Ideologies of Empire in Spain, Britain and France c. 1500–c. 1800*. New Haven, CT: Yale University Press, 1998.

Patton, Pamela, ed. *Envisioning Others: Race, Color, and the Visual in Iberia and Latin America*. Leiden: Brill, 2015.

Paz Espeso, Julián, ed. *Diversos de Castilla*. Madrid: Artes Gráficas, 1969.

Pease G. Y., Franklin. *Curacas, reciprocidad y riqueza*. Lima: Pontificia Universidad Católica del Perú 1992.

Pease G. Y., Franklin. "La noción de propiedad entre los Incas: Una aproximación." In *Etnografía e historia del mundo andino: continuidad y cambio*, edited by Shozo Masuda, 3–33. Tokyo: Tokyo University, 1986.

Penry, S. Elizabeth. "Pleitos coloniales: 'historizando' las fuentes sobre pueblos de indígenas de los Andes." in *Reducciones. La concentración forzada de las poblaciones indígenas en el Virreinato del Perú*, edited by Akira Saitō and Claudia Rosas Lauro, 439–73. Lima: Pontificia Universidad Católica del Perú, 2016.

Phillips, William D., Jr. *Slavery in Medieval and Early Modern Iberia*. Philadelphia: University of Pennsylvania Press, 2013.

Pick, Lucy K. *Conflict and Coexistence: Archbishop Rodrigo and the Muslims and Jews of Medieval Spain*. Ann Arbor: University of Michigan Press, 2004.

Pike, Ruth. "Black Rebels: The Cimarrons of Sixteenth-Century Panama." *The Americas* 64, no. 2 (2007): 243–66.

Pike, Ruth. *Enterprise and Adventure; the Genoese in Seville and the Opening of the New World*. Ithaca, NY: Cornell University Press, 1966.

Pike, Ruth. "An Urban Minority: The Moriscos of Seville." *International Journal of Middle East Studies* 2 (1971): 368–77.

Pollak, Martha D. *Cities at War in Early Modern Europe*. New York: Cambridge University Press, 2014.

Ponce Leiva, Pilar, ed. *Relaciones histórico-geográficas de la Audiencia de Quito, siglos XVI–XIX*. Madrid: Consejo Superior de Investigaciones Científicas, 1992.

Poole, Stafford. *Juan de Ovando: Governing the Spanish Empire in the Reign of Phillip II.* Norman: University of Oklahoma Press, 2004.

Porras Arboledas, Pedro A. "Documentos cristianos sobre mudéjares de Andalucía en los siglos XV y XVI." *Anaquel de estudios árabes* 3 (1992): 223–34.

Powers, David S. *Law, Society, and Culture in the Maghrib, 1300–1500.* Cambridge and New York: Cambridge University Press, 2002.

Powers, David S. "On Judicial Review in Islamic Law." *Law & Society Review* 26 (1992): 315.

Powers, David S. *Studies in Qur'an and Hadith: The Formation of the Islamic Law of Inheritance.* Berkeley: University of California Press, 1986.

Powers, Karen Vieira. *Andean Journeys: Migration, Ethnogenesis, and the State in Colonial Quito.* Albuquerque: University of New Mexico Press, 1995.

Powers, Karen Vieira. "A Battle of Wills: Inventing Chiefly Legitimacy in the Colonial North Andes." In *Dead Giveaways. Indigenous Testaments of Colonial Mesoamerica and the Andes*, edited by Susan Kellogg and Matthew Restall, 183–214. Salt Lake City: University of Utah Press, 1998.

Premo, Bianca. *Children of the Father King: Youth, Authority, and Legal Minority in Colonial Lima.* Chapel Hill: University of North Carolina Press, 2005.

Premo, Bianca, and Yanna Yannakakis. "A Court of Sticks and Branches: Indian Jurisdiction in Colonial Mexico and Beyond." *American Historical Review* 124, no. 1 (2019): 28–55.

Price, Richard. *Maroon Societies.* Baltimore: Johns Hopkins University Press, 1996.

Puente Luna, José Carlos de la. *Andean Cosmopolitans: Seeking Justice and Reward at the Spanish Royal Court.* Austin: University of Texas Press, 2018.

Puente Luna, José Carlos de la. "The Interpreter Admonishes the Viceroy: Translating Indigenous Interests at the Peruvian Court of the Marquis de Montesclaros." Paper presented at "The Tasks of the Translator: Developing a Sociocultural Framework for the Study of Translation across the Early Modern World," St. Louis University, 2017.

Puente Luna, José Carlos de la. "Of Widows, Furrows, and Seed: New Perspectives on Land and the Colonial Andean Commons." *Hispanic American Historical Review* 101, no. 3 (2021): 375–407.

Puente Luna, José Carlos de la. "That Which Belongs to All: Khipus, Community, and Indigenous Legal Activism in the Early Colonial Andes." *The Americas* 72, no. 1 (2015): 19–54.

Puente Luna, José Carlos de la, and Renzo Honores. "Guardianes de la real justicia: alcaldes de indios y justicia local en los Andes." *Histórica* 40, no. 2 (2016): 11–48.

Quijano Velasco, Francisco. "Las repúblicas de la monarquía: expresiones republicanas y constitucionalistas en la Nueva España. Alonso de La Veracruz, Bartolomé de Las Casas y Juan Zapata y Sandoval." PhD diss., Universidad Nacional Autónoma de México, 2013.

Quiroga, Vasco de. *Don Vasco de Quiroga: pensamiento jurídico: antología*. Edited by Rafael Aguayo Spencer and José Luis Soberanes Fernández. Mexico City: Universidad Nacional Autónoma de México, 1986.

Quiroga, Vasco de. *La Utopia en America*. Edited by Paz Serrano Gassent. Madrid: Historia 16, 1992.

Quiroz Chueca, Francisco. *Artesanos y manufactureros en Lima colonial*. Lima: Instituto de Estudios Peruanos/Banco Central de Reserva del Perú, 2008.

Ramírez, Susan E. *Provincial Patriarchs: Land Tenure and the Economics of Power in Colonial Peru*. Albuquerque: University of New Mexico Press, 1986.

Ramírez, Susan E. "Amores prohibidos: The Consequences of the Clash of Juridical Norms in Sixteenth Century Peru." *The Americas* 62, no. 1 (July 2005): 47–63.

Ramírez, Susan E. "The 'Dueño de Indios': Thoughts on the Consequences of the Shifting Bases of Power of the 'Curaca de Los Viejos Antiguos' under the Spanish in Sixteenth-Century Peru." *Hispanic American Historical Review* 67, no. 4 (1987): 575–610.

Ramírez, Susan E. *To Feed and Be Fed: The Cosmological Bases of Authority and Identity in the Andes*. Stanford, CA: Stanford University Press, 2005.

Ramírez, Susan E. *The World Upside Down: Cross-Cultural Contact and Conflict in Sixteenth-Century Peru*. Stanford, CA: Stanford University Press, 1996.

Ramos, Gabriela. *Death and Conversion in the Andes. Lima and Cuzco, 1532–1670*. Notre Dame, IN: University of Notre Dame Press, 2010.

Ramos, Gabriela. "Indigenous Intellectuals in Andean Colonial Cities." In *Indigenous Intellectuals: Knowledge, Power, and Colonial Culture in Mexico and the Andes*, edited by Yanna Yannakakis and Gabriela Ramos, 21–38. Durham, NC: Duke University Press, 2014.

Ramos, Gabriela. "Nuestra Señora de Copacabana. ¿Devoción india o intermediaria cultural?" In *Passeurs, mediadores culturales, y agentes de la primera globalización en el mundo ibérico, SS. XVI–XIX*, edited by Scarlett O'Phelan Godoy and Carmen Salazar-Soler, 163–79. Lima: Pontificia Universidad Católica del Perú, Instituto Francés de Estudios Andinos, 2005.

Ramos, Gabriela, and Yanna Yannakakis. *Indigenous Intellectuals: Knowledge, Power, and Colonial Culture in Mexico and the Andes*. Durham, NC: Duke University Press, 2014.

Rappaport, Joanne. *The Disappearing Mestizo: Configuring Difference in the Colonial New Kingdom of Granada*. Durham, NC: Duke University Press, 2014.

Rappaport, Joanne, and Tom Cummins. *Beyond the Lettered City: Indigenous Literacies in the Andes*. Durham, NC: Duke University Press, 2012.

Real Academia Española, *Diccionario de la lengua española*. Twenty-third edition of 2014. https:dle.es

Reséndez, Andrés. *The Other Slavery. The Uncovered Story of Indian Enslavement in America*. Boston: Houghton Mifflin, 2016.

Rocha, Gabriel de Ávilez. "Maroons in the Montes: Towards a Political Ecology of Marronage in the Sixteenth-Century Caribbean." In *Early Modern Black Diaspora Studies: A Critical Anthology*, edited by Cassander Smith, Nicholas Jones, and Miles Grier, 15–35. Cham: Palgrave Macmillan, 2018.

Rojas García, Reyes. "El comercio por escrito. prácticas escriturarias mercantiles en la Sevilla moderna (siglos XVI–XVII)." In *Les documents du commerce et des marchands entre Moyen Âge et Époque Moderne (XII–XVII siècle)*, edited by Cristina Mantegna and Olivier Poncet, 355–76. Rome: École Française de Rome, 2018.

Romero, Carlos A. "Libro de la visita general del Virrey D. Francisco de Toledo, 1570–75." *Histórica* 7 (1924): 113–216.

Romero Muñoz, Vicente. "La recopilación de las ordenanzas gremiales de Sevilla." *Revista de Trabajo* 3 (1950): 225–31.

Rostworowski de Diez Canseco, María. "Algunos comentarios hechos a las ordenanzas del Doctor Cuenca." *Historia y Cultura* 9 (1975): 119–54.

Rostworowski de Diez Canseco, María. *Conflicts over Coca Fields in XVIth-Century Perú*. Ann Arbor: University of Michigan, Museum of Anthropology, 1988.

Rostworowski de Diez Canseco, María. *Costa peruana prehispánica*. Lima: Instituto de Estudios Peruanos, 1989.

Rostworowski de Diez Canseco, María. *Curacas y sucesiones, Costa Norte*. Lima: Minerva, 1961.

Rostworowski de Diez Canseco, María. *Doña Francisca Pizarro. Una ilustre mestiza, 1534–1598*. Lima: Instituto de Estudios Peruanos, 1989.

Rostworowski de Diez Canseco, María. "Dos probanzas de Don Gonzalo, curaca de Lima (1555–1559)." *Revista Histórica* 33 (1983): 105–73.

Rostworowski de Diez Canseco, María. *Ensayos de historia andina*. Lima: Instituto de Estudios Peruanos, 1993.

Rostworowski de Diez Canseco, María. *Estructuras andinas del poder: ideología religiosa y política*. Lima: Instituto de Estudios Peruanos, 1983.

Rostworowski de Diez Canseco, María. *Obras completas: Pachacamac y señoríos indigenas de Lima y Canta*. Vol. II. Lima: Instituto de Estudios Peruanos, 2002.

Rostworowski de Diez Canseco, María. *Señoríos indígenas de Lima y Canta*. Lima: Instituto de Estudios Peruanos, 1978.

Rostworowski de Diez Canseco, María. "Succession, Cooptation to Kingship, and Royal Incest among the Inca." *Southwestern Journal of Anthropology* 16, no. 4 (1960): 417–27.

Rowe, Erin Kathleen. *Black Saints in Early Modern Global Catholicism*. New York: Cambridge University Press, 2019.

Rubin, Miri. *Cities of Strangers: Making Lives in Medieval Europe*. The Wiles Lectures. Cambridge: Cambridge University Press, 2020.

Ruggles, D. Fairchild. "Mothers of a Hybrid Dynasty: Race, Genealogy, and Acculturation in al-Andalus." *Journal of Medieval and Early Modern Studies* 34, no. 1 (2004): 65–94.

Ruiz, Teofilo F. *From Heaven to Earth: The Reordering of Castilian Society, 1150–1350.* Princeton, NJ: Princeton University Press, 2004.

Ruiz, Teofilo F. *Spanish Society 1400–1600.* Harlow, England: Longman, 2001.

Sáez, Emilio. *Colección diplomática de Sepúlveda.* Segovia: Diputación Provincial de Segovia, 1956.

Saitō, Akira, and Claudia Rosas Lauro. *Reducciones: la concentración forzada de las poblaciones indígenas en el Virreinato del Perú.* Lima: National Museum of Ethnology, Pontificia Universidad Católica del Perú, 2017.

Salamanca, Beatriz. "Placing Mobile Identities: Freedom to Wander and the Right to Travel in Early Modern Spain and Spanish America." PhD diss., University College London, 2019.

Salinas y Córdoba, Buenaventura de. *Memorial de las historias del nuevo mundo Piru [1631].* Edited by Warren L Cook. Lima: Universidad Nacional Mayor de San Marcos, 1957.

Salomon, Frank. *Native Lords of Quito in the Age of the Incas: The Political Economy of North-Andean Chiefdoms.* Cambridge and New York: Cambridge University Press, 1986.

Sánchez-Albornoz, Nicolás. "Los libertos en el reino Astur-Leonés." *Revista portuguesa de história* 4 (1949): 9–41.

Sánchez-Albornoz, Nicolás. "La mita de Lima. Magnitud y procedencia." *Historica* 12, no. 2 (December 1988): 193–210.

Sánchez Saus, Rafael. "Cádiz en la época medieval." In *Entre la leyenda y el olvido. Épocas antigua y media,* edited by Francisco Javier Lomas Salmonte and Rafael Sánchez Saus, 165–326. Madrid: Editorial Sílex, 1991.

Saunders, A. C. de C. M. *A Social History of Black Slaves and Freedmen in Portugal, 1441–1555.* Cambridge: Cambridge University Press, 2010.

Schwartz, Stuart. *Blood and Boundaries: The Limits of Religious and Racial Exclusion.* Boston: Brandeis University Press, 2020.

Scott, Heidi V. "A Mirage of Colonial Consensus: Resettlement Schemes in Early Spanish Peru." *Environment and Planning D: Space and Society* 22 (2004): 885–99.

Seed, Patricia. *Ceremonies of Possession in Europe's Conquest of the New World, 1492–1640.* Cambridge and New York: Cambridge University Press, 1995.

Sevilla [España]. *Ordenanzas de Sevilla. Recopilación de las ordenanzas de la muy noble y muy leal ciudad de Sevilla.* Sevilla: Juan Varela de Salamanca, 1527.

Soares, Mariza de Carvalho. "Art and the History of African Slave Folias in Brazil." In *Crossing Memories. Slavery and African Diaspora,* edited by Ana Lucia Araujo, Mariana P. Candido, and Paul E. Lovejoy, 209–36. Trenton, NJ: Africa World Press, 2011.

Soares, Mariza de Carvalho. *People of Faith: Slavery and African Catholics in Eighteenth-Century Rio de Janeiro*. Durham, NC: Duke University Press, 2011.

Soifer Irish, Maya. "Beyond Convivencia: Critical Reflections on the Historiography of Interfaith Relations in Christian Spain." *Journal of Medieval Iberian Studies* 1 (2009): 19–35.

Soifer Irish, Maya. "Ferrán Martínez's Speech at the Tribunal del Alcázar in Seville, 19 February, 1388." *Open Iberia/América: Teaching Anthology* (blog), 2020. https://hcommons.org/deposits/item/hc:32497/.

Soifer Irish, Maya. *Jews and Christians in Medieval Castile. Tradition, Coexistence, and Change*. Washington, DC: Catholic University of America Press, 2016.

Soifer Irish, Maya. "Toward 1391: The Anti-Jewish Preaching of Ferrán Martínez in Seville." In *The Medieval Roots of Anti-Semitism: Continuities and Discontinuities from the Middle Ages to the Present Day*, edited by Jonathan Adams and Cordelia Hess, 306–19. New York: Routledge, 2018.

Spain [Consejo de Indias]. *Recopilación de leyes de los reynos de Las Indias*. México: MAPorrúa, 1987.

Spalding, Karen. *De indio a campesino: cambios en la estructura social del Perú colonial*. Lima: Instituto de Estudios Peruanos, 1974.

Spalding, Karen. *Huarochirí, an Andean Society under Inca and Spanish Rule*. Stanford, CA: Stanford University Press, 1984.

Sparks, Randy. *The Two Princes of Calabar*. Cambridge, MA: Harvard University Press, 2009.

Stern, Steve J. *Peru's Indian Peoples and the Challenge of Spanish Conquest: Huamanga to 1640*. Madison: University of Wisconsin Press, 1982.

Stone, Erin Woodruff. "America's First Slave Revolt: Indians and African Slaves in Española, 1500–1534." *Ethnohistory* 60, no. 2 (April 1, 2013): 195–217.

Stow, Kenneth. "The Church and the Jews." In *The New Cambridge Medieval History*, edited by David Abulafia, 5:204–19. Cambridge: Cambridge University Press, 2008.

Suárez Bilbao, Fernando. "La comunidad judía y los procedimientos judiciales en la baja edad media." *Cuadernos de historia del derecho* 2 (1999): 99–132.

Suárez Bilbao, Fernando. *El fuero judiego en la España cristiana las fuentes jurídicas, siglos V–XV*. Madrid: Dykinson, 2000.

Suárez Alvarez, María Jesús. "El 'novilisimo Gremio' de Mareantes de Luarca." *Asturiensia medievalia* 2 (1975): 239–58.

Tardieu, Jean-Pierre. *Cimarrones de Panamá: la forja de una identidad afroamericana en el siglo XVI*. Madrid and Frankfurt am Main: Iberoamericana; Vervuert, 2009.

Tardieu, J.-P. "Le marronnage à Lima (1535–1650): Atermoiements et répression." *Revue historique* 278, no. 2 (1987): 293–319.

Tarifa Castilla, María Josefa. "Las ordenanzas del gremio de San José de Tudela en el siglo XVI." *Revista del Centro de Estudios Merindad de Tudela* 15 (2007): 53–72.

Tenorio Cerero, Nicolás. *El concejo de Sevilla*. Sevilla: Concejo de Sevilla, 1901.

Terraciano, Kevin. *The Mixtecs of Colonial Oaxaca: Ñudzahui History, Sixteenth through Eighteenth Centuries*. Stanford, CA: Stanford University Press, 2004.

Thornton, John. *Africa and Africans in the Making of the Atlantic World, 1400–1680*. Cambridge and New York: Cambridge University Press, 1992.

Tolan, John, and Maribel Fierro, eds. *The Legal Status of Dimmis in the Islamic West (Second/Eighth to Ninth/Fifteenth Centuries)*. Turnhout: BREPOLS, 2013.

Toledo, Francisco de. *Francisco de Toledo: disposiciones gubernativas para e virreinato de Peru, 1569–1580*. Sevilla: Escuela de Estudios Hispano-Americanos, 1996.

Toledo, Francisco de. *Relaciones de los vireyes y audiencias que han gobernado el Perú: Memorial y ordenanzas de d. Francisco de Toledo*. Vol. I. Lima: Imprenta del estado por J. E. del Campo, 1867.

Torres Balbás, Leopoldo. *Ciudades hispanomusulmanas*. Madrid: Ministerio de Asuntos Exteriores, Dirección General de Relaciones Culturales, Instituto Hispano-Arabe de Cultura, 1970.

Torres Fontes, Juan. "El alcalde mayor de las aljamas de moros en Castilla." *Anuario de historia de derecho español* (1962): 131–82.

Torres Saldamando, Enrique. "El primero y el último provincial de la Compañía de Jesús en el Perú." *Revista histórica* 1, no. 4 (1906): 445–65.

Trivellato, Francesca. *The Promise and Peril of Credit*. Princeton, NJ: Princeton University Press, 2019.

Trujillo (La Libertad). Concejo Provincial. *Actas del Cabildo de Trujillo*. Lima: Concejo Provincial de Trujillo, 1969.

Vaca de Castro, Cristobal. "Ordenanzas de Tambos [1543]." *Revista histórica* 3 (1908): 427–92.

Valerio, Miguel. "Kings of the Kongo, Slaves of the Virgin Mary: Black Religious Confraternities Performing Cultural Identity in the Early Modern Iberian Atlantic." PhD diss., The Ohio State University, 2017.

Valerio, Miguel. "A Mexican Sangamento? The First Afro-Christian Performance in the Americas." In *Afro-Catholic Festivals in the Americas*, edited by Cécile Fromont, 59–72. University Park: Pennsylvania State University Press, 2019.

Valerio, Miguel. *Sovereign Joy. Afro-Mexican Kings and Queens, 1539–1640*. Cambridge and New York: Cambridge University Press, 2022.

Valerio, Miguel. "'That There Be No Black Brotherhood': The Failed Suppression of Afro-Mexican Confraternities, 1568–1612." *Slavery and Abolition* 42, no. 2 (2020): 293–314.

Valle, Ivonne del. "A New Moses: Vasco de Quiroga's Hospitals and the Transformation of Indians from 'Bárbaros' to 'Pobres.'" In *Iberian Empires and the Roots of Globalization*, edited by Ivonne del Valle, Rachel Sarah O'Toole, and Anna More, 47–74. Nashville: Vanderbilt University Press, 2020.

van Deusen, Nancy. "The 'Alienated' Body: Slaves and Castas in the Hospital de San Bartolomé in Lima, 1680–1700." *The Americas* 56, no. 1 (1999): 1–30.

van Deusen, Nancy. *Between the Sacred and the Worldly: The Institutional and Cultural Practice of Recogimiento in Colonial Lima*. Stanford, CA: Stanford University Press, 2002.

van Deusen, Nancy. *Global Indios. The Indigenous Struggle for Justice in Sixteenth-Century Spain*. Durham, NC: Duke University Press, 2015.

van Deusen, Nancy. *The Souls of Purgatory*. Albuquerque, NM: University of New Mexico Press, 2004.

Vargas Ugarte, Rubén. *Historia del culto de María en iberoamérica y de sus imágenes y santuarios más celebrados*. Madrid: Talleres Gráficos Jura, 1956.

Varón Gabai, Rafael. *Curacas y encomenderos: acomodamiento nativo en Huaraz, siglos XVI y XVII*. Lima: P. L. Villanueva, 1980.

Varón Gabai, Rafael. *Francisco Pizarro and His Brothers: The Illusion of Power in Sixteenth-Century Peru*. Norman: University of Oklahoma Press, 1997.

Vassberg, David E. *Land and Society in Golden Age Castile*. Cambridge and New York: Cambridge University Press, 1984.

Velasco, Jesús R. *Dead Voice. Law, Philosophy, and Fiction in the Iberian Middle Ages*. Philadelphia: University of Pennsylvania Press, 2020.

Velasco Murillo, Dana. "The Creation of Indigenous Leadership in a Spanish Town: Zacatecas, Mexico, 1609–1752." *Ethnohistory* 56, no. 4 (2009): 669–98.

Velasco Murillo, Dana, Margarita Ochoa, and Mark Lentz, eds. *City Indians in Spain's American Empire: Urban Indigenous Society in Colonial Mesoamerica and Andean South America, 1530–1810*. Brighton: Sussex Academic Press, 2014.

Verastique, Bernardino. *Michoacan and Eden: Vasco de Quiroga and the Evangelization of Western Mexico*. Austin: University of Texas Press, 2000.

Vergara Ormeño, Teresa. "The Copacabana Indigenous Elite: Formation, Identity and Negotiations (Lima, 1590–1767)." PhD diss., University of Connecticut, 2018.

Vergara Ormeño, Teresa. "Growing Up Indian. Migration, Labor, and Life in Lima (1570–1640)." In *Raising an Empire: Children in Early Modern Iberia and Colonial Latin America*, edited by Bianca Premo and Ondina González, 75–106. Albuquerque: University of New Mexico Press, 2007.

Vergara Ormeño, Teresa. "Hombres, tierras y productos: Los valles comarcanos de Lima (1532–1650)." *Cuadernos de Investigación* 2 (1995): 5–45.

Vicéns, Belén. "Swearing by God: Muslim Oath-Taking in Late Medieval and Early Modern Christian Iberia." *Medieval Encounters* 20 (2014): 117–51.

Vila Vilar, Enriqueta. "Cimarronaje en Panamá y Cartagena. el costo de una guerrilla en el siglo XVII." *Cahiers du monde hispanique et luso-brésilien* 49 (1987): 77–92.

Villanueva Zubizarreta, Olatz, and Luis Araus Ballesteros. "La identidad musulmana de los mudéjares de la Cuenca del Duero a finales de la edad media." *Espacio, tiempo y forma* 27 (2014): 525–45.

Villaverde Amieva, Juan Carlos. "Un papel de Francisco Antonio González sobre 'códices escritos en castellano con caracteres árabes' y noticia de las copias modernas de Leyes de Moros." In *Aljamías. In Memoriam Álvaro Galmés de Fuentes y Iacob M. Hassán*, edited by Raquel Suárez García and Ignacio Ceballos Viro. Gijón: Ediciones Trea, 2012.

Villella, Peter B. *Indigenous Elites and Creole Identity in Colonial Mexico, 1500–1800*. New York: Cambridge University Press, 2016.

Viñuales Ferreiro, Gonzalo. "El repartimiento del 'servicio y medio servicio' de los mudéjares de Castilla en el último cuarto del siglo XV." *Al-Qantara* 24, no. 1 (2003): 179–202.

Viñuales Ferreiro, Gonzalo. "Los repartimientos del 'servicio y medio servicio' de los judíos de Castilla de 1484, 1490 y 1491." *Sefarad* 62 (2002): 185–206.

Voigt, Lisa. *Spectacular Wealth. The Festivals of Colonial South American Mining Towns*. Austin: University of Texas Press, 2016.

Vose, Robin. *Dominicans, Muslims and Jews in the Medieval Crown of Aragon*. Cambridge: Cambridge University Press, 2009.

Wachtel, Nathan. *The Vision of the Vanquished: The Spanish Conquest of Peru through Indian Eyes, 1530–1570*. Hassocks, Sussex: The Harvester Press, 1977.

Wagner, Klaus. "La Inquisición en Sevilla (1481–1524). Notas al margen de las actas notariales del Archivo de Protocolos de Sevilla referentes a los autos de fe celebrados en dicha ciudad." In *Homenaje al Professor Carriazo*, 439–60. Sevilla: Facultad de Filosofía y Letras, 1973.

Wagner, Klaus. *Regesto de documentos del Archivo de Protocolos de Sevilla referentes a judíos y moros*. Sevilla: Universidad de Sevilla, 1978.

Wagner, Klaus. "Un padrón desconocido de los mudéjares de Sevilla y la expulsión de 1502." *Al-Andalus* 36, no. 2 (1971): 373–82.

Walker, Tamara J. *Exquisite Slaves: Race, Clothing, and Status in Colonial Lima*. Cambridge: Cambridge University Press, 2017.

Walker, Tamara J. "The Queen of Los Congos: Slavery, Gender, and Confraternity Life in Late-Colonial Lima, Peru." *Journal of Family History* 40, no. 3 (2015): 305–22.

Wayno, Jeffrey M. "Rethinking the Fourth Lateran Council of 1215." *Speculum* 93, no. 3 (July 2018): 611–37.

Weismantel, Mary. "Maize Beer and Andean Social Transformations: Drunken Indians, Bread Babies, and Chosen Women." *Modern Language Notes* 106, no. 4 (1991): 861–79.

Wheat, David. *Atlantic Africa and the Spanish Caribbean, 1570–1640*. Chapel Hill: University of North Carolina Press, 2016.

Whittaker, Cord J. *Black Metaphors. How Modern Racism Emerged from Medieval Race-Thinking*. Philadelphia: University of Pennsylvania Press, 2019.

Wiegers, Gerard Albert. *Islamic Literature in Spanish and Aljamiado: Yça of Segovia (Fl. 1450), His Antecendents and Successors*. Leiden and New York: E. J. Brill, 1994.

Yannakakis, Yanna. "Indigenous People and Legal Culture in Spanish America." *History Compass* 11, no. 11 (2013): 931–47.

Zuloaga, Marina. *La conquista negociada: Guarangas, autoridades locales e imperio en Huaylas, Perú (1532–1610)*. Lima: IEP-IFEA, 2012.

Index

For the benefit of digital users, indexed terms that span two pages (e.g., 52–53) may, on occasion, appear on only one of those pages.

Page numbers followed by t or f indicate tables or figures, respectively. Page numbers followed by n indicate notes.

Comuneros, 7–8

concejos (city councils), 24, 33, 93, 288, *see also* cabildos,
　conflict resolution, 129–30
　Iberian beginnings, 3–4, 6

Conchucos, 270n.65

concivos, 243n.28

conflict resolution. *see also* litigation
　by concejos, 94
　jurisdictional interventions, 145–50
　venue shopping for, 129–30

confraternities (cofradías), 236–37, 287.
　for Christians of African heritage, 3–4,
　　67, 186, 187–91, 203–7
　festivals and processions, 188–91
　financial management, 232–33
　internal conflicts, 203–5, 232–33
　internal structures, 204–5, 213
　in Lima, 56–57, 203–7, 213
　and manumission, 86, 133
　as mutual aid societies, 86
　as republics, 203–7
　restrictions on, 67
　in Seville, 41

Confraternity of Preciosa Sangre, 187–88

Confraternity of San Ildefonso, 187–88

Confraternity of the Rosary, 187

Conga, María, 86–87

congregación, 61

conquest
　of Seville, 22–24
　Spanish, 135, 139–41, 143, 268n.22

constables, 213

contracts, 122, 250n.148. *see also* notarial records

Contreras, Francisco de, 224

Contreras, Juana Josefa de, 224

Contreras, María de, 72–73

Contreras, Miguel de, 67, 68f, 71–72, 81, 82

convents and monasteries
　service and slavery in, 69
　walls, 220

conversion to Christianity
　Black catechists, 187
　false, 189
　forced, 7, 11–12, 21, 32, 33, 56, 135–
　　36, 137–38
　as justification for invasion, 137–38
　as qualification for office, 139

conversos (converts from Judaism), 11–12,
　32, 93, 115, 125, 246n.72, 288

convivencia (coexistence), 2

Córdoba (Caliphate), 4–5

Córdoba, Alfonso de, 1

Córdoba, Bernarda de, 73

Córdoba, Juan de, 38–39

Cornejo, Juan González, 82

corporate communities, 106–9

Corpus Christi celebrations, 188–89

corrales, 65

corregidores (magistrates), 16, 94, 139, 288
　de los naturales, 70–71, 143, 144, 166–
　　70, 201–2, 212–13, 288

cortes (royal assemblies), 24, 142

Cortés, Hernando, 141, 142

Cortés, Juan, 212–13

Council of the Indies, 149

Council of Trent, 143

Council of Vienne, 245n.51

courts
　appeals courts (audiencias), 16, 139, 142
　civil, 129–30
　community litigation, 150–51
　of corregidor de los naturales del
　　Cercado, 166–70
　early attempts to redress colonial
　　wrongs, 135
　jurisdiction, 99–102, 129–30
　jurisdictional interventions, 145–50
　Juzgado General de Indios (General
　　Indian Court), 166
　municipal, 129–30
　oaths, 100
　property regimes, 151–54